DATE DUE

No Nā Mamo

Other Books by Malcolm Nāea Chun

From First People's Productions

Must We Wait in Despair, The 1867 Report of the ʻAhahui Lāʻau Lapaʻau of Wailuku, Maui on Native Hawaiian Health

Nā Kukui Pio ʻOle, The Inextinguishable Torches: The Biographies of Three Early Native Hawaiian Scholars: Davida Malo, S. N. Haleʻole and S. M. Kamakau

It Might Do Good: The Licensing of Medicinal Kāhuna

From the Hawaiʻi Department of Health

Ka Moʻolelo Laikini Laʻau Lapaʻau, The History of Licensing Traditional Native Practitioners

From Bess Press

Hawaiian Medicine Book, He Buke Laau Lapaau

From the Queen Liliʻuokalani Children's Center

He Buke Mele Kamaliʻi no ka Mōʻīwahine o Liliʻuokalani, A Children's Songbook in Honor of Queen Liliʻuokalani

Translations

Native Hawaiian Medicine, Vol. III (David Kaluna M. Kaʻaiakamanu.)

The History of Kanalu: Moʻokūʻauhau ʻElua. (Benjamin K. Nāmakaokeahi)

Ka Moʻolelo Hawaiʻi, Hawaiian Traditions (Davida Malo)

Nā Mea Hunahuna o ka Nūhou: Selected Articles from the Hawaiian Language Newspapers

No Nā Mamo

Traditional and Contemporary Hawaiian Beliefs and Practices

Malcolm Nāea Chun

University of Hawai'i Press
and
Curriculum Research & Development Group,
College of Education, University of Hawai'i at Mānoa
Honolulu
2011

Library of Congress Cataloging-in-Publication Data
Chun, Malcolm Naea.
No na mamo : traditional and contemporary Hawaiian beliefs and practices /
Malcolm Naea Chun.
    p. cm.
  Includes bibliographical references and index.
  ISBN 978-0-8248-3624-5 (hardcover : alk. paper)
    1. Hawaiian philosophy.   2. Hawaiians—Social life and customs.
I. Title.
DU624.65.C47 2011
996.9—dc22   2011016425
                                              CIP

This book builds on the work produced as part of Pihana Nā Mamo: The Native
Hawaiian Special Education Project (Grant Number: H221A000002) funded by the
U.S. Department of Education under the Native Hawaiian Education Program.

Text design and composition by Wayne M. Shishido, Publication Specialist, CRDG

Printed by Sheridan Books, Inc.

Distributed by University of Hawai'i Press
2840 Kolowalu Street
Honolulu, HI 96822-1888
www.uhpress.hawaii.edu

In Dedication & Memorial
Ho'ola'a 'ia me ka Ho'omana'o

Whether I do right or wrong, I do not know; but I follow my faith
which cannot be wicked, as it commands me never to do wrong.
–Kamehameha to Kotzebue, 1816

I dedicate this book to the many people who let me experience our culture and who taught me what they know. Some of these people I name here so that their memory will not be lost and their tenure among us will not have been insignificant.

William Nāea and Lily Akana, Emmaline Lau-Kong Young, Aina Keko'olani Keawe, Aldeline Maunupau Lee, Shigeru Naramoto, Mary Lindsey, David Ka'alakea, Moses K. Keale, Sr., Mary Kawena Pukui, Alice K. Holokai, George Holokai, Beatrice Kerr, Richard "Papa" Lyman, Jr., Andy Cummings, Malia Solomon, Rachel Mahuiki, Henry Auwae, Annie Kanahele, Elaine Mullaney, Charlie and Pua Hopkins, Eleanor Horswill Williamson, Alice Namakelua, John Keola Lake, Annie Brewster and Lilian Spencer, Johnny K. Almeida, Whakahuihui Vercoe, Donald Anderson, Rudy Leikaimana Mitchell, Hokulani Meatoga, Mary Lou Kekuewa, Manuhuia Bennett, Gabby Pahinui, Maiki Aiu Lake, Lydia Nāmahana Maioho, Beatrice Krauss, Po'omaikelani Kawananakoa, Albert and Bessie Like, Grace Cora Oness, Kenneth and Marae Emory, Henry Nalaielua, Herb Kawainui Kane, and Abraham Pi'ianāi'a.

This book is also dedicated to one of the most enthusiastic supporters of the Pihana Nā Mamo project and to Hawaiian culture. Cal Sakata was a special education teacher in the Hawai'i Department of Education. He came to all our retreats to give of himself, setting up equipment and even learning how to cook so he could be among us. Not a Hawaiian himself, Cal embodied the virtues and values set out in this book simply because he believed in them.

Contents

Illustrations

Several of us involved in this project, and myself in particular, have been amazed at what could be learned from looking at the images and journals of the earlier European and American explorers, even after all the "Cook books" and other historical analyses that have been written. Many of those authors were not intimately acquainted with Hawaiian culture, and, although their analyses reveal some exciting details, more can be elicited from a careful study.

I have been so taken with the images that I made special trips to the Dixson Library in Sydney, Australia and to the British Library and the British Museum Archives in London, England to see first-hand some of the original images Webber drew or painted during his visit as a member of Captain Cook's crew. The details in these images open your eyes to a different world than the one we learned of only through black and white prints. It is for this reason that we have devoted a section of this book to those original drawings, in color, if available, and in enlarged detail.

Over the years, it has been typical for publications to include full engravings, usually in black and white. A few books, either very academic or expensive coffee table books, have published colored engravings or original drawings. However, it is apparent that artists like Webber and Choris made multiple sketches of the scenes or events they depicted. Using pen, pencil, and watercolors, they made quick drawings of what was transpiring before them. Often, because of the need to conserve paper, many of these drawings would be crowded together on a single page. They would then make a composite sketch of the entire scene and color it in. This would explain the several detailed drawings that exist of the larger composite picture, sometimes with some smaller details added or left out. We have to recognize that these drawings, although from the vision and perspective of foreigners, are the first images we have of Native Hawaiians and of the islands.

Most of the images in this section were originally done in color and have been published, for the most part, in black and white. Seeing the original color is important because it reveals more cultural detail than was previously seen. Using the original sketches, both study and pre-engraving, also brings out details that the engravings do not have, as well as showing the artistic progression as they worked towards a final drawing. Engravers sometimes added or subtracted objects before the final engraving, and those details may be of great interest. Many publications only print the image to fit the page or text, and yet some of these images, especially the Webber drawings, were done on enormous sheets of paper providing room for detail. We can't reproduce them in the same size of the original, but we can, with computers, enhance the images to show some of the details we have been missing.

Several of the images in this section are not referred to in the text, but are published here because they depict some cultural material or event influential to Hawaiian culture, and because often they are not easily accessible. The Webber drawings of fish and birds have rarely been published in color and their absence had some early researchers wondering if the British had even seen live forest birds at all when they got here. This is a rare printing of these 1779 drawings by Webber that I first saw in the British Museum's Archives.

List of Illustrations

Color Plates

Foreword
Ka ʻŌlelo Mua

For more than fifteen years, Pihana Nā Mamo, a project funded by the U.S. Department of Education through the Native Hawaiian Education Act, was actively involved with Hawaiʻi Department of Education schools in improving educational results for Native Hawaiian children and youth. Through this work, we witnessed the powerful role that our rich Hawaiian culture and heritage, and in particular the revival of interest in Native Hawaiian culture and the desire to practice Hawaiian customs appropriately, played in motivating our students to learn and excel.

We came to understand that a first step to ensure such an outcome is to help students, teachers, parents, and community members gain a deeper understanding of the historical and cultural basis for the many Hawaiian customs and traditions. To this end, Malcolm Nāea Chun, a cultural specialist with the Curriculum Research & Development Group (CRDG) at the University of Hawaiʻi, researched and compiled valuable information for the Ka Wana series, a set of publications that provides a wealth of insight into the history, evolution, and meaning of many aspects of Hawaiian culture, beliefs, and practices.

For this work, Chun drew on first-hand accounts from early Hawaiian historians, early explorers and missionaries, and nineteenth century Hawaiian language publications, as well as his own insights built over a lifetime of engagement with the language and culture. The result was a series of monographs that guide us to a better understanding of the many complexities of Hawaiian culture, and in particular, the way we interact with it in the twenty-first century.

This book is a compilation of the original Ka Wana series with several exciting additions. The foundation of the Ka Wana series with its systematic portrayal of Hawaiian beliefs and practices remains. Of all the concepts that might serve as a unifying representative of the Native Hawaiian value system, Chun has chosen pono, an overarching idea that defines the right way to live and, for him, encompasses all the relevant ideas. It is pono that encircles and drives the other values, and so it is pono that begins and ends the discussion in this book and puts the Hawaiian world view into context. It is within this context that he defines and discusses aloha, welina, aʻo, ola, hoʻoponopono, and hoʻomana as elements that build our understanding of the ancient culture. Having established this cultural base, he then goes on to describe how it influenced cultural practices such as alakaʻi, kākāʻōlelo, and hoʻonohonoho, a term Chun uses to describe culturally influenced ways of managing resources. He addresses the traditional roles held by women and men in Hawaiʻi both before and after exposure to Western culture, as well as concepts of sexuality in traditional society, under the broad heading of kapu. The book ends with a discussion of hewa, defined explicitly by Malo as the opposite of pono. Throughout, Chun focuses on research-based descriptions of the ancient culture that predates today's often misappropriated, commodified, or trivialized interpretation of Hawaiian culture and on how traditional beliefs and practices do not have to be in conflict with modern life.

In a new "Afterword" written for this volume Chun revisits the themes found in the book and looks forward to what our next steps might be. He talks about his own experiences working with historical resources and shares his hope that Native Hawaiians will take this opportunity to seek out these resources for themselves as a way of deepening their own understanding of Hawaiian culture and traditions. Chun has also treated us to an article that he and editor Lori Ward wrote describing some of their experiences with the researching and writing of this book.

Production of the Ka Wana series and of this book represents the work of many collaborators. Mahalo to Pihana Nā Mamo co-directors Gloria S. Kishi and Hugh H. Dunn; the Pihana Nā Mamo ʻohana of the Hawaiʻi Department of Education and the Curriculum Research & Development Group in the College of Education, University of Hawaiʻi at Mānoa; and the U.S. Department of Education, which provided the funding for Pihana Nā Mamo.

Morris K. Lai, Principal Investigator
Pihana Nā Mamo

Editor's Preface
Ka ʻŌlelo Mua o ka Mea Hoʻoponopono

This book began as a compilation of the eleven books that make up the Ka Wana series published by CRDG from 2005 through 2010. We encountered many challenges throughout the process of creating these books. We have included an article in the appendix that describes some of these challenges because we felt it was as important to share the process as it was to share this very important material. In this preface, I want to add some explanation of some of the technical details involved in producing this work, both to help you understand why things look the way they do and to help readers who may want to use some of the historical resources we used for their own research understand some of the challenges they might encounter.

The overarching issue that led to so many of our challenges was the fact that we were trying to tell an indigenous story in an authentic voice, but also trying to fit that story into the formal publishing conventions that exist in a university setting. Added to this were many challenges presented by the nature of the source material we were using. One of the most basic tenets of Western publishing is consistency. We use style guides for this reason, not because there is anything inherently right or wrong in a given style, but so we can all agree on the same set of conventions and be consistent. This is not an issue in speech where language is fluid, constantly adapting to the time, place, and situation. Written language, on the other hand, is typically much more formal and much less variable. It is not an accident that in Albert Schütz's book on the history of Hawaiian language studies the chapter that details the writing of Hawaiian is titled "Reducing the Language to Writing."

We used the Modern Language Association's *MLA Handbook for Writers of Research Papers*, Sixth Edition for this book. Elements of this style you are most likely to notice are the use of single quotation marks for translations of single words or phrases and the citation style that uses the title to distinguish between works by the same author. Much more problematic was the need to create style conventions for issues that were not addressed in any of the standard style guides. While the grammar and style conventions we chose applied to original text, quotations were reproduced exactly as they appeared in the original.

One of the very basic issues, and one for which there would not seem to be any discussion needed, is spelling. We made the decision to use modern Hawaiian spelling for our original text, meaning that we use all the diacritical marks listed in the Pukui and Elbert *Hawaiian Dictionary* and in *Place Names of Hawaii*. However, the material quoted in the book comes from a variety of sources that were written over a period of many years and in many locations. As a result, there is little consistency in either the italicizing of Hawaiian words or the use of kahakō 'macrons' and 'okina 'glottal stops.' Other seeming inconsistencies arise from a mixture of American spelling conventions in our original texts and British spelling conventions in some of the quotes. You will also find words from eighteenth and nineteenth century sources that follow neither of these, but show some of historical paths a word may have taken en route to its current spelling. Finally, in quotes from the journals of some of the earliest visitors to Hawaiʻi, you will see a variety of spellings of Hawaiian words that were written phonetically to represent what the visitor thought he was hearing (we have provided translations for those that seemed especially indecipherable). We have done our best to keep all this straight and reproduce both historical and modern sources exactly as they were written, with the result that as a reader, you can see all the variation in both English and Hawaiian that has occurred in both time and place.

Grammar necessarily follows the conventions of English with a single exception. We chose to use Hawaiian forms for plural words; for example, we wrote hale, not hale[s] or hales. We believe that it is always clear from the context when a word is meant to be plural. On the other hand, we used English grammar for possessive forms, so you will see phrases like "Kaheiheimālie's use of this proverb."

Although the text is in English, we chose not to treat Hawaiian words as foreign, and therefore, not to italicize them. However, you will find Hawaiian words italicized when they are referred to rather than used. For example, "the word *aloha* is often used as a greeting," but "he expressed his aloha." Words from other languages, including Māori, Sāmoan, Tahitian, Latin, and Tewa, are also italicized.

Translation is another area where we had to make some decisions. Historical eras bring their own flavor to translations, and the author has occasionally provided an alternative translation for some of the historical material he referenced, either along with or in place of the original translation. He has also occasionally translated a historical reference written in Hawaiian and given just the translation. In these cases we have provided citations for the original Hawaiian text.

Finally, I want to provide some explanation about citations, especially for some of the historical sources. As mentioned above, we chose to use MLA style for this book, so citations use the title to distinguish between multiple works by a single author. In two cases, we found ourselves needing to cite multiple sources by a single author and with the same title: a series of columns written by Samuel Manaiakalani Kamakau in the newspaper *Ke Au Okoa* in 1870, and a series of reports by the missionaries to the *Religious Intelligencer* in the 1820s. In both of these cases, we have had to add the dates, often down to the day, to the citation. Similarly, citations of the two versions (1957 and 1986) of the Pukui and Elbert *Hawaiian Dictionary* are distinguished by date. Another complicated set of sources are the various versions of Captain James Cook and his crew's accounts of their 1778 and 1779 visits to Hawaiʻi (explained in more detail in the appendix). We have cited two of the published versions produced in the 1780s as well as additional material found a volume edited by J. C. Beaglehole in the 1960s and based on the original handwritten documents rather than the published accounts. In each of these cases, we have modified the standard citation formats to give you additional information that can help you to locate these fascinating documents.

Lori Ward, Managing Editor
Curriculum Research & Development Group

Preface
ʻŌlelo Haʻi Mua

> Do you believe I'm wearing a kukui lei? It's Hawaiian in looks
> —it's plastic made in Hong Kong. That's what became of a lot our beliefs.
> I wore this on purpose. I wanted you to know this is kukui nut.
> It's not kukui nut, but it's Hawaiian, but it's Hawaiian made
> in Hong Kong of plastic, and that's the way a lot of our beliefs
> and customs have become.
> attributed to Mary Kawena Pukui

Throughout the Americanization of the Hawaiian Islands, beginning in the nineteenth century and accelerating following statehood, the indigenous population of Native Hawaiians has sought to understand their role in the new society. Cultural revival and identification have gone beyond academic and intellectual arguments to a reality in communities and families and are now part of the political landscape of the islands. In asking the question "Who are we?" people are really asking how they see the world differently from others, and how this affects the way they make decisions. These are questions about a people's world view—how they see the world around them, and ultimately how they see themselves. A popular term to describe the answers to these questions is "values."

Values are concepts and ideas that are important to a people in defining who they are, what they are doing here, and where they are going. Values are often expressed through the importance people place on things held in common. In the United States, these may be things such as eating hot dogs, or playing sports like football, baseball, and basketball, or they may be things that bring a diverse group of people together such as freedom of speech or the right to vote.

In the 1960s, social workers at the Queen Liliʻuokalani Children's Center, funded by a trust created to benefit orphaned and destitute Native Hawaiian children, began to notice behaviors of their children and families that were quite different from the textbook cases they had been taught in school. A lot of these new situations had to do with Hawaiian cultural behavior and responses and involved dreams, traditional healing practices, and attitudes towards modern trained professionals.

In response, the center initiated a project to identify Hawaiian cultural and social practices and behaviors and to study them as they contrasted with their Western counterparts. The impact and influence of the resulting books, entitled *Nānā I Ke Kumu*, are still felt in Native Hawaiian communities, where the books are now a standard reference.

A decade later, state senator Kenneth F. Brown, a descendant of the nineteenth century historian John Papa ʻĪʻī, became interested in knowing and understanding more about Hawaiian values. Brown had been appointed to chair the bicentennial commemorations for the arrival of Captain James Cook in 1778. George Kanahele described his approach.

> [. . .] he [Brown] proposed a number of activities centered around a Bicentennial Conference on Hawaiian Values. The goal of the conference lay in "rediscovering the essence that was here upon the arrival of Cook. Our purpose will be to understand ourselves better by tracing the values of Hawaiʻi from the beginning of western influence. [. . .] This is a large order. A voyage of rediscovery back into the past can be a hazardous undertaking. It could flounder. The essence of that long ago society may elude us or its values prove forever lost. [. . .] The rewards of success hold such a promise for us that the journey is compelling, [. . .] The values we seek, then, could have meaning for our survival [. . .]" (*Kū Kanaka* 7)

The following year Kanahele heard a talk given by Rubellite Kawena Johnson, a professor of Hawaiian language and literature at the University of Hawaiʻi, at a humanities conference held in Honolulu wherein she submitted several questions that intrigued him. "Can traditional Hawaiian values be known? Are we able to discover them? Do we know what values motivated the ancient

Hawaiian society and to what extent they are present now in Hawaiian society? Moreover, do we know what values are proper for present-day Hawaiians in a multiethnic society?" Johnson had an impact on Kanahele's interest. He wrote

> She made a strong plea for the need to study traditional
> Hawaiian values. Not only can such values be uncovered,
> she said, but they must be. [...] She concluded that
> because now enough material about Hawai'i's old
> culture is available, the time for humanities scholars to
> really get involved "has arrived." (*Kū Kanaka* 9)

Brown and Kanahele were also greatly influenced by a similar movement they saw in Aotearoa 'New Zealand' among the Māori people and initiated a new project they called WAIAHA. The name came from a combination of the words wai 'who' and aha 'what' and represented the question "who and what is a Hawaiian?" Funded by a private corporation, the final result of the project was to be a series of books dealing with traditional and modern Hawaiian values. It had three goals: (1) to fill the gap in our knowledge and understanding of Hawaiian values, particularly in terms of the relevance of traditional values to today's world; (2) to stimulate wider interest among Hawaiians in learning about and maintaining those values that enhance our individual dignity as a people; and (3) to provide additional material to those parents or teachers who are involved in the teaching of values at home or in the classrooms where so little is taught. (Kanahele, G., *Hawaiian Values*, n. pag.)

Although the series did not materialize, the idea of the project was finally realized in a book called *Kū Kanaka* in which Kanahele attempted to answer those questions in depth through a study of Hawaiian values. He also recognized the limitations of this personal search and study.

> Yet our search is not ended. We have made a genuine
> start, but much more needs to be explored. We have not
> fully examined the whole scope of Hawaiian aesthetic
> values which, while they may have been perceived in
> early times as being more functional and technical than
> artistic, are viewed today primarily in aesthetic terms.

> Nor have we adequately considered the important
> ideas and values connected with the human body,
> either in terms of its health or as a means to knowing
> pleasure, recreation, and art. Nor have we devoted
> enough attention to the social customs and attitudes of
> Hawaiians, especially in ancient times [. . .]
>
> Perhaps a search of this kind is never over, in that each
> generation must launch its own quest. (*Kū Kanaka*
> 497–498)

As a young researcher and writer I had been involved in the early stages of the WAIAHA project and submitted one of the few articles to Dr. Kanahele. Mine was on the ʻohana, or extended family system. Later, as the cultural officer for the Office of Hawaiian Affairs, I hoped to advance the idea of a published series on culturally important things for Hawaiians to know today. We were able to publish two books from a dream list of thirteen, *Hoʻokipa* on traditional protocols and *Moʻokūʻauhau* on genealogies.

Later, as the cultural specialist for the Queen Liliʻuokalani Children's Center, I had the chance to revive this idea through the need to update the now classic work of *Nānā I Ke Kumu*. This was in 1992, and it was, by then, considered historical information. With greater economic, political, and social pressures on Hawaiian children and their families, we were seeing cases that involved Hawaiian cultural practices and behaviors foreign to both Hawaiian and non-Hawaiian workers. It was clear that these cultural issues needed to be considered in any programs designed to help Native Hawaiians deal with these stresses. We were having to re-adapt traditional healing practices like hoʻoponopono to accommodate changes such as family schedules, misunderstanding or not knowing Hawaiian language and concepts, and having non-Hawaiian family members. Although there was once again a great need for a series that would examine, in depth, key concepts and values for Native Hawaiians to understand and practice today, the trustees of the Center chose not to fund the publication.

By that time I had met the Rev. Dr. Martin Brokenleg, a Lakota, Episcopalian priest and practicing clinical psychologist, who had co-authored a small book entitled *Reclaiming Youth at Risk, Our Hope for the Future.* Martin proposed that by understanding and using traditional indigenous forms of behavioral development and practices, indigenous communities could help their young people overcome such influences as drugs and gangs through greater self-esteem and cultural awareness. He has been able to redefine values from individual, and sometimes disconnected words, to an interconnected concept more in tune with the ideas of extended family and peoplehood. Instead of having long lists of individual values, we are able to see, through four guide words, how those individual values are interconnected and interrelated with each other. Simply put, Martin proposes that a native young person needs a sense of belonging or grounding in his or her people or community. A native people are a people because they have an identity and culture that distinguishes them from others. By belonging to and identifying with this group they are able to receive, contribute, and be valued. For them to be able to contribute, they must be able to have mastery in a skill or knowledge. That mastery allows them to become independent by producing something of their own, and through that production and sharing, contribute to the group. Finally, in practicing generosity by contributing the products of their skill or knowledge, and by teaching the next generation, all the important individual values like compassion, patience, humbleness, and so on are brought into the process.

When I became the scholar-in-residence for the Hawai'i Department of Education's special education project called Pihana Nā Mamo, I was given the opportunity to put all of those ideas into practice by creating a series of publications for the teachers, parents, and children of Hawai'i. The Ka Wana series of books applied Martin's four guidelines of belonging, mastery, independence, and generosity in the context of Hawaiian culture and the Native Hawaiian people. The series included each of the chapters found in this book as a separate title, with the exception of "Aloha." As we completed the books it was obvious to me that the topic of aloha 'love' could not be left out of this series, and so we belatedly added it on.

The English subtitles are my translations of the Hawaiian and refer more to what is written than how those Hawaiian words are used in everyday speech. They represent what I believe is fundamental to seeing the world around us through Hawaiian vision, thought, and feelings, and how these influence how decisions and ideas are formed by Hawaiians. Each title is supported by historical and cultural examples taken from our oral and written literature, in most cases directly from primary sources. In the body of Hawaiian literature these are the writings of nineteenth century writers Davida Malo, Samuel Manaiakalani Kamakau, Ioane (John) Papa ʻĪʻī, and others who contributed to volumes of Hawaiian newspapers, books, manuscripts, and oral accounts recorded by explorers, adventurers, beachcombers, missionaries, and foreign visitors. They recorded the stories of how Hawaiians acted, reacted, responded, and behaved in different situations. It is a record that is available to each one of us to research—to check, double check, and review for ourselves.

Researching these accounts has, itself, been a rediscovery of how we see the world, and how we see it differently from others, much as Kenneth Brown envisioned in 1978. Careful examination of the words, written in Hawaiian and English, revealed what kind of example the events represented. For instance, the Pahikaua war is a noteworthy event as it appears to be a pivotal event in the life of the kingdom. The ʻAi Puaʻa war on Kauaʻi is less well-known in Hawaiian history. But both were important because had the outcomes of these civil wars been different, the development of the kingdom under the rule of the Kamehamehas might not have occurred. By reexamining carefully accounts of the Pahikaua war, I was able to find one of the earliest examples of the concept and practice of hoʻoponopono, although no mention of the term was used in the accounts. By examining what had been said and the reactions of those involved, a perfect match was revealed with the practice of hoʻoponopono used today, which shows us how, to our ancestors, this practice was as natural as breathing. This method of comparative analysis with a deep understanding of the cultural base is a unique way to use the combined disciplines of history and anthropology now championed by many scholars outside of these islands—Marshall Sahlins and Valerio Valeri of the University of Chicago, New Zealand Anthropologist Anne Salmond, and Australian historian Inga Clenndinnen to name just a few. These methods have demonstrated that cultural reconstruction of lost, forgotten, or misinterpreted events and behaviors can be understood once again from the world view of the indigenous culture. A good example of this methodology is the descriptions and analysis of a series of ceremonial welcomes that all involve circuit-like action in the chapter on Welina.

Since the Bishop Museum's publications of the writings of Samuel M. Kamakau, John Papa ʻĪʻī, and Z. P. Kepelino, and the re-printing of Malo, we have more resource materials than ever before. In recent years further primary materials translated from Hawaiian newspapers have been published: *Huakai Makaikai a Kaupo, Maui, A Visit to Kaupō, Maui* by Thomas K. Maunupau, originally published in *Nupepa Kuokoa* in 1922 and 1923 (1998); *Keaomelemele* by Moses Manu, originally published in *Nupepa Kuokoa* in 1884 and 1885 (2000) (the translation first appeared in 1979 in *Ke Alahou* edited by Marjorie Sinclair); *Kamehameha and His Warrior Kekūhaupiʻo* by the Rev. Stephen L. Desha, originally published in *Ka Hoku o Hawaii* from 1920 to 1924 (2000); *The History of Kanalu, Moʻokūʻauhau ʻElua* by Benjamin K. Nāmakaokeahi concerning the priesthood and star-lore of Kanalu, originally published in *Nupepa Kuokoa* in 1900 and 1901 (2004) and *Ka ʻOihana Lawaiʻa, Hawaiian Fishing Traditions* by Daniel Kahāʻulelio, originally published in *Nupepa Kuokoa* from 1902 (2006). In addition, the availability of online resources such as www.ulukau.org for quick access to the Hawaiian newspapers and other websites for unprecedented access to the journals of the explorers allows us to confidently agree with Rubellite Johnson that the time to uncover Hawaiian values has indeed arrived.

Years ago that was not the case, for Te Rangi Hiroa (Sir Peter Buck) commented to his dear friend Sir Apirana Ngata, in a letter dated November 4, 1930, that there was a need for a good study and publication about Hawaiian culture: "A comprehensive work on Hawaiian culture has never been done in spite of the huge quantity of printed material that deals with these islands" (Sorrenson III: 74). What he meant by culture was material culture, the arts and crafts especially found in the Bernice Pauahi Museum where he was the new director. He completed such a study, and it was published as *Arts and Crafts of Hawaii*. It was first published as a large single book with each chapter emphasizing a broad topic. Those who wanted to use the book to replicate the arts and crafts found the large book cumbersome to take to the workshop or out into the field, so the chapters were reprinted as small booklets. Each booklet was a different bright color so it could be easily identified on the shelf. What Johnson, and then Brown and Kanahele, realized is that this generation needs to understand and appreciate another important aspect of culture: our world view, both of everything around us and of ourselves, and it was this idea that has been developed into the Ka Wana series.

Our series was inspired by *Arts and Crafts of Hawaii*. It was also printed in small booklets with different colored covers. I had asked our graphic artist Robin Clark to look at kapa samples in Dr. William Brigham's extensive study on Hawaiian kapa 'barkcloth' so we could show what the Hawaiian color palette looked like. We called it the Ka Wana series after the kapa stamp of the wana or sea urchin, but there is no symbolism or double meaning in the use of this name for the series. It just is a beautiful graphic image and demonstrates the Native Hawaiian artist's ingenuity and creativeness.

As a younger reader I was always afraid of the massive books we had to read for English literature classes, like Dickens' *David Copperfield*. I never thought I would be able to finish them. I thought if we had the titles in smaller chapter-booklets like *Arts and Crafts of Hawaii*, our targeted readers would be more likely to finish them. However, both readers and libraries began to ask if we would put all of the booklets into one large book, just the opposite of what happened with *Arts and Crafts of Hawaii*.

Producing a large book after the series was finished gave us the rare opportunity to correct mistakes and to add new information that we are continuing to find. Ongoing research has led to the discovery of previously unknown material and to new insights that often come from connecting bits and pieces of information together that may originally have seemed unrelated. I am also very pleased that we were able to add a special color section so readers can see the details found in some of the earliest recorded images of Hawai'i. Many have been published before, but after examining the original watercolors and pencil sketches at the British Library, the British Museum Archives, and the Dixson Library of the State Library of New South Wales, I realized how much we have been missing, visually and culturally, by not looking at these originals. Most of the time we see engravings made from the original drawings so they could be mass-produced in print. But they are not the same, especially if they were not printed with the original hand-coloring. In addition to early images of life in Hawai'i, we have included Webber's drawings of fishes and birds made during Captain Cook's voyage. Although researchers have long known of their existence, they are rarely published. Equally important to the readers and researchers are detailed citations of each of images so that readers will not have difficulty in finding them to use in their own work. By compiling these early accounts and images from our ancestors and earliest visitors, it is our hope that they will become more accessible, not only to researchers and scholars, but to everyone. They are cultural and historical treasures given to all of us by our ancestors, Hawaiian and non-Hawaiian.

Knowing how our ancestors behaved begs the question of whether we are doing the same. If we are practicing our culture in a way similar to how they did, then we know that Hawaiian culture is very much alive today. If we do things differently than they did, we have to ask if those changes have been to our benefit, and whether we can reclaim what has been forgotten, lost, or suppressed. The touching of noses, or honi ihu, is a good example of this rediscovery. Today many Hawaiians do not recognize this as a traditional practice that has been replaced by a hug or a kiss. In fact, most English translations of primary sources call it kissing, hence implying lip-to-lip or lip-to-cheek. Some see the touching of noses as undue influence of the cultural exchanges with our Māori cousins from Aotearoa 'New Zealand,' but the historical and traditional record is very clear. This is a traditional Hawaiian practice. Should it be made the practice today? The answer is still uncertain, as there are an increasing number of Hawaiians invoking the traditional honi ihu, while many others retain hugs and kisses as a greeting.

How will these stories affect you? It is our hope that you may discover some new insights into how you see the world and interact with it. If you are a teacher working with Native Hawaiian families, this knowledge may help you to understand reactions and responses to your teaching. It is our hope that it can also provide you with tools and opportunities to use our cultural history to help these ʻohana learn from the traditions.

If you are a parent you may discover new ways to help your children develop a true and deep sense of belonging based on the cultural and historical treasures left to them by our ancestors. If you are a school administrator you may discover new ways of working with Native Hawaiian communities to overcome the many so-called obstacles to learning and retention, and to build a community on your campus.

If you are not Native Hawaiian you may begin a new journey to deeply understanding our people and our ways of living. You may find new cultural tools that could help your own family situations.

I have a vivid memory of myself as a very little boy in my grandfather's backyard on Makalapua Street, in what were then the outskirts of downtown Honolulu. From the wooden bench where I sat, the house was to my right and there was a tiny garden to the left with a little grassy mound. I was sitting there watching things because my grandfather had gone into a tall shed next to the house, and while he was in there he yelled out to me to keep still and to wait for him. I heard the sound of water hitting a bucket, and then he came out zipping up his pants and holding the bucket. He then went to a water faucet and began to fill the bucket with water, and then he took it to a plant and dumped everything around the plant. By that time I was at his side hanging on to his blue jeans. He looked down and said, pointing to the plant, "Baby, this is medicine that can make you well. Let's go back inside." Many years later I would learn that plant, which most people consider a weed, was the pōpolo, one of the first medicinal plants given to us by the god Kamakanuiahaʻilono. My grandfather did not teach me how to make medicines; instead, he gave me the greater gift of seeing the world through different eyes. It is this gift that, after such a long journey, is now made real in this book. E ola!

No Nā Mamo

1 Pono

The Way of Living

E mālama ʻia nā pono o ka ʻāina e nā ʻōpio.
The traditions of the land are preserved by the youth.
(Author's translation)

✥

Ua mau ke ea o ka ʻāina i ka pono.
Kamehameha III, July 31, 1843
The sovereignty of the Kingdom is perpetuated by justice.
(Author's translation)

✥

E ʻoni wale no ʻoukou i kuʻu pono, ʻaʻole e pau.
Kamehameha's dying statement
Try as you may to undo the good I have done, you cannot.
(Author's translation)

The current emphasis on "values" and the desire to understand what they mean are perplexing from the traditional Native Hawaiian world view. There are no words in Hawaiian for values, morals, or ethics. This lack is not uncommon in traditional cultures where moral or ethical practices were an integral part of everyday life.

However, there are many words for actions and expressions of what people today consider to be values. Words such as *aloha* 'love or compassion,' *lōkahi* 'unity,' *oiaʻiʻo* 'truth,' *haʻahaʻa* 'humbleness,' and *ahonui* 'patience' describe values that are prominent in Hawaiian life, even though none of these by themselves accurately describe the moral and ethical world of Native Hawaiians. You could list, and keep on listing, these concepts as values. But would everyone agree on them? Or would we keep adding more so that the list might never be complete? To avoid such a situation, some have attempted to describe these values in a holistic approach to show their connection to each other. In doing so we use catch-all phrases such as "a way of life," "quality of life," or "the circle of life."

But what do these phrases mean, and how do they describe the values inherent in a native world view? I think one of the best explanations comes from Brendtro, Brokenleg, and Van Bockern in their work, *Reclaiming Youth at Risk*. They offer some guiding principles to help in understanding the Lakota (Sioux) Indian world view. The terms they use to describe the interrelatedness of the many values of the traditional native world are belonging, mastery, independence, and generosity (37–45). By understanding what these words mean and how they are related to each other, I believe we can begin to discover what values are important in Hawaiian culture.

Belonging

If one asks Native Hawaiians what the most important thing in life should be, some might say it is aloha 'love or compassion.' But what does it mean to practice aloha, and more importantly, why should people practice it? The answer might be that aloha is vital since it is desirable to enjoy positive relationships with others. The cultural practice of being in a relationship with another person is central to the idea of belonging. A native people are a people because they have an identity and culture that distinguishes them from others. By belonging to and identifying with this group, they also are able to receive, contribute, and be valued.

According to Brendtro, Brokenleg, and Van Bockern, this desire for membership in the group explains youths' fascination with, and need to belong to, gangs. A community of people who no longer have the time and interest to involve youth in their way of life increase the chances that undesirable alternatives will be found to replace what may be missing in these young peoples' lives. Without sanctioned rites of passage that uphold the way of life of a native people, young people may not know when they are expected to behave as adults or how to assume grown-up responsibilities.

For example, in traditional native patterns of child development, older children often look after their younger relatives, and in doing so, learn and practice adult responsibilities. Such passing on of knowledge and skills was one of the most effective means in native cultures of nurturing maturity. This transfer of knowledge and skills from one generation to the next is perhaps the most important assurance that a people's cultural legacy continues. This is the essence of the proverb, "E mālama 'ia nā pono o ka 'āina e nā 'ōpio" or "The traditions of the land are preserved by the youth."

According to scholar Davida Malo, a person with knowledge and skills who contributed to the community was a kanaka, or a "person," or "somebody." This notion is further reinforced in the motto of King Kamehameha II. His motto "Hoʻokanaka," which some have translated as "to be a man," is really more expansive—"be someone, be a kanaka," not anybody, or nobody.

Mastery

Learning skills and developing gifts are fundamental for native youth. By developing talents, a person is able to become an active participant in the community. It also usually means that young people need to be in a relationship with a mentor or teacher who has such skills. Such relationships allow the student to take risks and make mistakes in a protected and controlled situation. These mentor-student relationships ensure that no one will get hurt and that persons are encouraged instead of discouraged.

We can see such teaching experiences exemplified in traditional Hawaiian ways of learning. Pukui, Haertig, and Lee described this process of learning.

> The elders well knew that: "*I ka nānā no a ʻike*, by observing, one learns. *I ka hoʻolohe no a hoʻomaopopo*, by listening, one commits to memory. *I ka hana no a ʻike*, by practice one masters the skill."
>
> To this a final directive was added: Never interrupt. Wait until the lesson is over and the elder gives you permission. Then—and not until then—*nīnau*. Ask questions. (II: 48)

This methodology was also clearly recorded by the historian Samuel Manaiakalani Kamakau when he described how such a practice was conducted in "the Hawaiian school of medical kahunas" (*Ka Poʻe Kahiko* 107).

> The foundation of the knowledge and skill of the *kahuna lapaʻau* was the god. [. . .] Second came prayer. [. . .] That was the first basic learned by the pupil, and the prayers were memorized by the pupil until he could say them

without hesitation while making offerings of food and praying ritually.

Third came [the diagnosing of diseases by means of] the *papa 'ili'ili*, the "table of pebbles." This was an arrangement of pebbles in the form of a man, from head to foot, until there was an outline of an entire man. The study of the pebbles began at the feet. [. . .]

While the teacher taught, the pupils sat alert and remembered carefully everything that was taught them. [. . .]

By the time the instruction with the 'ili'ili, the pebbles, was finished, the pupils knew thoroughly the symptoms and the "rules" [. . .] for treatment of the diseases. [. . .] Then the teacher would bring in a man who had many disorders and would call the pupils one by one to go and "feel," *haha*, for the diseases. If the diagnosis (*'ike haha*) was the same as that of the teacher, then the teacher knew that the pupil had knowledge of *haha*. (*Ka Po'e Kahiko* 108)

Independence

When a youngster has mastered a skill, he or she is not dependent upon his or her teacher or mentor anymore. The student can function "in-dependently," though the notion of independence in the traditional Hawaiian world differs from some contemporary views. Independence, particularly in the Western world, is a complete state of individuality and separation. As Handy and Pukui observed, "an individual alone is unthinkable, in the context of Hawaiian relationship" (75). This sense of independence arises from the results of one's labor and creativity. The resulting development of one's own style or ways implies that a person is ready, in his or her own right, to be a teacher and mentor to others, thus "in-dependent."

Generosity

When one is able to give back by teaching and mentoring others, this is being generous. A generous person is someone who is able to share knowledge and skills with his or her people and community. At this point, a person has come full circle in that, through this generosity, one is able to enjoy relationships with others and experience a sense of belonging.

Kamakau gives a vivid example of this cycle of life in his account of the High Chief Kaʻahumanu.

> [. . .] her mind ran in the same channels with those of the old counselors who had passed on before her. Whenever a member of family obtained land, whether a district, an *ahupuaʻa,* or some smaller division, the whole family were informed of it, and the property divided among them all. Each member worked for the good of the others and they thus learned to love each other. The home of one was the home of all, and they were all well acquainted with each other, as was common with the chiefs of old. This accounts for their devotion to each other. [. . .] This working for the common good of the family was a fine practice which it would be well for our people today to emulate. (*Ruling Chiefs* 314)

Pono

Quite possibly, the word in the Hawaiian language that best encompasses all of these principles is *pono.* This word is commonly used today in English conversation, as in the phrase *His talk was pono,* or as a means of farewell in the phrase *mālama pono* for the English "take care." The word is also part of the state's motto: Ua mau ke ea o ka ʻāina i ka pono 'The life of the land is perpetuated in righteousness.'

So important was this notion of pono that scholar Davida Malo devoted an entire chapter to it in his book on Hawaiian traditions. He did so in a very traditional Hawaiian manner, first describing what pono is not. He gives a long list of what he considers to be acts or actions that are not pono, that is, acts that are hewa. It is noteworthy to review a summary of this list in its latest translation.

> [. . .] But when the eye sees something and the heart desires it, then the thought will increase there [in the heart]. The source of this kuko [*desire*], liʻa [*a strong*

desire], ulukū [*nervousness*], ho'okaha [*to extort*],
ho'omakauli'i [*avarice*], 'i'ini [*craving*], and halaiwi [*to
look at longingly*] with the idea to secretly take and acquire
the object. These hewa were called 'aihue [*theft, to steal*].

[. . .] Desiring another person's wealth. [. . .] ho'ohalu [*to
stare wide eyed*], maka'ala [*watchful*], kia'i [*to look at*],
ho'okalakupua [*elusive*], ho'oeleiki [*to bear a grudge*],
ho'opa'ewa [*to cause wrong*], and ho'opā'ē'ē [*to cause one
to go astray*]. [. . .] These hewa were called pōwā [*robbery*]
and murder was the means to do so.

[. . .] Taking someone else's [possessions] [. . .] the first
thought was to pākaha [*to cheat*], lawe [*to take*], kipa
[*entice*], hao [*plunder*], uhuki [*to pull up or uproot*], kā'ili
[*snatch*] and 'ālunu [*greed*].

[. . .] ho'opunipuni [*lying*], wahahe'e [*deceit*], 'alapahi
[*falsehood*], pālau [*to tell tall tales*], kūkahekahu [*jest*],
palolo [*gossip*], [. . .] pahilau [*to tell lies*]

[. . .] 'aki [*malign*], 'aki'aki [*slander*], ni'ani'a [*false
accusations*], holoholo 'ōlelo [*gossip*], makauli'i [*covet*],
ka'ameha'i [*elusive*], kuene ["*belittling*," Emerson's
translation], poupou noho nio [*pretense to knowledge or
skill*], ho'olawelawe [*tempting*], luahele [*seduce*], kumakaia
[*to betray*], ho'olawehala 'ōpū 'ino'ino [*malicious accusation*],
lawe 'ōlelo [*tattle*], and pūonioni [[to be] *contentious*]

If a person thought badly of another [. . .] [there was]
huhū [*anger*], inaina [*temper*], 'a'aka [*bad temper*], kē'ē
[*shrieking angrily*], nanā [*quarrelsome*], kūkona [*being
crossed*], nāhoa [*defiant*], mākona [*nasty*], kala'ea [*rude*],
ho'olili [*provoking jealousy*], ho'omāku'e [*to scowl*],
ho'oko'iko'i [*to treat harshly*], ho'oweliweli [*to threaten*]

[. . .] If a person decided to kill someone due to a fault (hala),
then there were [. . .] pepehi [*murder*], hailuku [*stoning*],
hahau [*beating*], kula'i [*pushing over*], 'umi [*strangulation*],
ku'iku'i [*fighting*], papa'i [*hitting*], hāko'oko'o [*leaning on*],
ho'okonokono [*to entice*]

> [. . .] koaka [*indecent exposure*], pakaulei [*irresponsibility*],
> pākela ʻai [*gluttony*], palaualelo [*laziness*], lomaloma
> [*idleness*], [. . .] hāwāwā [*incompetency*], ʻaeʻa [*shiftlessness*],
> kūʻonoʻonoʻole [*ill-supplied*], limalima pilau [*one who
> handles dirty matter*], and kōʻalaʻala makehewa [*to waste
> food*]. (186–187)

These are all actions and expressions of hewa, a state of not being pono. Both *pono* and *hewa* describe actions that are done, or not done, to others.

Malo also provided a description, not a definition, of pono. According to Malo, pono is a state of being, rather than an action.

> It was pono when one's eyes saw something and one's
> heart desired it, but one was hoʻomanawanui [*patient*]
> and did not go to take it, but quickly left forgetting about
> it without even touching it. This was pono. (187)

We find more examples of a traditional understanding of pono in Malo's comments about the state of being a good or bad chief. He mentioned that "[T]hese were the aliʻi who were killed by the makaʻāinana because [they oppressed them]" (266). He listed several of the chiefs who were so killed and concludes, "Therefore, several of the traditional or old aliʻi feared the makaʻāinana, but the makaʻāinana faced death when the aliʻi was pono [*moral, proper or fair*]" (266).

One of these traditions of an oppressive chief is that of Halaeʻa of the district of Kaʻū. The full story was given to Mary Kawena Pukui by [Mrs.] Keliihue Alakihu of Kaʻū. Malo also cited this event. Told in more detail in the chapter on Alakaʻi, this tradition is most revealing because it gives a very detailed description of Hawaiian behavior as it relates to pono. Although the chief is oppressive, he is still the chief and sacred; therefore, for the people to overcome his oppression they must resort to a course of action in which they would remain pono. Their method is conceived and executed with ingenuity and brilliance.

The historian John Papa ʻĪʻī recounted an event that happened while Kamehameha lived in Honolulu that demonstrated his expression of pono.

> Once Kinopu gave a tribute of fish to Kamehameha's
> son, Kinau, at Moehonua's fish pond in Kalia. [. . .] the
> result was a catch so large that a great heap of fish lay
> spoiling upon the bank of the pond.
>
> The news of the huge catch reached Kamehameha, who
> was then with Kalanimoku, war leader and officer of
> the king's guard. The king said nothing at the time, but
> sat with bowed head and downcast eyes, apparently
> disapproving of such reckless waste. Had they caught
> enough for a meal, perhaps forty or twenty, nothing
> would have been said. However, Kalanimoku, apparently
> knowing why the king kept his head bowed, commanded
> Kinopu to release most of the fish. (49)

We can easily recognize from Malo's list that wasting food is
not pono. But that is the easy part of understanding the lesson of
this story. The reaction of Kamehameha is subtle. He does not say
a thing but shows his disapproval by bowing his head and keeping
his eyes down. This is an expression of the principle of pono. His
shame and sadness at the wasteful act, however, are made known by
Kalanimoku, someone who is aware of the principle of pono and is
sensitive to the situation. Through Kalanimoku's interpretation and
actions, the situation is corrected.

Another event illustrating the concept of pono happened on
the island of Oʻahu and involved Kamehameha, Kalanimoku, and
Kinopu. In this account, provided by ʻĪʻī and recounted in full in
the chapter on Alakaʻi, Kamehameha puts his own "son" [actually
nephew] to death for violating a kapu, an imposed chiefly restriction.
In this story, pono was exemplified by Liholiho's display of patience
when he chose not to retaliate against his father, a choice that showed
Kamehameha "the nature of a true chief" (Ii 51). According to Malo,
Kamehameha was well aware of what would make a person a true
chief. Malo noted, "An aliʻi would be known to only plunder, another
to up root things, another to kill and another to collect or to heap
things up. There were a few just aliʻi like Kamehameha I, [. . .] he was
a just and caring aliʻi" (177). In Hawaiian, the statement reads, "he
pue wale kahi alii uuku na [a]lii noho pono e like me Kamehameha I
he alii hoomalu pono ia" (33).

What made Kamehameha pono? It is not to be found in his warrior status and ability to conquer and unify the islands as it was for the paramount chief Kākuhihewa. Rather, it was Kamehameha's knowledge, appreciation, and understanding of pono. His awareness of the actions of former chiefs furthered his ability to make the appropriate and proper decisions to rule well. Kamehameha was not the first to proclaim a kānāwai 'edict or law' that protected the rights of all people, especially the elderly, women, and children, from being harmed or harassed upon the pathways. However, Kamehameha is seen by Hawaiians as being pono for doing so. A version of this event was recorded by Mary Kawena Pukui, as told to her by Kaluhuiokalani.

> On one occasion when Ka-meha-meha Ist was building a *heiau* (temple) and needed human sacrifices, sometimes as many as ten persons were made victims; [. . .] he started along the coast in a canoe with his retainers. At one place they saw two fishermen walking on the shore. Bidding his retainers remain at a distance, Ka-meha-meha endeavored to capture the men. When they saw they were being pursued both fled. Just as Ka-meha-meha was about to grasp the hindermost, his foot caught in a fissure of lava and he fell. The man he was after instantly struck him over the head with his paddle so hard a blow that the paddle was splintered. "Why don't you kill him?" said his companion. "Life is sacred to Kane," replied the man, quoting the old saying *"Ua kapu ke ola na Kane."*
>
> Ka-meha-meha had regained consciousness after the blow and heard what the two men were saying. He knew the man could easily have killed him by running a fish-spear through his body and that neither of the two had recognized him as their chief. The chief was so impressed with the reverence for life shown by the two men that he put an end to human sacrifice and promulgated the famous "Law of the splintered paddle,"—the *"Kanawai mamala-hoe,"*—which runs, "Let the old men, the women and children sleep (in safety) by the wayside, *"E hele ka elemakule, a me na luahine, a me na keiki, a moe i ka ala."* (Green 119)

Kamakau added to the above event.

> Here is an example of his leniency toward one who had
> injured him. At the time when he became ruling chief
> over all Hawaii, there were brought to him those men who
> had struck him with a paddle, together with their wives
> and children. All the chiefs said, "Let them be stoned to
> death!" Kamehameha replied, "The law of the broken
> paddle is declared: no chief or officer of execution is to
> take their lives. It is I who should by right be stoned."
> What a wonderful thing for a chief thus to mete out justice
> towards those who had injured him! (*Ruling Chiefs* 181)

Kamakau said that Kamehameha was renowned because he
"regulated the fishermen," "selected workers in wood," "selected strong
paddlers to paddle canoes, and he set masters over them to navigate
the canoes," "appointed commoners to the different land divisions to
cultivate," selected people skilled in cultural arts and crafts, "appointed
tax gatherers," "placed restrictions on sea fisheries," "appointed men
to serve under the different chiefs as stewards," "took the children of
commoners and trained them," "selected men to act as teachers in [. . .]
the arts of the kahuna," "built heiaus for his gods," "established yearly
feasts as a time for rest from labor," "always listened to the advice of
orators, diviners, kahunas, and men of skill," "loved pious people,"
and "respected his wives and gave them wealth and honor." Kamakau
further reported that, "He [Kamehameha] used himself to take part in
the work, no matter what kind it was." Kamehameha did all of this, "in
order that the people might speak of his kindness and of the pains he
took to care for the chiefs and people; the orators were instructed to
speak of his kind acts" (*Ruling Chiefs* 176–183). Another example given
by Kamakau demonstrated Kamehameha's respect and appreciation
of even the commoner. It is reported that late one night, Kamehameha
and a companion heard an old man preparing ʻawa to drink. They
listened as the man invoked his prayer which ended with a plea to "Let
Kamehameha, the good king, live to be old [. . .]." After the old man
had drunk the ʻawa, Kamehameha spoke.

> "Is all your ʻawa gone?" The old man answered, "The
> ʻawa is gone. I have only scraps left. Last evening I gave

most of it to the god, and since I could not sleep I awoke
and pounded a little and drank it without any food
(*pupu*) to eat after it." Kamehameha said, "I have a little
'awa; let my man bring you some." After they had gone
away he said to his companion, "Bring him forty 'awa
stocks (*pu'awa*), twenty bundles of *pa'i'ai* (*holo'ai*), five
tuna fish (*ahi*), forty *aku* fish, forty *mamaki* tapas, and
twenty heavy loin cloths (*malo uaua*)." When the things
were given to the old man he said, "It must have been
Kamehameha and his man who came here last night!"
(*Ruling Chiefs* 182)

Kamakau spoke of Kamehameha's behavior in the face of
temptation. He listed, as Malo had, what was regarded as wrong in
old Hawai'i: petty thieving, taking things without leave, robbery,
oppression, taking without return, stealing, and taking without the
knowledge of the owner. Kamehameha's actions were, of course, the
opposite.

It is told of Kamehameha that when he went out to find
tops for planting his field he went to the place of a chief
who owned a large planting of taro in upper Kuapehu.
He knew that the chief was not at home but had left a
favorite in charge. Landing at Ka'awaloa he walked up
to the chief's place, which was not far off, and found the
man in charge returned from the god house drunk with
'awa and fast asleep. Kamehameha sat down therefore
and began to rub his head. The man started up and
asked, "Who is there?" "It is I, Kamehameha, come to
ask Naihe for taro tops from Kuapehu." A wonderful
ruling chief indeed, who could have taken anything he
liked, but was thus kind and humble of heart! He was a
true Christian ruler. (*Ruling Chiefs* 205)

Much has been said about Kamehameha, in particular, because
he is so well known in traditional memory for his belief in and
practice of pono. The depth of his understanding and practice of
pono was a part of his life even at his death. It is said he almost
tauntingly remarked as a final statement, "Try as you may, you will
not be able to undo the good I have done!" Again, the statement

is better expressed in Hawaiian: "E ʻoni wale ʻoukou i kuʻu pono, ʻaʻole pau!" We see that Kamehameha's own summation of his life has been to strive for the ideal of pono, that in his final breath it is "pono" that he chooses to best describe his achievements and, indeed, his life.

If pono is the legacy of Kamehameha, then certainly the proverb, "E mālama ʻia nā pono o ka ʻāina e nā ʻōpio," or "The traditions of the land are preserved by the youth," takes on added meaning and importance. Over one hundred thirty years ago, Kamakau expressed alarm at the growing outside influence on Hawaiian communities.

> The Hawaiian people had the reputation of being a pious people who worshipped the god; hospitable, kindly, giving a welcome to strangers, affectionate, generous givers, who always invited strangers to sleep at the house and gave them food and fish without pay, and clothing for those who had little; a people ashamed to trade. This was their character before the coming of the foreigners and of Christianity to Hawaii. Now they are being taught to be close, stingy, hard-hearted, niggardly, to take pay for what is given and to be selfish. Some are following this teaching, but the larger part are still clinging to the old custom of hospitality. [. . .] How did the old Hawaiians acquire this character? They were a people who worshipped the god, who knew the story of the god, his power, wisdom, patience, good works, and long life; a people who knew of other lands and could distinguish good from evil; a people who knew the history of the ancient rulers and which had done right and which wrong. (*Ruling Chiefs* 201–202)

His insight leads us to the recognition that Hawaiian values are not merely a set of discrete behaviors from which one selects. Nor can one learn behaviors that reflect these values by signing up for workshops. One could argue that such a perspective would lead to lists of traits or characteristics that are so global and universal that they are shared and experienced by all of humanity—they are, after all, what makes us human. However, when they are practiced with an understanding and within the context of a native world view, demonstrating the interrelatedness and interdependencies of belonging, mastery, independence, and generosity, the result is Hawaiian.

Kamakau saw what could happen when people no longer "could distinguish good from evil" (*Ruling Chiefs* 202) and seemed adrift from being pono. The restoration of pono—the word for this is ho'oponopono—must be linked to the traditions and history of Hawai'i. It is a process that has developed to become more than "making things right." Today, it includes to restore and heal or hō'ola, literally "to give life," by mending the broken relationships between members of family, community, and perhaps even a people. Deep and clear understanding, appreciation, and awareness of pono are a start to that restoration.

2 Aloha

Traditions of Love and Affection

Ua ʻōlelo pinepine mai nō hoʻi ka poʻe kānaka Hawaiʻi
holokahiki e holo nei ma nā ʻāina ʻē, i ka poʻe
aloha nui (lāhui Hawaiʻi) ke loaʻa aku ma ko lākou wahi i noho ai.
Ua kāhāhā nui nā haole me nā kānaka i ka poʻe mau o ke
aloha o ka lāhui Hawaiʻi, iā lākou Hawaiʻi iho, "I hemo
wale ai nō kahi malo i ka hōhē o ka poʻe kahiko."
Kamakau, *Ke Kumu Aupuni*

It was often said of those Hawaiians who went overseas
that they were full of love (the Hawaiians) when they received
visitors wherever they lived. The English speaking people
and others were greatly taken by the hospitality (aloha)
of the Hawaiians as they were treated like other Hawaiians.
A malo (loin cloth) was only removed at the timidity of the people of old.
(Author's Translation)

✤

Aloha is the most important word in the Hawaiian language.
It encompasses a wide variety of meanings, all of which are
about hospitality and love. The spirit of Aloha guides the
Hawaiian people in their lives everyday.
Westin Vacation Services, from a letter to guests

H. M. Queen Liliʻuokalani's hānai daughter, Lydia Aholo, left a collection of audio recordings of her recollections of the queen that extend our insight into the queen's personal life beyond what she shows us in her own published biography, *Hawaii's Story by Hawaii's Queen*. One of the stories Aholo remembered was of Her Majesty returning to Honolulu in the spring of 1910. In a taped interview, she recollected how Liliʻuokalani "was met at the wharf by *haole, hapa-haole,* and Hawaiians" (Allen 380). Helena Allen wrote of this event from the taped interview in her biography of the queen.

> She stepped off the ship with Curtis Iaukea and was
> greeted with "Alo-o-oha!"
>
> Liliuokalani stopped, shocked, still. She stood
> unmoving until the cry melted away as if in chagrin.
> She looked down upon the crowd. "I greet you," she
> said in her rich musical voice, "with *aloha. Aloha*—that
> is the Hawaiian greeting." "Never," she told more than

one Hawaiian child, including the adults such as Lydia,
"never say *alo-o-oha*. It is a *haole* word. *Aloha* is ours,
as is its meaning." (380)

What did Her Majesty mean when she said that aloha and its
meaning belonged to Hawaiians while *alo-o-oha* belonged to non-
Hawaiians, and in particular, to the haoles, the term for English
speaking peoples? Does *aloha* have meaning that goes beyond a
simple greeting such as hello and goodbye? The Queen, through
Aholo and Allen, says that her greeting is *with aloha*. That would
indicate to me that aloha is something that qualifies the greeting.
Yet, this is followed directly by the short statement "*Aloha*—that is
the Hawaiian greeting," which says *aloha* itself is a type of greeting, a
Hawaiian greeting. What, then, is aloha?

Dictionaries and Definitions

In looking at how aloha is defined, it seems that we, like the
Queen, can distinguish between the Hawaiian word and what has
become the English word.

Merriam-Webster's Collegiate Dictionary (34), in a very brief
entry, says that *aloha* is "used as a greeting or farewell" and indicates
that *aloha* comes from the Hawaiian word for love. It gives a date
of 1820 for the first documented use of the word *aloha* in print in
English, and this makes sense when we consider that that year was
marked by the arrival of American missionaries to the islands. The
Oxford English Dictionary echoes this in a similarly short entry. It
gives the definition as "[l]ove, affection" and adds "used in Hawaii
esp. at greeting or parting" (60).

The oldest Hawaiian dictionary was compiled by the Rev. Lorrin
Andrews and published in 1865. He notes that the word *aloha* can be
used grammatically as noun, verb, or adjective, with all three usages
connoting love, affection, gratitude, kindness, compassion, etc. In
addition, he includes the meaning of "salute at meeting or parting."
Andrews does note, however, that "*Aloha*, as a word of salutation, is
modern; the ancient forms were anoai, welina, &c." (37).

The *Hawaiian Dictionary* by Pukui and Elbert (1986), the
currently recognized authority, lists over thirty possible uses or

meanings for *aloha* beginning with the familiar love and affection but also including compassion, mercy, sympathy, pity, kindness, and charity, among others, before going on to "greeting, salutation, regards." Examples such as "*Aloha ʻoe*, may you be loved or greeted" and "*Aloha kāua*, may there be friendship or love between us" make it clear that it was more than a casual greeting. Pukui and Elbert (1986) also distinguish between the meaning of *aloha* and a long string of uses that "were introduced after European times" (21).

Although both English dictionaries I consulted indicate that aloha is merely a greeting, everyday greetings are not usually full of the love and affection that is clearly part of the Hawaiian definitions. A typical greeting, then, particularly to someone you don't know, would not necessarily include the word *aloha*. "Hello, I want a tall, skinny, mocha to go. Thank you. Goodbye." In this situation you want to be nice and polite but probably not affectionate. It is not a coincidence that Merriam-Webster's gave the iconic date of the missionaries' arrival for their definition. We can see how the meanings of Hawaiian words began to change after this date in the writing of Laura Judd, the opinionated wife of the American missionary doctor Gerrit P. Judd. This entry is from her journal in Lāhainā in 1828 and talks about some important Hawaiian words and concepts she was learning.

> There is no word for "nature," or "virtue," or "enemy," or "gratitude," or "color." "Pono" means "goodness" in general, but nothing in particular. *So also "aloha" signifies "love," "affection," "good-will," and may perhaps be twisted into "thank you," or "gratitude."* (italics added for emphasis) (Judd 21)

Thank you? Judd is correct that there was no traditional word or concept for *thank you* until quite recently. *Mahalo* in old texts is used more to express admiration, praise, and esteem as the second meaning in the *Hawaiian Dictionary* describes (Pukui and Elbert, 1986: 218). Have *aloha* and *mahalo* undergone similar transformations, so that the original meaning is now merely a secondary meaning? Is love and affection now a secondary meaning to hello and goodbye? I believe the answers can be found in how *aloha* has been used by Hawaiians before and after contact with explorers and, later, missionaries.

The Romantic Traditions

Romance is an important part of Hawaiian traditions. Thomas Thrum, who edited Abraham Fornander's collections, first categorized the traditions found in those collections. He gave the title "love stories" to several that Martha Warren Beckwith would call "romance" stories, a categorization she used for her translation of *The Hawaiian Romance of Laieikawai*. In her in-depth analysis of Hawaiian mythology, in which she summarized many of the traditions presented by Fornander, she devoted several chapters to what she labeled "romance." These were traditions where heroine or hero sought, sometimes in very complicated ways, to have an intimate relationship with a lover—whether god or mortal.

Beckwith says that in the romance traditions,

> [l]ove and marriage are always the theme, and chiefs of unexceptionable rank—hence of divine ancestry—the actors [. . .]. The world in which such persons live in actual society, built up as it is out of fictional illusion, is here represented in all the complexity of natural form with which their island world keeps them constantly surrounded. (*Hawaiian Mythology* 489)

One of these romance traditions is a short story concerning Hoamakeikekula, told in Beckwith's abstract of the tale as collected by Fornander.

> "Companion-in-suffering-on-the-plain" is a beautiful woman of Kohala, Hawaii, born at Oioiapaiho, of parents of high rank, Hooleipalaoa and Pili. As she is in the form of an *ala* stone, she is cast out upon the trash; but her aunt has a dream, rescues her through a rainbow which guides her to the place, and wraps her in red *tapa* cloth. In 20 days she is a beautiful child. Until she is 20 she lives under a strict taboo; then, as she strings *lehua* blossoms in the woods, the *elepaio* bird comes in the form of a handsome man and carries her away in a fog

to be the bride of Kalamaula, chief's son of Kawaihae.
She asks for 30 days to consider it, and dreams each
night of a handsome man, with whom she falls in love.
She runs away and, accompanied by a rainbow, wanders
in the uplands of Pahulumoa until Puuhue finds her
and carries her home to his lord, the king of Kohala,
Puuonale, who turns out to be the man of her dream.
Her first child is the image Alelekinakina. (Haleʻole
655–656)

For analysis, we can refer to Fornander's much longer and more detailed telling of the story. The first use of the word *aloha* in the text is by Hoamakeikekula.

"Aloha oe." Aloha aku o Hoamakeikekula me ka leo
oluolu; "Aloha oe e kuu haku." (Fornander IV: 537)

"Love to you." Hoamakeikekula showed her love using
a gentle voice; "Love to you, oh my lord." (Author's
translation)

Some translators would say that *aloha* is used here as a greeting, but I see it as a sign of affection that we would miss if we did only translate it as "Greetings to you" or "Hello."

The next time *aloha* is used is to describe Hoamakeikekula's desire for some unknown male suitor whom she only dreams about.

A po iho, o kela uhane kana kane e moe ai, pela ko
laua *pili ana me ke aloha*, a me ka paa o ke aloha
ia Hoamakeikekula. (italics added for emphasis)
(Fornander IV: 539)

At night she would retire and dream of the same person.
Thus they were united in love, which became steadfast in
Hoamakeikekula. (Fornander IV: 538)

There are four words to focus upon in their relationship to each other: *pili* and *aloha*, and *paʻa* and *aloha*. *Pili* is to come close to, to be near to or to have a relationship with and *paʻa* is to be made firm, to be tight or to hold tight, and both describe what has happened to her. Hoamakeikekula has fallen in love in her dreams.

The Romance of ʻAukelenuiaikū is a long one. In it we can find many more examples of the use of *aloha*. This tradition is believed to be a very old one because one of the major characters is the older sister of the Pele clan, NāmakaoKahaʻi, and the events of ʻAukelenuiaikū occur before she expels her younger siblings from their homeland, causing them to journey to their new home, the Hawaiian islands. Even the name of NāmakaoKahaʻi invokes an old memory, for it literally means the "eyes of Kahaʻi." Kahaʻi, who had his eyes gouged out in far away Kahiki, is a name shared in traditions with several South Pacific islands including Tahiti, the Tuamotus, Rarotonga, and Māori Aotearoa. Beckwith includes Kahaʻi as one of five chiefs that are "the twenty-eighth to the thirty-second in descent from Wakea" (*Hawaiian Mythology* 238).

Beckwith's brief introduction to her own summation of the story gives a sense of how it fits the theme of romance.

> The romantic tale of Aukelenuiaiku is said to have originated in Kahiki and to be one of the most noted of all Hawaiian stories. It tells of the wooing of Namakaokahaʻi, older sister of Pele and related to the family of gods who rule the heavens, by a stranger chief who is aided by a moʻo ancestor to cross the seas, escape the jealousy of his brothers and every attack launched upon him by the goddess and her relatives, and finally to become her husband and rule over her desolated land. Later he becomes enamored of her younger sister [Pele] and eventually leaves the land and arrives ultimately at Hawaii. (*Hawaiian Mythology* 490)

As with the story of Hoamakeikekula, a greeting is the first indication of love (aloha), but in this case, as Andrews had described, we find that *welina* (*walina*) is used for greetings, not *aloha*. However, aloha is to be found in the quality of voice used to say the greeting and carries the intent of affection.

> A hiki lakou i mua o Aukelenuiaiku, kahea mai la o Aukelenuiaiku me ka leo aloha, penei: "E walina ia oe e Kanemoe; e walina ia oe e Kaneapua; E walina ia oe e Leapua; e walina ia oe e Kahaumana." Aloha mai la no

hoi lakou ia Aukelenuiaiku: "E walina hoi oe." Mahope
o ke aloha ana mai a Aukelenuiaiku ia lakou, [. . .].
(Fornander IV: 57)

They arrived before Aukelenuiaiku, Aukelenuiaiku called
out with a voice of affection, thus: "Greetings to you, oh
Kānemoe. Greetings to you, Kāneapua. Greetings to you,
Leapua. Greetings to you, Kahaumana." They all shared
their love with Aukelenuiaiku: "Greetings to you." After
this affection of Aukelenuiaiku was shown to them [. . .].
(Author's translation)

In this tradition of ʻAukelenuiaikū, whose characters are older
in genealogies than those of Hoamakeikekula, we also see that *aloha*
is not only a word for affection but also for deep emotion, as in this
account of NāmakaoKahaʻi's deep attachment to her favorite pet.

A ike ke ʻlii wahine ua make kana ilio, minamina iho la
ia me ke aloha, a kulou iho la i lalo e uwe ana i ke aloha.
(Fornander IV: 61)

And the female chief [NāmakaoKahaʻi] saw that her dog
[Moela] was dead, she was full of regret and love, and
she collapsed in love [for her pet]. (Author's translation)

I wanted to use this particular example because it also answers
a question that the earliest explorers had about Hawaiians and
animals as pets. They knew that dog was eaten but wondered whether
Hawaiians had any affection for the animals they raised? Was it only in
mythical traditions? The emotional bond (aloha) between Hawaiians
and their pets was confirmed by Captain Portlock when he wrote of an
incident on February 5, 1787 at Waimea on the island of Kauaʻi.

A remarkable circumstance, related by Mr. Goulding,
a volunteer in the service, shews the great regard the
natives have for their dogs: in walking a considerable way
along the shore, he met with an Indian and his wife; she
had two puppies, one at each breast: the oddity of the
circumstance induced him to endeavor to purchase one of
them, which the woman could not, by all his persuasions
or temptations, be induced to part with; but the sight of

some nails had such powerful attractions upon the man,
that he insisted upon her parting with one of them; at
last, with every sign of real sorrow she did, giving it at the
same time an affectionate embrace. Although he was at
this time a considerable way from the ship, the woman
would not part with him till they arrived where the boat
was lying to take him on board, and just upon his quitting
the shore she very earnestly intreated to have it once more
before they parted; upon his complying with which, she
immediately placed it at the breast, and after some time
returned it to him again. (188)

The romantic tradition of 'Aukelenuiaikū further demonstrates
other emotional qualities that *aloha* could be used to describe in the
following three examples, and again, it is important to see which
words are used with it. In this first example aloha is a quality of
'olu'olu or kindness. Why not just leave it alone? Because the story
teller wants to emphasize how much affection was held between
them.

> [. . .] ike mai la ka wahine me na kaikoeke, uwe mai la,
> a halawai ae la lakou me ka oluolu aloha. [. . .] ua uhi
> ia ko laua mau manao i ke aloha a me ke manao [. . .].
> (Fornander IV: 67)

> [. . .] the woman saw the relatives (in-laws), and she
> cried and they met with loving kindness. [. . .] both of
> their thoughts were covered in love and consideration [.
> . .]. (Author's translation)

In the next example the verb *komo* is used to tell how aloha
dwells in a person, for *komo* means to enter, as into a house, into a
car, or into your clothes.

> No keia mea, komo mai la ke aloha i loko o ka wahine
> no kana kane, [. . .]. (Fornander IV: 83)

> Because of this reply made by her husband, sadness
> entered the heart of Namakaokahai for him; [. . .].
> (Fornander IV: 82)

> For this reason, love had entered into the woman
> [NāmakaoKaha'i] for her husband [. . .]. (Author's
> translation)

Aloha is a real object and, actually, the subject in this sentence. This concept whereby an inanimate object becomes the subject reminds me of when I was teaching Hawaiian language and my students struggled with the concept of smell and fragrance. In English we might say, "I smell the scent of the jasmine flowers." But in Hawaiian the literal translation of the same sentence would be "The scent of the jasmine flowers came to me." We use the same thought when we talk about being sick. The commonality of these three inanimate objects is that they are external and overwhelming objects to the subject.

The last of these three examples links aloha with the physical display of crying. Here the characters in the story are crying over only greeting each other!

> Uwe iho la lakou a pau me ke aloha, hoi aku la a ka hale
> noho iho la. (Fornander IV: 99)

> [. . .] where they all met and wept over each other, and
> after their greeting [. . .] (Fornander IV: 98)

> They all cried with affection, and came back to stay at the
> house. (Author's translation)

Fornander translated this as "they all met and wept over each other." I presume Fornander thought it was unnecessary to include that the crying was done with affection (aloha), but for this discussion about aloha, it is important to note that aloha is expressed through tears.

Now, a final example demonstrates another aspect of the romance theme. This story uses another word: ho'oipoipo, or what some today might describe as "love-making," which might be appropriate as the causative ho'o- is used. Pukui and Elbert define the word ho'oipoipo as to "make love, court, woo; love; romantic" (1986: 103). If emotional crying is a physical expression of aloha, is the physical act of sex a similar expression?

A ua pili mai no ia hana mua i ka poe o neia mau la
e hooipoipo ana, a nolaila he hana no ia a ke keiki
Aukelenuiaiku [. . .]. (Fornander IV: 103)

[. . .] and that his scratches and bites came from another
source altogether. (Fornander IV: 102)

The people of those days were discreet about such action
to have sex, and therefore that is what Aukelenuiaiku's
son did [. . .]. (Author's translation)

I have heard some talk today about sex as "hana aloha" or an act
of love, but, as we see in the above example, there are specific words
for sexuality. Le‘ale‘a, for instance, not aloha, means sexual pleasure.
I suspect the translator, either Fornander or Thrum, was either too
embarrassed or too prudish to directly tell us what was going on in the
above example. Instead he, quite hilariously, lets us imagine what has
happened by describing the physical results of the sexual act. In this
story, emotional expressions of love are used with the word aloha, but,
what some today would consider as a physical act of love, that is, sex
and sexual pleasure, is not aloha. Sex has its own unique vocabulary.

The Ruling Chiefs of Hawai‘i

Fornander's collection of Hawaiian traditions was gathered at
about the same time as Kamakau's works were being published in
Hawaiian language newspapers in the mid- to late-nineteenth century.
Kamakau's historical accounts of the chiefs, later translated and re-
published as Ruling Chiefs of Hawaii, continue the usage of aloha going
back to "mythical" ancestors from the times of Wākea and Kaha‘i.
We find, in the following examples, a consistent use of aloha
similar to that found in the romance stories, where aloha is defined
as affection in the context of relationships, and in the third example,
once again tied to deep emotions that produce crying.

[. . .] ua paulele aku kona naau ia Umi, he malama i na
oleloao, he hoohaahaa ia ia iho imua o kona makuakane,
a i mua o kana poe kumuao nana e ao, a imua o ke
aloalii o kona makuakane, a ua aloha aku lakou ia ia.
(Kamakau, "Ka Moolelo Hawaii" 17 Nov. 1870: 1)

Liloa was inclined toward 'Umi who heeded all
instructions, served his father humbly, and was obedient
to his teachers and those in his father's court. They love
him. (Kamakau, *Ruling Chiefs* 9)

[. . .] a na ke akua ka hoi e aloha mai i kou noho ilihune
ana, aia no i ke akua ka uku mai ia oe. (Kamakau, "Ka
Moolelo Hawaii" 17 Nov. 1870: 1)

Though you may live in poverty, the god will have compassion
on you and reward you. (Kamakau, *Ruling Chiefs* 9)

[. . .] a ahiahi loa, hiki mai ana o Kaleioku me kona ohana,
a halawai pu lakou me ke aloha nui, a pau ka uwe ana [. . .]
(Kamakau, "Ka Moolelo Hawaii" 24 Nov. 1870: 1)

They greeted each other with affection, and after they
had finished weeping [. . .] (Kamakau, *Ruling Chiefs* 13)

At least in the following text the translator(s) have owned up to
say that ho'oipoipo is a sexual act without any association with aloha.
This further reinforces the distinction between the vocabularies of
sexuality and aloha.

A me na hooipoipo ana no ka ike mai i keia kanaka
maikai, [. . .] I ka launa hooipoipo ana. (Kamakau, "Ka
Moolelo Hawaii" 8 Dec. 1870: 1)

Noticing his handsome appearance, Kolea-moku made
love to him. (Kamakau, *Ruling Chiefs* 25)

In contrast to this example, we have another form of
qualification, the word *olioli* or *joy*, which is linked to aloha. In the
same story the parents express their great love (aloha nui) for their
daughter by preparing an 'aha'aina olioli, a joyous feast.

[. . .] ka ike ana mai o na makua i ka laua kaikamahine,
a me ka laua moopuna, alaila, ua haawi ae laua i ka
hauoli nui me ke aloha kuhohonu, no ka olioli i ka laua
kaikamahine a me ka laua moopuna, [. . .] a ua haawiia
he ahaaina olioli me ke aloha nui, [. . .] (Kamakau, "Ka
Moolelo Hawaii" 8 Dec. 1870, 1)

> When the parents saw their daughter and grandson
> they greeted them with the deepest affection and much
> rejoicing [. . .] [foods] were prepared for a feast to
> express happiness and love. (Kamakau, *Ruling Chiefs* 26)

We can see that aloha is a very strong emotion, although it is not always present where we might expect to find it. In the following example, even among relatives, there is no aloha, and the result is death without any remorse or caring.

> Ua make o Hoolaemakua ma ka hoomauhala o
> Kihapiilani i kona makuahonowai, no ke kokua ole ona,
> aole oia i aloha i ka puka a maka ana iwaho (hoehaa ua
> Oahu makaewaewa). (Kamakau, "Ka Moolelo Hawaii"
> 15 Dec. 1870: 1)

> Hoʻolaemakua was killed because Kiha-a-Piʻi-lani bore
> a grudge against him, his father-in-law, for not helping
> on his side. He felt no affection for him, [. . .] (Kamakau,
> *Ruling Chiefs* 31)

In the next example, the two paramount chiefs ʻmōʻī,ʼ actually met together ʻhālāwai pū,ʼ not just to greet each other, but because of affection and love ʻka hui aloha pū ʻana.ʼ

> [. . .] a ua halawai pu naʻlii Moi elua, a no ka hui aloha pu
> ana. (Kamakau, "Ka Moolelo Hawaii" 29 Dec. 1870: 1)

> The two ruling chiefs met and greeted each other with
> affection. (Kamakau, *Ruling Chiefs* 42)

Earlier, we saw the action of komo in relation to aloha as entering inside of the person. In the following example, we see the word *hū*, to well up or swell inside of a person, and it is due to hearing a chant that recalled companionship and loyalty during extremely hard times.

> [. . .] *ua hu mai ka manao aloha nui i ke alii.* (italics
> added for emphasis) (Kamakau, "Ka Moolelo Hawaii" 19
> Jan. 1871: 1)

When Kapa-'ihi was no longer a favorite to the chief he
reminded him of their life of poverty in the wilderness
of Kauai, where they wandered about hungry. *Therefore
great affection welled up in the chief*, and Kapa-'ihi-a-
hilina became a greater favorite than he was before.
(Kamakau, *Ruling Chiefs* 48)

Kapa'ihi had composed a chant for his chief, Lonoikamakahiki,
and this is its ending.

Aloha a haalele ia oe ke hele nei, [. . .]
Aloha wale ana ka wau ia oe iloko o ka ua hoa.
(Kamakau, "Ka Moolelo Hawaii" 19 Jan. 1871: 1)

Farewell, I leave you and go. [. . .]
I bid farewell to you, who remain in anger.
(Kamakau, *Ruling Chiefs* 52)

Upon hearing these words, how could it have been possible
for Lonoikamakahiki to have remained angry? He did not, and the
compassion and affection inside of him did indeed hū, or well up, to
make him recognize how loyal a companion Kapa'ihi had been and
how important this relationship was to him.

When Kamakau writes about the period of the kingdom, the
use of *aloha* becomes related more to the act of greeting. He did
reflect that in traditional times such affection in a relationship was
expressed in numerous ways, and he noted that hand shaking had
been introduced in the islands as a means of showing one's aloha in
greetings.

'O ke aloha kahiko a ka lāhui Hawai'i, 'o ka honi 'ana
ma nā ihu, 'o ke kūnou 'ana o ke po'o, a 'o ke aloha 'ana
ma ka waha, a 'o ka uē me ka waimaka, 'o ke ka'a 'ana i
lalo o ka lepo, 'o ke kukuli 'ana i nā kuli e ho'oha'aha'a iā
ia iho; a 'o ia ihola nā aloha i a'o 'ia e nā mākua kahiko
Hawai'i. Ua pili ka nui o ke aloha ma loko o nā hale
ali'i, a 'o ke aloha e pili ana i ke kua'āina, [. . .]. 'O ke
aloha lūlū lima, he aloha hou wale a'e nei nō ia mai nā
haole mai. Ua pāpā 'ia ke aloha Hawai'i [. . .]. (*Ke Kumu
Aupuni* 250)

The old Hawaiian ways of salutation were touching
noses, bowing the head, greeting with the mouth,
weeping, rolling on the ground, or kneeling as a sign
of submission. These were the forms taught by early
Hawaiian parents. There were other forms required in the
households of chiefs, but the country people expressed
their affection in these ways. (*Ruling Chiefs* 249)

Shaking of hands is a new expression of aloha brought
by the Euro-Americans. The Hawaiian way of aloha has
been around for a long time. (Author's translation)

In the early post-contact period of the kingdom we still find that
aloha remains a qualitative part of greetings and hospitality, as seen
in this example when Kaumualiʻi received the other island chiefs to
his island of Kauaʻi in 1821.

[. . .] ua hoʻokipa mai ʻo Kaumualiʻi me ke aloha [. . .]
(Kamakau, *Ke Kumu Aupuni* 255–256)

Ka-umu-aliʻi received them all, feasted them royally, and
gave them presents of clothing and whatever else they
wanted. (Kamakau, *Ruling Chiefs* 253)

When King Liholiho returned from visiting Kauaʻi in 1823, he
lived at Puʻuloa (Pearl Harbor) and was visited by the American
missionary Hiram Bingham. Kamakau tells us that when the king
welcomed (hoʻokipa) Bingham, it was Bingham who spoke of aloha,
not as a greeting, but as affection.

[. . .] a ua hoʻokipa nō ka mōʻī iā ia. Ua haʻi aku ʻo ia i
kona kuleana o ka hiki ʻana aku i mua o ka mōʻī, ʻo ia ʻo
ke "aloha," me ka ʻī aku, "He nui loa koʻu aloha iā ʻoe; he
aliʻi ʻōpiopio ʻoe, no laila, e haʻalele ʻoe i ka inu rama a
me nā hana leʻaleʻa ʻē aʻe [. . .] (*Ke Kumu Aupuni* 258)

[. . .] he received a visit from Mr. Bingham who said, "I
love you very much. You are but a young king, therefore
I want you to stop drinking and loose living and become
a good king, [. . .]" (*Ruling Chiefs* 255)

How do you do?

It didn't take long after the arrival of foreigners, especially the haole, or Americans and British, for the Hawaiians to pick up customs needed for easy communication. One of the Russian explorers, Lisianskii, noted in 1814 while offshore of the island of Hawai'i how Hawaiians were learning European greetings.

> On coming on deck, they shook hands with every one they saw, repeating the word, *how-lo-lo*, meaning, as I conceived, *how do you do*. (Barratt 55)

It is quite possible that foreigners, especially the American missionaries who settled in the islands in 1820 and needed to learn Hawaiian to communicate, influenced Hawaiians to change the way they expressed greetings. In a speech given by Kīna'u Kaho'ānokū (Elizabeth Ka'ahumanu) dated December 20, 1825, we discover *aloha* being used by the chiefs in the greetings where it was substituted for *welina*. This would appear to support the claims that the two words were by then being used interchangeably.

> E nā maka'āinana kahiko o māua me ku'u ali'i, mai Hawai'i a Kaua'i, aloha kākou a pau loa. (Kamakau, *Ke Aupuni Mō'ī* 96)
>
> [. . .] you old people of my own and of my king, from Hawaii to Kauai, greetings to you all. (Kamakau, *Ruling Chiefs* 321)

And she closed the speech by saying

> E aloha aku kākou i ke akua, [. . .]. Aloha maika'i kākou. (Kamakau, *Ke Aupuni Mō'ī* 96)
>
> Let us therefore love God [. . .]. (Kamakau, *Ruling Chiefs* 322)
>
> Best aloha to all of us. (Author's translation)

The Missionaries: Aloha kākou!

We can compare those native examples of how *aloha* was used with what the American missionaries experienced. They were prodigious writers, especially since it was their best means of soliciting funds from back home. Initial reports, in the form of letters published in local New England newspapers and other publications, showed that Hawaiians were using the word *aloha* in their own context as a sign of affection.

In one of the earliest reports from the island of Kaua'i, American missionaries Whitney and Ruggles wrote about an audience they had with the king, George Kaumuali'i, in 1820. In this account, they describe the king's outburst of affection for the care given to his son, who had been to the United States, followed by seemingly adopting them (probably the form of ho'okama). The original letter had been published in the *Connecticut Mirror* and was reprinted in the *Religious Intelligencer*.

> May 4. This morning early I went to the king's house, and was met at the door by himself and the queen, who took me by each arm, led me in and seated me between them upon the sofa; and after having several times put their noses to mine, the king enquired if it was true that I had lived with Hoomehoome (the real name of George) in America, and eat with him and slept with him, saying his son had told him many things that he could not fully understand, and that I had been his friend a long time, and would stay here and instruct his people to read. I told him it was true, and that the good people of America who loved his son and loved him and his people, had sent several men and women to instruct his people to read and work as they do in America. When I told him this, he with his wife broke out in one voice "*miti, miti, nove loah aloha America*;" [maika'i, maika'i, nui loa aloha America] that is, *good, good, very great love for America*; and then burst into tears. After a short time, he asked me how long I would be willing to stay and teach his island. I told him I wished to spend my life here and die here; he then embraced me again and said "*kacke vo'u oe, mahkooah oe o-ou wihena o ou mahkooah oe*," [ka ko'u 'oe, makua 'oe o'u, wahine ou makua 'oe] that is, *you my son, I your father, my wife you* [sic] *mother.* ("Return of Prince George to Atooi" 771)

An article taken from the *Nantucket Inquirer* gives an eyewitness account of a similar incident of aloha and the desire to establish a binding relationship through adoption.

> The natives appeared to have their curiosity much excited with the novelty of the scene, as we are the first white females who were ever on the island. We called at the door of an aged woman who knew not how to express her joy, but by saying "Aloha nooe roa nume oe makooah ori," [Aloha nui loa, you call (nume/name) me joyful parent (makua oli)] that is, I love you very much, you must call me your mother. She gave us a number of oranges; [. . .] ("Mission to the Sandwich Islands" 5 May 1821: 786)

But, in a description of the "First Sabbath at the Islands," the greeting custom of shaking hands is used, and *aloha* is now understood as "the usual compliment."

> April 1 [1820] To-day as we were near his residence at Toeaigh [Kailua] Bay, Krimakoo [Kalanimoku] and his wife, and two widows of Tamahamaha [Kamehameha], decently dressed, and attended with a considerable train of men and women, came on board the brig, having sent before them a present to Capt. B. of three hogs, and as many large bundles of sweet potatoes. They were introduced to the members of the mission family individually, and the mutual salutation of shaking hands, with the usual compliment "Aloha," passed pleasantly among us all. ("Mission to the Sandwich Islands" 7 April 1821: 725)

Kamakau wrote about Hawaiians being "he hookipa, he oluolu, he heahea, he aloha" (Kamakau, "Ka Moolelo O Kamehameha I" 1) and expressed that Hawaiians were "hospitable, kindly, giving a welcome to strangers, affectionate, generous givers, who always invited strangers to sleep at the house and gave them food and fish without pay, and clothing for those who had little; a people ashamed to trade" (Kamakau, *Ruling Chiefs* 201). How were hospitality, greetings, and poverty expressed in this culture? The missionaries experienced it and left this account in which one can hear their amazement at the importance of hospitality among the natives.

> March 17. This morning, Mr. Loomis, accompanied by William Beals, set out on an exploring tour to make the circuit of the island of Woahoo [Oʻahu], with the design of conversing with the inhabitants at their dwellings [. . .]. Last evening, Mr. Loomis and William Beals returned. The inhabitants uniformly appeared to be not only inoffensive, but friendly, and pleased to show them kindness when they had an opportunity. In some instances, where the poor natives were unable to afford them the refreshment which they needed, they wept with sympathy for the hungry travellers, and bade them welcome to the best their humble cottages afforded, both by night and by day. [. . .] Mr. Loomis saw some evidences of what may be called the remaining shreds of idolatry;—a shapeless stone or two, decorated with colored tappa [kapa], receiving the continual offerings of grass, leaves, &c. Returning from Wi-ma-ha [Waimea], they met the chief, Krimakoo [Kalanimoku], with about 200 men and women, proceeding to the work of cutting sandal wood. He gave them some fish and tara [taro] for refreshment. ("Extracts from the Journal of the Missionaries" 20 July 1822: 116–117)

In the same account, a somewhat humorous incident involving the visit of Liholiho, the king, who tested out Mr. Chamberlain's bed for size, also re-affirms the idea that the missionaries were equating *aloha* with their form of a goodbye.

> April 4. The king and several of his queens called upon us this morning. His majesty inspected our well, cook-house, &c. and pronounced them "miti" [maikaʻi]. Entering the house of Mr. Chamberlain, he threw himself upon a bed, where he lay and rolled from side to side, for about a quarter of an hour. He afterwards visited the other rooms, and appeared pleased with our habitations. [. . .] Giving us his "aloha," he jumped into our handcart, placing his back towards the forepart,

and, in this position, was drawn by his attendants to the
village. ("Extracts from the Journal of the Missionaries"
20 July 1822: 117)

The Hawaiians' signs of affection for each other were still being
observed by the missionaries, although it is hard to know whether what
they were seeing as a "customary salutation" was actually customary or
was merely interpreted that way through their cultural lens.

> Tamoree [Kaumuali'i], being early apprised of his
> arrival, rose, and, with apparent composure, dressed
> himself, and, in a small canoe, with two or three
> attendants, went out quietly on board the king's
> boat, gave him his friendly *aloha*, and the customary
> salutation of joining noses, (while the company
> expressed great joy at seeing Tamoree,) then conducted
> him ashore, and appropriated to his use a large and
> convenient house, well fitted for his reception, spread
> with the beautiful Onehow ['O Ni'ihau]-mats; and, at the
> young king's earnest request, lest his people at Woahoo
> [O'ahu] should conclude that he was drowned in the
> sea, or killed at Atooi [Kaua'i], despatched two of his
> vessels, a brig and a schooner, to inform them that he
> had escaped the dangers of the ocean, and landed here
> in security, where he waited for two of his wives to join
> him, as he had left all five of them behind. ("Extracts
> from the Journal of Mr. Bingham while at Atooi" 10
> Aug. 1822: 163)

A joint letter to the *Missionary Herald*, written by several of the
Honolulu missionaries and dated May 5, 1823, reminisced about
Ka'ahumanu's greeting to those who arrived in Waikīkī on the island
of O'ahu on Sunday, April 27, 1822. The letter was also published in
The Religious Intelligencer in June, 1824.

> [. . .] Kaahoomanoo said to us, "We bid you welcome to
> our islands;—our hearts are glad you come—very glad.
> We are glad too you come on Taboo day [Sunday], and
> have been with us in worship. Give our *aloha* to all the
> new teachers, and their *waihinas*, (wives,) and tell them

we bid them welcome."—She then offered to send a
waggon back with us, [. . .] she sent a large company of
men to carry us on their backs through some standing
water which crossed our path. [. . .] while we were
waiting for our boat, several hundred natives collected
around us, and nothing was heard but their hoarse
voices telling each other the story of our arrival. ("Letter
of the Reinforcement" 21)

Upon hearing the words of the queen regent giving her "aloha"
to them, did they understand that it meant her affection, or was this
being interpreted as her greetings?

There is some evidence that they understood it to be merely a
greeting, including this passage from another letter to the *Missionary
Herald* reprinted in the *Religious Intelligencer.*

We are desired to send our patrons, and the good people
of America, the affectionate AROHA, (*salutation,*) of the
king and queen, of *Taumuarii* and *Kaahumanu* [. . .].
("Sandwich Islands" 740)

The *Religious Intelligencer* reported in its August 14, 1824 issue
that "[t]he missionaries were responsible by agreement, for the port
charges at Hanaroorah; but the king generously remitted them"
(Journal of the Mission 166). The journal then printed a copy of the
king's letter to Captain Clasby, of their ship.

E Capt. Clasby. Eo.—Aroha oe. Eia kau wahi olelo ia oe.
Maitai no oe i kou haavi ana mai i ka kumu hou. Aole oe
e uku i ke ava a ore akahi. Aroha ino oe. RIHO-RIHO *I*—*i.*

To Capt. Clasby. Sir,—Love to you. This is my
communication to you. You have well done, that you
have brought hither the new missionaries. You shall
pay nothing on account of the harbor. Nothing at all.—
Grateful affection for you. RIHO-RIHO *I*—*i.* ("Journal of
the Mission" 166–167)

At this point in time I believe the missionaries were already
equating *aloha* with "the usual compliment" or greetings. They were,

after all, prominent and full-time residents in the islands and needed to replace their own salutations and friendly, or at least customary, hello with something from the indigenous language. *Aloha* appeared to be what they heard. And now, as documented by *Merriam-Webster's Collegiate Dictionary*, *aloha* means hello and goodbye.

Aloha ke Akua

Today, in a deeply Christian-influenced society, we are familiar with the concept of the love and compassion of Jesus, the Christ, but in post-contact Hawaiian society that was a new, and perhaps novel, idea. The missionaries' theology emphasized repentance and salvation more than the love of God and the compassion of his son.

> The Hawaiian people received them as parents their firstborn children. [. . .] They went to the missionaries in procession with gifts in their hands, saying, "What must we do in order that God may save us?" "You must repent of your sins, then Jesus Christ will save you." (Kamakau, *Ruling Chiefs* 248)

But we see from the mission accounts that this concept of Christian love and compassion soon became a part of the Hawaiian consciousness. In a letter from Honolulu dated January 11, 1823 it was reported that

> [t]he queen recited about half of Watt's catechism. Kahuhu [brother of John Papa ʻĪʻī] read with fluency a passage from the Bible.—Two others presented their first essay on composition; and Naihi handed in a declaration, written in his own hand, containing four words—"Aroka au ia Jehovo."—[Aloha au iā Iehova] *I love the Lord.* Opiia exhibited fair hand writing, and so did many others. Honorii gave an address to the pupils, [. . .] ("Letter from the Mission to the Corresponding Secretary" 165)

Puaʻaiti (Puaʻaiki) was a notable convert to Christianity for several reasons. He was blind and deformed. He had "learned the *hula* and the *lua* [. . .] and the *kake*" (Maurer 7), and he had become a dancer for the chiefs' court. He became interested in Christianity when he was told about the healing miracles of Jesus. When asked to perform the hula for the chiefs he refused on the grounds that "henceforth he would serve the king of heaven" (Maurer 4). Known as Blind Bartimea from the Biblical account of Bartimeus, a similar blind man, he "was admitted to the church at this place, on the second Sabbath of last month, [July 1825,] and received in baptism the name of Bartimeus Lalana. Lalana was added at the request of the chiefs. It is the native name for London, where the King and Queen of these islands died" ("Letter from Bartimeus Lalana" 689).

This sketch of Bartimea Lalana Puaaiki is from Oscar E. Maurer's *Three Early Christian Leaders of Hawaii*, where it is noted that it was "probably made in the United States for Mr. Bingham's story of Bartimea printed by the American Tract Society."

Bartimea wrote the following letter, labeled "Lahaina, Isle of Maui, Aug. 2d, 1825," which appears to be one of the earliest published lengthy Hawaiian texts by a Native Hawaiian, and he begins by saying "[l]ove to you." The *Religious Intelligencer* prefaced the Hawaiian translation by saying, "[b]elieving that a few sentences of Hawaiian would not be unacceptable to our readers, we copy the following from the beginning of Lalana's" ("Letter from Bartimeus Lalana" 689).

> Ke aloha akunei au ia o ikou, kaikua, ana, ikoulohe anae
> nei, ikou inoa Uali ke kaua, ikamakapo, Uama ka po,
> kamata okou kino Uamata pohoi, tamata okou kino,
> otamata nae, okou naau kai taa taa, Uapihaloa kula,
> kou kino, ita malamalama nui, o Jesu Kraist, Uahikimai
> nei, ua mala mala la, io maknounei [*sic*], kehoomala ma
> la ma, ia mai nei hoi, kamata, okou naau, eka Uhane
> Hemolele, Uauwiuwi ki ma inei hoi, Uama la ma la
> mala, ikou naau, Uahikimai nei no, keaoma mua, ikapoe,
> Missionary, ma Hawaii, tahiki ana mai, okeao. Aole ma
> kou, ima ke ma te, iti atu, enoho ana no, ma kou, ma
> ka po eleele loa, Ehuhu atu, ana ma kou, aeehookuke
> atu ana matou ia la tou ehelepela, i Oahukou wa hi, ilo
> waai, italima mana, oke Atua, ai ko na Aloha wale ana
> mai no ia ma kou, i Oahu, kou wa hi ilo he pono ai, Ua
> hoola hele, ia, kama te po, e Jesu, Alaida, alaela kamata,
> otau naau, Alaid a wau, mihi atu la, imua, ikealo, ote
> Atua Aleid a wau haa lele loa tu la, ikou, he wa, a me kou
> hoomaunauna anatu i ka olelo maitai a ke Akua. ("Letter
> from Bartimeus Lalana" 689–690)

> Love to you, Mr. B—. I loved you my elder brother as
> soon as I heard your name. We two are alike blind. Your
> natural eyes are blind: my natural eyes are blind also. But
> the eyes of your mind are widely open, and your body
> is completely filled with the great light of Jesus Christ.
> The same light has also burst in upon us here. The eyes
> of my heart are also enlightened by the Holy Spirit; but
> it is only a gleam of light which has yet entered. The day
> indeed dawned upon us formerly, on the arrival of the
> first company of missionaries. On Hawaii the day then
> dawned. We did not then rejoice at all; we continued in

perfect darkness: we were angry with them, and thrust
them away from us, saying, Begone! Oahu was the place
where I first heard of the powerful arm of Jehovah, and of
his great love to us. Oahu was the place where I attentively
listened to the story that Jesus went about to open blind
eyes. There the eyes of my heart opened a little—there I
repented in the presence of God—there I forsook my sins,
and ceased to scoff at the good word of God [. . .]. ("Letter
from Bartimeus Lalana" 689)

During this same period there were still examples being
observed and recorded by the missionaries of the various traditional
expressions of *aloha* being practiced. Religious instruction and the
development of formal, albeit missionary inspired, greetings did not
radically change or discontinue the traditional value of aloha.

From the Journal of Messrs. Richards and Stewart at Lāhainā
comes this story involving Noa ʻAuwae, a senior traditional
genealogist-historian of the king's court and a teacher to the scholar
Davida Malo.

Feb. 6 [1824] This evening Auwai [ʻAuwae] and wife
returned our call. They came in while we were at the
tea table, but could not be prevailed on to join us.—We
could not but be amused at the evident reason—the
poverty of our board in their eyes. A plate of toast,
with a little force meat, were the only articles, besides
the tea service, on the table, which, for half a dozen
persons, when compared with the variety and quantity
of food placed *four times a day* before the family of
a chief, appeared to them a most scanty repast. [. . .]
"*Aroha ino ia oukou.*" [Aloha ʻino iā ʻoukou] (great is
our compassion for you,) burst from their lips, and they
hastened their return to send us some fish and potatoes
immediately. ("Journal of Messrs. Richards and Stewart
at Lahinah" 24 Sept. 1825: 259)

The following rather rare account of how a commoner, Mauae
or Mauaʻe, was welcomed by his family as he guided a group of
missionaries along the trails on the island of Hawaiʻi was published

in the *Religious Intelligencer*, in part, we are told in the preface, to demonstrate the Hawaiians' humanity.

> We lately made some extracts from the *Tour round Hawai* [sic] by the Missionaries at the Sandwich Islands. The following specimen of Native affection may convince some of our misanthropists that these *heathen* are *men*. ("Affecting Scene" 488)

Mauaʻe was a member of the court of Governor Kuakini "who had been sent with canoe, and who, since leaving Honuapo, had acted as our guide" (Ellis 191). In this detailed account we can see the many forms of aloha expressed in his welcome. Most traditional accounts involved the lives of the chiefs, and so these observations of the family interactions of commoners gives another perspective, one that is just as highly emotional and has all the cultural elements that we find in the accounts of the chiefs.

> The old people from the houses welcomed him as he passed along, and numbers of the young men and women came out to meet him, saluted him by touching noses, and wept for joy at his arrival. Some took off his hat, and crowned him with a garland of flowers; others hung round his neck wreaths of a sweet scented plant, resembling ivy [maile], or necklaces composed of the nut of the fragrant pandanus [lei hala].—
>
> [. . .] His father, followed by his brothers and several other relations, came out, and met him, and under the shade of a wide-spreading kou tree, fell on his neck, and wept aloud for some minutes; ("Affecting Scene" 488)

A good example of the synthesis of traditional greetings and Christian faith is the custom that was invented by William Henry Uaua. He had been educated at Lāhaināluna School by the American missionaries and was probably a church member there, and later he became one of the first native converts to the Mormon Church (Church of Jesus Christ of Latter-day Saints) in the early 1850s. The story of how he began the use of *aloha* as a ceremonial greeting in his church was told by the late William Wallace, a Native Hawaiian professor at the Brigham Young University at Lāʻie on the north shore of the island of Oʻahu.

> Uaua was called, 1869, to preside in the Honolulu district, and, in that capacity, reported his stewardship semi-annually in mission conferences. In this connection, he participated in an event at Laie in 1870 which has had far-reaching effects. At conference in that year, Uaua introduced a practice which found a permanent place in Church meetings and elsewhere. As he stood at the pulpit, without speaking, he withdrew a folded handkerchief from his breast pocket. He carefully opened the handkerchief, held it by two corners and "shook it out" before the congregation, saying, "Aloha from the Honolulu Conference." He then placed the handkerchief flat on the pulpit, asked those assembled to send their aloha back to his conference in Honolulu by saying it aloud and in unison. He then folded up the cloth which now, symbolically, contained the greeting and returned it to his pocket. He then reported the affairs of his district. As the next speaker came to the pulpit, he repeated the "Aloha" greeting with his handkerchief before making his report. The practice became immediately popular and marks the beginning of a practice, found nowhere else in the world or the Church, wherein a speaker begins his remarks with "Aloha" to which the congregation responds aloud. (Wallace)

Aloha kekahi i kekahi (Ioane 13:34)

There have been tremendous changes in the teaching and practice of Christianity since the arrival of the missionaries. Early on Native Hawaiians engaged in enculturation as they reconciled their traditional faith and culture with the Western world and Christianity. The earliest Christian prayer composed by a Native Hawaiian is credited to a former warrior, KaʻeleoWaipiʻo, who fought against Kamehameha at the concluding battle of conquest on the island Oʻahu. He was spared his life by appealing to Kamehameha's wife, Queen Kaʻahumanu, for refuge. It is reported that he used the same musical chant used for ʻanāʻanā, or sorcery, for his prayer to

Christ, "a prayer of salvation and a prayer used on a day of trouble or distress" (Chun, "Creation" 117). Robert Schreiter, in his book *Constructing Local Theologies*, discusses this in terms of similarities, noting that "[i]n this case, the elements in the invading culture are seen as analogous to those in the receiving culture" (152). He goes on,

> From the perspective of the local culture, this manner
> of incorporation provides the easiest accommodation
> of the foreign elements intruding upon it. The culture's
> own messages, and to a great extent its own codes, have
> remained intact, and the receiving culture may even
> believe that it has understood the intent of the incoming
> church. (153)

The theological dogma of the early missionaries emphasized seeking conversion through repentance and salvation to gain new coverts. This would ultimately change as the mission was ended and the churches converted to localized governance and to a philosophy that exemplified God's love and compassion through his son Jesus. In this new era converts became full members and church leaders. But it was slow in coming, for the first Native Hawaiian minister of the mother church of Kawaiahaʻo, the Rev. Akaiko Akana, was not "welcomed" until 1917 (Damon 110). There have been Native Hawaiian ministers since that time.

The crystallization of enculturation could be seen when Hawaiʻi became the fiftieth state in the union and the late Rev. Abraham Akaka was the minister of Kawaiahaʻo Church. Akaka was giving the invocation for the Territorial Senate at ʻIolani Palace when the news broke out of admission to the United States, and he could hear the firecrackers and sirens outside. The next morning at his parish of Kawaiahaʻo, diagonally across the street, a packed house gathered for prayer and celebration listened to his sermon entitled "Aloha ke Akua." He wove elements of the traditional concept of aloha with those of Christianity, something the early missionary clerics never even considered, and to these, added concepts of the diversity of the modern world to expound upon an idea and define the "Aloha State."

Akaka used the analogy of an old mele hula for Pele, "Hakuʻi i ka uahi o ka lua, [. . .] There is a fire underground," to evoke the image of the "lifting of the clouds of smoke, as the opportunity to affirm positively the basic Gospel [. . .] to see that Hawaii has potential moral and spiritual contributions to make to our nation and to our world" as "living witnesses of what we really are in Hawaii, of the spirit of Aloha [. . .]." And that led him to define what that spirit is.

> We do not understand the meaning of Aloha until we realize its foundation in the power of God at work in the world. Since the coming of our missionaries in 1820, the name for God to our people has been Aloha. One of the first sentences I learned from my mother in my childhood was this from Holy Scripture: "Aloha ke Akua"—in other words, "God is Aloha." Aloha is the power of God seeking to unite what is separated in the world—the power that unites heart with heart, soul with soul, life with life, culture with culture, race with race, nation with nation. Aloha is the power that can reunite when a quarrel has brought separation; aloha is the power that reunites a man with himself when he has become separated from the image of God within.

> Thus, when a person or a people live in the spirit of Aloha they live in the spirit of God. And among such a people, whose lives so affirm their inner being, we see the working of the Scripture: "All things work together for good to them who love God . . . from the Aloha of God came his Son that we might have life and that we might have it more abundantly."

> Aloha consists of this new attitude of heart, above negativism, above legalism. It is the unconditional desire to promote the true good of other people in a friendly spirit, out of a sense of kinship. Aloha seeks to do good, with no conditions attached. We do not do good only to those who do good to us. One of the sweetest things about the love of God, about Aloha, is that it welcomes the stranger and seeks his good. A person who has the spirit of Aloha loves even when the love is not returned. And such is the love of God.

> This is the meaning of Aloha. (Akaka n. pag.)

Archbishop Desmond Tutu told a well-known story about the missionaries and native Christians, saying that the missionaries gave the Bible and took the land. I have heard a similar explanation used in Hawai'i, that Hawaiians are so full of the spirit of aloha that they gave all their lands away. This small episode in the development of Hawaiian Christianity shows how the traditional concept of aloha had changed, whether good or bad. Akaka, in his sermon, also acknowledged that statehood "brings silent fears" especially for Native Hawaiians.

> There are fears that Hawaii as a state will be motivated by economic greed; that statehood will turn Hawaii (as someone has said) into a great big spiritual junkyard filled with smashed dreams, worn-out illusions; that it will make the Hawaiian people lonely, confused, insecure, empty, anxious, restless, disillusioned—a wistful people. (Akaka n. pag.)

In this brief statement from his sermon, was Akaka hinting at the future commercialization of tourism and its possible tragic consequences for Hawaiian culture and his precious spirit of aloha? Answers to that question have been debated since statehood and continued to be debated quietly as we marked the 50th anniversary of statehood and moved on. It is a bigger debate than I can wisely summarize here. Instead, I want to return to where I began with Her Majesty the Queen and her thoughts about *aloha*.

Aloha 'Oe

Earlier I asked the question, "What did Her Majesty mean that *aloha* and its meaning belonged to Hawaiians while *alo-o-oha* belonged to non-Hawaiians?" To understand the motivations and actions of H. M. Queen Lili'uokalani it must be understood that she was a Christian monarch, something that was demonstrated particularly through her experiences of imprisonment at 'Iolani Palace. Locked up in her own private bedroom, overseen by guards and spies of the provisional government, she was allowed only two books: the Bible and the Book of Common Prayer. Few visitors were allowed to see her, and the ministers of her own church were not among them. Instead, she was visited by the Anglican bishop and nuns who had given her refuge when she was accused of fermenting a counter-revolution against the provisional government.

Imprisoned, Her Majesty used the time to write and compose, and the first project she took upon herself was to rewrite *Aloha ʻOe*. As described by Allen (148) and Hui Hānai (Liliʻuokalani, *The Queen's Songbook* 38), she had first composed this song around 1878 after witnessing an emotional goodbye at the Boyd ranch in Maunawili on the island of Oʻahu. In 1883 it was "sung for the first time in the United States, sung by the beautiful Hawaiian singer Nani Alapai. The song soon swept the nation, and later the world" (Allen 188).

At the time of the re-write, some interpreted it as a "farewell to her country" and some as "a great love song" (Allen 346), but Allen contends there is another meaning underscoring the Christian influence in the queen's life.

The sheet music of *Aloha ʻOe* was published in San Francisco in 1890 or 1891. Today, reproductions of this original sheet music can be purchased at the ʻIolani Palace gift shop.

There however were, as in all true Hawaiian songs, three
interpretations. The obvious one: beautiful description
of the rain, the cliffs, the flowers. The analogy the
Hawaiians knew: union of man-woman-nature-gods.
And the mystical, the *kahuna* knew: the union of all-in-
all, the "Christ" revelation of man's individual unity with
God. Therefore only a few of the older, knowledgeable
Hawaiians recognized the meaning of the rain striking
the *lehua* blossom signifying marital union and unity
of the people and the land, and further the mystical
marriage of Christ, revealed in the old *mele*, but also in
Revelations. (Allen 346)

It is obvious there was a difference between the two usages of the
same word to her. Her culture and faith determined that there is a
greater depth and quality to the word *aloha* than what was expressed
when it was surreptitiously used as a greeting. A little-remembered
incident occurred in the spring of 1910 that captures the depth of her
understanding of the concept of aloha. Lili'uokalani was returning
to the islands after lobbying for seven months to stop the process
of annexation. Her efforts had not been successful, and the islands
would soon become part of the United States of America. She
disembarked from the ship and was greeted by a large crowd.

David Kawananakoa went aboard the *Gaelic* to escort
Liliuokalani down the gang plank. A small tent-like
enclosure had been placed on deck to protect the "ex-
queen" from "prying eyes," [. . .] She wore black from
her plumed hat to toes that moved straight forward in
Onipaa.

She paused for a moment and looked down upon
the upturned faces of the Hawaiians. Tears flowed
uninhibitedly from the eyes of both men and women.
There was a total silence, permeated with a love that
enveloped the crowd and the queen. Liliuokalani paused
[. . .]. Then her musical voice rich with emotion broke
the silence.

"*Aloha.*" (Allen 362)

I think the message we are getting, through Lydia Aholo's reminiscences and Helena Allen's words, from all these examples, and especially from Liliʻuokalani's reactions, is that aloha is special because it upholds, reaffirms, and binds relationships. Aloha should not be taken lightly. It should not be used casually or frivolously. She reminded her bandmaster and confidant Henri Berger that this song of farewell, "Aloha ʻOe," she had introduced to the world was not to be sung at her funeral as a funeral dirge.

> The funeral song, because it best symbolized her life,
> should have been "The Queen's Prayer." But it was not
> included in the service. (Allen 399)

I have been hoping to show this depth and quality in this story of the traditional roots of aloha and its usage by Hawaiians. In doing so, I have discovered how the word has evolved from a truly Hawaiian word, to one changed by outside influences, and finally to yet another form of usage, similar but still different.

All these changes should make us not just pause, but stop for a reality check as to how much we really know and understand about the word *aloha*. Is it just "hello," or is it "my love to you?" That may seem trivial to some, but this appropriation, sometimes politely called cultural borrowing, of aloha into a haole or Euro-American salutation has made it an international word. It may not be the *most* important word for Hawaiians, as Westin Vacation Services claims, but it certainly is one of the most renowned, easily recognized, and, perhaps, exotic words to everyone else around the world, and one that has become a very marketable and economically profitable one, too.

3 Welina

Traditional and Contemporary Ways of Welcome and Hospitality

Mai! Mai! Komo mai maloko nei.
E noho iho a kuʻu ka luhi, hele e ʻai.
Come! Come! Come inside here. Sit down and rest till your
weariness is gone from you, then have something to eat.
Pukui, *ʻOlelo Noʻeau*

✄

Inā hoʻi he huakaʻi kā kāua na ke aloha, he aloha mai nōhoʻi ko uka.
Kalola to Kalaniʻōpuʻu

✄

Ēa! Hele loa nō ka, ʻaʻole ka e aloha mai.
Kanikaniula to Eleio

I love to tell this story now, but when we were little kids it scared the heck out of us, though I suppose it was meant to do so. I had an aunt who was a school teacher in Kona, and her time spent there enabled her to be a very good story teller. She loved to tell stories of Pele, the goddess of the volcano. Even if we had heard the stories over and over again, they were so entertaining and spooky, especially at a bedtime gathering after a large family meal.

This is her story: In a small village on the mountain slopes there lived several families. In one home they welcomed all the strangers who passed by and stopped to ask for rest and refreshments. Further down the pathway there was another household that was just the opposite. They did not trust anyone who came by their house and would not share any food or water, or even their shade.

One day an old woman came walking through the village and stopped by the first house. She was warmly greeted and given some food and water. She rested for a while and then said good-bye and journeyed down the pathway. She then stopped at the second house, called out, and asked if anyone was home. There was only the sound of the wind whistling through the house. She called out again and again. Finally a voice yelled back, "Go away! You are not welcome here. We don't have enough food and water for you, old woman!"

The old woman felt very hurt by these words and hurried off down the pathway.

A few nights later, the elder of the first household had a dream in which he was visited by the old woman. She told him that they must place four white flags around their house to mark the boundaries of their property. They were told not to let their neighbors know what they were doing or the reasons for doing so.

The next day they planted white flags at the four corners of their property and waited for the old woman to pass by again. Instead, the volcano erupted, and as the ground shook, lava flowed down the mountain slope. As it sped downwards, it broke into a fork and passed around the home marked with the white flags. The household that would not greet anyone, however, was covered by the lava flow, killing everyone in it.

The old woman was none other than Pele, the goddess of the volcano, in the form of an old woman. As we listened in the stillness of the night, we were admonished: "That is why you must welcome all who pass by and stop at your doorway, especially an old woman, for you never know if it is Pele herself."

Why do we continue to tell these stories? Perhaps today some view them merely as "ghost stories" to entertain young children or enjoyable legends used to share a little Hawaiian culture. I believe, however, that is not why such stories were shared. The moral of the Pele story, for example, is not to invoke fear of Pele and her anger, but to teach that old people who traveled long distances needed to receive rest and refreshment during their journey. In more general terms, it is to remind people of the importance of being hospitable by emphasizing opposite behavior (hewa) and its eventual consequences, for we know, as Mary Kawena Pukui remarked, "Hospitality was typical of all Hawaiians on all of the islands. My own parents, our relatives, friends and associates were always glad to share whatever they had, be it little or large" (Handy and Pukui 186).

Hawaiian Welcoming Traditions and Practices

In Hawaiian traditions, we find many reminders of the importance of welcoming visitors. One well-known account is related to the meaning of the place name Nānākuli on the leeward side of Oʻahu.

Although the compound name Nānā-kuli appears to have several meanings, the most widely known was recorded by Mary Kawena Pukui during an interview with informant Simeona Nawaʻa. He shared that he had gotten his information from "a native woman of Waiʻanae who told him why this place was so named."

> Because of the great scarcity of water and vegetable food, they were ashamed to greet passing strangers. They remained out of sight as much as possible. Sometimes they met people before they were able to hide, so they just looked at strangers with expressionless faces and acted as though they were stone deaf and did not hear the greeting. This was so that the strangers would not ask for water which they did not have in that locality.
>
> The strangers would go on to the other places and mention the peculiar, deaf people who just stared and they would be told that the people were not deaf but ashamed of their inability to be hospitable. So the place they lived was called Nana, or look, and kuli, deaf — that is, Deaf mutes who just look. (Sterling and Summers 61–62)

A similar idea is to be found in the tradition of Kūlepe.

> Kulepe once upon a time set out from Oahu and landed at Kalaupapa in Molokai and proceeded to the first house seen by him, where he found the people eating with their heads bowed down, and who never looked up to see who the stranger was. Kulepe was hungry and this was the reason why he called at this house. [. . .]
>
> After a while Kulepe again called out: (He did this with the hope of being able to get the people to invite him to sit down with them and take some food, without asking outright for the food.)
>
> Say, Molokai, raise your paddles.
> When you look down, the darkness you see is pili grass,
> And the black things, the heads of people.
>
> These words of Kulepe were meant for themselves, on account of the way they gormandized the food and fish;

of the fingers dipping the poi and raising them aloft
[the raised paddles], while the dishes were loaded with
fish, that only the dark color of the hair was manifest
as their heads were bowed [the pili grass and the dark
heads], and of their eating and then whistling. (Fornander
V: 172)

In Hawaiian proverbs or wisdom statements, we find several
references to such a lack of hospitality in certain communities. The
following are but a few more examples:

Oʻahu maka ʻewaʻewa (Oʻahu with indifferent eyes) was "a term
of reproach to Oʻahu people, said to have been said by Hiʻiaka when
her Oʻahu relatives refused to help her mend a canoe for a journey to
Kauaʻi" (Pukui and Elbert 1986: 42).

Kalaoa ʻai pōʻeleʻele (Kalaoa eats in the dark) describes the people
of Kalaoa in east Hilo on the island of Hawaiʻi. They "were noted for
their lack of hospitality. To avoid having to ask visitors or passers-by
to partake of food with them, they ate in the dark where they could
not be seen" (Pukui, ʻŌlelo Noʻeau 155).

Na ka puaʻa e ʻai; a na ka puaʻa ana paha e ʻai ([It is] for the pigs
to eat; and perhaps the pigs will taste [you]) is based upon a story of
a missionary and his two Hawaiian companions. They had reached
Keonepoko in the district of Puna on the island of Hawaiʻi and were
hungry and tired. "Seeing some natives removing cooked breadfruit
from an *imu*, they asked if they could have some. 'No,' said the
natives, 'it is for the pigs to eat.' So the visitors moved on. Not long
after, leprosy broke out among the people of Puna. The first to
contract it were taken to Oʻahu and later on to Kalaupapa. Others
died at home and were buried. When the last ones finally died, there
was no one to bury them, and the pigs feasted on their bodies. Thus,
justice was served" (Pukui, ʻŌlelo Noʻeau 244).

Hoʻohewahewa ke aloha, aia i Puna i Nānāwale (Love failed to
recognize him, for it is gone to Puna, to Nānāwale) (Pukui, ʻŌlelo
Noʻeau 113) is a proverb that uses a word play on the place name
of Nānā-wale or literally "only looking." It was considered rude or
insulting for a person not to call out or greet another, particularly if
they knew each other.

Mū ka waha heahea ʻole (Silent is the mouth of the inhospitable) (Pukui, *ʻŌlelo Noʻeau* 239) is another such proverb.

In the tradition of the man-eating ghost of Oʻahu, Hanaaumoe, hospitality is used as a device to entice travelers to land ashore only to be later eaten.

> This is the only island that is without ghosts, the island of Halalii. Come ashore, we have food ashore [. . .], and we also have women. The canoe men can have as many as two or three, while your chief, Kahaookamoku shall have five, therefore you must come ashore. (Fornander V: 428)

The Need for Kānāwai in Traditional Society

This need to be reminded to show hospitality may seem surprising given Hawaiʻi's image as the "aloha" state. In traditional Hawaiʻi, there were several kānāwai ʻedicts or laws' proclaimed by the paramount chiefs to ensure the safety of children and of the weak or elderly. One might have assumed that such protections were an inherent part of traditional society. But we cannot assume that this was always the case.

The kānāwai Nīʻaupiʻo Kolowalu, issued during the reign of Kūaliʻi on the island of Oʻahu, "provided that old men and old women could go and sleep [in safety] on the highway, and also that farmers and fishermen had to welcome strangers and feed the hungry" (Kamakau, *Ka Poʻe Kahiko* 14). Kamehameha proclaimed a similar kānāwai called Māmalahoe stating, "Let the old men, the old women, and the children sleep [in safety] on the highway" (Kamakau, *Ka Poʻe Kahiko* 15). This became the kānāwai of the kingdom when Kamehameha brought all the islands under one rule.

It is clear from the traditions that people sometimes had to be reminded of the proper manner in which to treat strangers. Laws were enacted to ensure the daily practice of acceptable public behavior since such actions could not always be guaranteed. Stories and legends also served to reinforce desired social behaviors related to welcome and hospitality, stories that we can read today to help us understand how these behaviors fit into daily life.

Hospitality in Traditional Society

In the tradition of the high chief Lonoikamakahiki, we are told of his return to the island of Hawai'i. He stopped by the island of Maui and was "royally welcomed" by the reigning chief Kamalālāwalu. Kamakau's recollection of this event gives an interesting description of the preparation of the chiefs' food by their head stewards.

> Kama's stewards and food-preparers made their chief's food ready. Lono did not say what he wished for the evening. [. . .] Kama's food and 'awa had been prepared beforehand, but the food that Lono wished was not ready. Lono asked for his broiled chicken, and his head steward answered, "It is not ready." The chief felt ashamed because his food was not ready. Maui's chief made Hawaii's feel humiliated by showing the readiness of his servants. Lono gave his steward, named Puapua-kea, a blow that drew blood from his nose. The meal was to be served in the chief's eating house, but nothing was ready there.
>
> Puapua-kea, still bleeding, [. . .] made a fire [. . .]. He tore pieces of 'awa, put them in his mouth, grasped the chicken, tore off a wing, rubbed salt on it, and placed it on the fire; tore off a leg and laid it on the fire. He had one ball of 'awa and then a second which was enough. The steward said, "The chief did not say anything to the servant. If he had, the servant would have deserved the beating." The chicken cooked very quickly, and the 'awa was ready in a cup before the 'awa of the chief of Maui had time to take effect. (*Ruling Chiefs* 53)

Although we are given a good idea about the preparation of foods, this is more about a contest between chiefs and retainers for prestige than about hospitality. In another royal welcome from *The History of Kanalu*, we have this image of a welcome.

> Kahikoluamea, the old man said, "Is the food for the visitor ready?" The head steward replied, "It is ready." The eating mat of the chiefs and the visitor chief was set down. They ate with great honor, the council of chiefs for Pilika'aka'a. (Nāmakaokeahi English 66)

Later on there is another welcome for the prophet, Pāʻao.

> [. . .] it was evening as the canoes entered [into the
> bay] and the drums ʻOwela and Kukona were sounded
> for the arrival of Pāʻao. The drum Kaiuli on board
> of Pāʻao's canoe was sounded [in reply]. The drum,
> ʻOmaʻo also on board was sounded and the conch shell
> Kīhapū was blown. The menehune saw their chiefly lord,
> Pāʻao. The signs and omens of the lofty sky (lewa nuʻu)
> of the priest chiefs of the darkness were again opened
> (wehe hou).
>
> The canoes beached ashore of the island, the canoe
> of Pāʻao. Pāʻao quickly was engulfed by the people.
> When [they] were done looking at each other, Pāʻao
> entered into his house with the chiefs. All the food was
> prepared "to fill the pit of anger."
>
> The chiefs sat together in unity with the peace of Kāne
> [. . .]. (Nāmakaokeahi English 100)

The use of drums and conch shell as signals of approach and
welcome for these canoes is most interesting, but what is lacking is
the detail of how they greeted each other: what did they eat, and what
happened during this ritual encounter? I believe that information was
so commonplace that it is not important for the story teller to describe
those details. For this, we have to wait until people arrive who see those
actions as important to remember and record, our first tourists.

The details and descriptions given in the various accounts
of Captain Cook's "discovery" of the Hawaiian islands are
extraordinary, rather than everyday, events simply because Cook
was received by the chiefs not as a stranger but as a form of the god
Lonoikamakahiki, or Lono. But when the ships first sighted land,
which was the island of Kauaʻi, we are told

> Some canoes came out, their crews shouting and
> gesturing in amazement, and when they came
> alongside Cook gave them red cloth, nails and trinkets.
> They seemed delighted by these gifts, particularly the
> iron, and some of them handed up their loincloths as

return presents. The sailors were [. . .] thrilled when
their visitors assured them that there were plenty of
pigs, chickens, breadfruit, sweet potatoes, plantains,
sugar-cane and coconuts on their island. The canoes
contained piles of stones, but when they found that
the strangers were friendly, the Hawai'ians threw their
missiles into the ocean. (Salmond, *The Trial* 380)

This was not a royal welcome, and the defensive weapons
indicate the occupants of the canoes were not all that sure of what
and whom they were approaching, but things would dramatically
change once the strangers came ashore and the chiefs of Kaua'i were
in charge.

Several hundred people had gathered on the beach, and
when Cook went ashore, accompanied by a guard of
marines, they fell flat on their faces—the *kapu moe*, or
ritual prostration. They remained in this position until
he signalled to them to rise, and then presented him
with a great many small pigs, and plantain branches.
(Salmond, *The Trial* 382)

Captain Clerke of the Discovery had been sick when the ships
arrived at Kealakekua Bay on the island of Hawai'i and went ashore
later than the rest of the party. His welcome was still a chiefly one, for
he is presented with a feather cloak and draped with kapa. Salmond
provides a bit more detail.

When they [Captain Clerke and Dr. Samwell] arrived
at the chiefs' settlement, Palea hurried out to meet
them. He was accompanied by an attendant carrying a
pig, a chicken and a coconut, and as he greeted them
he draped a piece of red cloth around Captain Clerke's
neck, and put a piece of white cloth around Samwell's
shoulders. While his attendant slaughtered two pigs
and cooked them for their breakfast, Palea went off and
soon returned with a splendid red and yellow feather
cloak which he put around Clerke's shoulders, tying
a piece of red cloth around his waist. He set the table
himself, spreading plantain leaves on the ground and

a piece of fresh white bark-cloth, with five coconuts
stripped of their rind, two wooden dishes filled with
pork and two platters of cold sweet potatoes. He tore
the pork to pieces, chewing it and offering to feed them
by hand [. . .]. (*The Trial* 401)

What was shown, without the fine presentations of gifts to
Clerke, is very similar to the later accounts of the missionaries,
who came as settlers rather than as tourists. Their curiosity and
desire to know more about native culture and behavior, for various
reasons including their own surprise, led to some of the most
detailed descriptions of traditional hospitality, and it all verifies how
commonplace hospitality was.

Tamoree [Kaumuali'i], being early apprised of his
[Liholiho, the King] arrival, rose, and, with apparent
composure, dressed himself, and, in a small canoe,
with two or three attendants, went out quietly on
board the king's boat, gave him his friendly *aloha*,
and the customary salutation of joining noses, (while
the company expressed great joy at seeing Tamoree,)
then conducted him ashore, and appropriated to his
use a large and convenient house, well fitted for his
reception, spread with the beautiful Onehow [Ni'ihau]
- mats; and, at the young king's earnest request, lest
his people at Woahoo [O'ahu] should conclude that
he was drowned in the sea, or killed at Atooi [Kaua'i],
despatched two of his vessels, a brig and schooner, to
inform them [. . .]. ("Extracts from the Journal of Mr.
Bingham while at Atooi" 10 Aug. 1822: 163)

Unlike the encounter with Cook's expedition, the arrival of the
American missionaries forty-two years later brought people who
came as residents rather than tourists. Also unlike Cook's expedition,
the missionaries did not arrive on a "cruise ship" but had to be
lodged wherever they went. Without inns or hotels, they had to seek
accommodations among the villages where they stopped.

The inhabitants treated us hospitably. Coming thirsty
to the foot of fort hill, I asked the natives, whose huts

line the shore, for a *neoo* (cocoa-nut). One of them ran
to a tree and brought me a large one, containing nearly
a quart of milk. He tore off the thick, fibrous husk with
his teeth, and cracked the shell for me, and I walked
along, up and down the hill, draining the milk, and
eating the meat of my cocoa-nut and sharing it with my
companions. We then sailed up the river a mile or two
[. . .] and walked back to the river's mouth, where the
head men of the place had prepared a dinner for us. A
pig, baked with hot stones covered in the ground, set
before us on a large shallow wooden tray; taro, baked
in the same manner, pounded and laid on green leaves;
bannanas [*sic*], rich and yellow, handed to us as ripe
fruit; and water served to us in a tumbler made of the
neck of a gourd, composed our dinner, which, reclined
on the mats, we received with thanksgiving. ("Extracts
from the Journal of Mr. Bingham while at Atooi" 17
Aug. 1822: 177–178)

The most impressive description of a traditional welcome and
the following hospitality is given by the Reverend William Ellis,
reprinted in the *Religious Intelligencer*, when his traveling party is
received at the home village of their guide, Mauae. This is not a royal
or chiefly welcome or a welcoming of strangers, but a homecoming
for a native-born son.

We approached Kaimu. This was the birth place of
Mauae, a young man who accompanied the deputation,
and the residence of most of his relations. He walked
before us as we entered the village. The old people
from the houses welcomed him as he passed along, and
numbers of the young men and women came out to
meet him, saluted him by touching noses, and wept for
joy at his arrival. Some took off his hat, and crowned
him with a garland of flowers; others hung round his
neck wreaths of a sweet scented plant, resembling
ivy [maile], or necklaces composed of the nut of the
fragrant pandanus [lei hala].—When we reached the
house where his sister lived, she ran to meet him, threw
her arms round his neck, and having affectionately

embraced him, walked hand and hand with him through
the village. Multitudes of young people and children
followed, chanting his name, the names of his parents,
the place and circumstances of his birth, and the most
remarkable events in the history of his family, in a lively
song, which he afterward informed us, was composed
at his birth. [. . .] His father, followed by his brothers
and several other relations, came out, and met him, and
under the shade of a wide-spreading kou tree, fell on
his neck, and wept aloud for some minutes; after which
they took him by the hand, and led him though a neat
little garden into the house. He seated himself on a mat
on the floor, while his brothers and sisters gather [*sic*]
round him. Some unloosed his sandals. [*sic*] and rubbed
his limbs; others clasped his hand, frequently saluting
it by touching it with their noses; others brought him a
calabash of water, or a lighted tobacco pipe. One of his
sisters, in particular, seemed considerably affected. She
clasped his hand, and sat for some time weeping by his
side. At this we should have been surprised, had we not
known it to be the usual manner among the South Sea
Islanders of expressing unusual joy or grief. [. . .] On first
reaching the house, we had thrown ourselves down on a
mat, and remained silent spectators, not however without
being considerably affected by the interesting scene. We
had been sitting in the house about an hour, when a small
hog nicely baked under ground, with some good sweet
potatoes, was brought in for dinner, of which we were
kindly invited to partake. ("Affecting Scene" 488)

The deep affection that exists within families can also be seen in
this account of the chief Kaʻiana when he located his father living on
Niʻihau. The moment must have affected David Samwell deeply, for
he wrote this poignant description of the moment on Friday, March
12, 1779.

Taiana, the Man who came in the Resolution from
Atowai, met his father who lives upon this Island &
whom he had not seen for some time; their meeting
was truly affectionate, they sat down & threw their

Arms round each other and wept aloud at the same time
repeating some words, they continued thus giving vent
to their passions for about a quarter of an hour with
a croud of people about them, they then saluted each
other by touching their Noses; the Son while he had
his arms round his father put a Toi which he happened
to have about him into his Maro or girdle as a present.
(Beaglehole 1,229–1,230)

William Ellis, like many of the missionaries, traveled extensively
around the islands, and in doing so, he often invoked Hawaiian
hospitality for food, water, and shelter. Ellis gave this very important
description of a welcome.

A transient visitor on arriving among them will generally
have an entertainment provided, of which the persons
who furnish it seldom partake. The family with which we
lodged were, however, induced to join us this evening at
supper, though contrary to their ideas of propriety. (247)

He added,

Connected with this, another custom, equally at variance
with our views of hospitality, is practised by the guests, who
invariably carry away all that remains of the entertainment,
however abundant it may have been. (247)

What Ellis means by "entertainment" is food and drink. The
prevailing custom he describes is that when "entertainment" can be
provided, it all belongs to the guest, even after the meal is over, so that
the guest will have something to take on the journey. Hiram Bingham
confirmed this practice in his journal when he wrote that "[i]n many
cases, the host sits by, while travelling guests make their meal and stow
for subsequent meals the residue of what is set before them" (193).

In the tradition of Niho'oleki, we are told that one day his friend
Kamapua'a intended to pay a visit.

Before Nihooleki set out on a certain day to fish he gave
his wife the following instruction: "In case a man with
the dropsy should come, call him in as he is my friend."

After Nihooleki had started, Kamapuaa arrived and
came and looked in at the door. "You filthy man,
begone," said the wife of Nihooleki. Kamapuaa with the
men that carried him down, went over to the hog pen
and there waited for the return of Nihooleki his friend.
When Nihooleki returned with the fish, he came and
kissed his friend, and then turned to his wife and said:
"You are indeed strange. I told you to take good care
of my friend, but you have not done so. Never mind,
you may stay, but I am going along with my friend." He
then told his friend to give some of the fish to the men
who brought him down. (Fornander IV: 496)

Why is hospitality valued so much among Hawaiians? The most
obvious reason is that people traveled long distances and could not
carry heavy loads of food and water with them, especially when
traveling on foot through hot and arid places such as Nānākuli. One
of the most familiar calls in the Hawaiian language, still retained
today, is "Mai! Hele mai! E ʻai!" ʻCome. Come here and eat!' or "E
komo mai e ʻai!" ʻCome inside and eat!'

The Importance of Relationships

In these accounts, we note the emergence of another compelling
reason to offer greetings and display hospitality, the importance of
establishing and maintaining relationships with others. One of the
most descriptive accounts of the importance of such relationships
and the emotional quality of aloha that binds people is found in the
battle of Kakanilua.

In this battle, Kalaniʻōpuʻu and the chiefs of Hawaiʻi invade
Maui to attack Kahekili, his chiefs, and his people. When it appears
the invading forces are to be routed and defeated, Kalaniʻōpuʻu
appeals to his wife, Kalola, to intervene in order to save his remaining
warriors and chiefs. (There is a more detailed discussion of this event
in the chapter on Hoʻoponopono.)

When Ka-lani-ʻopuʻu saw that the forces of Hawaii were
surrounded by Ka-hekili's men he said to Ka-lola his
chiefess, "O Hono-ka-wai-lani! we shall all be killed.

Do go up to your brother Ka-hekili to sue for peace."
Ka-lola answered, "It will not do any good for me to go,
for we came to deal death. If we had come offering love
we should have been received with affection. I can do
nothing. Our only hope lies in Ka-lani-kau-i-ke-aouli
Kiwalaʻo." (Kamakau, *Ruling Chiefs* 88)

In ancient Hawaiʻi, personal ties and relationships were
sometimes readily established by the simple gesture of greeting
a person by his or her name. This is illustrated in the legend of
ʻAukelenuiaikū.

> When the birds arrived in the presence of
> Aukelenuiaiku, he greeted them one by one saying:
> "My greetings to you, Kanemoe. My greetings to you,
> Kaneapua. My greetings to you, Leapua. My greetings
> to you, Kahaumana." At this they all returned the
> greeting, saying: "Our greetings to you." After greeting
> Aukelenuiaiku, they fell to conversing in low tones
> between themselves, wondering how it was possible
> that their names were known. After a while Kanemoe
> said: "How wonderful! How did he come to know our
> names? And what are we going to give him for this?"
> (Fornander IV: 56)

Another example of the importance of greetings and establishing
a relationship is the story of Eleio, a fast runner on his way to Kaupō
on the island of Maui. This occurred when he overtook a woman
named Kanikaniaula.

> Upon his arrival at Kaupo one day he found a woman
> by the name of Kanikaniaula sitting by the roadside,
> but he passed right along without noticing her.
> Kanikaniaula at this want of respect on the part of Eleio
> called out after him: "Say, are you going to pass right
> along without greetings?" When Eleio heard this call he
> turned back and greeted her. Kanikaniaula then invited
> him to the house which invitation was accepted by
> Eleio. (Fornander IV: 482)

In the tradition of 'Umi, an 'ōlelo aloha 'message of love' is requested to be conveyed to another chief. This message is deemed to be of the utmost importance.

> When Omaokamau was about ready to make his return, Piikea called Omaokamau, to whom she gave her love message, saying: "Omaokamau, you are about to return to the presence of the great king of Hawaii. When you meet him, give him my love." (Fornander IV: 216)

Similarly in the tradition of Kila, this dialogue of an actual greeting is given:

> At this Kila addressed her saying: "My greetings to you, Kanepohihi."
> Kanepohihi replied: "The same to you."
> Kila continued: "Your grandchild and lord send you aloha greetings."
> Kanepohihi asked: "Who is this grandchild and lord of mine?"
> Kila answered: "Moikeha."
> Kanepohihi again asked: "Is Moikeha then still alive?"
> Kila replied: "He is still alive."
> Kanepohihi again asked: "What is he doing?"
> Kila then chanted the following in a pleasing way: [. . .]."
> (Fornander IV: 162)

We can see in a traditional account of the chief Kihapi'ilani, told by Fornander (V: 179) and re-translated by the author, how the renewal of one's relationships immediately commands hospitality.

> [. . .] Upon arriving at the house, Kihapiilani began to wail and wept tears. Umi said, "Who among us is related to you, is it I or is it her?" Kihapiilani said, "It is your wife." Piikea said, "I do not recognize you." Kihapiilani replied, "Lonoapii is the eldest, then Piikea, Kihawahine, and Kihapiilani. I am Kihapiilani your youngest." Piikea jumped up crying. She ordered Umi to prepare some food for his brother-in-law. Kihapiilani ate with these friends until he was full. (Author's translation)

Ceremonial Welcomes

It is important to note that the levels of formality and intimacy of greetings between two people, whether family members or friends, change with the rank and status of a person. This has been shown in the types of welcomes for chiefs, like Lono and Cook, and for ordinary people like Mauae. We have also seen this in the account of the battle of Kakanilua where the presence of Kīwalaʻō, a young boy of high status, altered the outcome of the battle. Kamakau noted such differences in his descriptions of greetings between chiefs and those between common people. He observed that

> The old Hawaiian ways of salutation were touching
> noses, bowing the head, greeting with the mouth,
> weeping, rolling on the ground, or kneeling as a sign of
> submission. These were forms taught by early Hawaiian
> parents. *There were other forms required in the
> households of chiefs, but the country people expressed
> their affection in these ways.* Even when in modern
> times the old ways have been discountenanced the
> country people still keep up the ways of their ancestors.
> (italics added for emphasis) (Kamakau, *Ruling Chiefs* 249)

Many times these welcomes and greetings are public, involving large numbers of people. Such encounters become ceremonial and full of rituals. These rituals are oftentimes quite elaborate in order to bestow the respect and honor commanded by the status and rank of the guest. Ceremonies such as these often create a production worthy of remembrance.

We have already seen one detailed account of such a ceremonial welcome from *The History of Kanalu* when the drums and conch were sounded for the arrival of Pāʻao. Fornander provides another in the tradition of Moikeha.

> Late in the evening the people of Kau heard the beating
> of a drum together with the notes of a kaeke flute [ʻohe
> kaʻeke], which startled them and they rushed out to see
> where these sounds came from. When they got outside
> they saw that these sounds came from aboard of a
> double canoe. Upon seeing this the people remarked: "It

is the canoe of the god Kupulupulu. These sounds came from that canoe." When the people heard that it was Kupulupulu's canoe they prepared food and swine as offerings to the god. (Fornander IV: 154)

During the first encounters with Captain Cook, this was remembered.

> The chief Kiʻikikiʻ and the kahuna Ku-ʻohu, each clothed in a fine girdle of tapa cloth about the loins and a red tapa garment caught about the neck, stepped forward with the left fist clenched and, advancing before Captain Cook, stepped back a pace and bowed as they murmured a prayer; then, seizing his hands, they knelt down and the tabu was freed. (Kamakau, *Ruling Chiefs* 93)

Before Captain Cook arrived at Kealakekua Bay on the island of Hawaiʻi, he had, as described above, had several encounters with Native Hawaiians, both chiefs and commoners. There were presentations of what appear to be gifts to Cook, such as a small pig, fruits and vegetables, and even some material things like kapa 'bark cloth' and ʻawa drinking bowls.

David Samwell, a surgeon on Cook's ship, described a most unusual ceremonial welcome that seems to mimic the ceremonial throwing of spears, called kāʻili, to welcome the high chief back to shore during the Makahiki festival, but here the priest uses stones or pebbles instead of spears.

> [. . .] and dining at a Priest's House whose name is Kaimekee [Kaʻimikiʻi], I shall describe his method of receiving and entertaining us. As we went along we were much crouded by the Indians, who flocked about us in great Numbers merely to satisfy their Curiosity; approaching the Priests House we saw him come out, who perceiving us surrounded by the Indians & judging that they were no welcome Companions to us immediately threw large Stones in the midst of them, some of them lighting close to us, had we not been a little acquainted with the Character of these people we shou'd have concluded that he was pelting us. This

unmannerly salute put the rabble to flight and Kaimekee
waved his hands to us to invite us to his House, into
which we were introduced by himself; he desired us to
sit down while he withdrew, he returned back in a very
short time with two or three attendants, they entered
the court yard singing, the Priest himself holding in his
Hand a small pig, another man carrying some cocoa
nuts & a third a fine new matt. After repeating a few
Verses & being answered by his Attendants Kaimekee
presented the Pig & Cocoa nuts to us, which we accepted
of and made him a Present of some Toies & c in return.
(Beaglehole 1162–1163)

While ships were anchored at Kealakekua Bay on Monday,
January 25, 1779, "[i]n the afternoon, Terreeoboo [Kalaniʻōpuʻu]
arrived, and visited the ships in a private manner, attended only by one
canoe, in which were his wife and children. He staid on board till near
ten o'clock, when he returned to the village of Kowrowa [Kaʻawaloa]"
(King, J. 16). Samwell gave this description of the high chief

He seems to be above 60 years of age, is very tall &
thin, seemingly much Emaciated by Debaucheries,
tottering as he walks along, his Skin is very scurfy and
his Eyes sore with drinking Ava; he was attended by his
Queen whose name is Kanee-cappo-rei [Kaneikapolei,
ftn. 3], his two young Sons & many of his Courtiers.
(Beaglehole 1168)

But then at noon the next day, Tuesday the 26th, something
tremendous happened.

[. . .] the king, in a large canoe, attended by two others,
set out from the village, and paddled toward the ships in
great state. Their appearance was grand and magnificent.
In the first canoe was Terreeoboo and his chiefs, dressed
in their rich feathered clokes and helmets, and armed
with long spears and daggers; in the second, came the
venerable Kaoo [Kaʻuʻu or Kaʻōʻō], the chief of the
priests, and his brethren, with their idols displayed
on red cloth. These idols were busts of a gigantic size,

made of wicker-work, and curiously covered with small
feathers of various colours, wrought in the same manner
with their cloaks. Their eyes were made of large pearl
oysters, with a black nut fixed in the centre; their mouths
were set with a double row of the fangs of dogs [. . .].
The third canoe was filled with hogs and various sorts of
vegetables. As they went along, the priests in the centre
canoe sung their hymns with great solemnity; and after
paddling round the ships, instead of going on board, as
was expected, they made toward the shore at the beach
where we were stationed. (King, J. 16–17)

On the shore Kalaniʻōpuʻu put his feather cloak over Cook and
put a feather helmet on his head. Then five or six feather cloaks were
set before him on the ground, and the four pigs, fruits, and vegetables
were brought to him. King wrote, "this part of the ceremony was
concluded by the king's exchanging names with Captain Cook"
(King, J. 17). Was this a ceremony to exchange names, a formal and
ceremonial welcome to Cook, or both? Sahlins saw the ceremony that
preceded the exchange as a royal welcome, and he noted "it was of a
kind that would be repeated by Kamehameha for Vancouver" (*How
Natives Think* 69). Being that Kamehameha was with Kalaniʻōpuʻu,
and more than likely on the welcoming canoe, it would be reasonable
that he would employ a similar welcome for another British captain.
But the journal of Captain Portlock, who came to the islands seven
years after Cook, but whose ships stayed mostly off Maui, Oʻahu, and
Kauaʻi, also describes such a welcome. On Friday, December 1, 1786
Captain Portlock was visited by Kahekili at Maunalua Bay on the
island of Oʻahu, and Portlock recorded this account.

The old man [a priest] informed me, that in a short time
the king (who had just arrived in the bay with a large fleet
of canoes) would be on board to pay me a visit, and that
when he returned again on shore the taboo would be taken
off [. . .]. The priest left us about ten o'clock, and returned
again at eleven in his own canoe, accompanied by many
others both large and small. In a very large canoe, paddled
by sixteen stout men, was the king himself, attended by
many of the principal chiefs. [. . .] [A]fter paddling three

times round the ship in great state, [he] came on board
without the least appearance of fear, and would not suffer
any of his retinue to follow him till he had got permission
for their admittance, which I gave to eight or ten of the
principal chiefs. The king brought me a few hogs and
some vegetables by way of present [. . .]. (155–156)

Kahekili's visit to Portlock's ship echoes the events witnessed
by King in 1779. Since there was no exchange of names, and since
Kahekili went on board, we can guess that it was the "stately"
paddling of large double-hulled canoes full of chiefs around the ship
that was a ceremonial welcome. And indeed, it seems to be the pro
forma welcome Kamehameha employs when Vancouver arrives.
These "royal welcomes" bring up more questions about traditional
protocol than we can discover answers to: Why did Kalani'ōpu'u first
visit the ship "privately" with his family, then enact a tremendous
ceremony the next day? Why circle the ships? Why were the feather
gods, whose size was never seen again, brought out in this manner?
What was the meaning of the ritual involving gods and offerings?

We find further clues in this account of an incident that also
involved circling, and that Cook took to be religious in nature, that
occurred while Cook was on Ni'ihau.

As soon as we got upon a rising ground, I stopped
to look round me; and observed a woman, on the
opposite side of the valley where I landed, calling to
her countrymen who attended me. Upon this, the
Chief began to mutter something which I supposed
was a prayer; and the two men, who carried the pigs,
continued to walk round me all the time, making, at
least, a dozen circuits before the other had finished
his oraison [sic]. This ceremony being performed, we
proceeded; and, presently, met people coming from all
parts, who, on being called to by my attendants, threw
themselves prostrate on their faces, till I was out of sight.
(Cook 217–218)

Another recollection of something similar to this circuit-like
action would be the movement of the akua loa and akua poko of the

makahiki celebrations. They move around the island in a clock-wise and counter-clock-wise manner, respectively. Valeri gives a very good and concise description of the movements.

> On the twenty-fourth of Welehu, the *akua loa* and the *akua poko* begin their circuit. The circuit of the first god lasts twenty-three days, as long as the Makahiki festival proper; that of the second god lasts four days, as long as the so-called *kapu Makahiki*. The *akua loa* travels clockwise, keeping the interior on its right; the *akua poko* travels in the opposite direction, with the sea at its right. When it reaches the boundary of the district it returns. As the *akua loa* travels, all the land to the left of the road (i.e., the land under cultivation) is taboo; if someone enters it he is condemned to pay a pig but is not put to death. (206–207)

The scholars who have poured over the historical record don't tell us why the gods move in a circuit, regardless of which way the gods are going, nor do the early Native Hawaiian scholars comment on this activity. Perhaps the circular travel might mimic the original travels of Lonoikamakahiki, but there is nothing to back that up, not even in the tradition of Lonoikamakahiki. So, why the circular movement? Listening to an interview recorded by Clinton Kanahele with a Native Hawaiian elder, Luka Kinolau, I have a much more persuasive hypothesis.

Kanahele recorded the interview on June 29, 1970. Kinolau tells him a remarkable story of how she lost her grandfather and hence was hānai[ed] 'raised' by her grandmother, who was a traditional practitioner of hāhā 'diagnosis by palpation.'

> My parents, I don't know my parents because when I was very small my Chinese sire died. My grandmother was Manoa, and her husband was Kaiama. [. . .] My grandfather was a fisherman, fisherman. He always went fishing. One day he came home and he told my grandmother, "Say, I have been bewitched." My grandmother asked, "Who bewitched you?" "So and so." He divulged her name. My grandmother then said, "Dear, you are going to fall into trouble. You had

not better go fishing. You don't go." My grandmother
reiterated, "You don't go fishing. You stay home." Then
my grandfather said, "How are we going to live? What
shall be our means of support?" My grandmother replied,
"I have saved some money of ours. I have indeed saved.
We have enough." My grandfather prized the night for
it was a good fishing night. So he went fishing. He went
and he never returned. The canoe floated ashore. My
grandfather had perished. My grandmother knew the
woman who had bewitched him because that woman had
circled his canoe once, once, twice, thrice, four times, five
times, and stood and then circled again, once, five times,
stopped. [. . .] [T]he canoe drifted home into our port.
My grandmother went and got the fish, and we pulled
the canoe on dry land. My grandmother began to weep.
She walked around that canoe as that other woman had
done. She circled this canoe, and she wept; she circled
again, and wept. That woman died. (Kanahele, C. 3–4)

Fortunately, the interview was done in Hawaiian, for we do
not have any Hawaiian text for the Cook, Portlock, or Vancouver
examples or even a term for what this circuit is called. Kinolau says
that her grandfather was "haihaia" and Kanahele translated this as
"bewitched"—a remarkable and significant fact. Haihaiā is not a
commonly used word today, and in the Pukui and Elbert dictionary
we find that its first usage comes from the Bible in 1 and 2 Timothy
as "the unholy" or "to increase unto more ungodliness" (47).

If one thought that the root word might be haiā, the first usage of
that word is a "retainer or follower of a chief," and the second usage
points back to haihaiā. The second usage of haihaiā comes from
the writings of Kamakau concerning the priesthood of sorcerers or
"kahuna ʻanāʻanā," a priest who could counter the sorcery of another
"by acting insane (eating poison, going naked), thus diverting the
god's curses to himself [the kahuna] and freeing the victim" (Pukui
and Elbert 1986: 47).

Kamakau described a haihaiā as a method of healing to counter
an act of sorcery. The text is "ʻimi ke ola ma ka haihaia" and was
translated as seeking a cure "by acting ʻinsanely.'" (*Ka Poʻe Kahiko*

140). In the endnotes Lorrin Andrew's (1865) definition of the word
is given with further explanation from Mary Kawena Pukui. Her
explanation that the counter-sorcerer not only takes on the curses
of the victim but also "does battle against the forces of destruction"
(Kamakau, *Ka Poʻe Kahiko* 141) became part of the definition in the
1986 Pukui and Elbert *Hawaiian Dictionary* for haihaiā.

However, if we look closer at Kamakau's description we find that
the kahuna can also "go naked in a circuit around the house, and on
out onto the highway [. . .] (Kamakau, *Ka Poʻe Kahiko* 140). The term
Kamakau uses is kaʻapuni, or "circuit," ("Ka Moolelo Hawaii" 15
Sept., 1870: 1). So the element of a circling movement is part of the
meaning of haihaiā.

Were the Hawaiians using some form of counter-sorcery upon
these foreigners or aliens in their midst? If we knew what the priest
or chiefs were chanting, we might be able to better understand the
nature of this ceremony, but we don't know. In fact, the actions that
follow do not concur with what Kamakau has described as the rites of
haihaiā. Instead I would argue that we need to go back to Andrews'
first usage of the word, which was also cited in the footnotes to
Kamakau's description. Andrew says that it means to "court the favor
of the gods" (Andrews 122, Kamakau, *Ka Poʻe Kahiko* 141. ftn. 12).

I have not seen any records later than Vancouver's visit of an
event like those welcomes. When the Russian explorer Otto von
Kotzebue arrived at Kailua Kona during Kamehameha's latter years,
he is not greeted with the same accord; in fact Kamehameha was
wary of the Russians' intentions and their arrival. Perhaps if we had
known about this before we might be doing ceremonial welcomes
today a bit differently. But times were changing and when another
Russian, Golovnin, arrived in the islands, he saw that Hawaiians were
already integrating new customs with the traditional ones.

> Encountering Europeans, they bow and shake hands
> according to our customs, but among themselves they
> observe their own custom of rubbing noses and holding
> hands. (Golovnin 210)

Looking at the context of each of the greetings upon the water
by the paramount chiefs and priests, we can see they involved several

common elements: a large fleet of canoes; a main double hulled canoe transporting the paramount chief; chanting either by priests or chief; other canoes following with gifts, particularly food; the giving of gifts, including extremely esteemed goods made with feathers; and even the exchange of names. All these point to the circuit or circuits used in the beginning of the ceremony as being propitious.

Despite the differences that leave us with more questions than answers, these accounts of the rituals of welcome emphasize certain common elements:

- 🌾 the need to acknowledge another person's presence by the offering of greetings,
- 🌾 the importance of demonstrating signs of recognition by remembering a person's name or by physical contact such as the honi ihu (*touching of noses*), and
- 🌾 the need to display hospitality through the offering of food, drink, and rest.

The essence of these greetings and offers of hospitality are

> [. . .] a value held in common and shared by Hawaiians, but perhaps not practiced by all. At first it might seem unusual or strange that these admonitions, in proverb and story, would be so necessary to re-enforce in such a society. However, if Hawaiians place such a high value on hospitality, then non-conformity by a few might seriously damage or destroy those values. After all, the act of hospitality is indeed a serious act in which one's resources are shared and one's privacy opened to public scrutiny. (Office of Hawaiian Affairs 16)

Contemporary Protocol

The process of rituals in welcoming guests is what we have come to regard as protocol. Today this practice is synonymous with the Native Hawaiian people and these islands, an image that is possibly heightened by the tourist industry and the promotion of the "aloha spirit." Ironically, this welcoming of guests is perhaps the most prominent legacy of the ancient practices of hospitality.

Native American author Vine Deloria Jr., in his critical analysis of the impact of Western culture and Christianity on native culture, traditions, and religion, described why hospitality is so important to native peoples.

> It is with respect to the attitude displayed toward strangers
> that a community's psychic identity can be determined.
> A community that is uncertain about itself must destroy
> in self-defense to prevent any conceivable threat to its
> existence, whereas a community that has a stable identity
> accords to other communities the dignity of distinct
> existence, which it wishes to receive itself. (*God is Red* 217)

Deloria suggested that greetings and hospitality are not only for individuals and families but also indicative of a community's or a people's view of the world and of others. In essence, the manner in which we welcome others, particularly strangers, defines who we are, how we see ourselves, and how much confidence we have in our beliefs. Some societies remain hesitant and suspicious of any outside influences and change.

A society or community that is open and welcoming to strangers is so because its members are strong and steadfast in their self-identification. Thus, outside influences and behaviors can be adapted or easily dismissed without much harm to their way of life. Such a society can be generous because it is "rewarded" by the acceptance and recognition of its culture (identity) by the visitor (guests) as the way things are done in that place.

A Recent Hawaiian Welcome Ceremony

Deloria's views were put to the test in July 1985 when an event compelled a very serious review of traditional Hawaiian hospitality and welcoming ceremonies. A delegation of Māori people was scheduled to visit Hawai'i on their way back to Aotearoa 'New Zealand' after opening an exhibition of Māori treasures and art in San Francisco. The group included fifty elders and leaders and a cultural performing group. Their arrival in Hawai'i was to coincide with the opening of an exhibition honoring a former Bishop Museum director and Māori, Te Rangi Hiroa (Sir Peter Buck).

At the invitation of the Bishop Museum's director, the Culture Division of the Office of Hawaiian Affairs arranged the welcome ceremony. As the officer for the Culture Division, I collaborated with the museum staff to organize a welcome committee. Members of the committee were selected for their skills in culture, language, and the performing arts, and the committee included people skilled in chanting, which today has survived only in the form of the hula.

We all had a vision for the welcome, but we wanted to be sure that our plans would be true to traditions and not merely reflective of our own assumptions and prejudices. The next six months were used to conduct research to rediscover traditional rituals of welcome. Several of us on the committee, having lived in Aotearoa and stayed on marae, were experienced with the Māori *kawa,* or ceremonial welcomes. We wanted to have a ceremony that would emphasize specifically Hawaiian cultural practices, yet contain elements that would be familiar to the Māori so they would also be able to contribute to the occasion.

What was proposed was to consider the museum by its Hawaiian name as the house of Princess Bernice Pauahi. The garden entrance to the museum would be our courtyard, or "malae," where the rituals of encounter would be held. These rituals would include greetings, chants, the genealogy of the Kamehameha dynasty for Princess Pauahi, and words of welcome. A kapu sign of the crossed pūloʻuloʻu or "tabu stick" would be set before the entrance doors of the museum building to prohibit any entry until the greetings were completed. Only then would the Māori and Hawaiian elders enter to bless the exhibit. When this was over, everyone gathered would be invited into the "house" and the museum's Great Hall to join in speeches and songs in both Māori and Hawaiian.

The welcome was recounted from the Māori perspective by Dr. Hirini (Sidney) Moko Mead in the publication describing the Te Māori exhibition's journey throughout the United States.

> We learnt that the Hawaiians had set up a protocol committee to discuss in fine detail the kawa [ceremonial protocol] for the opening of CELEBRATING THE MAORI on 18 July and to work out what they would do for the event. [. . .]

During the meeting, the function of kawa was of course paramount in our minds. Kawa allows certain activities of high symbolic value to occur in an orderly way, so our task was to work out procedures that would be understood and accepted by the participants. [. . .] Some understanding was absolutely essential if the opening ceremony was to be a success. So the two sides talked about the procedures and very soon reached some understanding. [. . .]

The ceremony was to begin at 4:00 p.m., and we arrived in two buses. We were led on to the grounds of the museum and towards the entrance [. . .]. [N]o words can really convey the great feelings of expectation, excitement and sheer delight in the coming together of Hawaiian and Maori in a series of rituals.

The Hawaiian welcome ceremony called *heahea* began with a chant of greeting [. . .]. It was actually difficult for the Maori group to sit still and not respond with either karanga [responding chants] or speeches. Our responses were to come after the opening rituals for the exhibitions.

Several times our warriors pranced towards the door [to the museum], and several times we had to call them

back because the rahui [prohibition posts] was still in
place. [. . .] In point of fact, we were feeling our way and
sometimes getting ahead of the set procedures. But at no
time did we actually break the flow of the rituals. [. . .]

The newspapers described the event in a number of
ways. [. . .] The Honolulu ADVERTISER (19 July 1985)
said, 'Hawaiians and New Zealand Maori, among the
closest of cousins, joined together yesterday and became
one people. Their unique exchange of greetings opened
the Bishop Museum's "Celebrating the Maori" exhibit in
a spectacular fashion.' (Mead 91–96)

Hoʻokipa, the Expression of Hospitality

The experience of researching, planning, and executing the
events of that day lead to the first in what was hoped to be a series on
Hawaiian cultural traditions and practices by the Office of Hawaiian
Affairs. The office published a booklet called *Hoʻokipa, Hawaiian
Hospitality* as a means of sharing the information that was compiled
and used.

In the introduction of the booklet, the late Moses Keale, Sr., then
chairman of the Office of Hawaiian Affairs, described the feeling of
that time.

At the Museum, for the first time in generations,
perhaps even since we had left Kahiki, the homeland,
such a large number of Hawaiians and Maoris met as
hanauna, as relatives. The warmth, the aloha of the
occasion was profound and it brings back so many
good memories about the Maori people.

What we learned from these occasions was a need
to express what exactly is hoʻokipa [. . .]. (Office of
Hawaiian Affairs 3)

Like many other cultural practices, there is no exact term for
welcomes, especially ceremonial ones. The closest Hawaiian term
may be hoʻokipa, or hospitality. There are certain key elements
to hoʻokipa. The foremost is the greetings. Informally, it is to call
out to the other person, or to "kāhea." In more formal settings, we
rediscovered the term heahea. This call might be a simple greeting
of aloha, or it might be a more traditional and lesser-used greeting
known as welina. The call may be extended into a chant based on the
closeness of the relationships or on the status and rank of the people
involved.

Chants

Mary Kawena Pukui recorded one such chant from her home
district of Kaʻū, on the island of Hawaiʻi:

He mai!
He mai e kuʻu pua lehua o ka wao,
I pohai ʻia e na manu o uka,
Kuʻu lehua i mohala i ka ua o Haʻao,
Ua ao ka hale nei, ua hiki mai la ʻoe.
Mai! mai! Eia no makou nei.
(Handy and Pukui 172)

Welcome!
Welcome, my lehua flower of the forest
Surrounded by the birds of the uplands
My lehua that bloomed in the rain of Haʻao
Light comes to our house, for you are here.
Welcome! Welcome! Here we are.
(Author's translation)

In the hula, similar chants are used. Those chants mostly come from the traditions of Pele and Hiʻiaka, telling of the younger sister Hiʻiaka's ventures across the islands stopping to find rest and food. Many times she was not greeted with open hospitality. For instance, on the island of Kauaʻi she chanted

> Kunihi ka mauna i ka laʻi e,
> O Wai-ale-ale la i Wai-lua,
> Huki aʻe la i ka lani
> Ka papa au-wai o ka Wai-kini;
> Alai ia aʻe la e Nou-nou,
> Nalo ka Ipu-haʻa,
> Ka laula mauka o Kapaʻa, e!
> Mai paʻa i ka leo!
> He ole ka hea mai, e!
> (Emerson 40)

> *Steep is the mountain in the calm,*
> *Waiʻaleʻale at Wailua,*
> *Twisted towards the heavens*
> *The water courses of Waikini;*
> *Blocked by Nounou,*
> *Ipuhaʻa disappears,*
> *The upland broadness of Kapaʻa!*
> *Don't be silent!*
> *And not call!*
> (Author's translation)

In planning the first welcome for the Māori at the museum, we recognized the importance of chanting and the familiarity kumu hula 'hula instructors' and chanters would have with these chants. We followed the words of Mary Kawena Pukui who noted that, "With favourite children and with chiefs, the *heahea* was followed by the name-chant (*mele inoa*) of that individual or of his family" (Handy and Pukui 172). We also utilized the concept that we were at the "House of Pauahi" by using a name chant for Pauahi and reciting the genealogy of the Kamehamehas.

There is one major difference between welcomes and the hula in the use of these chants. In the hālau hula 'hula school,' or at the kahua hula 'dance stage,' these songs of welcome and calling are used as passwords for someone to enter. Some have carried this idea, as well as the Māori *kawa* or "protocol," over into contemporary welcomes so that visitors must call for permission to enter. Some even recite their genealogies during a welcome, a practice that was used on the island of Oʻahu at genealogical houses or schools called Hale Nauā. Again, the reciting of the genealogy was to ask for permission to enter.

> The purpose of this hale (nauā) was to ask and discuss (ʻike pono) the relationship of anyone to the aliʻi nui. This is what was done at this hale. When it came time to enter into this hale, the aliʻi sat inside. Two persons sat outside of the pā lāʻau [wooden fence]. There were many people inside with the aliʻi nui [in the hale] and those persons skilled in genealogies were also inside with the aliʻi nui.
>
> When a person came to enter into the aliʻi(ʻs) hale, the people outside called out, Here is so and so, who enters. Then those inside would call out, Who are you, so and so, nauā. Who is your parent, nauā. Who is your parent, nauā. This person would reply, So and so is my parent. (Malo 262)

Handy and Pukui noted that "there was no set chant of welcome; each person made up his own for the occasion. [. . .] The purpose of the *heahea* was to make a person feel welcome. When the *heahea* was lacking, a guest felt unwanted and ashamed to come" (172).

Handy and Pukui also distinguished another form of heahea, "a loud wail of welcome (*uwe*)," used for more intimate friends and relatives.

> The words of the *uwe* were spontaneous and not memorized, and they expressed the affection of the host for the returned traveller. Loved ones, home, the hills and the sea, places where they had been together, loved ones who had passed on during his absence might be mentioned. One person might do the wailing while others sat about and wept silently, or one adult followed another in uttering the *uwe*. (173)

Hoʻokipa, as we have seen many times in the traditional accounts, is not about asking or gaining permission. Welcoming a person or persons is not about defending one's position or place, but about extending hospitality. Therefore it should not be about permission. Instead, it is calling for recognition, pili aloha, or love.

There were certain physical ways to express that aloha. Some of these were defined by Kamakau: "The old Hawaiian ways of salutation were touching noses, bowing the head, greeting with the mouth, weeping, rolling on the ground, or kneeling as a sign of submission. These were forms taught by early Hawaiian parents" (*Ruling Chiefs* 249).

John Papa ʻĪʻī wrote one of the most poignant examples of this expression when he, as a young boy, had to leave his parents to begin his new life in the king's court.

> His mother said, "Do not think of us. The chief alone
> must be your father and your mother. From him
> shall come your vegetable food, your meat, your tapa
> coverings, and malos."
>
> The boy asked, "May I not come and see you sometimes
> when you are as near as you are now?"
>
> "It will be all right to do so at the proper time," she
> replied, "but it would be much better for you to remain
> with the chief with no thought of us, whether we are as
> near as we are now or far away."
>
> While they talked, the sun passed to the opposite side of
> Mount Kaala, and his mother said, "Night has come for you."
>
> "Homai ka ihu (embrace me; literally, give the nose),"
> replied the boy. (56)

Honi Ihu

Today most people have adopted Western expressions such as kissing, handshakes, and hugging. Having had my nose touched, rubbed, and sometimes crushed while living among the Māori, I find it an amusing sight to watch adult Hawaiian men greet each other with true affection. Most of the time they do not know exactly how this should be expressed, as handshaking is too formal, and kissing, for the most part, is too personal. Many resort to a good bear hug.

The honi ihu, or the touching of the nose, is an expression that exchanges the breath of the two, sharing the scent of familiarity, and conveys the closeness of that relationship. It is physical contact, but it does not have the same intimate connotation as "kissing"

does in the contemporary mind.

A wonderful example of how such an expression can define this relationship is to be found in the journal of Captain James King of the *Discovery*, who accompanied Captain Cook on his third voyage in the Pacific. On Saturday, February 13, 1779, Palea, a favorite of Kalaniʻōpuʻu who was trying to help the British explorers, was mistakenly assaulted by some crew members who thought he was responsible for some stolen items. Although Palea had been knocked down, he was able to get up in

Moses K. Keale Sr., then chair of the Office of Hawaiian Affairs, welcomed a Māori elder at the grounds of Kawaiahaʻo Plaza with a honi ihu.

time to stop a counter attack by Hawaiians against the crew. After helping to restore some order,

> he followed them [the crew] in his canoe, with a midshipman's cap, and some other trifling articles of the plunder, and, with much apparent concern at what happened, asked, if the *Orono* would kill him, and whether he would permit him to come on board the next day? On being assured, that he should be well received, he joined noses (as their custom is) with the officers, in token of friendship, and paddled over to the village of Kowrowa [Kaʻawaloa] (40).

Both a sign of departure and of friendship, the honi ihu, as this early account demonstrates, is without doubt part and parcel of our culture and who we are.

Lei

The giving of floral lei was a traditional practice, but we find few references to lei in greetings or ceremonial welcomes. (One exception is the account by the Rev. William Ellis of Mauaʻe's return to his home village.) The many different methods of haku lei 'lei making,' particularly for the chiefs, would indicate that lei were not tied until presented to the intended wearer. This manner of presentation respected the concept that a person's head and back were sacred and precluded the casting of the lei over the head as is usually done today. Pukui added, "One must never ask for a *lei* which another person was wearing. It was proper, however, if one were wearing a *lei*, to take it off one's self to garland a near relative or someone held in esteem" (Handy and Pukui 182).

Preparation of Food

The preparation and distribution of food are critical when hospitality is requested. Again, we have seen in traditional accounts the importance of nourishment for a stranger or visitor who had traveled great distances. My aunties who lived in Kakaʻako remembered when Mary Kawena Pukui would visit them, stand at the wooden fence, and call out to them from the gate to let them know she had arrived. Someone would rush to the kitchen to prepare some food and drink, for they did not know if she had come from nearby Mānoa or as far away as her birth place in Kaʻū on the island of Hawaiʻi. Pukui stated that in Kaʻū, "[a]s soon as he [the visitor] was seated, he was asked to have something to eat (*E ʻai*). If the stranger was hungry, he accepted, but if he was not, he declined" (Handy and Pukui 172). And as Ellis had suggested before, the custom is also to have food ready for the visitors to take home or for their journey after their stay has ended. "Entertainment," as Ellis called it, is more important than speeches and protocol for relatives and friends or those who traveled far.

Role of Children

The role of children in traditional society was well understood. Handy and Pukui noted, "Children did not run around and make noise during the *uwe* [greetings of cries and wailing] but sat quietly near a parent or grandparent. Older ones, able to help with the preparation of food, hurried off to prepare and serve the guest as soon as the *uwe* was over. The younger ones waited to be called forward to meet the guest" (173).

Yet, children could have a participatory role in the welcome of dignitaries and very special persons. One such role children played is described in the account of the visitation of Queen Liliʻuokalani to the island of Kauaʻi shortly after her coronation in 1891. A special song, entitled *E o e Liliʻu*, a mele inoa, was composed in her honor by Miss Pelelia Castro. It was sung by five girls when Her Majesty visited the community of Anahola. It was said that "the Queen was so pleased and touched that she burst into tears. The children were summoned several times to different places that the Queen was visiting to sing the song again" (Chun, *He Buke Mele* Introduction).

Hoʻokupu

Today, particularly with the visitation of dignitaries, a hoʻokupu 'tribute' is presented. Recent and continuing research is rediscovering accounts of such tributes. Traditionally, hoʻokupu were obligatory tributes given to high chiefs. The descriptions of hoʻokipa do not indicate that hoʻokupu was given at the time of the greetings. Part of the reason for this may be that a hoʻokupu appears to have been a massive undertaking, requiring the gathering of the people, the collection of the "gifts," or sometimes even the taxes to be given to the high chief. A missionary's eyewitness account of such a presentation recorded the following:

> Monday, 30. Reached the beach, this evening just in time to witness a novel and interesting sight—the presentation to the king of a tax levied on a district on the windward side of the island. It consisted of a procession of not less than 150 persons led by the headman, or overseer of the district. They were all neatly dressed in new tapa, and walked in a single file, the first 20 men bearing each a baked pig, or dog, neatly and ingeniously wrapped in and ornamented with green leaves. These were followed by fifty others, bearing 30 immense calabashes of *poi*, 20 of which were suspended each on a long pole, and carried by two men, and 10 others on the shoulders of the same number of men. Then came females to the number of 70, or 80, each bearing on her shoulder a large package of tapa, or native cloth. The whole was deposited in

front of the royal tent, and the company, with hundreds
who followed them, seated themselves in a circle, at a
respectful distance, apparently with the expectation, that
the king would present himself.

In the course of half an hour he left his tent, and paced
the large mat in front of it for 15 or 20 minutes. He
appeared with dignity, and we could not but remark
the similarity of his air and whole appearance to that of
persons of high rank in our own country [. . .]. ("Journal
of Messrs. Richards and Stewart at Lahinah" 19 March
1825: 658)

Kamakau recorded this account of a hoʻokupu given in honor of
Kamehameha by Kahekili Keʻeaumoku in 1808 at Awāwamalu Bay
on the island of Oʻahu.

He announced that he was giving a tribute to
Kamehameha, and so all of the people of his lands on
Oahu and Maui prepared the tribute.

The treasures given were food, pigs, dogs, kapa, skirts,
loin cloths, nets, olona fiber, feather capes, helmets, O-o
and mamo feathers and pearls. [. . .]

Putting together all the people from the many districts
that came, there must have been four thousand people
gathered.

No treasures or riches of the chief were spared for this
tribute. The chief's people said, "The poor will survive." [. . .]

This tribute did not become a burden to the people. It
was not considered a burden because of the generosity of
the chief. (Kamakau, I Ka Wa 41–43)

Customary items today are based upon the ideal of these
traditional items. These modern-day counterparts may include items
such as food wrapped in kī-leaf bundles called pūʻolo. Lei, especially
uncommon ones, are many times given to honored visitors. Other
modern day gifts such as books and "traditional" handicrafts

are considered appropriate to be presented as hoʻokupu. Some "transitional" gift items presented today are Hawaiian quilts, which have replaced traditional kapa 'bark cloth,' and canoe paddles and bowls made from native hard woods.

Former State Senator Kenneth Brown, a descendant of John Papa ʻĪʻī, presents a canoe paddle to Sir Howard Morrison at the opening of a Māori-Hawaiian Trade Show at the Sheraton Waikīkī Hotel.

Speeches and Welcome

Influences of the Māori *kawa* and the hālau hula are noticeable in contemporary welcome ceremonies. The elements of speech making followed by chants or songs are traditional components of the *kawa*. A speech given without a chant or song 'waiata' is considered dry or without the relish, added either to give the words more emphasis or to ease the serious nature of the speech.

The long process of welcoming in both speeches and chants, particularly when chants are used as passwords for permission, is derived from the experiences of the *kawa* and the hālau. The traditional accounts do not support the long wait for a visitor to be greeted and to receive food and drink.

The welcoming of strangers and relations is an extremely important function and practice in Hawaiian society because it reinforces the concept of relationships as articulated in the word aloha. It has developed into a means of Hawaiian self-identification and expression and is further nurtured today by the commercial tourist industry.

This was a dramatic point observed by James Kekela, the Hawaiian missionary to the Marquesas Islands, who compared the hospitality of the Tahitians and Samoans. "Then again, the people take no interest in welcoming strangers, but the Hawaiians living here saw us at once and came to welcome us with demonstrations of affection, and have helped us in every way, giving us food of all kinds and bringing us pigs and fowl as we do to strangers in Hawaii" (Kamakau, *Ruling Chiefs* 244).

When the relationship has been established through verbal acknowledgment, it is then immediately followed by expressions of hospitality through physical contact and the offering of food and drink. How simple or elaborate those expressions are depends upon their appropriateness to the persons being greeted. Beyond these key elements of hoʻokipa, the most essential ingredient is to create a true sense of aloha and ensure that such aloha is conveyed.

4 Aʻo

Educational Traditions

There was mana in the old days, and those people who were
correctly taught had real mana; eyewitnesses could not say
that their mana was false (wahaheʻe).
Kamakau, *Ruling Chiefs of Hawaii*

✖

Nānā ka maka; hoʻolohe ka pepeiao, paʻa ka waha.
Observe with the eyes; listen with the ears, shut the mouth
[Thus one learns].
Pukui, *ʻŌlelo Noʻeau*

✖

Haʻaloʻu knew no man who understands deep things should go
unrecompensed, for knowledge is not to be scattered about freely and
"the laborer is worthy of his hire."
Kamakau, *Ruling Chiefs of Hawaii*

Aʻo is the word for education, but it means much more.
It implies both to learn (aʻo mai) and to teach (aʻo aku). This
sense of receiving and giving supports the idea that relationships
and belonging are primary actions in traditional Hawaiian
society and culture. It is the idea that as one learns and becomes
skilled (mastery), knowledge and skill are to be used and shared
with others (generosity). This builds relationships of mutual
dependence and support, bringing families and community
together. And yet, having knowledge and skills gives one a sense
of independence and identity within the family and community.
This concept is expressed in a Māori proverb, first introduced to
me by the Chief Judge of the Waitangi Tribunal, the Honorable
Eddie Durie: Hō atu taonga, hoki mai taonga, a gift given is a gift
returned. This symbolizes that the building of a relationship that
becomes mutual and long-lasting is as important as the gift itself.

What traditions we have about ancient education come from
the "literature" [both oral and written] of the chiefs and priests
and describe how they were trained for their roles. We know about
everyday labor, like farming and fishing, and the techniques that were
used, but we have no detailed accounts of how people were taught
those skills, perhaps because they were indeed everyday and ordinary.

Native historian John Papa ʻĪʻī described his own education. It was supported by his parents and intended to prepare him to become a skilled and well-trained servant of the king.

> From the time he was little, Ii was taught by his father, Kuaena, the rules of good behavior, in preparation for his position in the royal court, where he was destined to go at the age of ten. They brought him up carefully, instructing him in all things, and saw to it that he was quick and capable, [. . .] (Ii 22)

This does not mean that our view of traditional learning and teaching is elitist; on the contrary, we shall see that there are certain common patterns of education throughout traditional society and culture.

Traditional Patterns of Education

Traditional patterns of education were first articulated by Mary Kawena Pukui in her work on the Queen Liliʻuokalani Children's Center's culture project. In *Nānā I Ke Kumu* she revealed that there are five responses that students have to learning and teaching.

> The elders well knew that: "*I ka nānā no a ʻike*, by observing, one learns. *I ka hoʻolohe no a hoʻomaopopo*, by listening, one commits to memory. *I ka hana no a ʻike*, by practice one masters the skill."

> To this a final directive was added: Never interrupt. Wait until the lesson is over and the elder gives you permission. Then—and not until then—nīnau. Ask questions. (Pukui, Haertig, and Lee 48)

1. **Observation**, or "nānā" or "ʻike," is crucial in island life. The ability to look at the sea and to see where the schools of fish were located, or if there were any at all, led to great skill in fishing. Such skill was developed over time while gazing at the currents and waves, and from the observations of teachers or mentors. Today's television cooking programs demonstrate this technique of learning by taking the viewer through the various stages of preparation to the end result.

In the tradition of the chief 'Umi it was remembered that a fisherman-warrior on the opposing side knew of an impending attack because of what he had just observed.

> [. . .] a o kekahi kanaka lawaia nui no Puueo, aia no oia
> i ka lawaia kolo huki heenehu' i kai; ike oia i ka lepo o
> ka wai i ka moana; ua puiwa kona manao, a manao iho
> la, he kaua aia ma ka mauna, a oia ke kumu i lepo ai ka
> wai; [. . .]

> There was a great fisherman from Puueo engaged with
> a large net at the heenehu' fishing grounds, who
> noticed the dirty water of the sea and was surprised
> at the fact. He thought that there was war in the
> mountains which was the cause of the dirt in the
> stream. (Fornander IV: 224–225)

It was his ability to deduce, by putting together the facts that the fresh water coming from the mountains was muddy although it was not raining up there, that the streams were probably being crossed by many feet, hence a war party was on its way.

Handy and Pukui describe a similar deductive skill in Ka'ū on the island of Hawai'i.

> [. . .] these men, who sharply watched every sign of
> ocean and air, the fact that here the flow (*au moana*) of
> ocean around the island came together from east and west
> alongshore, pushed by whatsoever wind—trade winds
> (*ko'olau*), southerlies (*kona*), north-westerlies (*kiu*). And
> they knew that here ran the big fish they treasured most
> for subsistence—'*ahi* (tuna), *aku* (bonito), *a'u* (swordfish),
> *ulua* (*Caranx*) and *mahimahi* (dolphin fish), and the
> smaller but much relished '*opelu* (mackerel). (223)

2. **Listening**, or "ho'olohe," is another important aspect of learning. As with observation, listening requires one to be attentive and patient. Such skills would be fully utilized in traditional "schools," particularly those of the kāhuna where students had to memorize prayers and chants, without the aid of writing or printed materials. Laura Judd, wife of the missionary

doctor Geritt P. Judd, came to this conclusion when she entered into her journal for April 28, 1828 that, "[t]he aged are fond of committing to memory, and repeating in concert. [. . .] Their power of memory is wonderful, acquired, as I suppose, by the habit of committing and reciting traditions, and the genealogies of their kings and priests" (Judd 17).

3.   **Reflection**, or to consider what has been done, is a polite way to translate the term paʻa ka waha, literally to "shut one's mouth." Instead of jumping to conclusions, it is better for one to reflect on all the options, putting the experiences of observing and listening together.

4.   Actually **doing** the task, or hana ka lima, literally "the hands create or do," was the next step. Having seen the stages necessary to create something, having heard the instructions and reflected on them, the time came to actually do it by one's self. Mistakes could be experienced and corrected as part of the learning process without harm. Kamakau, in his detailed analysis of the training of students for the priesthood gives this description.

> [. . .] until the pupil knew as much as his teacher, then
> the teacher would say to the pupil, "Concentrate your
> prayers (*E kia ko pule*) on that solid cliff and make it
> slide," and the pupil would concentrate on the cliff until
> it crumbled. (*Ka Poʻe Kahiko* 121)

5.   **Questioning**, or "nīnau," encouraged from the start in many cultures, is thought of as something a person would consider almost as the last expression of learning. Having experienced seeing, listening, reflecting, and doing, a student may have answered many of the trivial questions, leaving only the most important to be asked of one's teacher or mentor.

These are in a deliberate order and form an approach that is different from the methods of inquiry we find in education today.

Looking at all of the five parts together, we see how this process can work: Through discerning and careful observation 'nānā, hoʻolohe, and paʻa ka waha' a child learns under the tutelage of a master, a concept similar to mentorship. This system allows for the careful transmission of knowledge and skills from generation to generation as well as for the development of an interpersonal relationship wherein a child may experience the care and guidance of a mature adult.

In the next phase, experiential participation allows the child to demonstrate the abilities he or she has developed through observation. The child can be tested to see if he or she has learned well, or has even improved upon the tradition. Mistakes made during this period can be corrected either by the student or by the master, and the child is given opportunities to practice his or her acquired skills while still under careful guidance.

Then and only then are questions allowed, for by this time the child will have focused on the most important points that he or she may not understand. This is an economical usage of the master's time and helps the child develop self-teaching abilities. The end results are the mastery of skills and the gaining of knowledge; the expression of independent learning under careful guidance; the creation of a sense of belonging as the transmission of skills and knowledge from one generation to the next is done through an interpersonal relationship; and the fostering of a desire for generosity in sharing one's skills and knowledge with those willing to learn. In addition to teaching a child specific skills, this system teaches a process that serves the child well through the transition from adolescence to adulthood.

Professional Training of Young Experts

The training of young persons to become experts, or "kāhuna," was different, perhaps because these skills dealt with the precise memorization of long prayers and chants and had to do with religion. We are sure of this because Kamakau provides great detail on how students were educated to become expert healers, particularly in diagnosing and treating an illness by palpation 'hāhā.' In this case the founder of the practice had followers (students), and they established a center and herbal farm in Kukuihā'ele on the island of Hawai'i.

> There were kapus connected with learning the art of healing by the *haha* method. An apprentice must first release (*huikala*) any kapus that he was under pertaining

A circle of students and their teacher are shown gathered in front of what might be a hale moku in an engraving based on a painting by Dr. William Ellis.

to his own *ʻaumakua* before entering the Lonopuha profession (*ʻoihana* Lonopuha). The training was given under kapu, and sometimes in a special house, such as an *ulu hale*, a *moku hale*, or a *hale lau*. The pupils were taught the laws and rules of the practice until they obtained knowledge and skill, and if they had listened to and observed these laws [. . .]

In learning the medical arts, including that of Lonopuha, the first thing was to learn the prayers. These were the foundation and the guide to knowledge and skill whereby a man learned to heal and to recognize the mysterious things inside a sick man. The god was the guide to all things, the giver of boundless life; therefore every person who was learning the arts depended upon the god. [. . .]

In some countries of the world, medical practitioners are not like the Hawaiian ones. [. . .] Some are medical experts, not through the mana of God, but through their being guided by visual proof (*ma ko lakou alaka'i 'ikemaka*) in their search for knowledge. In the Hawaiian school of medical kahunas, the god was the foundation, and secondly came prayers. Third came schooling in the kinds of diseases; fourth, in the kinds of remedies; fifth, in the art of killing; and sixth, in the art of saving.

The foundation of knowledge and skill of the *kahuna lapa'au* was the god. It was he who knew without error the treatment; it was he who pointed out the nature of the ailment and the things that pertained to this or that disease of man.

Second came prayer. [. . .]

After the prayer of thanksgiving (*pule ho'omaika'i*) for the mana of the god came the prayer of rememberance (*pule ho'omana'o*) for those who had belonged to the order of the medical kahunas of Lonopuha and for the long-time kahunas [. . .]. (Kamakau, *Ka Po'e Kahiko* 106–107)

Kamakau also tells of the ratio of teacher to pupil at these professional schools. "Each teacher had from three to five pupils. The teacher, too, lived under kapu" (*Ka Po'e Kahiko* 121).

Educational Tools

When a learning system is not based upon literacy, other learning senses such as memorization, careful observation, and practice must be enhanced. Those skills were perfected in the "classroom."

[. . .] a *moku hale*, a house set apart for this training, was built, and there his course of instruction began. [. . .] All he did was to learn the prayers, and to pray continuously (*kuili*) night and day until the prayers were so memorized that they would slip from his mouth as easily as an *olioli* or *mele*, without hesitating or stammering. (Kamakau, *Ka Po'e Kahiko* 120–121)

To help students refine their skills, some educational tools were used to give a "graphic illustration" of the idea. During the process

The use of pebbles for the training of the kahuna hāhā

of learning to heal by hāhā 'palpation or feeling,' students were introduced to a large diagram of the human body laid out in pebbles.

> Third came [the diagnosing of diseases by means of] the *papa ʻiliʻili*, the "table of pebbles." This was an arrangement of pebbles in the form of a man, from head to foot, until there was an outline of an entire man. The study of the pebbles began at the feet. [. . .]

> While the teacher taught, the pupils sat alert and
> remembered carefully every thing that was taught them. [. . .]

> By the time the instructon with the *'ili'ili*, the pebbles,
> was finished, the pupils knew thoroughly the symptoms
> and the "rules" (*na kulana ma'i a me na loina*) for
> treatment of the diseases [. . .]. (Kamakau, *Ka Po'e
> Kahiko* 108)

The use of such a "table of pebbles" was evidently not the
exclusive tool of the kāhuna hāhā. We find it mentioned in, of all
places, a book on the use of medicinal herbs, that such a table of
pebbles was used for teaching astronomy and that the foundation of
the "table" was a mat made from the makaloa sedge 'reeds.'

> The instruction of astronomy and Hāhā healing were
> done on Makaloa mats that had been woven [for that
> purpose]. These arts of old Hawai'i were good things and
> [people] were taught by arranging small 'Alā pebbles
> given individual names, on some 365 meshes of the mat.

> This was also the same way for the practice of the hāhā
> priests to use the same number of pebbles to show the
> Hāhā chart (papa Hāhā) as were used in the Lani-honua
> chart (*astronomy*). (Chun, *Native Hawaiian Medicine* 213)

We also know that in astronomy an 'umeke or "calabash" was
carefully prepared by a teacher to be used for teaching the positions
of the stars.

> Take the lower part of a gourd or hula drum (hokeo),
> rounded as a wheel, on which several lines are to be
> marked (burned in), as described hereafter. [. . .] The
> teacher will mark the positions of all these stars on the
> gourd. [. . .]

> During the nights from Kaloa to Mauli (the dark nights of
> the moon), are the best times for observation. Spread out
> a mat, lie down with your face upward, and contemplate
> the dark-bright sections of Kane and Kanaloa, and the
> navigating stars contained within them. [. . .]

You will also study the regulations of the ocean, the
movements of the tides, floods, ebbs and eddies, the art
of righting upset canoes, "Ke kamaihulipu," and learn
to swim from one island to another. All this knowledge
contemplate frequently, and remember it by heart, so
that it may be useful to you on the rough, the dark and
unfriendly ocean. (qtd. in Johnson and Mahelona 72–73)

Experimentation

We know today that a powerful event can be caused when
creativity, innovation, risk, an element of challenge, and courage—
the elements of experimentation—go beyond the boundaries of the
accepted norms and come together to forge something new and
possibly revolutionary. Scientific and technological advances are most
often the results of such events, and we now fully recognize that this
process occurred in Hawaiʻi before the arrival of Captain James Cook
in 1778.

Palaha was the first teacher to have thought of the
benefits of the enema. This is how Palaha reasoned:
When the water of a stream is stagnant, it is filthy; when
a freshet comes, the water becomes clean—all the trash
and filth are gone. So it is in filthy pools—when fresh
water comes in, the filth is removed. Palaha meditated
on this, and when he understood it, he gave an enema
to a dog. Seeing the benefits of the enema, he thought
of the illness of his father Puheke. By experimenting, he
found the benefits of the enema given below (*hahano
malalo*) and the purgative given above (*hoʻonaha iho
maluna*), and which illnesses to treat by means of
loosening the bowels, and how to check the action of
the bowels. When Puheke died, Palaha cut his father
open, according to his father's wish that he look inside
and see what the disease was and what its symptoms
were. Because of his work Palaha became famous in the
order of the *kahuna kapaʻau* [*sic*], and he and his father
entered into the line of succession of Lonopuha kahunas
(*papa moʻo kahuna Lonopuha*). (Kamakau, *Ka Poʻe
Kahiko* 111–112)

There is another, slightly different, version of the same tradition.

> There was a man named Palaha who was sick. His
> son, Palapuheke, tried to cure him, but his father died.
> Palapuheke cut open his father's stomach and saw a
> large accumulation of filth had collected inside of his
> father. He believed that this accumulation was the cause
> for the failure of the medicine to work.
>
> Palapuheke saw that this situation was similar with
> nature. He observed how the soil in the uplands
> accumulated and became filthy in the streams, but when
> it rained the water washed the soil away. He also saw
> the soil being washed out to sea during the high tide.
> Reflecting upon these events, Palapuheke got a water
> gourd with a long spout, placed some medicines in it
> and inserted it into a dog. The enema purged the dog. He
> tried the enema on a woman, and it also worked. Lastly
> Palapuheke tried it on a man and it worked too. (Chun,
> *Hawaiian Medicine Book* 54–55)

These two versions of the same tradition are full of important information. It is obvious that the son has employed the skills of good observation and deduction. The deduction part is tremendously important because he was able to piece together the sequence of actions of the fresh water, and reflecting upon it he was able to come to a conclusion. If we go back to those guiding principles of traditional education, we see how important reflection 'pa'a ka waha' is to the process—not purely being quiet and attentive but also allowing the creative process of thinking to take place.

This is not the end of this analysis, for the son then does something people usually do not relate to indigenous cultures. He conducted a scientific experiment to ensure that his discovery would work. The son takes this whole procedure up another notch and conducts an autopsy on his father, as instructed, for the sole purpose of scientific discovery. That is a major point in our re-discovery of traditional learning, because people often would like to believe that indigenous peoples, unlike peoples of the Western world, stumbled upon their discoveries and inventions.

This became a tremendously important event in our culture for we have been led to believe that the cutting up of the human body was not performed here, although sub-incision was done to young boys as a ritual to maturity. This entire story demonstrates the fact that localized self-directed discovery for the sake of knowledge, which is the basis for the scientific revolution and much of the world's attitudes about education, was part of what some have called a primitive society.

Indeed, the son and father were entered into the memory of the priesthood. We have the complete chants of this priesthood, and in the prayers of thanksgiving and remembrance are these lines:

> The priests who gather during the night,
> Lonopuha and Milu Koomea,
> Nahilipuna, Nahiliwai,
> Keanuiki, Keanunui,
> Keanuohua, Piipii,
> Palaha, Palapuheke,
> Maiaea, Kalaniwahine, (Chun, *Hawaiian Medicine Book* 49)

Demonstrating Mastery

In the few examples to be found in the traditions about instruction between a teacher and students, there are some that describe how a teacher determined the student's mastery. In the practice of the kāhuna hāhā 'medicinal practitioners who used palpation,' after intense training using a physical diagram of pebbles to represent a person's body and illnesses, Kamakau says,

> [t]hen the teacher would bring in a man who had many disorders and would call the pupils one by one to go and "feel," *haha*, for the diseases. If the diagnosis (*'ike haha*) was the same as that of the teacher, then the teacher knew that the pupil had knowledge of *haha*. (*Ka Poʻe Kahiko* 108)

In the practice of 'anāʻanā 'practice of inflicting illness or death through prayers,' after rigorous training in learning prayers, a ritual called 'ailolo that used a baked pig from each student to divine a message of the student's proficiency was invoked. According to

Kamakau "[i]f a pig was all right, but an eye had fallen out or the throat was cracked [. . .] [t]hat pupil should not practice what he had been taught, for he would have an insatiable greed for other people's property [. . .]" (*Ka Po'e Kahiko* 121). A similar ceremony is said to be part of the training for traditional hula dancers. Nathaniel Emerson describes it in his account of the hula, *Unwritten Literature of Hawaii.*

> Now comes the pith of the ceremony: the novitiates sit
> down to the feast of ai-lolo, theirs the place of honor, at
> the head of the table, next the kuahu [altar]. The ho'o-
> pa'a, acting as carver, [. . .] sets an equal portion before
> each novitiate. Each one must eat all that is set before
> him. It is a mystical rite, a sacrament; [. . .] The kumu
> lifts the tabu by uttering a prayer—always a song—and
> declares the place and the feast free, [. . .] The pupils
> have been graduated from the school of the halau; they
> are now members of the great guild of hula dancers.
> (34–35)

The next stage in their initiation is what Emerson called their "début" or "uniki" when they "present themselves to the breathless audience" (Emerson 35).

A friend of mine at the university was ending her training with her kumu hula 'hula master or instructor' and invited me to attend her 'ūniki at the music department's auditorium. She had been trained in the traditional or ancient forms of hula, and the 'ūniki was the opportunity for her to demonstrate her proficiency in the various styles of dance as well as to utilize the instruments that she had to make. It was a long time ago, but I recall how nervous she was until she began to chant the prayers invoking the god/goddess of hula, Laka, and then the individual chants to put on her apparel for the performances. Those chants, as they should have been, were ho'oulu, that is, meant to inspire and bring the spirit of the hula into her; in fact, her name was Ho'oulu.

Evaluation of mastery did not have to be purely demonstrative. In a less formal situation John Papa 'Ī'ī recalled how he had been "tested" by his uncle, Papa. He recalled that

> [a]bout two or three weeks after the trip to Ewa, on the
> day of Muku, the last day of the lunar month, all of the
> chiefs went to Waikiki to surf. When evening came they
> went to Leahi, where the royal parent, Kamehameha,
> had a house separate from that of Liholiho. Ii and Papa
> shared the house of the young chief. When the sun grew
> warm the next day, which is Hilo, Papa called Ii to come
> and sit beside him, where he lay face down at the end of
> the house. The young chief, who occupied the other half
> of the house, was watching. (55)

The setting ʻĪʻī describes is disarming, non-threatening, and a far
cry from the formality that is used today for almost any examination
or interview. The informality of it all should indicate to the boy that
this is all conversation and not an examination of any sorts. Then,

> Papa asked his nephew which he would choose between
> Kamokupanee (Expanding Island) and Lualewa
> (Without Foundation). The boy was unable to answer,
> for he did not understand the question. Then he
> was told that Kamokupanee meant the father chief,
> Kamehameha, and Lualewa meant the young chief,
> Liholiho. (55)

The examination question is coded in poetic or indirect language
that whatever the answer the boy chooses would be indirect and not
insulting to the actual persons being referred to, but the metaphor is
too indirect and instead of, perhaps, sidestepping the issue, ʻĪʻī admits
he doesn't understand it at all. Unlike modern testing where the boy
could be seen as failing the test for not understanding the method
being used, Papa reveals the true nature of the test—choosing sides
and loyalty of one chief over another. It is evident that ʻĪʻī recalled
how difficult the moment was, especially with the young chief
Liholiho present, but the boy answers.

> He was embarrassed about being asked such a question in
> the presence of one of the chiefs; but he replied, "The father
> chief is the wealthy one. The young chief has no wealth."
> Then he added, "Perhaps I shall remain with Lualewa."

When Papa replied, "This chief of ours is without
wealth," the boy said, "The chief without wealth should
be obeyed, and when he becomes wealthy, the servant
becomes wealthy too." (55)

'Ī'ī not only answers the question, he demonstrates to his
uncle that he understands the gravity of the question and gives his
reasoning, to which, "[a]ll of those present approved of this reasoning,
the young chief included" (Ii 55). Those gathered must have been
pleased because of the loyalty the boy showed in his choice, but I
also think they, especially Papa, were taken with how he came to his
conclusion. If he had chosen the king, Kamehameha, then he would
side with immediate favors and provisions, but in the longer run, who
would provide for him? By choosing the son and heir, he demonstrated
the virtue of patience and with Liholiho present also loyalty.

Educating the New Leadership

The education of young chiefs was different from that of the
priests, for it centered upon leadership in politics, the military,
and religion. Leadership in politics requires the art and skill of
governance; in the military, the ability to direct battle and to fight;
and in religion, the knowledge and skill to conduct rituals and
ceremonies as a chief-priest. We do not have as detailed accounts
of the education of the young chiefs as Kamakau has given for the
priesthood. Malo gives a glimpse of the intensity of their training,
especially for warfare, but whether or not the young chief would
choose to heed and interpret advice was another matter.

An early description of their introduction to their roles as leaders
is told by the native scholar Davida Malo.

[. . .] during the youth of the ali'i 'aimoku [*paramount
chief of district or island*], they were sent out to live with
wise and skilled people, and to listen first to the words of
experts and to the important things that would benefit
their rule. They were to first show bravery in combat and
in wisdom and to do these things without any hesitation.

Furthermore, [these young people] would initially live
with another ali'i in a state of poverty, starvation and

famine so they would remember what these conditions
of life were like. Some were taught to take care of the
people using great patience and they were even belittled
below the position of the maka'āinana. (173)

Once again we see, even with the rank and status of chiefs, the
elements of traditional education being employed when Malo states,
"to *listen* first to the words of experts." We presume this process
followed that of other young boys who probably were educated in the
hale mua, the men's house, where they became familiar with several
religious ceremonies and where, it is assumed, skills in fishing and
other tasks were taught, and many traditions told.

Another virtue acquired from mentorship and experiential
learning is shown in this account of how the young warrior
Kekūhaupi'o learned to wrestle with a niuhi or "tiger shark." And
although this is another example of the chief and priestly ways of
education, the story underlines the importance of how youth can
acquire the virtue of patience.

When Kekūhaupi'o saw this large-mouthed fish he
mentally prepared himself for an immediate leap, but his
teacher spoke: *E Kekūhaupi'o ē*, don't hasten to leap into
the fight with your opponent, but let us play with him.
[. . .] When he has swallowed enough, then my chiefly
pupil, the fight will be more equitable. This is something
good for you to learn: in the future when you fight an
opponent, don't hasten to leap forward, but first study
his nature to enable you to learn his weakness, then it
will be easy for you to secure him by one of the methods
you have learned. [. . .]

As Kekūhaupi'o again prepared to leap his teacher again
said: *E Kekūhaupi'o ē*, don't be too hasty—listen well to
me—when I tell you to leap, attempt to dive under this
fish [. . .], but not just at this moment as the sea has not
cleared. [. . .]

Kekūhaupi'o was impatient with these words for he
greatly wished to leap into the fight [. . .].

> Kekūhaupi'o's teacher stared intently at the shark and how
> he gobbled the greasy sea water. [...] When he saw that the
> time was right he ordered the men to drop the sail and the
> order was quickly carried out. [...] Leap forth, Kekūhaupi'o
> and fight with this famous fish [...]. (Desha 9–10)

We have but a glimpse of what was emphasized and passed down to the young chiefs from the post-contact period during Kamehameha's reign. The inference is that these traditions and ideals were probably still handed down from generations before, comprising, as Malo states, "the important things that would benefit their rule" (173).

> Whenever there was a meeting in the Ahuena house
> in the evening, the king instructed the heir carefully
> as to how to do things, describing the lives of former
> rulers such as Keakealaniwahine, Kalaniopuu, Koihala,
> Kamalalawalu, Kauhiakama, and Hakau. Thus Liholiho
> learned the results of abuse and disregard of the welfare
> of chiefs and commoners and about farming and fishing
> and things of like nature. In the discussions with the
> king the heir derived understanding which has passed
> down to his heirs of today. (Ii 129)

The traditions of those named chiefs are remembered as examples of certain qualities, good and bad. For instance, Keākealaniwahine is remembered because she was the first female chief to become a paramount chief with the equal rights and responsibilities of any male paramount chief before her; Ko'ihala is well remembered as one of the despotic or abusive chiefs from the Ka'ū district of the island of Hawai'i, and Hākau is remembered as the abusive older brother of the high chief 'Umi, ancestor of the Kamehamehas.

This recollection of the importance of knowing events of past ali'i was important to Kamehameha when he met with his equal, Kaumuali'i, from the independent island of Kaua'i, in 1810. This encounter was risky and full of plots and intrigue.

> It was in the year 1810 [...] that a discussion was held
> between the chiefs and Kamehameha pertaining to
> the advisability of Kaumualii's coming to meet him.

Meanwhile the chiefs plotted to have Kaumualii put to
death when he arrived [. . .]. However, Kamehameha
did not approve of the plot, for he had often heard of the
hospitality accorded to the chiefs of the eastern islands
when they went to Kauai. (Ii 81)

What he remembered was the tradition of the chiefs called the
hua, described in the chapter on Alaka'i. It was one of the traditions
of chiefs probably told to him as a young boy being trained to rule. In
fact we know from 'Ī'ī that his training had begun many years before
the age at which a young chief would be allowed to exercise his rank
and status.

There were many things to show that Kamehameha was
a ruling chief, though he was not yet ready to rule. He
was too young, being about 19 or 20 years old, and the
custom then was just as it is now. (Ii 6)

A Kingdom of Learning

He aupuni palapala ko'u; o ke kanaka pono 'oia ko'u kanaka.
Mine is the kingdom of education; the righteous man is my man.
- Kamehameha III

Nani nā lehua kāpili wai a ka manu,
Nani nā lehua lū lehua o ka manu,
Nani nā pua o ka 'ae'ae,
Nani nā 'ulu hua pala i ka lau,
Nani nā ki'owai o Kalawari,
Nani wai o ua nei i ka pali,
Pākū akula i nā pali,
Hio nā lua o nā wai i ka makani,
Noho pākū i ke kuahiwi,
E ho'i ma Hiku i ka uka,
Ka lālā i ka wai la ku'ua,
Ku'ua mai manu'u kelekele
Ho'okela mai e ka la,
'O Maku'ukaokao, 'o Makilihoehoe,
E ka lālā i ka na'auao la ku'ua,
Ho'onu'u iho a kū kahauli.

Beautiful are the lehua of the nectar of the birds,
Beautiful are the lehua scattered by the birds,

Beautiful are the flowers of the ʻaeʻae,
Beautiful are the ripe ʻulu fruit among the leaves,
Beautiful are the pools of Calvary,
Beautiful is the water of the rain in the heights,
That hides the cliffs,
The water on the leaves is shaken off in the wind,
That grows like a veil in the mountain range,
Going to Hiku in the uplands,
The branching of the water, released,
Flowing forth that swells and makes it muddy
The sun is glorious,
Makuʻukaokao, Makilihoehoe
Whose learning flows like a stream,
Eager these to be honored men.

The historian Samuel Manaiakalani Kamakau cited this mele ʻchant,ʼ particularly the last two lines, "Whose learning flows like a stream, Eager these to be honored men," because it illustrated his point that there was a time when, "[p]arents would then be anxious to have their children educated, or, if they had no children, would adopt others and educate them to bring honor to the name of such parents" (*Ruling Chiefs* 373).

Some may find such a claim to be remarkable or even bewildering in light of the difficulties and challenges presented in education today. But Kamakau was an eye-witness to that time.

> [. . .] the government of learning moved along quickly so that within half a year there were thousands of persons who knew how to read, write, and spell. The governor of Kauai had his own teacher, so had the governor of Maui, and this humble writer was one of those who taught. Many of these old-time teachers are still living. Of the pupils who entered the first, second, and third classes at Lahainaluna, half of were elementary teachers whose knowledge and capacity had been tested before the missionary teachers, and the chiefs had selected from among them those whom each wished to educate at Lahainaluna. That is how the government of learning moved ahead. (*Ruling Chiefs* 424)

This government of learning had been proclaimed in 1824 by the ten- or eleven-year-old king, His Majesty King Kamehameha III, at Honuakaha, in Honolulu. "Chiefs and people, give ear to my remarks. My kingdom shall be a kingdom of learning" (Kamakau, *Ruling Chiefs* 319). However, Hawaiians were learning how to read and write years before the arrival of the first company of American missionaries. There is a tendency to forget that there were some forty-two years of continuous encounters and exchanges between the Hawaiian population and Euro-American explorers, adventures, traders, and beachcombers as well as Chinese, African-Americans, and Tahitians before the first missionaries arrived.

This new technology was known as palapala, probably derived from the word *pala* or *kāpala* which depicts the action of stamping or blotting designs upon kapa 'barkcloth,' and hence, printing. David Samwell observed an exchange between some women who were making kapa and the British and recorded the event in his journal. But, Samwell went further and is perhaps the first foreigner to have given instructions to the Hawaiians, in this case a group of women, in literacy.

> [. . .] they call it 'cappara' [kapala] & always gave the same appellation to our writing, & the Young Women would frequently take the pens out of our hands and shew us that they could 'cappara' as well as us, and gave us to understand that our pens were much inferior to their brushes; they looked upon a written sheet of paper as a piece of Cloth marked in various figures according to our own fancy and the fashion of our Country, and seeing some of us frequently employed at this Work they thought that making Cloth was the chief part of our Business – tho' at last they came to understand that our Characters had some meaning in them which theirs wanted, from seeing us put words down and the Names of things which we asked of them & I dont remember ever having seen them express more pleasure & astonishment than they did at hearing one of their Songs repeated which I had wrote down on a piece of paper. (Beaglehole 1,187)

Captain King must have been with Samwell for he describes it almost in the same language, but he says the word used was *kipparee* [kipali?].

> The business of painting belongs entirely to the women,
> and is called *kipparee*; and it is remarkable, that they
> always gave the same name to our writing. The young
> women would often take the pen out of our hands, and
> shew us, that they knew the use of it as well as we did; at
> the same time telling us, that our pens were not so good
> as theirs. They looked upon a sheet of written paper, as
> a piece of cloth striped after the fashion of our country,
> and it was not without the utmost difficulty, that we
> could make them understand, that our figures had a
> meaning in them which theirs had not. (King, J. 149)

When the first printing press began operation, the word for printing changed to pa'i, that is, to strike hard or to hit hard, as with the kapa beater upon the wood anvil. Even the word for writing probably came from the same source as tattoo or "kākau," again, to set a mark as on a kapa or on the skin. The cleverness, even the genius, of the Hawaiian mind, in this appropriation and adaptation of such a new skill, was to keenly observe how close it was to the traditional technology of kapa making, and that it was indeed not an untouchable icon, but a powerful new technology that they could, indeed, gain access to.

We know that arrival of the first company of American missionaries was a very tenuous affair and it took at least three years to establish themselves in the islands. In a journal of one of the missionaries sent to King Kaumuali'i on the island of Kaua'i, this dialogue was recorded.

> This morning Tamoree sent for me-said his interpreter
> was going away to be gone several days, and he wished
> to say a few things to me before he went. I want to know
> if you love Hoomehoome [Humehume], if you love me,
> if you like to stay here and learn my people. I assured
> him that I loved his son and him, and I wished to spend
> my life in doing them good, [. . .]. Hoomehoome tell

me so, says he; he then shed tears freely and said, I love
Hoomehoome. I love him very much more than my
other children. I thought he was dead; I cry many times
because I think he was dead. Some Captains tell me he
live in America, but I not believe; I say no, he dead, he
no come back. But he live, he come again; my heart very
glad. I want my son to help me; he speaks English and
can do my business. But he is young; young men are
sometimes wild, they want advice. I want you stay here
and help Hoomehoome, and when vessels come you and
Hoomehoome go on board and trade, so I make you
chief. ("Return of Prince George to Atooi" 771–772)

The chiefs clearly understood the power of this new technology
and tried to gain access to it. And learning, like today's latest
computer-related technology, just was not readily available on
the open market. We know that it took nearly three years for the
missionaries to develop a standardized alphabet, and then only after
seeking the consultation and assistance of the Revs. William Ellis,
Daniel Tyerman, and George Bennett of the London Missionary
Society (LMS) based in Tahiti. We also know now that with the
LMS consultants came, unexpectedly, several Tahitian Christians
who were supposed to have disembarked at some other islands off
Tahiti, but due to a storm, had journeyed all the way to Hawai'i
with their English colleagues. Their close genetic, ancestral, and
linguistic ties to the Hawaiians opened a means of communication,
which the missionaries had struggled with for the first two years. The
once inaccessible technology now came with translation, and more
importantly, teachers for the chiefs. Again, as Kamakau recounts
the situation, "As soon as the chiefs saw what a good thing it was to
know how to read and write, each chief took teachers into his home
to teach the chiefs of his household" (*Ruling Chiefs* 248).

With access now guaranteed, Kamakau would report, "Before
the end of the year the old people over eighty and ninety years old
were reading the Bible. [. . .] When the missionaries began to settle in
the outer districts they found that people already knew how to read"
(*Ruling Chiefs* 249). Cultural anthropologist Marshall Sahlins found
this native school system to be significant to the continuance of

Hawaiian culture. He described "quasi-ritual centers, corresponding in their organization to the hierarchy and segmentations of the system of chiefship," to which he added, "And all this had been accomplished without benefit of clergy" (Kirch and Sahlins I: 92).

Widespread literacy was first accomplished by instruction within the household or compound of the chief. The brightest of his household and retainers became teachers who were sent to villages and settlements where they established schools on behalf of their chief and for the "government of learning." The Rev. Sheldon Dibble wrote this account of one such scholar named Mo'o.

> A young man named Moo, pipe-lighter to Hoapili, being regarded as a rather bright scholar, Hoapili sent him to Hawaii to be teacher for the district of Puna—a district nearly or quite as large as a county in the state of Massachusetts. He took a central post and collected a school. As soon as his scholars had made a little proficiency he sent out the best of them to the right hand and to the left, to be teachers of other schools, and he continued their course till every village of Puna was furnished with a teacher. A process something after this sort was simultaneously going on from Hawaii to Kauai. (217)

We return again to the words of Kamakau.

> In his speech at Honuakaha he [Kamehameha III] proclaimed "The government of learning" in which chiefs should teach commoners and each one teach another. Teachers were distributed about the islands, and only those who could not walk stayed away from school. Some schools had a hundred, some a thousand pupils. From children to bearded men, all were gathered into the schools. Buildings went up over night to serve as school houses; if a landlord refused to build he lost his post. A line separated those who could read from those who could not. The concert exercises by which they were taught delighted the people. The rhythmical sound of the voices in unison as they rose and fell was like that of the breakers that rise and fall at Waialua or like the beat of the stick hula in the time of Pele-io-holani and Ka-lani-'opu'u. (*Ruling Chiefs* 422–423)

Kamakau also revealed the simple methodology used, perhaps based upon the rote methods used in the memorization of chants, prayers, and oratory.

> Reading aloud in unison was the method used. [. . .] The quickest pupils were advanced, and this made the pupils ambitious to be at the head. The teachers made great strides in their methods of teaching, not only in reading but also in writing. All followed the same method and drilled good behavior into the pupils. (*Ruling Chiefs* 249)

> The study of letters was taken up universally from the king's own household to the remotest country dwelling. Schools were established all over Oahu conducted like the schools of the hula in old days. After the second or third week they would hold all-night and all-day sessions, and as April 19 of each year approached, when all gathered for the yearly exhibition (*hoʻike*), from Kepukaki you could see the lights burning all the way from Nuʻuanu Pali to Kaimuki. Each school vied with the others to make the best showing on the day of the exhibition, and the winner would receive acclaim from the public. (*Ruling Chiefs* 270)

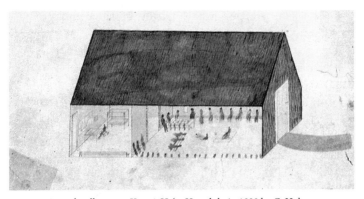

First mission schoolhouse at KawaiaHaʻo, Honolulu in 1820 by G. Holmes

At first the missionaries seemed to employ an examination at the schools where students would publicly demonstrate their new skills and competence. One of the earliest accounts of such an examination is found in a letter from the Honolulu station dated January 11, 1823. They proudly told of the attendance of 12 chiefs at the examination.

> Nahienaena, and Opiia, one of the wives of the late king, with her present husband, Laanui, bore an interesting part of the examination. Nor was the king's copy-book, with its fair, neat pages, and his communication before alluded to, which was read to the assembly, less interesting. [. . .] The queen recited about half of Watt's catechism. Kahuhu [brother of John Papa 'Ī'ī] read with fluency a passage from the Bible.—Two others presented their first essay on composition; and Naihi handed in a declaration, written in his own hand, containing four words—"Aroka [*sic*] au ia Jehovo." [*sic*] [Aloha au iā Iehova]—*I love the Lord*. Opiia exhibited fair hand writing, and so did many others. ("Letter from the Mission to the Corresponding Secretary" 165)

This system of examination developed into more of a public festival or hōʻike 'exhibition' in later years. The Rev. Tinker described a hōʻike in 1831.

> The shell horn blowing early for examination of the schools, in the meeting house. About 2,000 scholars present, some wrapped in large quantity of native cloth, with wreaths of evergreen about their heads and hanging towards their feet [maile or fern lei?] - others dressed in calico and silk with large necklaces of braided hair and wreaths of red and yellow and green feathers very beautiful and expensive.

> [. . .] The King and chiefs were present, and examined among the rest. They read in various books, and 450 in 4 rows wrote the same sentence at the same time on slates. They perform with some ceremony. In this exercise, one of the teachers cried out with as much importance as an orderly serjeant . . . and immediately the whole company began to sit up straight. At the next order, they stood on their feet. At the next they "handled" slates or "presented"—i.e. they held them resting on the left arm as a musician would place his fiddle. At the next order, they

brought their pencils to bear upon the broadsides of their
slates ready for action. Mr. Bingham then put into the
crier's ear the sentence to be written, which he proclaimed
with all his might and a movement of the 450 pencils
commenced which from their creaking was like the music
of machinery lacking oil. (Kuykendall 108–109)

These were major events, not like the hula performances and
exhibitions that the missionaries were trying to discourage. In fact,
Honolulu schools held their hōʻike quarterly according to the Rev.
Dibble, who describes how much preparation was done prior to a
major hōʻike.

Several weeks previous to an examination were spent both
by teachers and scholars as a special season of preparation.
Months, perhaps, may have passed with scarcely a school,
but the stimulus of an approaching examination had power
to call in every scholar and to make them day after day
patiently attentive to what was taught them.

The time approaches to assemble. Food must be baked
for the journey and for the occasion, sufficient to last one
or two weeks. The scholar wraps his food in one bundle
and his best suit of kapas in another and balances the
two with a stick on his shoulder. [. . .] From fifty to one
hundred schools, in the same style, arrive. Some find
lodgings with the residents of the town or neighborhood,
but most are obliged to construct small huts of leaves or
grass [. . .]. The day of examination arrives. The chiefs
are present in their gayest dresses and scholars in their
newest kapas. No house will contain the assembly. The
meeting house is chosen as being the largest. (220)

Laura Judd also witnessed a hōʻike and entered into her journal,
with her frank and honest style, her amazement and the ability of
Hawaiians to grasp literacy.

The grand annual exhibition of all the schools on this
island is to be held at the church. Adults compose these
schools, as the children are not yet tamed. The people
come from each district in procession, headed by the

principal man of the land (konohiki), all dressed in one uniform color of native cloth. [. . .] the "kihei" for men, and the "pau" for women.

It is astonishing how so many have learned to read with so few books. They teach each other, making use of banana leaves, smooth stones, and the wet sand on the sea beach, as tablets. Some read equally well with the book upside down or sidewise, as four or five of them learn from the same book with one teacher, crowding around him as closely as possible. (17)

In 1840, during the visit of the American scientific expedition, both Captain Wilkes and the medical doctor, Charles Pickering, remarked on the excellent performances of Hawaiian students.

At an examination in the old church, there were seven hundred children, and as many more parents. The attraction that drew together such numbers, was a feast, which I understood was given annually. The scholars had banners, with various mottoes, in Hawaiian, (which were translated to me,) as emblematical of purity, good conduct, steadfast in faith, &c. [. . .] On my arrival at the church, I found several tables set out, one for the accommodation of the chiefs, furnished as we see for a 4th of July lunch at home, with hams, turkeys, chickens, pies, &c. The common people's children took their poe and raw fish on the floor. [. . .] It was a joyous sight to see fifteen hundred human beings so happy and gratified by this molasses feast: poe and raw fish were the only additions. The latter are everyday food, so that the molasses constituted the special treat. So great is the fondness of the natives for it, that I was told many are induced to send their children to school, merely to entitle them to be present at this feast. [. . .] At the schools, it has been observed that the scholars are extremely fond of calculations in arithmetic, and possess extraordinary talent in that way. So great is their fondness for it, that in some schools the teachers have had recourse to depriving them of the study as a punishment. (Wilkes IV: 56–58)

Pickering must have visited Lāhaināluna where he was shown the engravings that the students were becoming famous for, and so accomplished that some of them became involved in forging the local currency at the school.

> Engraving, was an unexpected accomplishment to find among Polynesians: and some drawings of ships were shown to me, which exhibited a neatness and a correctness in minute detail, not often met with. I witnessed at the mission schools, the remarkable universal talent and fondness for mathematical pursuits; [. . .] Printing, too, was conducted by natives [. . .]. (Pickering 88)

Of his own education Kamakau proudly admits that he did not have such a formal education until he entered Lahainaluna High School.

> I had no teacher to teach me the alphabet and numbers [. . .] No one ever taught me to add, multiply, subtract, or to divide [. . .]. I entered high school without taking up the preparatory steps. [. . .] [t]he pupils themselves taught each other with great patience. (*Ruling Chiefs* 409)

At a world exposition in Paris during the late 1860s, the Kingdom of Hawai'i had an exhibit. Kamakau noted that it was the only government from the Pacific represented.

> The European governments are astonished to see the sign outside the Hawaiian room at the exposition. They cannot believe it. A race of man-eaters are the Hawaiian people, are they not? And do they really have a government? And have they a room here? Then they examine the exhibit and see a cloak made out of bird feathers, a wreath of bird feathers, and a number of other objects from ancient times. They see the products of the country—sugar, molasses, rice, coffee. At the office of the Hawaiian government they find books from the first *pi-a-pa* primer to books large and small, the Bible, and newspaper files beginning with the *Lama Hawaii* and the *Kumu Hawaii* and ending with the *Au 'Oko'a*

and the *Ku'oko'a*. Books for education, books of laws
from the beginning to the present time. The office has a
quantity of Hawaiian manuscripts. The men interested
in education look at each other and say, "This cannibal
island is ahead in literacy; and the enlightened countries
of Europe are behind it!" (*Ruling Chiefs* 420)

He was not merely boasting. "Between 1824 and 1846 about 80
books were published covering 65,444 pages. In 1827 a beginning
was made in printing the Bible; in 1832 the New Testament was
printed; in 1839 the whole Bible was in the hands of the Hawaiians"
(Kamakau, *Ruling Chiefs* 405). But the picture was not as rosy as
it might seem. The 1832 statistics of the general minutes of the
Sandwich Island Mission report a total of 23,127 readers, but then
the numbers began to dramatically decline, and two years later were
down to less than half that number (Kirch and Sahlins I: 124). Sahlins
believes this was due to the waning authority and control of the
chiefs over the commoners. He says, "Early on reports came in from
O'ahu and the other islands that church attendance on Sundays had
fallen off markedly and the schools were being abandoned wholesale
by students and teachers alike. The 'peculiar school system,' wrote
Rev. Dibble, 'crumbled into ruins'" (Kirch and Sahlins I: 123).
Something had gone wrong. Sahlins is right in pointing out that the
exact date cannot be precisely attributed, but it occurred in the early-
to mid-1830s. Again, we turn to Kamakau's eyewitness account:

But how about the people who strive for an education
today? They are no better off than the unlearned; luckless
fishermen who make no better catch than the ignorant.
After graduating from high school they turn to hard
labor for a living. (*Ruling Chiefs* 373)

In the school they may have learned navigation
and know all the rules by which to find latitude and
longitude by the sextant, by the sun and Mercury, by
the moon and stars, by heaving the lead, and all other
means of directing the ship into the desired haven. But
upon emerging from the school and seeking a place
in which to show their skill, what do they find? Some

become school teachers, some preachers, some are in
government, some make a living in ways suited to the
uneducated, but the larger number become idlers. Many
of them would like to go into something worth-while but
are prevented by poverty, and cannot take up any kind
of work they would be fitted for. [. . .] They are just lost
like one hidden away in a clump of grass [. . .]. All this
learning concerning the circuit of the sun, the planets,
the comet, [. . .]—of what good is it? Where is it leading?
(*Ruling Chiefs* 375)

This history lesson on the development of literacy in the
Hawaiian Islands should be understood in the same manner that
Kamehameha, as a young man, related to the traditions of several
generations before his time in his quest to unify the islands. It can be
history, prophecy, and a forewarning.

The seeming tremendous success of the new technology of
palapala was due to several factors:

- government sanction and sponsorship;
- authority and encouragement of the chiefs;
- culturally based instruction that comprised role models,
  mentoring and training for teachers, group learning, drilling
  and group activities, and the recognition of achievements;
  and
- supportive publications and materials.

Beyond the political implications of the times, what appears to
be a contributing factor to the later utter disinterest was the lack of
any relevant and appropriate applications or jobs. If we are to be
like Kamehameha and understand this story as a possible means for
developing new strategies to accomplish the once obtainable goal,
then we need to understand the importance of the factors mentioned
above, and, particularly, how they fit into a culturally based model.

The success of the early Hawaiian schools, from the descriptions
given by Kamakau, can be easily related to the tremendous success and
enthusiasm we see today in the very traditional descendants of those
schools: hālau hula and canoe clubs. They impress upon children and

young people not only some fundamental principles of education, but also cultural traditions, behavioral and moral values, and responsibility as they reach adulthood. This is culturally based education using many of the methods described in this book. We need to explore and exploit these methods and to support the re-discovery of these skills with appropriate and interesting publications and materials, ensuring their relevance to our children's discovery of their world and their future.

5 Ola

Traditional Concepts of Health and Healing

Ua ola loko i ke aloha.
Love gives life within.
Pukui, *ʻŌlelo Noʻeau*

✂

E ola, ola ka lani
Ola ka honua, ola ka mauna
Ola ka moana, ola ke [a]lii
Ola ka moana, ola ke [a]lii
Ola ke kahuna, ola ke kilo
Ola na makaainana
Ola ka ai, ola ka iʻa
Hoola i na mea ulu o ka aina
Amama, amama, ua noa, lele wale.

Let it live, the sky exists
The earth exists, the mountain exists
The sea exists, the chief lives on
The sea exists, the chief lives on
The priest lives on, the observer [of the stars] lives on
The people live on
The crops flourish, the sea life flourish
The living things on the land flourish
Ended, ended, freed, depart.

Ending to "A Prayer for Healing" taught by the priest Naluhoʻomana
to the chiefs from *The History of Kanalu*

The word ola has come to be understood as health and to refer to a state of well-being. But the meaning of ola is so much more. It is life. It is to be alive. We are only now beginning to rediscover the importance of the concept of ola and all that it means.

The earliest recorded information about Native Hawaiian health comes from the descriptions of the physical features and appearance of Native Hawaiians as seen by Haole (American or European) explorers and adventurers, including observations about the general state of health in Hawaiʻi. Captain King of the *Discovery*, sister ship to Cook's *Resolution* on his third and final voyage in 1779, wrote, "[t]hey seem to have few native diseases among them" (Barrow

429), and in 1818 Russian explorer Captain Vasilli Mikahailovich Golovnin on the *Kamchatka* re-confirmed that observation. "The climate of the Sandwich Islands is hot but very healthy; epidemics and infections are unknown to the inhabitants" (Golovnin 219).

Kamakau, writing in the mid-nineteenth-century, concurred with them.

> In very ancient times many people observed the rules of the art of healing (*ʻoihana kahuna lapaʻau*), but in later times most of them abandoned medical practices because there was not much sickness within the race. Foreigners (*malihini*) had not yet come from other lands; there were no fatal diseases (*luku*), no epidemics (*ahulau*), no contagious diseases (*maʻi lele*), no diseases that eat away the body (*maʻi ʻaʻai*), no venereal diseases (*maʻi pala a me ke kaokao*). (*Ka Poʻe Kahiko* 109)

And he adds,

> It was a common thing to see old men and women of a hundred years and over, wrinkled and flabby-skinned, with eyelids hanging shut. One does not see such people today. (*Ruling Chiefs* 172)

Native accounts about health became more frequent with the introduction of literacy and also, tragically, of foreign diseases. Davida Malo writes that there had been a great illness, an ahulau or epidemic, in early Hawaiian traditions during the reign of the chief Waia, who was the son of Hāloa. This illness was called ikipuahola, and it was followed by another illness called hailepo.

Then, in 1804, an epidemic of devastating proportions appeared as predicted a year before by a traditional practitioner named Kama and told to his son, Kūaʻuaʻu, a practitioner for Kamehameha. Malo preserved the dialogue between father and son.

> "I am dying. Do you know of the great illness that is coming? You will become exhausted treating [for this illness], because it is the [same] illness that came during the time of Waia. This illness is the ikipuahola that wiped out Hawaiʻi leaving only twenty six survivors." (296)

Kamakau gives this description of the epidemic.

> It was a very virulent pestilence, and those who contracted
> it died quickly. A person on the highway would die before
> he could reach home. One might go for food and water
> and die so suddenly that those at home did not know what
> had happened. The body turned black at death. A few
> died a lingering death, but never longer than twenty-four
> hours; if they were able to hold out for a day they had a
> fair chance to live. Those who lived generally lost their
> hair, hence the illness was called "Head stripped bare"
> (Poʻo-kole).*[1] Kamehameha contracted the disease, but
> managed to live through it. His counselors all died, and
> many of the chiefs and their families. (*Ruling Chiefs* 189)

So great was the impact of this epidemic upon Hawaiian society
that it was decided that even the chiefs needed to know what to do.
A "method of training promising members of the court as medical
kahunas" was commenced "because of the great death rate among
chiefs and commoners in the year 1806, perhaps owing to the terrible
ʻokuʻu disease [. . .]" (Ii 46). "Among [the] other chiefs trained [. . .]
were Ka-lani-moku and Boki Ka-maʻuleʻule. Others were educated in
the art of healing chronic diseases" (Kamakau, *Ruling Chiefs* 179).

The high chief Boki, who was governor of the island of Oʻahu,
would follow up this training many years later by convening a
gathering of prominent traditional practitioners when he "returned
and lived at his place at Beretania [in Honolulu] and devoted himself
to medicine, in which he was proficient, and all those joined him
who were skilled in placing pebbles [in diagnosis], such [as] Kaao,
Kuauau, Kinopu, Kahiole, Nahinu, Kekaha, Hewahewa, and their
followers and other kahunas besides" (Kamakau, *Ruling Chiefs* 291).

There were several epidemics that followed: from 1824 to 1826
there were "epidemics of cough" that killed thousands; in 1832 there
was whooping cough that again claimed thousands of lives; in 1840
the first case of leprosy was reported; from 1845 to 1849 there were
epidemics of diarrhea, influenza, measles, and whooping cough that
killed over ten thousand (Blaisdell, *History* 2).

The first smallpox epidemic appeared in 1853 and killed close to
one-tenth of the native population. Kamakau's eyewitness account is

a very different picture of native health than what King and Golovnin had seen, and this situation became particularly difficult because the government, by then under mission and foreign counsel, could do very little to intervene.

> The smallpox came, and dead bodies lay stacked like kindling wood, red as singed hogs. Shame upon those who brought the disease and upon the foreign doctors who allowed their landing! [. . .] Everywhere there was mourning and lamentation.

> [. . .] A hundred were stricken in a day; scarcely one out of ten lived. The writer went into the hospital and saw for himself how fatal the disease was, even under foreign doctors. [. . .] The writer himself saved over a hundred persons [. . .], and some are living today whom he treated at Kipahulu where the government could not care for patients. [. . .]

> From the last week in June until September the disease raged in Honolulu. The dead fell like dried *kukui* twigs tossed down by the wind. Day by day from morning till night horse-drawn carts went about from street to street of the town, and the dead were stacked up like a load of wood, some in coffins, but most of them just piled in, wrapped in cloth with heads and legs sticking out. (*Ruling Chiefs* 416–417)

Native Hawaiians struggled to comprehend what had happened and was happening. In response to this tragedy, and with few foreign doctors available, they once again looked back, as the generation before had done, to largely forgotten traditions. A group of eight Native Hawaiians on the island of Maui founded an association to investigate what could be done to intervene and stem the tide of depopulation and disease. They met on December 20, 1866 in Wailuku and began a series of meetings that would attempt to determine "if traditional Native medicines, which would be cheaper and [more] abundant, were the answer to their problems" (Chun, *Must We Wait in Despair* iii) and to develop an action plan to present to the government's Board of Health.

One of the conclusions reached by their President J. W. H. Kauwahi would be considered quite naïve in light of what we now know of infectious diseases, but at that time it certainly reflected the immense bewilderment Native Hawaiians faced in trying to rationalize the devastation from foreign things.

> Our fashions today are very different and people have
> been completely won over to this different way of living.
> If one slightly changes and succumbs to ignorance, then
> it is likely that he or she will get sick and eventually die,
> and that is the case for foreign foods, like bread, tea and
> other foods; because those who were accustomed to
> the more traditional ways of dressing and eating would
> rest upon couches and beds and they would take care
> of themselves when they were feverish and perspiring.
> They would not undress and they would go on bathing
> or swimming just for fun while they were still sick.
> But, the Hawaiian people have mixed the new and old
> ways together and in doing so they have become more
> susceptible to those illnesses familiar and new to them.
> Therefore, the mixing of these two types of illnesses
> internally has developed into a hybrid, that is [one made
> up of] the traditional illnesses contracted due to their
> way of living and the food they ate, and the introduced
> illnesses which are contracted due to the change of
> clothing and improper health care. These type [sic] of
> illnesses have mixed and become deadly because there
> are no doctors or traditional practitioners who know
> the medicines to treat these hybrid illnesses. [. . .] I have
> reached this conclusion after having observed the habits
> of our people and their reactions. (Chun, *Must We Wait
> in Despair* xxxii)

The members of the association were educated at the mission high school, and none of them were traditional healers, so they decided to investigate which traditional healing practices could be the answer to their problem. Incredibly for that time, they began, on their own, a systematic oral history, interviewing at least twenty-two living traditional practitioners, many of whom were the students of

Kūaʻuaʻu and others of the previous generation. Those interviews were conducted in Hawaiian and were recorded in the field, and then each report was sent to the recording secretary of the association at Wailuku and finally written into a ledger book. The association did this to prevent any allegations of fraud, quackery, and abuse towards traditional healing practices and to overcome a skepticism and prejudice in a Christian era suspicious of back-sliding to former pagan ways, because as Davida Malo had explained earlier about traditional healing practices, "Healing the sick was done through worshiping the god" (207).

In 1868, perhaps due to the work of this association, for several of their members were also members of parliament, a law was passed, over the objections of the professional medical community, to allow for the licensing of traditional healers. And in 1886, King Kalākaua broadened the licensing process with the creation of a "Hawaiian Board of Health, consisting of five kahunas, appointed by the king, with the power to issue certificates to native kahunas to practice 'native medicine'" (qtd. in Chun, *Ka Moʻolelo Laikini* 5).

The Curious Case of ʻAwa

In the face of new health problems, we are attempting again to rediscover the wisdom and skills of traditional healing. Our appreciation and understanding of traditional healing practices are no better, for we view those practices, many times unwittingly, with new prejudices and skepticism arising out of modern attitudes about clinical medicine or with misplaced nostalgia and inventive romanticism.

The recent controversy over the use and abuse of ʻawa, or kava, is a good example of modern perceptions of the use of traditional plant materials. The controversy was spurred by two reports, one from the U.S. Food and Drug Administration (FDA) and the other a German government report, warning of possible serious liver damage due to ʻawa usage. The reporting of the issue starkly illustrates two areas of contrast between traditional and modern cultures—the use of ʻawa outside of any cultural context and the focus on benefits—both the therapeutic benefits of the plant itself and economic benefits of ʻawa as an industry. The latter was clearly described in a news report.

Kava is promoted to relieve anxiety, stress and insomnia.
A member of the pepper family, it has long been used as
a ceremonial drink in the South Pacific; until recently its
biggest danger seemed to be in drinking too much of the
sedative before driving. Then, about two years ago, kava
in pill form suddenly boomed, bringing in about $30
million in sales — and Europe reported liver damage.
(Daranciang A1)

In this controversy it is the ceremonial use contrasted to the
contemporary pill usage that interests me, because the reports did
not consider any of the original cultural traditions of using ʻawa,
especially since islands where ʻawa is being grown for export are the
very places where it is traditionally drunk with rituals and prayers:
Hawaiʻi, Sāmoa, Tonga, and Fiji.

The use of ʻawa in traditional culture involves its preparation as
well as its consumption. King was the first person to give a detailed
account of the way that ʻawa was prepared in Hawaiʻi.

Whilst the *ava* is chewing, of which they always drink
before they begin their repast, the person of the highest
rank takes the lead in a sort of hymn, in which he is
presently joined by one, two, or more of the company;
the rest moving their bodies, and striking their hands
gently together, in concert with the fingers. When the *ava*
is ready, cups of it are handed about to those who do not
join in the song, which they keep in their hands till it is
ended; when, uniting in one loud response, they drink off
their cup. The performers of the hymn are then served
with *ava*, who drink it after a repetition of the same
ceremony; and, if there be present one of a very superior
rank, a cup is, last of all, presented to him, which, after
chanting some time alone, and being answered by the
rest, and pouring a little out on the ground, he drinks off.
A piece of the flesh that is dressed, is next cut off, without
any selection of the part of the animal; which, together
with some of the vegetables, being deposited at the foot of
the image of the *Eatooa*, and a hymn chanted, their meal
commences. (King, J. 161)

Although he does not tell us how long this ceremony took, we can assume from his description of singing, serving, and drinking that it had taken a considerable amount of time. And we can tell by the serving of food to the participants that this is not only a religious or ceremonial event, but also a communal one. The surgeon, David Samwell, also described the preparation of ʻawa but in a less ceremonial way, led by Palea, the aikāne to Kalaniʻōpuʻu.

> Parea before he eat [*sic*] any meat drank a cup of Ava, but this he did as if he had been taking a dose of Physic, his Servant immediately supplying him with water to wash his mouth & a piece of Sugar Cane to take the Taste off. In preparing the Ava they mix no water with it except one mouthful, which he who chews it takes to wash his Mouth, & this he spits into the bowl among the chewed root. They did not sing before drinking it as others had done along side the Ship. (Beaglehole 1166)

Her Majesty Queen Sālote of Tonga compared this ritual to the Eucharist or Holy Communion when she explained the origins of ʻawa.

> The drinking of *kava* is thus a communion. It commemorates not only the sacrifice of the people for their king, but also the sympathy and appreciation of the king for his people. But life is not ruled by love alone. The story of the *kava* includes the bad with the good, the bitter with the sweet. [. . .] So the story of the *kava* and the drinking of it expresses not only the good aspect of relations between the king and people, but also doubts and suspicions as well. (Bott 93)

One must realize that the traditional use of ʻawa is communal and religious because ʻawa is sacred. It was given by the gods. As Kamakau reports, "ʻAwa is the oldest drink native to Hawaii, but this itself is not very old, for it was Lono who brought it to Ololo-i-mehani, and Kane and Kanaloa brought it here and planted it at Alanapo *mauka* of Keʻei on Hawaii" (*Ruling Chiefs* 193). Kamakau also says that "ʻAwa was a refuge and an absolution. Over the ʻawa cup were handed down the tabus and laws of the chiefs, the tabus of the gods, and the laws of the gods governing solemn vows and here the wrongdoer received absolution of his wrongdoing" (*The Works* 43). ʻAwa, like the cup of wine, deserves respect, but it also can be abused.

Without any ritual or ceremony, a concentrated pill of ʻawa is, literally, all too easy to take. This approach follows a seemingly popular attitude about individual cures for individual ailments and illnesses. You can see this perception in action at a drug store counter when someone is looking for something to take for aches, a cold, or a fever and a running nose. How do you invoke the sacred when you only have to pop a pill?

Time magazine reported that

> [i]n sleepless, stress-rattled America, consumers spend more than $50 million on kava—kava drinks, kava drops, kava capsules, kava candy and kava tea. [. . .] [Kava] didn't catch on in the U.S. until 1996, when a group of herbal-product purveyors called the Kava General Committee decided to pool their resources and make kava America's herb du jour. That year, supported by a heavy promotional campaign, retailers moved $15 million worth of the stuff [. . .] [as] kava vaulted out of the health-food ghetto and into the aisles of supermarkets and K Marts. (Grossman 58)

This marketing strategy runs directly counter to the traditional use of plant materials for various types of illnesses, which is evident when you look over the complex and compound prescriptions and recipes traditional practitioners have recorded since the early 1900s. Again, we can compare what has been recorded of traditional native pharmaceutics to the trendy way people talk of and take a single plant material like ʻawa or noni for all kinds of ailments. It should make you wonder what has happened to the state of traditional native medicine.

The two reports point out how this easy modern use of ʻawa is dangerous because it can lead to over indulgence and abuse. It is noted in the *Time* article that "some of the cases reported in Europe were complicated by extraneous factors; some patients had been taking extremely high doses of kava over long periods of time, or using it with alcohol, or taking it on top of a pre-existing liver condition" (Grossman 58).

Abuse of ʻawa was not unheard of in traditional culture. Kamakau reports that one use of ʻawa was for the purpose of losing weight.

> Ka poʻe kahiko liked ʻawa as a means of reducing weight. When a man saw himself growing too fat, or perhaps constantly being sick, then ʻawa was the thing to restore health or to slim the body. The way to do it was to drink ʻawa like the ʻaumakua or the kaula prophets, that is, copiously, until the skin scaled.

> Such a man looked for a place where grew very potent ʻawa, ʻawa ʻona, and obtained a large quantity. When the drinking of the ʻawa began, all foods — ʻai and iʻa — were prohibited until after the ʻawa treatment had been taken; only then could he eat. It was also tabu to go out in the sun and rain, for the feet would crack if wet in water or mud. [. . .] When the drinking of the ʻawa ended, sea water was drunk. When all the effects of the ʻawa were gone, the body was slender, the illness gone, and the body restored to health. (The Works 43)

Several captains also noted the abuse of ʻawa by chiefs and priests in their journals. Captain James King, of the Discovery, wrote this account of the abuse of ʻawa in March of 1779.

> The Erees [aliʻi] are very free from these complaints; but many of them suffer still more dreadful effects from the immoderate use of the ava. Those who were the most affected by it, had their bodies covered with a white scurf, their eyes red and inflamed, their limbs emaciated, the whole frame trembling and paralytic, accompanied with a disability to raise the head. Though this drug does not appear universally to shorten life, as was evident from the cases of Terreeoboo, Kaoo, and some other Chiefs, who were very old men; yet it invariably brings on an early and decrepid old age. [. . .] The young son

of Terreeoboo, who was about twelve years old, used to
boast of his being admitted to drink *ava*, and shewed
[showed] us, with great triumph, a small spot in his side
that was growing scaly. (126–127)

Portlock, the next foreigner to arrive in the islands after Cook's
death in 1779, described the degree of consumption of 'awa and its
effects on Kahekili, the paramount chief of Maui and Oʻahu.

On the 3d [of December] Taheeterre [Kahekili] paid
me another visit attended as before, and brought his
customary present of a few hogs, vegetables, and cocoa-
nuts. [. . .] [A]ccording to his usual custom, drank vast
quantities of yava, which kept him in a most wretched
condition; he seemed quite debilitated, and his body was
entirely covered with a kind of leprous scurf. (157)

The results of their abuse did not appear to be life threatening,
however, because they did not combine 'awa with alcohol, nor could
they take the concentrated dosage found in pills. And even if they
were over-indulging, they still had to go through some ceremony
and ritual in which socialization also occurred, and therefore slowed
consumption. King did intervene with some of the chiefs and priests
to stop the abuse, and he discovered that recovery was quick, noting
that "Our good friends, Kaireekeea and old Kaoo, were persuaded by
us to refrain from it; and they recovered amazingly during the short
time we afterward remained in the island" (127).

Ceremony, ritual, and socialization can have the effect of
deterring overindulgence and abuse in the following ways.

    ∽ Individual prayers, salutations, stories, and songs do prolong
the time period over which an individual's intake of 'awa
occurs. Kamakau gives this commentary in his description of
how a farmer prepared 'awa.

When the cup was filled, a prayer was offered with
gladness—for the afflictions and the blessings received
from the gods, and for their help to their offspring in this
world and in the bright world beyond. (*The Works* 42)

∽ Even when only one person prepared and drank ʻawa, there was a prayer of thanksgiving or salutation. Kamakau gives us this example from the time of Kamehameha.

> At midnight an old man rose up to pound ʻawa. Hearing the pounding, the chief and his companion came up close to the house. After pounding away for some time on some scraps of ʻawa, the old man strained the ʻawa and poured it into the cup. Then he prayed for the preservation of all the chiefs, and after that he prayed for the preservation of all the chiefesses, then for the life of Kamehameha, saying, "Let Kamehameha, the good king, live to be old, until his eyebrows are wrinkled like a rat's, his skin parched like the dry hala leaf, until he lies helpless, so let him live, O god, and let me live also." The old man drank the ʻawa. At the end of the prayer Kamehameha asked, "Is all your ʻawa gone?" The old man answered, "The ʻawa is gone. I have only scraps left. Last evening I gave most of it to the god, and since I could not sleep I awoke and pounded a little and drank it without any food (*pupu*) to eat after it." (*Ruling Chiefs* 182)

∽ Despite this example, ʻawa is generally taken with food. It is not taken by itself; the small morsels taken with ʻawa were called pūpū perhaps after the inclusion of little shellfish ʻpūpū.' Other foods could include kalo ʻtaro,' maiʻa ʻbanana,' and kō ʻsugar cane,' all of which have a sweet taste, which, it was thought, would counteract the bitterness of ʻawa. Kamakau describes other foods to be served with ʻawa in the following account.

> Then the heads of *kahala, uku, mokuleʻia* and *ulua* fishes, and the *kumu* and *ʻopule lauli* fishes which had been wrapped in ti leaves and cooked were taken out of the *imu* and laid on the eating mat. A bunch of dead-ripe bananas, sections of sugar cane just on the point of souring, sweet potatoes ridged in shape and deep red in color, were all ready at the eating place. (*The Works* 42)

    ꙰ The social drinking of 'awa not only emphasizes sharing, it also serves to limit one's intake. Further diluting of the potency of the 'awa depends on the number of people, which determines the amount each person has to drink. I experienced this in 1984 in Suva, Fiji when boarding students invited me to an all-night kava, or "grog," party around an enormous tānoa, or "wooden bowl." The cup of kava was served, then food passed around, more water was mixed after each round, and people would stop before or after a cup to tell a story or to sing a song.

The controversy over 'awa is no different from the story of another native plant of the Americas, tobacco. Used ceremonially as a purifying and medicinal agent for many Native American peoples, it was transformed by non-native peoples into a secular and pleasure-inducing habit. Overindulgence, abuse, and addiction have transformed this plant from the purifying medicine of the new world to one of the leading causes of cancer around the world. In hindsight we have learned that when what once was sacred and special is reduced to the everyday and ordinary, disastrous consequences are likely to follow. Such disasters will occur if fundamental cultural knowledge is not recognized, understood, and respected.

The State of Being Ma'i and Ola

I suspect that modern attitudes toward traditional health care 'ola' might be similar to the attitudes we've seen toward the use of 'awa and tobacco. But, as in those cases, if we recognize and respect the full range of cultural knowledge in the way our Hawaiian ancestors diagnosed illnesses, I think we can see that there is a great depth to the concept that is expressed when we talk of the state of being ola. They considered the opposite of ola, which is ma'i, or "being sick," and discovered five forms of sickness.

    ꙰ There is a "true" or "real" sickness such as a cold, flu, or HIV/AIDS that is caused by a virus or bacteria.
    ꙰ Physical injury such as broken bones and/or cuts is another form of illness.

We are very familiar with these two types of maʻi today. However, a person could also be sick for other reasons.

- ❧ Sickness can come from retribution or revenge that occurs when someone is angry, probably for something that has occurred to them, and is directing the blame at the sick person.
- ❧ Family problems that involve ancestral spirits, ghosts, or something else supernatural can cause a person to become sick.
- ❧ Finally, there are illnesses known only to a single family and not to any "outsiders." Today we might recognize this type of illness as genetic, psychological, or psychosomatic.

Ola and maʻi do not just affect or concern an individual; they affect one's (extended) family, especially if the family relationships are very close.

> This certainly is true of "spirit/ghost sickness," "Hawaiian sickness" and "retribution sickness" whose cultural cause is the breaking of some type of kapu (*prohibition or sacred things*), but also can be understood as being "more involved with a breakdown in the social relationships" than of the body. These cultural or social "sicknesses" reveal, through their painful physical and mental forms, any conflict between individuals, families and groups. These "sicknesses" also serve as a control or deterrent to "socially undesirable behavior," by invoking the possibility of punishment through physical or mental discomfort. (Chun, *Ola* 1)

Being sick was more than aches and pains. It involved the whole body, mind, and environment holistically. Having described the opposite of ola, we must then look at the causative form of ola, which is hoʻōla, 'to heal and to cure.' Treating a patient probably involved one or more of the following:

- ❧ There were frequent and lengthy consultations with the patient and with his or her family and extended family during the entire process of healing.

- During these consultations people were encouraged to air any grievances which might be causing tensions within the family, especially any problems concerning illnesses, and other difficulties.
- There were several ways a practitioner could diagnosis a patient: by palpation 'feeling' for the illness, by visual examination 'alawa maka,' and/or through prayer 'kāhea' for divine help in determining the illness and discovering the cure.
- Traditionally rituals, prayers, offerings, and the constant feeding of people involved in the consultation and healing process were done.
- A treatment was revealed to the practitioner through prayer and/or physical diagnosis.
- A patient received different treatments, first to address any natural or physical illnesses and then, if necessary, for any of the other types of illness described above, until the patient was cured.

Much of this process involved significant participation from the patient and family, so that all were fully aware of what was occurring. This process made them feel that they were contributing to the patient's recovery. Therefore, at the conclusion of the treatment, not only was the patient healed and a possible "wrong" way of living corrected, but the family, even the extended family, was also restored to its norm. The successful results would be cause for a display and celebration in the form of a public or community feast.

Today many people would call this process hoʻoponopono, with the idea that it is a process for the treatment of psychosomatic illness, and they might be surprised to discover that it was the way to diagnosis physical illnesses as well. This broader perspective comes from the recognition that

> illness to Hawaiians was not just a lack of physical well-being. It was generally thought to be induced through a medium by magic or sorcery. Sacred *mana* as well as physical strength was lost in illness. The means to correct or to help such illness was to counter it through chants, prayers, and medicines in order to restore an

ill person to physical, mental, and spiritual health and
to regain the lost *mana*. (Chun, "Understanding La'au
Lapa'au" n. pag.)

Diet

Diet is another aspect of ola. Food is not just nutrients to sustain
life. It is also medicine. As the popular adage goes, "You are what
you eat," hence my own adage, "food is medicine." Medicine and
food were integral and related in traditional healing practices. After
the ordeal of purging, food was used to help regain strength and
to restore the patient to better health. In later traditional practices,
certain foods, such as the deep-sea fishes aku 'skipjack,' 'ahi 'tuna,' or
mahimahi, were also banned during treatment.

What was the Hawaiian diet? Dr. Kekuni Blaisdell gives this
description.

> The maka'āinana diet of old was mainly i'a (fish) and
> other sea foods, such as 'opihi, pāpa'i (crab), ula (lobster)
> and wana (sea urchin); kalo (taro), 'uala (sweet potato),
> uhi (yam), 'ulu (breadfruit), leafy vegetables, like lū'au
> (taro leaf) and hō'i'o (fern), limu (algae relish); some
> fruit, like mai'a (banana), 'ohi'a'ai (mountain apple)
> and niu (coconut); and occasional moa (chicken). Pua'a
> (pig) and 'īlio (dog) were consumed only on special feast
> occasions by nā maka'āinana. There was no pipi (beef),
> hipa (mutton or lamb), kāmano (salmon), halakahiki
> (pineapple), mīkana (papaya), guava, mango, pastry,
> ice cream, butter, cheese, mayonnaise, ketchup, shoyu,
> candy, french fries, soft drinks, beer or other alcoholic
> beverages. ("Ho'okē 'Ai" 23)

We might look at this diet as being particularly bland, but then
most of the European cuisine was too, until the age of exploration
that began some five hundred years ago. Accounts of European
explorers and castaways who settled into the local community and
hosted or were guests at shared meals provide some details about
the Hawaiian diet, eating habits, and food preparation, and about
how encounters with foreigners were increasingly changing the way
Hawaiians ate.

We have this account from King who, as part of Cook's expedition, was one of the first foreigners to observe the Hawaiian way of life.

> The food of the lower class of people consists principally
> of fish, and vegetables; such as yams, sweet-potatoes,
> tarrow, plantains, sugar-canes, and bread-fruit. To
> these, the people of a higher rank add the flesh of hogs
> and dogs, dressed in the same manner as at the Society
> Islands. They also eat fowls of the same domestic kind
> with ours; but they are neither plentiful, nor much
> esteemed by them. [. . .] Their fish they salt, and preserve
> in gourd-shells; not, as we at first imagined, for the
> purpose of providing against any temporary scarcity,
> but from the preference they give to salted meats. For we
> also found, that the Erees used to pickle pieces of pork
> in the same manner, and esteemed it a great delicacy.
> (King, J. 140–141)

Russian explorer Captain Iurii F. Lisianskii of the *Neva* gave this detailed description of the Hawaiian diet and methods of food preparation in 1804.

> [Their] diet consists of swine and dog meat, fish, fowl,
> coconuts, sweet potato, bananas, taro, and yams.
> Sometimes they eat fish raw; but everything else they bake.
> The women are forbidden pork, coconuts, and bananas.
> The men may eat anything. They do not kill swine with
> a knife but stifle them by tying a rope around the snout.
> The animal is prepared for eating as follows. A hole is dug.
> One or two rows of stones are placed in it and a fire is lit
> on them (fire is obtained by friction). More stones are so
> positioned that the air can freely circulate around them.
> When the stones are very hot, they are spread out evenly
> and covered with a thin layer of leaves or reeds. The beast
> is placed on it and turned over until all the bristles have
> disappeared. If any hairs still remain, they are scraped off
> with knives or shells. Having thus cleaned the carcass,
> the natives next open up the belly and remove the viscera
> while the fire is laid again. As soon as the stones are hot in

the pit again, they take them out, leaving one layer only, on which they duly spread leaves and then the hog. Hot stones wrapped in leaves are put into the disembowelled beast, which is covered over with leaves and more hot stones. Sand or earth is finally scattered on top. The animal is thus left until baked. Tubers are prepared in the same manner, with the difference, however, that water is poured over them before they are covered with hot stones. (Barratt 47)

The Sandwich Islanders use salt and are very fond of salted fish and meat. They also prepare little balls of taro-root flour,*[2] for consumption on long journeys. By soaking these in fresh or salt water, they produce something rather like meal dough. (Barratt 48)

David Samwell's entry of how they served up the baked pork completes this description of how they prepared the underground baked pig that today is called kālua pig.

They use the slit bark of the Sugar Cane for Knives, with which they cut the Meat down to the Joints and then tear them asunder after which every one falls to with his Hands. (Beaglehole 1163)

Archibald Campbell, one of the early Europeans to live in the islands for an extended period of time, made these observations of his day-to-day encounters.

Fish are often eaten raw, seasoned with salt water. When cooked, they are either done in their usual manner, under ground, or broiled, by putting them, wrapt in leaves, upon the fire. When the leaves are burnt, they consider them ready.

They preserve pork by taking out the bones, and rubbing it well with salt; after which it is made up in rolls, and dried. [. . .] The sugar-cane, which they chew, is also a general article of food. (131–132)

Vasilii Nikolaevich Berkh, on the *Nadezhda*, another ship from the same Russian voyage of 1804, wrote in regard to the introduction of breadfruit to Europe by the crew of Cook's earlier voyages.

> Some thirty years ago, there was rather a commotion
> in Europe about the breadfruit tree. In reality, the
> breadfruit is far less nourishing than yams or taro are
> and, besides, the tree does not always fruit, being easily
> damaged by cold air. The roots of yams and taro, on
> the other hand, may always be had in abundance, never
> spoil, and are so soft that the very biggest root can be
> made into small grains within five minutes. (Barratt 106)

And he added, again contrary to Cook's description of it being a "disagreeable mess, from its sourness" (Barrow 336) that "it is my own opinion that taro root is the most nourishing foodstuff on earth" (Barratt 106–107).

We can presume that the meals of the high chiefs were opulent in comparison to everyone else, but Samwell noted that some of the chiefs, in particular Palea, did not like fish. He observed one day that, "It appears that the Chiefs look upon it as beneath them to eat fish, for some being offered to Parea one day he refused it and told us it was the food of the Women" (Beaglehole 1184). Campbell also observed, "The king's mode of life was very simple" (92). He described Kamehameha's dinner as consisting of "a dish of poe, or taro pudding, [. . .] salt fish and consecrated pork from the morai [. . .]. He concluded his meal by drinking half a glass of rum; but the bottle was immediately sent away, the liquor being tabooed, or interdicted to his guests" (93). Campbell added that "breakfast and supper consisted of fish and sweet potatoes" (93). He also noted that Kamehameha kept a regular meal schedule, for "he breakfasted at eight, dined at noon, and supped at sunset" (92). This was no doubt a result of foreign influence, for Golovnin wrote that "they still cannot acquire the habit of regular meals and eat only when the stomach demands it" (210).

One eating habit that all observers seem to have noticed and commented on was the 'ai kapu, an edict preventing women from eating with men and prohibiting all women from eating certain food items, which remained in effect until 1819. Lisianskii called it "a most odd custom" that "[n]ot only are women forbidden to eat in a house where a man is eating; they may not even enter that house. A man may be in a female dining place, but may not touch food" (Barratt

47). Golovnin wrote the following in October, 1818 just before the end of the kapu.

> The women, by the way, regardless of their rank, are forbidden to use pork in their food, although those belonging to the nobler ranks may eat dogs, chickens, wild fowl, and fish. It must be noted here that these people do not consider dog meat unclean. The chiefs eat it, and Tameamea [Kamehameha] himself prefers it to pork; almost every day he is served a fat roasted pup for dinner. (208)

> A woman, however, no matter how noble her rank, may not break a single one of the prohibitions imposed upon her sex. The wife of the first chief of the entire region around Karekekua visited me; her long silk dress of an old-fashioned European style and an expensive looking white shawl were proof enough that she was "a lady of noble rank," but when we sat down to eat with the chiefs I could not persuade her even to stay in the cabin, let alone dine with us. All she answered was: "Tabu," which means forbidden, and she ate on the quarterdeck with the wife of another chief. Their meal consisted of a dough made of taro root flour and raw fish, which they dipped in sea water instead of vinegar. They would not touch a morsel of our food except biscuits and cheese [. . .]. (209)

One exception Lisianskii described was in the "[o]utdoors, in the fields or on a craft for example, the sexes may eat together unless the food be a pudding made from taro roots" (Barratt 47). And Campbell noted, "They [women] are never permitted to eat with the men, except when at sea, and then not out of the same dish" (135).

Golovnin saw some subtle changes in food preparation when he noted, "Whereas formerly meat and vegetables were baked in pits in the ground by means of hot rocks, some of their dishes are now prepared our way, being boiled and fried." And he saw a serious problem of alcoholic consumption; "The common people are also given to this destructive vice, and at present on the Island of Woahoo, where most ships touch, some of the provisions are paid for in alcoholic drinks as if there were a fixed form of exchange" (210).

Another important factor we must consider with regard to the traditional diet and food preparation is that there was no refrigeration. Having things fresh, especially meats, meant there were very few processed foods, unless it was preserved by salting or drying in the sun or wind. Indeed, as we have seen, Captain King observed that salt meats were a preferred source of protein for meals.

Without refrigeration there can be no fresh meat leftovers, unless one would tempt having a very bad stomachache and food poisoning. This means the land and the ocean served as the pantry for sources of protein. But a fisherman or farmer would not want to gather too much of a catch or harvest for a daily meal lest the food spoil or be wasted. Storage could be used, again for preserved foods, and for tuber crops like sweet potato or paʻi ʻai (mashed, cooked taro root without added water), but not for a long period of time.

Therefore, the Hawaiian diet was probably high in fiber and low in fat, processed sugars, and salts. Only on infrequent, special occasions, such as communal and public feasts, would there be an excess of foods, especially fatty foods like pigs, chickens, and dogs. Even then, we can appreciate the great sacrifice the roasting and eating of an animal represented when we consider the tremendous effort, time, and resources it took to raise it, and to slaughter and cook it, and remember that with no refrigeration any leftovers went to waste. Blaisdell warned of the dangers brought on by the insidious change of diet.

> One main difference between the nutrition of *kahiko loa* and modern Hawaiʻi is that there were almost no processed and preserved foods, such as we have today. Long ago, some salted and dried fish, yes, but certainly not the supermarket canned foods, such as Spam, pastries, frozen foods, fast junk foods, such as "french fries," dairy products, sauces, and snacks, such as see moy, of today [. . .]. ("He Mau Ninau Ola" 15)

A Sacred Link

We have seen many of the elements that make up the concept of ola: understanding the causes of sickness, various means of treatment, and the idea that what we eat affects our health. But there is still more to understand. Hoʻōla has another connotation as it relates to healing. As a verb, it can mean to spare, and as a noun, salvation, healer, or, even, savior (Pukui and Elbert 1986: 283). These meanings have strong religious connotations, especially in the Christian faith, but they should not be disregarded when it comes to traditional health.

This meaning of ola is similar to the idea described in the story of Jesus and the Samaritan woman at the well in the Gospel according to John 4: 1–26.

> "Sir," the woman said, "you don't have anything to get water with. The well is deep. Where can you get this living water? [. . .]" Jesus answered, "All who drink this water will be thirsty again. But those who drink the water I give them will never thirst. In fact, the water I give them will become a spring of water in them. It will flow up into eternal life." (*Holy Bible*, John 4: 11–14)

While the woman thinks this conversation is about the physical "living" or flowing water, Jesus is using the image of water to represent eternal life. It is not just the daily bread or water that makes up living, but something else. I believe a similar understanding is to be found in ola, when we speak of life and living.

This type of healing (hoʻōla) centers upon a threefold relationship between the Divine, or what most people name God(s) and spirits; people, as a community, extended family, family, and individual; and the intermediary, the healer.

This relationship is beautifully explained in Tonga where they consider the principal causative agent of all sickness to be the *avanga* (spirits). Traditionally, it requires three agents, or vehicles, to complete the cycle of health, illness, and restoration or death. These three forms are the *vaka* 'vessel or canoe,' which is the messenger, and may actually be the medicine or cure; the *taula* 'anchor,' which is interpreted as the priest or medium; and the *faletapu* 'the house' where the priest conducts his or her ritual. This relationship of the divine to the practitioner and then to the patient is very similar to the process Kamakau described concerning the training of healing practitioners.

> In the Hawaiian school of medical kahunas [practitioners
> or priests], the god was the foundation, and secondly came
> prayers. Third came schooling in the kinds of diseases;
> fourth, in the kinds of remedies; fifth, in the art of killing;
> and sixth, in the art of saving. (*Ka Poʻe Kahiko* 107)

Even with elaborate training, the traditional practitioners'
abilities are recognized as a gift from God or inherited through one's
ancestors. Unlike contemporary faith healers, a native practitioner
works through a process of healing rather than an instantaneous act.
It is for these reasons that traditional practitioners are respected for
their knowledge but also feared because of their intimate relationship
with the divine. They can be dangerous and powerful, or as the late
Rev. Dr. Abraham Akaka once reminded me, "no phony baloney."

In this form of medical practice, there is no ethic for fees or any
obligation of gifts, because healing is seen as a gift from the divine.
For the practitioner, the power to heal should be payment enough.
Even makana aloha, or gifts for service such as a bag of rice and
other foodstuffs, are not asked for and are resisted if they are seen as
payment for services. If money is given, it is usually turned over to
churches or charities rather than kept.

Central to this is the idea that the process of healing cannot be
complete without the recognition of where the power to heal came
from. Kamakau termed the prayers used by kāhuna engaged in
the process of diagnosis and the use of medicinal herbs as prayers
of "remembrance" and "thanksgiving" *(Ka Poʻe Kahiko* 107). The
kāhuna, when reciting these prayers, were recalling their ancestral
beginnings and later giving thanks to and acknowledgment of the
gods associated with the healing arts.

In contemporary times the invocation of the Christian God
and personal or family spirits ʻʻāumākuaʼ reinforces this cultural
continuity and recognition. The duality is not a contradiction but
a genuine expression of experience; after all, the mana ʻpowerʼ of
medicines comes from the divine, through revelation such as dreams,
through ancestral inheritance, and even through the Holy Bible
during contemporary forms of healing such as wehe i ka Baibala. This
type of mana implies a different presence of the divine, being of a
more personal nature than that of a distant hovering God.

Medical science, in particular the pharmaceutical industry, continues today to re-examine the forest, wild plants, and *materia medica* used by indigenous peoples, and in rare instances they do make some amazing discoveries. Even the World Health Organization is now recognizing that the traditional practitioner is a valued and important resource. The difficulty for the modern researcher is to see beyond the material into the power of religion and the divine.

"And there is no health in us"

This phrase comes from the middle of a confessional evening prayer in the *Book of Common Prayer*. It sums up the state of the total inadequacy of a person at the end of the day having forgotten or not finished things that should have been done. It also sums up the state of ola that we are living in today.

In 1922, the Hawaiian language newspaper *Nupepa Kuokoa* published an article about the need to rediscover traditional healing ("Eia Mai Kekahi"). It begins by lamenting the past, then calls for a renewal for the future.

> Here we are living in the modern world, but we have not taken notice of the value of the knowledge our ancestors had of medicines, and we regret it very much. The medicinal priesthood was closely related to the agents of God, who are today the ministers, the leaders of all the priests. Several of these ministers have followed in the ways of their predecessors, and thus has come the saying, 'When the high priest has completed his work, then the medicine of the practitioner begins.' [. . .] Our ancestors who have departed into the night were full of knowledge and skill. They searched for and found the very understanding of the principles of healing the sick, and of the various types of illnesses revealed through the process of using different cures. Not only did they subscribe to these treatments, but they also tended the sick, prescribed steam baths, which are widely talked about and practiced by families today, and prescribed purging. [. . .] As we look upon our lives today, and

remember the dim past, we will see how dynamic this
kind of healing is, because the medical school that stands
with its door open to both the light and the darkness,
that is, the future and the past, is one that is found also
in the mountains, the ridges, the hills, and the valleys
down to the sea. These were the places where our elders
found their medicines without having to buy them, so
unlike today when we have to go to the drug store to buy
the medicines prescribed by licensed doctors.

This process was even more flexible than today, because
one did not have to pay the practitioners as one does
nowadays. Cure or not, one has to pay the doctor
today, and for some patients the doctor might not
know what is ailing you. He will treat you by trying out
some medicines, but the greater part of the problem is
that there is not a real consultative process to discover
the symptoms of the illness. This has led to wrong
prescriptions.

It has been reasoned that we should be sending young
Hawaiians to learn to become doctors. It is also good
for our elders to teach their grandchildren the secrets of
native healing so they can benefit families and friends.
This transmission of knowledge seems to have ceased
as more and more Hawaiians are seeking to get rich fast
like in the old trading days, about a hundred years ago
when people sought and amassed money only to bury it
in the ground for worms to eat.

What would you do in the forest if you do not know
of the great wealth that is there for you to treat the
aches of your body? [. . .] Therefore, it is to our benefit,
as Hawaiians, to recognize again the practices of our
ancestors. Happy is the family who lives in poverty and
a friend arrives to share his skill in healing [. . .]. So was
the healing of our ancestors. (Author's translation)

We, too, are recognizing the value and appropriate use of
traditional health and healing.

Overindulgence and abuse were not the norm of traditional life. Although they did exist in traditional times, we did not see the wide-spread effects such as obesity or addiction to alcohol, tobacco, or other drugs that are a part of everyday life today. The traditional lifestyle, which included intensive food preparation, incorporated both a healthy diet and a significant amount of exercise into daily life.

Changes to one's diet and exercise are actions an individual can do right now. Without farming, fishing, and the more intensive food preparation such as pounding kalo root into poi or cooking in an imu, there is little daily exercise in gathering and preparing foods. It is not surprising, then, that obesity is epidemic and the government must create guidelines that advise us to exercise for at least sixty minutes per day, and to make that exercise very strenuous at least three days per week. Because healthy diet and exercise patterns are not an integral part of our lives today, they must become a matter of discipline. Discipline is not a popular word these days, but it really just means creating habits, and the difficult part of a habit is keeping it up. Help is available in the form of diet plans and exercise programs, but all of these come at a cost.

There are many popular, and sometimes faddish, diet plans available; most of them marketed as conveniences that try to make dieting easier. Some are actually based on the traditional Native Hawaiian diet updated to reflect diet and food changes. Similarly, health clubs and weight-loss programs utilize a group or a team effort for mutual support, fun, and a sense of achievement. But, ironically, many of these fail us because they become an additional burden rather than an integral part of our lives.

Healthy activities can also involve our family, friends, and even co-workers, and can be a physical and emotional expression of taking care of each other. In traditional health care, neither food preparation nor healing were an individual experience but something that concerned and involved the entire ʻohana. Learning, as a family, some basic elements about traditional health and healing may free one from the dependence on and costs of these diets and exercise programs. There are three simple elements in the traditional diet that must be understood. The first is a focus on the complex carbohydrates of kalo and ʻuala (taro and sweet potato); the second

Henry "Papa" Auwae and associate Sabrina Mahelona conduct a traditional medicine workshop at Hōnaunau on the island of Hawai'i.

is that proteins are centered upon fish and not fatty meats; and the third element is always having fresh, rather than highly processed, foods. We must remember that feasting was done on appropriate occasions and was not an everyday occurrence. Therefore, fatty and rich foods were to be enjoyed but only for a brief moment.

In health care, too, a return to a family and community focus rather than individual professional practices can benefit all of us. Collaborative programs need to be developed that can provide sound research, testing, and educational use of traditional healing practices that focus on families and communities. This approach must start with preservation and perpetuation of the cultural knowledge our ancestors had.

Our understanding of Native Hawaiian health is greatly indebted to the documented legacy provided by Native Hawaiians and others, and today's traditional practitioners need to continue to document their practices as a historical record for the future.

Almost all native plants found on the islands were used to some extent for medicinal recipes, but urban and commercial encroachment has diminished the open fields and forests. The availability of adequate amounts of fresh material is, therefore, at risk. Plants in home gardens are needed to fill that niche, as are large gardens and collections maintained solely for this purpose.

A community-based approach must also encourage practitioners to engage in the study and practice of traditional culture and health. Finding health care with professionals who understand traditional healing practices can be difficult. One of the major factors leading to the avoidance of medical professionals by Native Hawaiians has been the lack of understanding, sensitivity, and appreciation of traditional concepts by health professionals and institutions. In addition, some present-day practitioners of traditional healing, who seek to equate their practice with modern medicine, particularly in terms of fees and status, become enmeshed in governmental and professional regulations, standards, liability, and a myriad of other problems that plague the medical profession today, thereby alienating their fellow Native Hawaiians. The use of traditional healing practices for non-life-threatening ailments can help low-income families and communities with health care that is readily available and affordable. As we are increasingly learning, there is a crucial role that traditional healing can play in the larger health care picture.

All of the above may lead us to a perfect state of ola, but ola should actually be living one's life in pono, because if you are not, then you are unhealthy, in one form or another. Ola is a *way* of living, rather than simply a state of being healthy. Whether one is religious or not, having guidelines for living, which are a measure of what should or should not be done and the reasons for making those choices, gives us a sense of direction and purpose for living. This is what pono is all about, and the re-discovery of that way of living will no doubt also become a road to ola, to better health.

Endnotes
[1] *Ka Nupepa Kuʻokoʻa,* July 20, 1867.
[2] *ʻai paʻa.* Dried baked taro or sweet potato, known as *ʻao,* was also used thus.

6 Ho'oponopono

Traditional Ways of Healing to Make Things Right Again

We forgave and were forgiven, thrashing out
every grudge, peeve or sentiment among us.
In this way, we became a very closely bound family unit.
Pukui

Hawaiian historian Samuel Manaiakalani Kamakau described what families in pre-contact and pre-Christian Hawai'i did to seek reconciliation and forgiveness.

> The Hawaiians are said to be a people consecrated to the gods; the *'aumakua* gods were "born," and from them man was born [. . .].

> When trouble came upon a family for doing wrong against an *'aumakua* god [. . .] the cause for this trouble was shown to them by dreams, or visions, or through other signs sent by the god. It was pointed out to them what sacrifices to offer, and what gifts to present, to show their repentance for the wrong committed by the family. They were to go to the *Pohaku o Kane*, their *pu'uhonua*, where they were to make offerings to atone for their wrong doing *(mohai hala)* and to pacify the god *(mohai ho'olu'olu)*. (*Ka Po'e Kahiko* 32)

He also observed

> The *Pohaku o Kane*, the Stone of Kane, was a place of refuge, a *pu'uhonua*, for each family from generation to generation. It was not a heiau; it was a single stone monument [. . .] and a *kuahu* altar with ti and other greenery planted about. There the family went to obtain relief. (*Ka Po'e Kahiko* 32)

When the high chiefs ended the state religious system in 1819, places of refuge such as Pōhaku o Kāne gradually ceased to be used and other forms of seeking reconciliation developed. Today, a descendant of those early forms of reconciliation is still practiced.

It survives largely through the efforts and determination of Mary
Kawena Pukui, formerly a translator and consultant at the Bernice
Pauahi Bishop Museum.

When interviewed by the museum nearly fifty years ago, Pukui
spoke of a way in which Hawaiians were able, on a course to healing,
to "set to right first" mental problems. The interview was tape-
recorded and transcribed. Pukui called this way of mental cleansing
hoʻoponopono.

She noted in the interview, "Today, the hoʻoponopono remains
only a fond memory since the death of my mother in 1942. [. . .]
The hoʻoponopono is rare today and is regarded as a silly remnant
of heathenism by most people and squelched at every turn"
(*Hoʻoponopono*, audiotape). Pukui was afraid that this way of life
would soon be forgotten.

From the mid 1960s through the early 1970s, Pukui had the
opportunity to ensure that this part of Hawaiian culture would not
die. She collaborated with mental health professionals and social
workers at the Queen Liliʻuokalani Children's Center to codify
the cultural practice in systematic terms that could be understood
and learned by modern professionals and families. She wanted

Mary Kawena Pukui in a photograph by Fritz Henle

to ensure that Hawaiian families would once again be able to use
hoʻoponopono.

A Hawaiian Way of Healing

What is hoʻoponopono? Why is it so special and important?
Pukui described it in these words.

> My people believed that the taking of medicine was of
> little help without first removing any and all mental
> obstructions. [. . .] When a problem arose in the
> family affecting an individual or the group as a whole,
> every member of the immediate family turned to the
> hoʻoponopono. [. . .] Every one of us searched our
> hearts for any hard feelings of one against the other and
> did some thorough mental housecleaning. We forgave
> and were forgiven, thrashing out every grudge, peeve
> or sentiment among us. In this way, we became a very
> closely bound family unit. (*Hoʻoponopono*, audiotape)

According to Pukui, only then would the afflicted family
members be ready to be healed. The burden of the problems needed
to be lifted from their minds before their bodies were ready for
medical treatment.

The word *hoʻoponopono* itself hints at such a process. The root of
the word is *pono*, which has a multitude of meanings. In the Andrews
dictionary, compiled throughout the middle of the nineteenth
century, *pono* is defined as "to be good, to be just, to be morally
upright," and, directly relevant to its use in *hoʻoponopono*, "to be
well, i. e., in bodily health" (490). The scholar Davida Malo indicated
that pono was the absolute model of good behavior and values in
traditional Hawaiian society. All persons, including chiefs, strived to
be pono.

> There were also many thoughts considered to be pono
> maoli [*truly pono*], but misfortune could quickly come
> about. It was pono when one's eyes saw something and
> one's heart desired it, but one was hoʻomanawanui [*patient*]
> and did not go to take it, but quickly left forgetting about it
> without even touching it. This was pono.

Furthermore, it was not considered correct behavior to grab things, to lie, to flock into a person's doorway, to look longingly at something, or to beg for someone's things. This was pono.

There were several other things considered to be pono: being well supplied, not being shiftless, not exposing oneself to others, not being irresponsible, and not eating someone else's food. This was pono.

Furthermore it was pono for a husband and wife to live together, to have children, friends [. . .]

These things were considered pono: not to over indulge in pleasure and fun [. . .]

These were things a person could do to greatly improve (pono) the quality of life (ka noho ʻana ma keia ola ʻana). Great was the pono of these things. (187–188)

When a word in Hawaiian is repeated, as the word *pono* is in *hoʻoponopono* it is done to give emphasis and underscore its importance. The prefix *hoʻo–* is a causative, adding the sense of "to do something" or "to make something happen." Hence, the term *hoʻoponopono* is "to make very pono."

A year before being interviewed, Pukui had worked on the publication of a modern Hawaiian-English dictionary. In this 1957 publication, hoʻoponopono is described as "Mental cleansing: the old Hawaiian method of clearing the mind of a sick person by family discussion, examination, and prayer" (Pukui and Elbert 1957: 314).

Following Pukui's work on the publication *Nānā I Ke Kumu* with the Culture Committee at Queen Liliʻuokalani Children's Center, the 1986 revised *Hawaiian Dictionary* described hoʻoponopono as "Mental cleansing: family conferences in which relationships were set right [. . .] through prayer, discussion, confession, repentance, and mutual restitution and forgiveness [. . .]" (1986: 341). Pukui had pointed out that hoʻoponopono is directly related to healing and good health. An understanding of traditional wellness and healing is critical to give clarity to this cultural concept and the process of hoʻoponopono.

We know that traditional Hawaiian ideas about being sick are complex and not easily correlated with Western concepts of illness. In Hawaiian terms, being ill is more than being injured or affected by a physical ailment or disease. People believed that sickness could be inflicted by spirits or by the breaking of a kapu. These types of sicknesses were made known through painful physical and mental forms or even through conflicts between individuals, families, and groups.

The treatment, or healing, of these types of sicknesses is very complicated and requires great skill and flexibility. Diagnosis involves the consultation of the healer with the sick person, his or her family, and even the extended family or community. In many situations the healer is also a relative of the ill person.

A traditional healer uses his or her skills in observation and dialogue to gain an understanding of the family's or group's insights in order to determine the degree and type of sickness and the approaches to be used for healing. Without such a collaborative diagnosis, it would be extremely difficult to pinpoint the type of illness and to allay any doubts or fears on the part of the ill person. These consultative diagnoses serve to improve the chances of healing. This approach is not only holistic, it also targets the root causes for sickness instead of just its symptoms or manifestations, such as being tired or having a cold.

> [The] key element to this process is the often and lengthy consultations with the patient, his or her family and extended family, where "a sick person is not treated as an isolate, but rather (he or she) is considered in the context of family relationships." It is during these sessions that people are encouraged to air any grievances which might be causing tension within the family, problems concerning illnesses, and other difficulties encountered so that the appropriate treatment may be revealed. (Chun, *Ola* 2)

The airing out of the patient's and the family's mistakes and transgression mirrors what a student learning to be a traditional healer must do. He or she must forgive him or herself of previous wrongs before entering into the priesthood to the forgiveness (reconciliation) of others. But we find that it was the kahuna 'anā'anā kuni, a class of priest not usually thought of today as being associated with healing, who were responsible to forgive (kalahala) the trespasses of other people. Kamakau points out that kalahala, a term that Hawaiian Christianity associates with "forgiveness," was "one of his duties."

> [. . .] One of his duties as a *kahuna ʻanaʻana* in his practice of *kuni* (*iloko o kana ʻoihana kuni*) was to *kalahala*—remove the grounds for offense within the victim, and so remove (*wehe*) the affliction (*make*) sent by another. (*Ka Poʻe Kahiko* 122)

This lesser known aspect of traditional healing practices is corroborated by Kamakau's contemporary Zepherin Kahōāliʻi Kepelino in a brief article entitled "Te Tala." Although the translators of this article rendered it as "counter-sorcery," te tala literally means "to untie," and hence, in the case of hoʻoponopono, to forgive. Inserting it into the translation gives us support to Kamakau's statement.

> Forgiveness (te Tala) is something associated with all the priests involved with sorcery. The skilled guardian of sorcery was able to counter (te tana ʻana) the sorcery of another. This was the true priest and one who was not able to do so was unskilled (holona).
>
> There were two important things in sorcery: causing death (ʻo te tala mate) and restoring health (ʻo te tala ola). [. . .] This is what is first done: he first examines (hoʻotolotolo) himself, to see what errors and deeds he has done wrong against the person who wants to harm him. (Author's translation from Kirtley and Moʻokini 59)

The implication of this information for this discussion of hoʻoponopono is that we see its possible development as a family practice from a merger of two forms of traditional healing. It is possible that this merger took place after the original two practices had decreased due to modernization and the spread of Christianity.

The radical changes to Hawaiian society and culture that may have led to the development and evolution of hoʻoponopono have also led to its near demise. The findings of the Culture Committee at Queen Liliʻuokalani Children's Center indicated that common understandings of hoʻoponopono were greatly lacking.

Many Hawaiians came to believe their time honored
method of family therapy was "a stupid, heathen thing."
Some practiced *ho'oponopono* secretly. As time went
on, Hawaiians remembered, not *ho'oponopono* but
only bits and pieces of it. Or grafted-on innovations.
Or mutations. Or complete distortions of concept,
procedure and vocabulary.

In the past five years, Center staff members have
compiled an almost unbelievable list of incomplete or
distorted explanations of what *ho'oponopono* is. Most—but
not all—come from clients. (Pukui, Haertig, and Lee 69)

In order to dispel these mistaken beliefs and to gain a better
knowledge of ho'oponopono, it is important that one understands
historical and traditional Hawaiian roots of the healing and
peacemaking processes.

Traditional Accounts of the Process of Healing and Peacemaking

The process of consulting and counseling was used by the early
Hawaiians for healing of the greater community, especially during
times of crisis. This form of peacemaking had no particular name,
but its similarities to ho'oponopono are remarkable. With a better
understanding of the process of ho'oponopono, we are now able to
revisit known historical events where the elements can be observed
in action. There are several significant occurrences that have been
recorded and that provide a powerful image of the effectiveness of
this process.

Through interviews with living informants recorded by
Kamakau, the earliest account recalls a battle between Alapa'i, the
paramount chief of Hawai'i, and the chiefs of O'ahu allied with
Peleiōhōlani of Kaua'i. The battle was to take place on the beach of
NāoneaLa'a in Kāne'ohe on the island of O'ahu.

Now there was a certain wise counselor named Na-'ili,
brother to Ka-maka'i-moku the mother of Ka-lani-'ōpu'u
and Keoua, who was the chief in charge of Wai'anae. [. . .]
Said Na-'ili to Pele-io-holani, "It would be best for you to

put an end to this war and you two become acquainted with Alapaʻi," and he continued, "You can stop this war if you will, for the chiefs of Maui and Hawaii are related to you and that not distantly, for they are your own cousins." "Is Alapaʻi related to me?" asked Pele-io-holani. "You are a god, and on one side you are related," answered Na-ʻili. So Pele-io-holani consented to a meeting with Alapaʻi.

At this time the fighting was going on at Kaulekola in Kaneʻohe, and Na-ʻili went down to stop the fighting. Approaching Ka-lani-ʻopuʻu and Keoua he kissed their hands and asked, "Where is your uncle?" Ka-lani-ʻopuʻu said, "Alapaʻi? He is at the seacoast at Waihaukalua." "Then stop the fighting and let us go down to the seacoast." The two consented and went down with Na-ʻili to the coast with the chiefs and fighting men of Hawaii, and those of Oahu and Kauai also retired. There Na-ʻili met Alapaʻi, and the two wailed over each other affectionately. "What brings you here?" said Alapaʻi. "I have come to stay the battle while you go to meet Pele-io-holani." "Does he consent?" "Yes," answered Na-ʻili. So Alapaʻi agreed to stay the battle and go to meet Pele-io-holani. Then Na-ʻili laid down the terms of the conference. They were to meet at Naonealaʻa. The Hawaiian forces were to remain in their canoes; not one was to land on pain of death except Alapaʻi himself, and he was to land without weapon in his hand; likewise in the forces of Kauai and Oahu, if even a single chief bore arms, he was to die.

The beach of NāoneaLaʻa, Kāneʻohe, Oʻahu

It was the custom, when blood relatives went to war with each other and both sides suffered reverses, for some expert in genealogies to suggest a conference to end the war; then a meeting of both sides would take place. So it was that Pele-io-holani and Alapaʻi met at Naonealaʻa in Kaneʻohe, Koʻolaupoko, on Kaʻelo 13, 1737, corresponding to our January. The two hosts met, splendidly dressed in cloaks of bird feathers and in helmet-shaped head coverings beautifully decorated with feathers of birds. Red feather cloaks were to be seen on all sides. Both chiefs were attired in a way to inspire admiration and awe, and the day was one of rejoicing for the end of a dreadful conflict. [. . .] Between the two chiefs stood the counselor Na-ʻili, who first addressed Pele-io-holani saying, "When you and Alapaʻi meet, if he embraces and kisses you let Alapaʻi put his arms below yours, lest he gain the victory over you." [. . .] Alapaʻi declared an end of war, with all things as they were before, the chiefs of Maui and Molokai to be at peace with those of Oahu and Kauai, so also those of Hawaii. Thus ended the meeting of Pele-io-holani with Alapaʻi. (*Ruling Chiefs* 71–72)

However, within a year the two sides were at odds again. Kamakau describes Alapaʻi's reaction: "I thought that this was a family quarrel, but it seems to be a real war of rebellion!" (*Ruling Chiefs* 74). However, Kamakau noted, "[t]he two ruling chiefs met there again, face to face, to end the war and become friends again, so great had been the slaughter on both sides. . . Perhaps the reason for this friendliness on the part of the two chiefs was the close relationship that existed between them" (*Ruling Chiefs* 74).

What can we learn from the above description that helps to identify the process of mending a broken relationship? How does it work?

- ❧ It takes a wise counselor who knows or is familiar with all parties involved [a genealogist] to go beyond blind rivalries and emotions.
- ❧ It takes the willingness and consent of all parties to stop the fighting and agree to meet.

     ↣ A conference is called. Ground rules and the meeting site are established and agreed upon by the participants.

     ↣ All involved are eyewitnesses to the outcomes.

     ↣ The peace returns the situation to what it was before the conflict began.

Kamakau's description of the second outbreak of fighting illustrates that such agreements were not always kept, perhaps because there were deeper causes that remained unaddressed. However, once again the process of meeting was used to bring the parties to peace.

The next event illustrates early forms of ho'oponopono that took place on the island of Maui when the chiefs of Hawai'i set out to conquer Kahekili, the paramount chief of Maui. It was known as the battle of Kakanilua.

Having established a massive fleet of canoes offshore on the leeward coast of the island, the first wave of eight hundred warriors attacked on the shoreline dressed with feather capes that reflected the colors of the rainbow: red, yellow, and dark green-blue. They moved across the plains and towards the sand dune hills. Their helmets stood out like the crescent moon, but when they reached the sand dunes, they were caught in an ambush like fish that had entered the gates of a fishpond. They were immediately surrounded by a fine-meshed net made up of the defending Maui warriors. These forces had swarmed behind the sand dunes cutting off the invading force from the rear. They were routed and the dead were piled up like tree branches or fish caught up in a net. It was said that only two of the eight hundred warriors escaped.

While this was occurring, the chief of the invading warriors, Kalani'ōpu'u, remained offshore on a canoe where he boasted and bragged of how his warriors must have reached their goal. He was shocked by the incredible news that the two surviving warriors brought to him.

A war council was held with the remaining warriors and war chiefs to prepare for the next day's battle. The second wave of invaders was caught in a trap. It was reported that the spears rained down upon the warriors like thick waves that pound the shoreline at high tide. The dead were picked up like grasshoppers to be burnt in huge piles. It was at that moment Kalaniʻōpuʻu sought a means to stop the killing.

> When Ka-lani-ʻopuʻu saw that the forces of Hawaii were surrounded by Ka-hekili's men he said to Ka-lola his chiefess, "Oh Hono-ka-wailani! we shall all be killed. Do go up to your brother Ka-hekili to sue for peace." Ka-lola answered, "It will not do any good for me to go, for we came to deal death. If we had come offering love we should have been received with affection. I can do nothing. Our only hope lies in Ka-lani-kau-i-ke-aouli Kiwalaʻo." "Perhaps Ka-hekili will kill my child," said Ka-lani-ʻopuʻu. "Ka-hekili will not kill him. We will send Ka-hekili's half brothers with him, Ka-meʻe-ia-moku and Ka-manawa." So Kiwalaʻo was dressed in the garments of a chief and attended by Ka-meʻe-ia-moku bearing the spittoon and Ka-manawa carrying the *kahili*. (Kamakau, *Ruling Chiefs* 88)

The young boy, who appeared as if he were covered by a rainbow, walked into the midst of the battlefield. Warriors on both sides lay down on the ground because Kīwalaʻō's rank demanded such respect. Kamakau commented, "The soldiers of Maui wished to ignore the tabu, regretting the cessation of the fighting, but Kiwalaʻo continued on to Wailuku" (Kamakau, *Ruling Chiefs* 88). When they reached the Maui chief Kahekili, they saw that he was surrounded not by warriors but by old men and women and children.

> When the twins and Kiwalaʻo saw the multitude they said, "We imagined that he was in the midst of a school of fish, but it is only red sea moss." When, at the arrival of Kiwalaʻo, Ka-hekili heard the words, "Here is your child," he turned his face upward [as a sign of a favorable reception]. Kiwalaʻo entered and sat on his chest; and they kissed each other and wailed. Afterward the twins crawled forward and kissed the hands of Ka-hekili. Kiwalaʻo, being tabu, could not be addressed directly. Ka-hekili accordingly asked them, "Why do you bring the chief here? If you are in trouble you should have come up

here yourselves, lest without my knowledge your chief be killed." The twins answered, "We do not believe that the chief will be killed. It is we who would have been killed had we left the chief at the shore. The chief has been sent to ask for life. Grant us our lives. If the chief dies, we two will die with him (*moe-pu'u*). So our royal brother commanded." Ka-hekili replied, "There is no death to be dealt out here. Let live! Let the battle cease!" and he asked, "Where is your sister [referring to Ka-lola]?" "At the shore, at Kihepuko'a, and it was she who sent us to the chief," answered Ka-manawa. Then Ka-hekili said to his followers, "Take the fish of Kanaha and Mau'oni and the vegetable food of Nawaieha down to Kiheipuko'a." So the two chiefs became reconciled [. . .]." (Kamakau, *Ruling Chiefs* 88–89)

John Papa 'Ī'ī, wrote about the same event with a slight difference.

Kalola, the mother of Kiwalao, was there with her brother Kahekili; and while they were conversing with Oulu a voice proclaiming the *kapu moe,* or prostrating kapu, was heard. "The chief Kiwalao must be approaching," said Kahekili. "Remove my head covering (a wig) quickly." Then Kahekili saw that Keawe a Heulu was in front with the kapu stick and that behind Kiwalao were Kahekili's younger cousins, Kamanawa and Kameeiamoku, one with a feather cape and kahili, and the other with the spittoon and mat, so he said to his sister, "Wait before you remove my wig, for it is a retainer who comes first. When our 'young one,' Kiwalao, comes up, that will be the proper time to remove it."

[. . .] Then Kiwalao met Kahekili, and an order was given to stop the fighting." (11)

Once again, there are some key characteristics present that should be noted.

    ∺ Someone is looked to as a bridge or mediator with the other side.

- ॐ Knowledge of relationships, status, rank, symbols, and a person's behavior and mannerisms are extremely important tools.
- ॐ Knowing what to say and how to say it are critical for mutual understanding.
- ॐ The bonds of relationship are primary.
- ॐ Generosity is a key outcome when relationships are mended.

'Ī'ī also describes an interesting familial event that occurred when Kamehameha was a young man. Today the basis for this family quarrel may seem archaic and incongruous with modern morals and values, but in the context of Hawaiian traditional culture, it reveals a deep understanding of Hawaiian thought and behavior.

> Because his [Kamehameha's] physique was perfect and his features well formed and admirable, the women took a great fancy to him, as they did also to his younger brother Kalaimamahu. They were the handsomest men of those days, and the chiefesses gave them many gifts. Thus beautiful physiques and handsome features earned them a livelihood. This led to trouble with their uncle Kalaniopuu, for they were taken by Kaneikapolei, wife of Kalaniopuu. This happened twice, the first time with Kalaimamahu and the second time with Kamehameha. It was probably in this way that Kaoleioku was conceived. Their uncle was "peeved" and would not allow his nephews to see his face. Keawemauhili, who stepped in as mediator, told his half brother Kalaniopuu to stop resenting his nephews because everyone knew that a woman was like an easily opened calabash, or a container with a removable lid. Upon these words, Kalaniopuu's anger ceased, and he sent for his nephews to come and see him. (7)

There are a few elements of note in this event.

- ॐ The intervention of a relative as a mediator when some obvious problem has caused a disruption in family life is useful.

- ❧ Well chosen words are used to cause a reconsideration of the problem.
- ❧ There is an immediate end to hostility and a call to gather to restore or mend the broken relationship.

The following event occurred during the reign of Kamehameha III when he was still a youth and under the guardianship of his cousins and relatives. As a sacred chief and king, his older relatives sought influence over him to further their own personal and political ambitions. The resulting conflict first took place in 'Ewa on the island of O'ahu and quickly spread to Honolulu. An attempt was made to hold a council in which the two sides could air their differences.

> A few days later a council of chiefs was held at the stone house at Pohukaina where were gathered chiefs, commoners, and foreigners to discuss financial matters. Three chiefesses spoke for the chiefs, Ke-ahi-kuni Ke-kau-'onohi, Ka-ho'ano-ku Kina'u, Kuini Liliha. Ke-kau-'onohi opened with the words which appear so often in newspapers today and which I then heard for the first time— "Hawaii of Keawe, Maui of Kama-lala-walu, Oahu of Kakuhihewa, Kauai of Manokalanipo." She spoke of the goodness of God, of guarding what was good and forsaking what was evil, of not worshipping other gods; Jehovah alone was the one true God. Kina'u spoke in the same way. Then Liliha spoke to the people: "Chiefs and people of my chief, hear me. The stink of my name and that of my husband Boki has spread from Hawaii to Kauai. It is said that we do evil and that we have led the young king to do evil, and so he has been taken away from me. But we are not guilty; it is the white people and the naval officers who are guilty; it is they who tempted the king, and the blame has been put upon me. But I admit I have done wrong." At these words both natives and foreigners shed tears. Then Ka-heihei-malie, who had been sitting on the stairway during the council, rose and spoke about the goodness of God and urged the people to listen to the words

of Kaʻahu-manu and Kau-i-ke-aouli and of Nahi-
ʻenaʻena. Then she added, drawing a figure from the
communal method of fishing for sword fish, "In the
time of Kamehameha the fisherman swam together in
a row, and if one got out of line or lagged behind he
was struck by the sharp nose of the fish. So those who
do not follow God's word and do not obey our king,
but fall out of line, they shall be struck by the sharp
sword of the law, so do not lag behind lest you be
hurt." As these words fell upon the ears of the people,
they applied them to Liliha and raised an uproar
and talked of war against Ka-ʻahu-manu and the
chiefs. When the chiefesses had gone back to Maui,
preparations were actually made for the war which
was called the Pahikaua [. . .]" (Kamakau, *Ruling
Chiefs* 300–301)

During an interview I had with Stephen Boggs, we talked about
our work in analyzing the events of the Pahikaua war. We both
agreed that Liliha's speech, wherein she had admitted that she had
been wrong, was the pivotal point of this meeting. Then he asked
what the Hawaiian meaning for the word *mihi* was. In my answer
I wanted to make a distinction between the Hawaiian and Māori
usages, and to distinguish any post-missionary influences. I said that
mihi is the recognition that one has done something wrong. It is
more like a confession of guilt than an apology. It is the recognition
by someone that he or she has been the cause of that situation, and
for some it might be the first time they have come to that realization.
That is why a haku 'head of family' works so hard to bring about a
mihi, which is a pivotal point in the process of hoʻoponopono.

What more can we discover about the tools and methods of this
process?

- Be careful, that is, be full of care, in choosing one's words and
  in how those words are spoken.
- Listen attentively to what others have to say and be extremely
  careful to hear what another shares.
- Receive genuine words of regret, confession, or guilt with
  understanding and love.

* Dropping one's personal agenda or wants can bring everyone back together.

* This process can easily fail if everyone is not totally committed to a successful outcome.

There are several common elements in the events described above that highlight tools people were able to use to resolve conflicts.

* One of the most important, yet least obvious, skills is to recognize that something is wrong; that is, a person or persons are upset or hurt and are in need of healing. This recognition is based upon having a common understanding and knowledge of the other person(s) and good intuition. The need becomes recognizable because the relationship between persons is strained and not the same as it was previously. What is desired is the return to that previous positive relationship.

* There is a proverb that says, "In the word there is life and in the word there is death." In a cultural context, it stresses how important it is that one's word is "good," or what is said is meant. Thus one needs to be very careful of what one says and how one says it. Many times that means having some knowledge about the person or people gathered. One has to think and reflect about the best way in which to say what one wants people to hear.

* Listening is crucial to the process. Listening is not an easy task, especially if one does not agree with what is being said, or does not understand and wants to ask a question. Listening means paying attention to what the other person is saying, and waiting until that person is finished speaking before asking questions or thinking about a response.

* It is important to review, understand, and accept the things that are common and shared between everyone gathered, and to recognize how important it is to maintain positive relationships.

* As much as the above are important tools, they must be guided by a deep emotional understanding based on trust, sincerity, and honesty. Without these guiding principles no amount of discussion and listening will ever lead to any understanding or healing. It will all be hidden by miscommunication and lies, adding to the causes of the trouble.

- ❧ A useful way of disarming the quarreling parties is by getting away from the scene of the problem and using a third party to avoid direct conflict; provide leadership, guidance and direction; and allow each side to say all that they have to say and to listen to all that is said.
- ❧ It is important to establish the appropriate ground rules to ensure that there is a feeling of trust, safety, and care.
- ❧ All those involved must commit to the process, agree to the ground rules, and want an outcome that would restore the broken relationships and provide healing.

However, it must be understood that this process was not, and is not, used for the resolution of violence and abusive behavior. In traditional times during the kingdom, and still today, acts such as murder, abuse, robbery, and other violent crimes were handled by the chiefs, and later, the courts under the law. The Reverend William Ellis reported during his brief stay in the islands that

> [i]n cases of assault or murder, except when committed by their own chief, the family and friends of the injured party are, by common consent, justified in retaliating. When they are too weak to attack the offender, they seek the aid of their neighbours, appeal to the chief of the district, or the king [. . .]. (306)

Ho'oponopono could be used thereafter as a process for the transition to incarceration or to address the victims and their families. Again, we return to the primary purpose of ho'oponopono, which is the restoring of relationships; it is not about who is right or who is wrong.

The Process of Setting Things to Right

Ho'oponopono as a process for setting things to right, largely credited to Mary Kawena Pukui, is not a modern concept. The historical overview demonstrates that this cultural practice was being used during pre- and post-contact periods. This practice appears to have been continuously used and refined by Hawaiians in family, community, and religious (now mostly Christian) life.

In the historical overview, we have seen the use of a mediator to work with conflicting parties, particularly in the second account of the Pahikaua War. The story illustrated how the words of each person, spoken without thought, led to the outburst of emotions that became the root of the problem. When these accounts are compared with the description of hoʻoponopono as practiced by the ʻohana 'family' of Mary Kawena Pukui in Kaʻū on the island of Hawaiʻi, we can see how certain related practices and processes emerged. There is even evidence of retaining the pre-missionary period practices of including the ʻaumakua, as seen in the accounts of the Pōhaku a Kāne.

> When a problem arose in the family affecting an individual or the group as a whole, every member of the immediate family turned to the hoʻoponopono. The problem might be lack of employment, physical illness, ill luck or whatever. If it was an illness, the ailing person was asked whether he had a feeling of resentment against anyone, or had committed a deed that he should not have. If he had, he confessed and explained. Then he was asked whether he was convinced that it was wrong and, if he did, a prayer was offered asking forgiveness of God or gods. The person against whom the feeling of resentment was directed was asked to forgive him, also. If he, in turn, bore an ill will and had thought or spoken evil against him, he must ask to be pardoned. First the patient confessed and was forgiven, then he in turn forgave the trespasses of the others against him. A mutual feeling of affection and willingness to cooperate had to exist in the family and the household before anything further could be done. So it was between the family and the ʻaumakua, all obstructions had to be removed. The current of affection and cooperation had to flow freely between the ʻaumakua and the family also.

The process of hoʻoponopono sometimes took from
one to several hours depending on the natures of the
individual, whether quick to anger and to curse, or the
reverse.

If the process would be lengthy it would be broken up in
shorter sessions with periods of rest between so as not to
exhaust the patient. [. . .] One did a lot of self-examining
during a hoʻoponopono whether one was the patient or
not. (Pukui, *Hoʻoponopono*, audiotape)

The codification, that is, the detailed description and explanation,
of this process with the publication of *Nānā I Ke Kumu* in 1972,
led to wider recognition and use of hoʻoponopono. Its revival from
that time until the present has seen an evolution of the process
towards a social work, group therapy, or psychological orientation
and away from what appears to be its original intent as a step in
the process of traditional healing. This shift away from its historical
roots was reinforced with state legislation in 1965 that eliminated
the recognition of Native Hawaiian healing and contributed to the
demise of the knowledge and skills of traditional healing.

Current practice has seen the role of mediator, facilitator, or
haku fall upon religious leaders and trained professionals such
as social workers and lawyers. More recently, a wide range of
interested persons have attended training workshops or classes on
hoʻoponopono. Pukui noted that "most hoʻoponopono did not go
beyond the door of our house [. . .] (b)ut with some [other families]
a kahuna from outside handled the hoʻoponopono" (*Hoʻoponopono*,
audiotape). Recently, there have even been suggestions that
practitioners of hoʻoponopono should be licensed as are other
health-related professionals, although this would be contrary to
Pukui's desire that hoʻoponopono be retained as a cultural family
practice rather than as a professional activity.

In her interview, Pukui spoke of certain terms being used that
described "periods of time" during the process. These included "ku
i ka mihi, or repentances; ku i ka pule, [which] set a special period
of time for prayers; kukulu kumuhana, or present the problem to
God; and hoʻomalu (a sheltering) with no loud boisterous talking,

arguments, or going to places of pleasure until the kahuna saw fit to lift the probationary periods" (*Ho'oponopono*, audiotape).

These terms became descriptive of the stages of the ho'oponopono process as it developed into a "clinical" model. The descriptions of these developmental stages proved to be especially helpful to those unfamiliar with Hawaiian traditional cultural practices. The descriptions of these terms were further defined through the discussions of the Culture Committee at the Queen Lili'uokalani Children's Center and published in 1972 in *Nana I Ke Kumu, Volume I.*

> hihia—entangled or entanglement; snarl or snarled; enmeshed (71)
>
> kūkulu kumuhana—the pooling of strengths, emotional, psychological and spiritual, for a shared purpose. Group dynamics characterized by spiritual elements and directed to a positive goal. A unified, unifying force. In broad context, a group, national, or worldwide spiritual force, constructive and helpful in nature. In *ho'oponopono*, the uniting of family members in a spiritual force to help an ill or troubled member.
>
> Secondary meaning: statement of problem and procedures for seeking a solution, as in opening explanation of *ho'oponopono*. (78)
>
> mahiki—to peel off; to pry; as to peel the bark of a tree to judge the wood beneath; to scrape at the skin to remove a tiny insect burrowed beneath the epidermis. Also, to cast out, as of a spirit. (75)
>
> ho'omalu—to shelter, protect, make peace, keep quiet, control, suspend. A period of peace and quiet. Silent period. (77)
>
> mihi—repentance, confession, apology; to repent, confess, apologize. (73)
>
> kala—to release, untie, unbind, let go. (74)
>
> (Pukui, Haertig, and Lee I: 71–78)

Each term, then, became linked to a stage in the hoʻoponopono process. Depending upon the progression and development encountered at each stage, the process could either move on or become circular, being repeated as many times as needed. Some have compared this circular movement to peeling away the layers of an onion, oftentimes leading to another layer upon other layers.

Cordage: A Cultural Analogy

One cultural analogy to the process of hoʻoponopono is the making of cordage and the use of that cordage to make an ʻupena, or "fish net." This is a useful analogy since the terms hihia (entanglement) and kala (to unbind, untie, to forgive or let go) are used in hoʻoponopono.

Around the age of seven or eight, I learned how to make fishing nets using cordage, a bamboo shuttle needle, a small rectangle of press board for a gauge, and a nail to hold down the net.

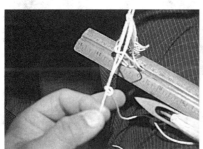 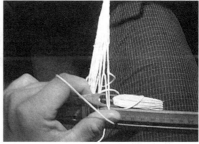

The left photo shows how an individual knot is tied and secured, while the right photo shows how a knot is made with several rows completed.

The making of traditional cordage from plant material involves extracting the individual strands of fiber and then rolling and twisting several strands to make up a strong piece of cordage. These collective strands can then be used to make stronger cordage by either twisting them together or actually weaving them. I see the ʻohana in a very similar way: made up from individual fibers but bound together for strength and purpose.

The making of a fish net is a very simple task with the most critical skill being the tying of a tight and secure knot—in fact, several knots—in a straight row. When I first learned this skill, I would often discover after tying down several rows that one or two knots in previous rows were loose. One could go back and try to tighten the knots, but usually that wouldn't work, as it left the triangular holes between knots loose and capable of expanding so that a fish or crab could easily escape.

Unfortunately, the solution to this problem was undoing all the knots, working back to the one or two knots that were loose, then re-doing all that work. Making such mistakes taught me some very valuable lessons:

- ❧ I needed to be very careful about the work that I did, making sure that each knot was tight and secure.
- ❧ I needed to be patient.
- ❧ There was no sense in getting angry since mistakes do happen, even if you are being careful.

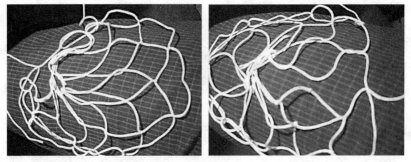

The photo on the left shows tight knots and perfect holes in the beginning stages of a net, while the photo on the right shows a mistake where the knot is not tied correctly.

These lessons also apply to the process of hoʻoponopono.

We all make mistakes every day of our lives. How do we go about "untangling" these problems, big or small? Through hoʻoponopono we are given a chance to undo both minor and major mistakes by literally going back through events in our lives, back to "knots" that may have been done "wrong," or at least not completed in a desired manner. By correcting those wrongs or mistakes, we can then proceed towards completing our own "net," or life itself.

Contemporary Applications

With the revival of, and growing respect for, traditional Hawaiian cultural practices, interest in utilizing hoʻoponopono in contemporary situations has increased. Several publications and graduate student papers have detailed its practice and demonstrated its application, especially in the mental health field. Family courts have offered hoʻoponopono as a cultural option for Hawaiian families in mediating child custody cases and in marital counseling.

The Boggs and Chun article on hoʻoponopono in the aptly titled *Disentangling* demonstrated that its continued practice suggests the continuing vitality of Hawaiian culture and social structure, contrary to the belief that they had disappeared and were dead. Shook concluded in her book that "The Hawaiian family certainly deserves to receive the gifts of its own tradition. Furthermore [. . .] [the] potential of *hoʻoponopono* could expand our understanding of the uses [. . .] and allow for the sharing of this Hawaiian gift" (101).

The recent development of "restorative justice" or "family conferencing" in Aotearoa (New Zealand) appears to fulfill Shook's insight and prediction that, "Further study could also shed light on the understanding of therapeutic universals" and "could provide valuable insights into understanding basic principles about assisting people in establishing harmonious interpersonal and social relationships" (101–102).

Based upon similar traditional practices of the Māori and Sāmoan communities in New Zealand, the ideas of restorative justice are emerging. Briefly, restorative justice is based on a process that is indigenous, places victims at the center of the justice equation, offers healing to all involved, and lays responsibility for crime in the hands of those who commit it (Consedine 161–164).

Family conferencing has adapted the skills and tools of traditional peacemaking and healing to contemporary life. Family conferencing is increasingly being used in communities throughout the United States and Canada to provide a community and family-based option, particularly for non-violent crimes, as a means to ease the burden of the courts.

One account of family conferencing was told by the late Reverend Flora Tuhaka of Aotearoa (New Zealand). An incident occurred in a small township on a Saturday when a Māori teenager vandalized the local bus company. The damage was severe enough that the bus company had to stop its service to the town until the damages were fixed. When the youth was caught, he was headed for criminal charges in court. The bus owner intervened and requested that he would rather have a family conference so that he could speak to the teenager face-to-face and confront him with the consequences of his actions. At the meeting the owner told of how much disruption was done to the lives of people in the town, some who were the teenager's friends and relatives. The teenager responded that he was sorry, never imagining how much damage he had done by just goofing off because he had nothing better to do during his free time.

Instead of having the offender spend time in a youth facility, the bus owner asked that the youth spend his Saturdays at the company cleaning the place and the buses until he had "paid off" the damages. The idea was that this would provide structure to the teenager's free time, teach him how important the bus service is to the people, and allow him to get to know his own neighbors. The teenager not only "did his time," but after he graduated from school, the bus owner offered him a job at the company because he had performed so well and the owner had gotten to know him.

There is no moral to this true story, but there are some important lessons: many mistakes in life can be corrected, good counsel can be productive in discovering truth, and broken lives and relationships can be mended instead of dismissed and wasted.

Nearly a half century ago, Pukui shared a vision of the re-emergence of ho'oponopono as an important cultural practice to help Hawaiian families heal and strengthen their bonds. Today these very skills and tools have immense educational and social implications if practiced in contemporary life, especially among its youth. Its power and influence lies in the recognition of our basic humanity and the need for healing in every moment of our lives.

7 Ho‘omana

Understanding the Sacred and Spiritual

E nihi ka hele mai ho‘opā mai pulale i ka ‘ike
a ka maka o inaina ke akua.
Traditional Hawaiian proverb attributed to Pele

Walk softly along the trail and don't touch anything, don't look
in places you shouldn't or else the god[dess] will be angry.
(Author's translation)

When one hears talk about Hawaiian religion, there should be an inner voice that says, "This is not the same thing as religion as I know it today." Today traditional Hawaiian religion is neither organized nor institutionalized like many world religions, and what is left of its temples and places of worship are only the foundation walls and house sites.

Yet what remains of Hawaiian religion can have great meaning and importance. Why is this? The Hawaiian scholar Davida Malo tried to explain in his writings on Hawaiian traditions, *Ka Mo‘olelo Hawai‘i*, that what he knew as religion, or ho‘omana, was to be found in almost all aspects of Hawaiian culture and life. He described the building of canoes, hunting of birds for feathers, farming, fishing, the conception and initiation of chiefly children (that is, boys), healing, and even sorcery and dancing as acts of ho‘omana.

It appears all aspects of Hawaiian culture that required prayer are linked to ho‘omana. In fact, the term *kahuna*, which is usually translated as priest, actually is intended for a person who happens to be an expert in his or her tasks involving prayer and rituals. Hence, an architect 'kahuna kuhikuhi pu‘uone,' a canoe builder 'kahuna kālai wa‘a,' and a traditional healer 'kahuna lā‘au lapa‘au' are all experts who knew the prayers involved in their work. The prayers were necessary to begin and complete their tasks.

Although Hawaiian religion no longer involves organized temple worship, one can see elements of ho‘omana when Hawaiian groups begin and end their meetings or gatherings with prayer or when someone is called to bless a house or property. So what is ho‘omana?

Re-creation of a paehumu, or circle of major gods, at Pu'uhonua o Hōnaunau, Hawai'i

Ho'omana is the word Malo used to describe religious activity and, sometimes, worship. Malo was one of the earliest Native Hawaiians to discuss traditional religious practices. He was well qualified for the task, having been trained, prior to the establishment of Christianity in the islands, as a genealogist. That training would make him familiar with much of the lore associated with the gods, chiefs, culture, and society. When the missionaries were established in Hawai'i, Malo became one of their most avid students of history, which was the closest subject they had to traditional genealogies.

Malo's writings were not made public until after 1898, so his descriptions of ho'omana were not a part of the discussions about religion in early (post-contact) Hawai'i. In those discussions, religion was seen as organized and institutional, that is, conforming to familiar Christian definitions and judgments, and the discussion was, therefore, focused on the worship of a particular akua 'deity' and on major religious ceremonies and rituals at the large stone-walled temples.

Ho'omana comes from the root word *mana*, which is not an easy word to translate into modern concepts. A lot of people, in particular anthropologists, have written whole studies attempting to do so. In the Pukui and Elbert *Hawaiian Dictionary* it is described as a "supernatural or divine [. . .] miraculous power" (1986: 235). The prefix *ho'o-* is a causative that adds the meaning "to do" or "to make happen" or, in the case of many Hawaiian cultural activities, to "imbue with." Thus, literally, ho'omana means "to cause something to have mana."

This explanation makes sense if you are using prayers, because prayers are meant, when chanted or invoked, to cause something to happen that you yourself cannot do alone. This use of ho'omana as worship or religion may not actually be too far from what is meant by religion if we go back to the Latin roots of *religio* 'linking back to' as in *to rely upon*. A prayer may be a message, but it takes an agent who has heard the prayer to cause something to happen.

Again, Malo pointed out this relationship.

> Eia wale no ka (ke) kanaka mau akua e like maka ai, o na kii laau, a me na kii pohaku i kalai lima ia, ma ka manao ana o ke kanaka, i hoopii aku ai, i ua mau kii la ma ke ano maoli o ke akua ma ka lani ana i manao ai i akua nona iho, ina o ka lani e hana i ke kii a like me ko kalani. (49)

> The gods of the people only looked like what they were seen through the wood and stone images carved by hand from what the carver thought they looked like as the shapes of the gods in the heavens. If the god was from the heavens then the image was created to look like the heavens. (195)

And,

> Alaila, lalau ke kahuna, i ka ai, a kaumaha aku i ka lani, aole i na kii la, no ka mea, ua manao ia, aia no ma ka lani ke akua, he mea hoomanao wale no ua kii la, e ku ana, imua o ke anaina kanaka a pau. (104)

> Then, the priest seized the food and offered it up to the heavens and not to the image, because it was believed that the god dwelled in the heavens. The image was only a representation [of the god] as it stood before all those gathered. (Author's translation)

He is saying some important things here that we cannot let go right away. First, contrary to the popular Christian prejudices, the wooden and stone images were images, not idols. (There is a tendency for members of a religion, when set on conversion, to harshly prejudge another religion rather than try to understand it.) When one is beholding the golden statue of Buddha, is one worshipping an idol or is one reminded, by the position and hand placements of the Buddha, of one's spiritual journey? Do Christians worship a cross set on or above an altar, or is the cross merely to help the worshipper remember and reflect on the suffering and resurrection of Christ?

Reconstruction of Hale o Lono heiau at Waimea, Oʻahu by archaeologist and cultural consultant Rudy Mitchell

Second, and more important, he is making the point that it is the relationship with something greater than yourself that should be the focus of a prayer or ritual. A wooden or stone image is just a piece of wood or rock until it is hoʻomana, imbued with mana, or in the religious-poetic language "when the god dwells ʻnohoʻ in the object." Hence, certain trees, stones, rocks, and places could become sacred when mana is invoked and the divine intervenes.

The relationship with the divine and the use of prayer as a means of communication are the first two elements Kamakau said were essential in "the Hawaiian school of medical kahunas, [. . .] [t]he foundation of the knowledge and skill [. . .] was the god. [. . .] Second came prayer." (*Ka Poʻe Kahiko* 107).

Kamakau stated that by using both prayer and skill, an able student could

> concentrate on the cliff until it crumbled. He would concentrate his prayer on a hard rock and it broke up as if nothing, just as if a roll of powder had been inserted into the rock and had broken it to fragments. He would concentrate his prayer upon a grove of trees and the trees would wither. He would concentrate his prayer upon a whale and it would be cast up on land. He would concentrate his prayer upon a shark that had eaten a man, and the wicked shark, and the man, would land on shore. The mana of the [. . .] prayers was his, and the mana was made manifest. (*Ka Poʻe Kahiko* 121)

Whether or not a student, or even a master kahuna, could accomplish such a task is not the point. Kamakau's statement shows how important prayer can be for an expert to be able to cause mana, to hoʻomana, in his or her particular task.

Prayers and ceremonial rituals were both personal and communal, although there were differences for the kanaka 'ordinary person' and the aliʻi 'chiefs.' The prayers of the kanaka did not involve the service of kāhuna or kahu akua 'guardians of gods,' whereas the aliʻi were dependent upon the kāhuna, for the aliʻi did not recite their own prayers. This distinction is clearly brought out in Malo's description of the rites concerning sub-incision of boys of "proper" families and of the high chiefs.

> Pela no e hana ia ai na keiki a ka poe haipule, a me ka poe koikoi, a me ka poe hanohano, a me ka poe kahuna, a me ka poe alii haahaa, he okoa ka hana ana i na keiki a ka poe alii, kiekie a o na keiki a kekahi poe, aole no i hana ia pela, e lawe wale aku no ka lakou mau keiki imua, a e kahe wale iho no me ka hoomana ole i ke akua. (52)

> That was the way it was done for boys of religious
> families, those of rank and prestige of kahuna(s) and
> the lesser aliʻi (aliʻi haʻahaʻa). The procedure for boys of
> higher aliʻi (aliʻi kiʻekiʻe) was different from the boys of
> others. It was not done in this manner. Their [the others]
> boys were only taken to the mua and cut without any
> religious rites to the god. (199)

However, not all of traditional Hawaiian society was religious. Malo tells us that there were people who had no gods and survived without them: "those who had no god did not worship at all" (273). These ʻaiā were listed in a prayer for purification as persons whom the kahuna would seek to dispel or chase away 'hemu' (Malo 54, 201–202). Here Malo is speaking of certain purification rituals where these ʻaiā were not welcome, but his mention of them as a group also tells us quite clearly that there were non-religious or irreligious persons in traditional Hawaiian society. This statement has several implications:

- Contrary to popular belief, being Hawaiian did not necessarily mean you had to be religious or practice religious rituals.
- Traditional Hawaiian society practiced a high level of tolerance for behavior contrary to that of most of society.
- Religious practices and behavior had to be reinforced as being positive and good, and people had to be constantly reminded of their responsibilities.

The Kapu System of Prohibitions and Restrictions

The kapu system is another part of Hawaiian religious belief and practice that has been popularized and misunderstood. The very word *kapu* brings to mind for many today certain images related to what people think of as traditional Hawaiian religion. These may include stone-walled temples, huge carved wooden images, and things one is, or is not, supposed to do for fear of divine punishment. Landowners used to place imposing signs with the word KAPU across their vacant property.

Although related to the divine, the establishment of the kapu system did not directly impose any religious belief or ritual. It did regulate how people worshipped. Today this might be similar to the idea of the separation of men and women worshipping in a mosque, or other distinctions that men, more than women, may have with regard to religious worship and leadership. And like those examples, the establishment of the kapu system was not divinely inspired but was imposed by those in power.

The Reverend Ellis, in the early 1820s, was able to learn about kapu in his travels and noted the following.

> It is a distinct word from rahui, to prohibit, as the ohelo berries at Kirauea were said to be prohibited, being tabu na Pele, sacred for Pele, and is opposed to the word noa, which means general or common. (278)

And,

> [a]lthough employed for civil as well as sacred purposes, the tabu was entirely a religious ceremony, and could be imposed only by the priests. (279)

When I was much younger, the Nuʻuanu Pali tunnels were the only direct route through the Koʻolau mountain range between Honolulu and the windward side of the island. We would go over for lūʻau 'traditional feasts' and come back home at night through the Pali tunnel. However, as a form of homage to the pig god, Kamapuaʻa, who came from this island, we never carried any form of pork during those trips. We were afraid that if we did, our car would stop, and we would be stranded. How could anyone even consider such an idea, for even in those days it was a multilane highway full of fast cars. But we, as well as a whole lot of others, did. That is a lāhui. No priests or official sanctions were needed; it was a popular belief.

Kapu is another matter. It all began with one of the traditions about Wākea and Papa, an ancestral couple of the Hawaiian people, not gods but actual human beings in Hawaiian genealogies. This particular tradition says that Wākea wanted to sleep with his own daughter, Hoʻohōkūkalani, but he could not think of a way to do so without his wife, Papa, knowing.

So upon the advice of his kahuna pule 'expert in prayers,' Komoawa (or Komoʻawa), he declared that there would be four

sacred nights a month. During that time Wākea and Papa would
be separated as husband and wife, and certain foods would be
prohibited 'kapu' for women to eat. This separation would give
Wākea the opportunity to go off and to sleep with Ho'ohokukalani.

Papa agreed. The kahuna pule would wake Wākea in the early
morning before Papa got up. However, in the end, Wākea could not
wake up from his sleep, even when the kahuna pule tried several
times. Malo provides us with Komoawa's chant.

> E ala au aku, e ala au mai, e ala makia, o
> makia a hanohano i ke aka, o ke ake kuhea, o
> keakekieihikina, Ku kahikinailunakalani, kaopuaulu
> nui, kaopuamakolu uakaua, kahe ka wai, mukeha,
> Oiliolalapaikalaiponiponihaaikamea, mokapawa, lele ka
> hoku, haule kalani moakaka, i ke ao malamalama Ala
> mai mai uao [. . .]. (121)

> "I awaken [you] there, I awaken [you] here. Concentrate
> upon waking up. Catch your breath. Breathe this
> morning. The desire to call out and look at the east. [?]
> The east appears up in the heavens, the large rain cloud,
> the heavy laden clouds rain, water flows, the flashing [of
> lightning] appears in the purple heavens humbling one.
> [?] The dawn breaks and the stars fly away. The clear
> sky falls to the bright light. The person who is the go-
> between wakes you up." (294)

When Wākea finally did wake up in the morning sunlight, he
had to cover himself up with a kapa 'sheet of bark cloth' to hide
himself from Papa's sight as he returned to the mua 'men's house'
where he should have been for the religious ceremonies of those
sacred nights. Papa saw him and they quarreled. They were separated,
but the division of foods, houses, and eating remained as kapu.

In a version recorded by Kepelino we find the following.

> As the chiefess sat that morning in her own house,
> Wakea covered his head with the sleeping-tapa, ran from
> Ho'ohoku-ka-lani and came to Papa.

> Papa was puzzled by Wakea's manner. She ran to meet her
> daughter and Ho'ohoku-ka-lani related all that Wakea had

done that night. The chiefess was very angry and she came
to the house where the sin had been committed. Outside
the house she found Wakea, they quarreled, and Papa
related to Wakea everything that her daughter had told her.
When Wakea heard all the shameful things he had done he
was ashamed and angry, and he beat the chiefess and spat
in her face and their union was broken.

At that time disagreement arose among the chiefs, the manner
of worship was changed, laws were made and proclaimed
throughout all the land. Here are the laws of class I:

1. It is not right for a man to eat with his wife.
2. It is not right for a woman to enter the *mua* or house of worship.
3. It is not right for women to go to the men's eating house.
4. It is not right for women to eat bananas except the *pupuulu* and
   the *iholena* varieties.
5. Women must not eat pork, the yellow coconut, the *ulua* fish, the
   kumu fish, the *niuhi* shark, the whale, the porpoise, the spotted
   sting-ray [hahalua, hihimanu], the *kailepo*; all these things were
   dedicated to God, hence women could not eat them.

Here are the laws of class II:

1. There is to be one house (the *noa)* for the wife and the husband, etc.
2. There is to be a house (called *mua*) for the men's eating house.
3. There is to be a heiau for the images.
4. There are to be a two eating houses, one for the men and another
   for the women.
5. There is to be a house (called *kua*) for tapa beating.
6. There is to be a house (called *pea*) for the separation of the woman
   when she is unclean. (64)

This became the core of what we know of as traditional Hawaiian
social structure:

- ⮞ the separation of women and men in eating, working, and
  living;
- ⮞ the desire of the aliʻi to have children through their closest
  relatives as a means of ensuring high rank and stature;

     ➤ the dominance of men and masculinity in religious activities (most or all priests are alleged to be male as are the "major" gods); and

     ➤ the increased power of the kahuna in charge of religious activities.

This is illustrated in the relevant lines found in the Hawaiian creation chant "Kumulipo."

> Papa-seeking-earth
> Papa-seeking-heaven
> Great-Papa-giving-birth-to-islands
> Papa lived with Wakea
> Born was the woman Ha'alolo
> Born was the jealousy, anger
> Papa was deceived by Wakea
> He ordered the sun, the moon
> The night of Kane for the younger
> The night to Hilo for the first-born
> Taboo was the house platform, the place for sitting
> Taboo the house where Wakea lived
> Taboo was intercourse with the divine parent
> Taboo the taro plant ['ape], the acrid one
> Taboo the poisonous 'akia plant
> Taboo the narcotic auhuhu plant
> Taboo the medicinal uhaloa [plant]
> Taboo the bitter part of the taro leaf [la'alo]
> Taboo the taro stalk that stood by the woman's taboo house
> Haloa was buried [there], a long taro stalk grew
> The offspring of Haloa [born] into the day
> Came forth (Beckwith 124–125)

The plants mentioned in the Kumulipo are not the same as those found in Malo and Kepelino. Those mentioned in the Kumulipo are believed to have chemical properties or bitterness that associate them with matters of life and death or with communicating with the spiritual world. They are called "ka 'ai lani makua" (Beckwith 233), or "elder chiefly or heavenly foods."

The kapu system of prohibitions lasted until the third or fourth of October, 1819, an amazing forty-one years after Captain Cook's arrival at Waimea, Kaua'i, although Barrère suggests it is early

November based upon Kuykendall's reading of Marin's journal (*Kamehameha* 33). The ali'i themselves ended this system of privilege, and ironically, the highest ranking of them at that time was a woman, Keōpūolani. Kamakau noted, "This was a strange thing for a tabu chiefess to do, one for whom these tabus were made and who had the benefit of them" (*Ruling Chiefs* 224).

There are several theories as to why this system was ended, but I favor the thought that the female ali'i, particularly Keōpūolani and Ka'ahumanu, who were the wives of Kamehameha, determined that this was the best way in which to ensure that Kamehameha's children and grandchildren would rule the Kingdom. By ending this privilege system they ended the system that also determined who could rule, a system that had allowed, and perhaps even encouraged, rebellion among siblings.

As interesting as those thoughts are, it is what happened after the overthrow of the kapu system that deals with traditional Hawaiian religion. It is assumed that the overthrow of the kapu system also ended traditional religious practices, perhaps because these two events happened at the same time, or perhaps because the image of the kapu system as the Hawaiian religion is so strong in the imagination of non-Hawaiians.

The missionaries, upon their arrival in 1820, just after the end of the kapu, proclaimed joyously

> [t]hey have indeed thrown away their idols as worthless things, unable to save them, but they have not heard of Jesus; no Christian has yet said to them, there is a God in heaven who made them and the world, nor pointed them to the Saviour, "the Lamb of God, who taketh away the sins of the world." ("Return of Prince George to Atooi" 770)

Organized Hawaiian Religion Ends

Very soon the missionaries would discover what had actually happened as they settled into Hawaiian society.

> They [natives who were trading] replied that Reho reho the king had heard of the great God of white men, and had spoken of him; and that all the chiefs but one

had agreed to destroy their idols, because they were
convinced, that they could do no good, since they
could not even save the king. Idol worship is therefore
prohibited and the priesthood entirely abolished.
("Mission to the Sandwich Islands" 7 April 1821: 725)

This was all confirmed when they were introduced to the kahuna
nui 'high priest,' Hewahewa, who had proclaimed the end of the
kapu.

In the course of the day, as we passed near the place where
several chiefs were spending their idle hours in gambling,
we were favoured with an introduction to Havahava, the
late high priest. He received us kindly. On his introduction
to Mr. Brigham, he expressed much satisfaction in
meeting with a *brother priest* from America, still pleasantly
claiming that distinction for himself. He assures us that
he will be our friend. Who could have expected that such
would have been our first interview with the man, whose
influence we had been accustomed to dread more than any
other in the islands; whom we had regarded, and could
now hardly avoid regarding, as a destroyer of his fellow
men. But he seemed much pleased in speaking of the
demolition of the *Moreeahs* and idols.

About five months ago [this would place the event in
November, 1819] the young king consulted him with
respect to the expediency of breaking *taboo*; and asked
him to tell frankly and plainly whether it would be good
or bad; assuring him, at the same time, that he would
be guided by his word. Havahava readily replied, *"miti
[maika'i]," it would be good*, adding that he knew there is
but one *Akooah* [God,] who is in heaven, and that their
wooden Gods could not save them, nor do them any
good. He publicly renounced idolatry, and with his own
hand set fire to th[e] *moreeah*. The king no more observed
their superstitious *taboos*. Thus the heads of the civil
and the religious institutions agreed in abolishing that
forbidding but tottering taboo system [. . .]. ("Mission to
the Sandwich Islands" 14 April 1821: 739)

But the missionaries still believed the kapu was all one system, and so the popular myth began. Kamakau would later show the differentiation of the kapu, giving three classifications: kapu aupuni 'kapus of the kingdom,' kapu hoʻolaʻa 'kapus of consecration,' and kapu liʻiliʻi 'minor kapus.' He related that the kapu "applied to everybody and were set up by Wakea *ma*" (*Ka Poʻe Kahiko* 89).

The other lesser kapu (kapu liʻiliʻi) belong, he says, "to those persons with shark, *mano, ʻaumakua* and those whom they had transfigured and whose spirits (*haili*) had entered into *mano* bodies [. . .] to those with *moʻo ʻaumakua* [. . .] [and to] those with volcanic *ʻaumakua* (*ʻaumakua pele*) [. . .]" (Kamakau, *Ka Poʻe Kahiko* 89).

Nā ʻAumākua—Guardians of the Family

ʻAumākua are forms of nature—shark 'manō,' lizard 'moʻo,' volcano 'Pele,' and owl 'pueo'—that were part of traditional religious belief, but not necessarily part of the temple or priestly worship. The ending of temple worship and the consequent destruction of the temples and images did not necessarily affect or stop the belief in ʻaumākua. It appears, in fact, to be the only native form of religious belief that survived the ending of the kapu to be encountered by the missionaries upon their arrival.

> From the side of the mountain on your right, as you pass up the valley, a torrent of water issues, and descends, it would seem, two or three hundred feet, bounding and foaming down the almost perpendicular rocks. Here, the natives say, is the residence of the *Akooah Mo-o*, or the *Reptile god*, which resembles a large shark, devours men, and lives in the ground and in the water. Many of the natives have attempted to describe this Akooah, and they generally exhibit a great degree of earnestness and credulity respecting it. All the evidence that appears of the existence of the large reptile, which devours men, rests upon the testimony of a single man, who escaped, however, to tell the story.
>
> The principal reptile, which the island affords, is a small lizard, about six inches in length, inoffensive, but numerous. It is sometimes called an Akooah, and has

heretofore been worshipped. ("Extracts from the Journal
of the Missionaries" 13 July 1822: 99)

Several of the missionaries, at various times, ventured up to the
active volcano, Kīlauea, just as tourists do today. When the Rev. Ellis
and party got close to the area, their guide told them of the lāhui, a
prohibition on certain forms of behavior, that needed to be followed
lest the volcano (Pele) erupt in anger.

> He [Makoa] objected strongly to our going thither, as we
> should most likely be mischievous, and offend Pele or
> Nahoaarii, [nā hoa ali'i] gods of the volcano, by plucking
> the ohelo, (sacred berries,) digging up the sand, or
> throwing stones into the crater [. . .]. (Ellis 141)

> [. . .] the natives requested us not to kaha, a heru ka one
> [helu ke one], strike, scratch, or dig the sand, assuring us
> it would displease Pele [. . .]. (Ellis 166)

On several occasions the missionaries would encounter the kahu
akua 'guardians of the god,' whom they perceived to be a challenge
and opposition.

> She [kahu akua of Pele] answered, "He is your good
> God, (or best God), and it is right that you should
> worship him; but Pele is my deity, and the great goddess
> of Hawaii. Kirauea is the place of her abode. Ohiaotelani
> (the northern peak of the volcano) is one corner of her
> house." (Ellis 216)

Of the many 'aumakua forms, the presence of Pele endures as
long as the lava flows from Kīlauea, and being one of the patron
deities associated with the hula, her memory is constant in the
chants and dances. The physical activity of the volcano with its
uncontrollable nature continues to manifest the spirit of the
'aumakua to more than her descendants. In the late 1980s the
possibility of harnessing geothermal energy brought together
various persons who claimed an 'aumakua relationship to Pele with
environmentalists to oppose drilling into the volcanic areas. A local
newspaper reported on this cultural-political mix.

Nā ʻaumākua by Joseph Feher from *Ka Poʻe Kahiko, The People of Old* by Samuel Manaiakalani Kamakau

Long after many have forgotten other Hawaiian spirits, Pele remains an active and controversial part of Big Island life. One native group, the Pele Defense Fund, has gone to the state Supreme Court, trying to stop geothermal drilling, which they fear will extinguish the islands creative force and thus the heart of their Hawaiian religion.

Other Hawaiians say belief in Pele keeps Big Island hearts afraid. "We are praying to God that through his spirit he will break through the darkness on this island," said Rev. Henry Kahalakili, pastor of Hilo's Glad Tidings Church.

"I will do everything I can to lead my people out of bondage, and Pele worship is nothing more than bondage." (Hartwell A8)

For examples of the shark 'aumakua we need to turn to Kamakau.

> Kaneikokala was a shark famous for his good deeds. If a canoe was wrecked in the ocean and broken to pieces, and someone called for Kaneikokala, he would appear and save them [...]. (*Ka Po'e Kahiko* 87)

And,

> The body of the god was separate from his body as a shark, but the *kokala* fish was consecrated to him in the ancient worship of him by the ancestors. Their descendants may have heard of Kaneikokala, although they do not worship him; but to this day, the whole district of Kahikinui, Maui, with the exception of *malihini*, will run away if they see a *kokala* fish cooking, or even the smoke from the cooking; and they will eat no "food" or "fish" that has come in contact with it. If they ate food, or crossed the smoke, or touched things that had been in contact with *kokala* fish, they might die. (*Ka Po'e Kahiko* 87)

Not all the 'aumākua were benevolent and helpful. Kamakau tells us that even the kahu 'guardians' of Pele were afraid of too many deceased persons becoming deified, and this forced the kahu to do things in secret. This was no different he says with the other forms, especially the sharks.

> Some were evil, some were man-eaters, some were as fierce and untameable as lions, who even devoured their own *kahu* who had transfigured and deified them. [...] Others who were worshiped (*ho'omana 'ia*) became beloved friends if their *kanawai* were properly obeyed; they became defenders and guides in times of trouble and danger [...]. (*Ka Po'e Kahiko* 76)

Part of the reason this belief system in the 'aumākua was able to survive is the fact that it was not part of the temple worship but, as Ellis discovered, a relationship that was much closer and more personal.

Respecting family idols, the natives in general suppose
that after the death of any member of a family, the spirit
of the departed hovers about the places of its former
resort, appears to the survivors sometimes in a dream,
and watches over their destinies; hence they worship an
image with which they imagine the spirit is in some way
connected. (197)

Kamakau, when he discusses the ʻaumakua of Pele (volcano),
underscores how important this family connection and the use of
hoʻomana are.

> If one of these ʻaumakua is in the family of a person,
> they are all in his family [as they are related to each
> other]. Through giving birth in human form, one of
> them joins a person's blood to theirs [. . .]; they are all
> ʻaumakua. The kuleana does not come by consecrating
> a spirit to be one's god (hoʻolaʻa), or by pretending to be
> possessed by a god (hoʻonohonoho akua) and feigning
> insanity (hoʻopupule) and speaking in whispers, or
> bowing down and worshiping them, as some do, or
> by calling upon them to come and inspire him as he
> wishes. Only through the blood lineage (koko i eweewe
> mai) of the ancestors does the kuleana come. (Ka Poʻe
> Kahiko 66)

In his discussion of another ʻaumakua form, the owl, Kamakau
emphasizes the difference between the natural object, in this case the
owl, and the owl as a god. As I have earlier explained, it is the task of
"hoʻo-mana" to imbue something with mana—something that did
not have mana before—and through prayers and rites it becomes full
of mana.

> The owl itself is a worthless thing; it is eaten by the
> people of Kula, Maui, and Naʻalehu in Ka-ʻu, Hawaii,
> and thrown about on the road. The owl itself is not a
> god—it has no mana. The god is separate. Kukauakahi
> is the main god (poʻo akua nui) who is consecrated in
> the body of the owl and who shows his mana in the
> worthless body of the owl. [. . .]

> Is the owl a god? The writer of this history says that the
> owl is not a god—it is the form (*haili*) taken by a god. The
> owl is a humble bird among the birds of Hawaii, but it
> was consecrated, and was made kapu to certain people,
> but the *po'e kahiko* knew that the god itself was a different
> thing. (Kamakau, *Ka Po'e Kahiko* 88)

Long before Kamakau wrote these judgments, Captain Cook, on his first visit to the island of Niihau, in February 1778, observed the following, "A particular veneration seemed to be paid here to owls, which they have very tame [. . .]" (Cook 219) What does he mean by "tame?" I would consider that the people there had captured the owls and treated them with special care as we do household pets. It may be that our cats, dogs, and other dependent animals are the closest things we have to help us understand this 'aumākua relationship.

These descriptions of the 'aumākua tell us certain things.

- ❧ There is a very real and cherished relationship between a family and their departed relative or ancestor that is maintained through an ancestral symbol or form.
- ❧ In this relationship, the living relatives are obligated not only to care for their 'aumakua, but also to keep the kapu 'prohibitions' of their 'aumakua, such as not eating the body form of that 'aumakua.
- ❧ As living relations and ancestors have personal names, so do the 'aumākua. They are not generic.
- ❧ Not all natural forms that the 'aumākua can take as its shape, such as sharks or owls, are in fact 'aumākua. Kamakau is very clear on this point.
- ❧ Not all 'aumākua are helpful guardians of their living relations. They can actually harm or kill those who invoke them.

These are important cultural elements that seem to be forgotten today, allowing for a casual re-invention of who and what the 'aumākua are. This was brought to issue in the early 1990s when there were several shark attacks in the islands that brought the concept of 'aumākua to the attention of the general public, particularly when the reaction was to hunt the killer sharks.

This little known painting by Juliette May Fraser entitled "Haunted Woods" shows the very small night marchers in the left foreground. The 'aumākua of the forest witness the procession of ghostly chiefs and retainers.

Local newspapers reported on a protester who was against the shark hunt. "[S]tate officials refuse to say whether the shark hunt will resume over the protests of native Hawaiians who fear that certain sharks designated as *'aumakuas*, or family guardians, will be killed as well" (Neil A3).

The controversy was broadened when two respected Hawaiians responded to the claims of the protester. One of them, Rubellite Johnson, told the newspapers that "the concept of seeking out and killing a shark that has attacked people is fully supported in Hawaiian tradition. There is a 'common revulsion' toward such animals. [. . .] The purpose of the hunt is vindication. Restitution is implied. It is reciprocity" (TenBruggencate A4).

The article explained further that,

> Sharks were an integral part of life in old Hawaii. They were hunted for sport. They were revered as family gods or guardians. They were fished for food, for their tough, sand papery skins, and for their teeth, which were used for knives and affixed to weapons. (TenBruggencate A4)

And, Johnson stressed,

> "The important point is no matter what the class of animal or individual animal, the aumakua is the spirit of the ancestor."

> [. . .] Some modern Hawaiians may know the class of aumakua with which they are associated, without knowing details or an individual. [. . .] Because of intermarriage, many people may have several classes of aumakua in their family lines.

> But once a member of the family no longer actively cares for an aumakua creature, the relationship changes.

> "The remembrance of the name of the aumakua shark remains through tradition, but the kahu hanai no longer contacts the shark. After many generations, you don't expect that particular shark to still be alive [. . .]." (TenBruggencate A4)

There are many accounts of shark hunting. (See the chapter on A'o for the tradition of how the warrior Kekūhaupi'o learned to hunt sharks.) One of the earliest historical accounts was noted by Captain Nathaniel Portlock on Tuesday, December 5, 1786 as his ship was off southeast O'ahu.

> Numbers of sharks were about the ship, four or five of which we caught, and after taking out the livers they were given to the Indians [Hawaiians], who thought them very

acceptable presents, particularly the old priest, who got
two of the largest, and having ordered them to be carefully
lashed in his canoe, was going to send them on shore. [.
. .] one of the sharks not being securely fastened, fell out
of the canoe, and sunk to the bottom in eleven fathoms
water; at the same time there were several large hungry
ones swimming about, yet an Indian went down with a
rope, slung the dead shark, and afterwards hauled him
into his canoe, without any apparent fear of the others
that surrounded him. I found that sharks were esteemed
valuable, as they answer a variety of purposes; they salt the
shark, and seem very fond of it, the skin serves for a cover
to their drum-heads, and the teeth they fix in wooden
instruments which they use as knives. (159)

Of the eating of sharks, the niuhi shark was prohibited for
women to eat under the kapu imposed by Wākea. This type of shark
was apparently sought after as indicated by the following traditions.

My wife's grandfather also told me that fishing for *niuhi*
sharks furnished food for the chiefs, as in ancient times it was
an offense punishable by death for a commoner to secrete
some of it as food for himself. The only persons entitled to
fish for the *niuhi* were the chiefs' fishermen. (Desha 13)

Some of the chiefs under Kamehameha, such as Alapaʻi-
malo-iki and Ka-uhi-wawae-ono, were murdering chiefs
who did not keep the law against killing men, but went out
with their men to catch people for shark bait. If they found a
man or even a woman out at night they would kill him and
keep the body until it decayed and use it for shark bait. [. . .]
At Keala and Kalahiki in South Kona, at Hamakuapoko on
Maui, and at Puʻuloa on Oahu, people were killed by them
for shark bait. (Kamakau, *Ruling Chiefs* 232)

Mahope o laila, holo aku la o Kalaepuni me na lawaia a
Keawenuiaumi, ma waho ae o Kalahiki, he kupalupalu
mano ka lakou lawaia. A makaukau na mano a pau loa
malalo o na waa o lakou, huki na lawaia a Keawenuiaumi
i ka mano i luna o na waa, lele iho la o Kalaepuni i waena
o na mano, a pepehi iho la i na mano i laka mai ma ke

kupalu ana, a lanakila o Kalaepuni maluna o na mano a
pau loa. Alaila, olelo iho o Kalaepuni i kana olelo kaena
penei: "Ma keia hope aku, e hoolilo ana wau i oʻu mau
lima i makau kihele mano! A e hoolilo au i na mano a
pau, i lehu i loko o kuu poho lima." [. . .].

Kalaepuni went out fishing with some of Keawenuiaumi's
fishermen to the fishing grounds outside of Kalahiki; they
went out shark fishing. After some of the bait was thrown
out the sharks began to gather under the canoe, when the
baited hooks were let down and several sharks were caught
and hauled into the canoe. While Keawenuiaumi's men were
hauling the sharks up, Kalaepuni jumped out amongst the
sharks that were gathered under the canoe and began to fight
them, killing them all. After killing all the sharks, Kalaepuni
began boasting, saying: "Henceforth I shall use my hands as
hooks for catching sharks and shall make all sharks as dust in
my hands." (Fornander V: 200–201)

However, a mere eight years after the protests of the early 1990s,
protests against the killing of sharks for "cultural" reasons were again
reported in the newspapers.

The agency also said it would prepare a report on the
cultural aspects of sharks and shark fishing following
complaints by Native Hawaiians, who say shark finning
is an affront to their beliefs that a shark is an ʻaumakua,
or a personal god. ("Agency to Reassess" A3)

Then another situation over the disposal of a whale carcass
brought a similar charge. A whale was taken out into the ocean for
disposal. The headlines read "Native Hawaiians see the action as a
victory for their spirituality."

Hawaiian spirituality overcame scientific inquiry
yesterday as a dead dwarf sperm whale was buried at sea
rather than brought back to land to determine the cause
of its death. [. . .]

Finally, the spirituality of the Hawaiian people is
respected. It was very, very encouraging," Maxwell

[a Hawaiian cultural specialist] said. "It's a cultural
and spiritual thing over anything else. (Kubota,
"Officials" A6)

A year later another pygmy sperm whale washed ashore on the
south side of the island of Maui at Oneuli Beach and was taken,
probably for health and safety reasons, to the Puʻunēnē landfill to
be dumped. A Hawaiian cultural specialist on the island said that
"he [was] upset about the way" in which the whale was disposed
of "without the benefit of a cultural blessing" as it "is part of the
spiritual essence of the ocean and should have been returned to the
ocean" (Kubota, "Whale Sanctuary" A7).

The issue persisted, and a few days later, the specialist said that it
was a " 'wasteful practice' [. . .] not in keeping with Hawaiian culture
and its respect for ocean life, including sharks, which are regarded
by Hawaiians as guardians or aumakua" (Kubota, "Wasteful
Practices" A6).

Unlike with sharks, we know that our ancestors did not hunt
whales until modern technology, in the form of the whaling ships
and harpoons, came to the islands. What about the bodies of dead
whales that washed up on shore? We do know what our ancestors did
because Kamakau tells us.

> [. . .] Ka-hekili's request for Kualoa and the ivory that
> drifted ashore [. . .]. Some approved [. . .]. [Ka-ʻopulupulu,
> the kahuna] said, "O chief! if you give away these things
> your authority will be lost, and you will cease to be a
> ruler. To Kualoa [it] belong[s] [. . .]. Without the ivory
> that drifts ashore you could not offer to the gods the first
> victim slain in battle; it would be for Ka-hekili to offer it
> on Maui, and the rule would become his. You would be
> no longer ruler." (Kamakau, *Ruling Chiefs* 129)

Since the whale could not be hunted, how else would they
have obtained the whale's tooth unless it drifted ashore and was
made kapu in the name of the sovereign or ruling chief to be
used for offerings and chiefly ornaments? Kahahana's high priest,
Kaʻopulupulu, does not want his aliʻi to give up this right, for it
would amount to his loss of sovereignty as ruler.

It is apparent that some Native Hawaiians want to protect the whale by granting it special status as ʻaumakua like the shark. The difficulty here is that it is a completely modern invention. If Hawaiian culture and spirituality are to be consulted in the treatment of beached whales today, the result should be the claim by Native Hawaiians of the right of sovereignty to use the ivory as their ancestors did.

The pre-eminent problem, as summed up by one of the newspaper accounts on the shark attacks, is "the dilemma facing modern-day Hawaiians is that while family traditions claim shark aumakua, very few families have continued the practice of being in contact with their aumakua" (Ashizawa A4).

According to the newspaper account, it was this "inability of modern Hawaiians to recognize a family guardian spirit in the form of a shark" (Ashizawa A4) that alarmed the protester about the planned hunt by the state. Of course, the fact that this was not the case in the first newspaper reports, but what the protester then began to say after others had brought attention to longstanding religious traditions, further reveals the dilemma.

> [H]e has seen reefs killed and fish stocks depleted by runoff from sugar plantations and golf courses, the denial of access to beaches and a headlong rush to develop once-pristine land for the tourist industry.

> "What was dear to my father I cannot show to my three grandsons—how to pick limu, how to catch a certain fish, how to build a house in the ocean to feed the fish and taking only what you need. I'm 54 years old and now I have to break the law to get to the ocean." (Neil A3)

Traditional Hawaiian religious beliefs, as Kamakau wrote of the ʻaumākua, still persist to this day. Modern Hawaiians continue to work out cultural identity and practices with present-day beliefs and realities, but we must keep clear several points.

- ❧ A belief system needs to be believed and practiced, not just invoked for a particular purpose and/or cause.
- ❧ From the newspaper reports, we have seen how traditions about the ʻaumākua were being used for environmental

concerns, and as noble as that may be, that use distorted those traditions. If there had not been some public response to clarify the historical accuracy of the traditions, they might have been accepted by a whole new generation of people in a new way: as the beliefs of romantically and environmentally friendly natives whose great ancestors lived in the "garden" protecting and safeguarding nature.

- ❧ Practice means having unhindered access to be able to establish and maintain a relationship with the divine.
- ❧ It is quite clear that the lack of knowledge, ability, and access to opportunities to practice traditional ways has led to the need for understanding and renewed practice. But with population growth and heavy use of the ocean for recreational activities, it would be very difficult to ensure and maintain such an intimate relationship as with an ʻaumakua without curious on-lookers.
- ❧ Like many indigenous belief systems, traditional Hawaiian religious beliefs involve the harnessing, invoking, and imbuing of the world with the mana 'power' of the divine. That means having the ability and knowledge to communicate (prayers and rituals), as well as taking on responsibilities to maintain and nurture that relationship.
- ❧ One of the key points made over and over again about the ʻaumākua is that they have personal names and are not just a type of animal or form. They are uncle so-and-so or great-great grandfather so-and-so. This spiritual relationship is reflected in the word *hoʻomana* for without the mana, as Kamakau wrote, an owl is just an owl, and it tastes good, too.

There is a very real danger today of re-inventing these traditions for questionable motives and "quick fixes." The results can be very funny, but, sadly, they also can greatly diminish what mana does exist within remaining traditional beliefs.

Pī Kai—House Blessings and Purification

Fortunately, there is great potential for the creativity and survival of our beliefs in this modern day. A good example is the widely accepted practice, especially with businesses and families, to have "house blessings" done in a traditional Hawaiian way. We find this religious practice described in Ellis.

> Offerings were made to the gods, and presents to the priest, who entered the house, uttered prayers, went through other ceremonies, and slept in it before the owner took possession, in order to prevent evil spirits from resorting to it, and to secure its inmates from the effects of incantation. (Ellis 228)

In most ceremonies today, not only are prayers invoked (although I haven't heard of anyone sleeping in the house the night before), but also a wooden calabash filled with salt water to sprinkle the building or house is used. This, too, is a traditional religious practice called pī kai (sprinkle with salt or sea water) or pī wai (sprinkle with fresh water and turmeric root). We can find this in both Kamakau and Malo.

> Another good use for sea water was to secure forgiveness (*huikala*). When someone in the family broke an oath sworn against another (*ho'ohiki 'ino*) [. . .] then the *pikai,* or sprinkling with salt water, was the remedy to remove [the repercussions from the breaking of the oath]. This is how it was done. A basin or bowl of real sea water, or of water to which salt had been added, in which were placed 'awa rootlets (*huluhulu 'awa*) and *olena*, was the water to absolve and cleanse (*kalahala e huikala*) the family for the defilement (*haumia*) caused by the one who had broken his oath.
>
> Any defilement pertaining to the house, to fishing, tapa printing, tapa beating, farming, or *wauke* cultivation, from which trouble had resulted, could be cleansed with pikai; it purified and caused an end to defilement. Implements of labor could also be cleansed of their defilement by *pikai*. (Kamakau, *Ka Po'e Kahiko* 114)

Malo states that it was a kahuna pule heiau 'a priest in charge of the temple prayers' who conducted the ceremony for purification.

> When this kahuna arrived with a po'i [*covered bowl*] full of salt [sea] water. There was some limu kala in this bowl. Some used 'Ōlena [*Tumeric*] in the bowl. The kahuna then

stood in front of the people who were sitting in a row. He prayed [. . .]. Then the kahuna sprinkled the fresh water (wai) mixed with ʻŌlena upon all the people, and the purification ceremony was over and the defilement was ended. (201–202)

Hawaiian blessing of land and buildings is a very profound indication that traditional beliefs and a world view or culture endure for Native Hawaiians. This is furthered by the near universal acceptance of the practice by business, government, and individuals in the islands, either having or attending such blessings, performed as traditional, or as Christian Hawaiian, ceremonies.

Astonishing Food of the Land

During and after the overthrow of the Hawaiian Kingdom, Her Majesty Queen Liliʻuokalani urged her supporters not to act violently against the revolutionaries. At this urging, many of the native citizens protested using non-violent means. Since they were banned from displaying the Hawaiian flag, they made wooden shields to hold in public, wore Hawaiian patriotic ribbons and hat bands, and composed songs of protest. One of those songs is sung today as "Kaulana Nā Pua." It contains the following stanza.

> Ua lawa mākou i ka pōhaku
> I ka ʻai kamahaʻo o ka ʻāina.
>
> We are satisfied with the stones,
> Astonishing food of the land.
> (Elbert and Mahoe 64)

I can think of two traditions in which stones were placed into kī leaf parcels after the food that was originally in the parcels had been eaten. One is the tradition of the despotic chief Koihala (Koʻihala). The chief kept moving from place to place with no regard for his retainers who carried his meal. They became exhausted and hungry, and so they ate the food they had been carrying around. After eating the food, they placed stones inside of the kī leaf wrapped parcels and awaited their chief who had seen them eating his food. When he arrived demanding his food, his own retainers stoned him to death (Green 89).

The other is a similar use of the 'ai pōhaku, or stone bundled foods, by the friends and followers of 'Umi to kill and entomb his older brother, the abusive chief Hākau (Fornander IV: 200–205).

The most well-known, and in fact internationally known, tradition about stones is the belief that taking stones from the volcano will displease Pele and cause bad luck. The National Park Service has many letters and returned stones from visitors to demonstrate the power of the tradition. But, remember what Ellis told us about the lāhui imposed for Pele at Kīlauea.

> [. . .] the natives requested us not to kaha, a heru ka one,
> [helu ke one] strike, scratch, or dig the sand, assuring us
> it would displease Pele [. . .]. (166)

There is no mention of stones. It has been admitted that this tradition was, wisely, created by a park ranger fearing the tremendous loss of lava rocks from the national park, especially over time, with the thousands of souvenir-hunting visitors.

A more locally known stone tradition has been the offering and depositing of stones wrapped in kī leaves, sometimes to the extreme of being bundled like a laulau 'kī leaf-wrapped food bundle' at historical and sacred sites, mostly traditional temples and shrines.

Archaeologists are alarmed at this religious act, not because of the intent, but because like the park ranger, they are concerned that, over the years, additional piles of stone will alter the site. And, like in the park, a careful reading of the traditions shows that this is not a practice that was traditionally done. If we go back to the tradition of Wākea and Papa and look at the list of prohibited foods, which are the foods used for temple offerings, we will not find stones on that list.

When did we start to feed the gods and spirits stones? Are we, like the retainers of Ko'ihala, waiting to stone the next visitor to death, or are we stockpiling weapons? It is possible that someone once left an offering weighed down by a stone wrapped with a kī leaf so that the offering wouldn't be blown or knocked down, and as others came to the site and noticed the stone wrapped with a kī leaf, they imitated it and a new tradition began.

Recently there have been increased conflicts over what is "sacred" and what is not, especially with recent laws and sensitivities

A rain god located on the 'Ulupalakua Ranch, sometimes called Lono. The late Rev. David Ka'alakea, who worked as a ranch hand, said that offerings were made to it to cause clouds to form over Kaho'olawe that would then move over Kula, Maui and bring rains in the afternoon. The recent offerings seen below the image are stones wrapped in kī leaves.

to museum collections and traditional burial sites. The intent of many of these laws is to address a history of looting and destruction of Native American sites, the insensitivity accorded native peoples and their traditions, the reparations of collections of items acquired in such a manner, and the protection of existing sites and materials.

However, in the late 1990s several cases pitted Hawaiians against Hawaiians over the claim of what is sacred. A good example of this type of conflict occurred when a museum in Providence, Rhode Island decided to put an old carved Hawaiian image, identified as a decorated canoe haka used to hold spears or fishing poles, up for sale for the sum of $200,000. The Office of Hawaiian Affairs and a group called Hui Mālama i Nā Kūpuna o Hawai'i Nei sued to stop the sale under the Native American Graves Protection and Repatriation Act. Their claim was that "the object was an 'aumakua, an ancestral deity relied upon by present-day descendants for guidance and protection" (Wright A31).

This claim was challenged by the museum's expert witnesses, including Herb Kawainui Kane, "famous in Hawaii as an artist and one of the creators and the first captain of the voyaging canoe Hokule'a."

> Kane said "it is uncomfortable to me" to be testifying
> against the claims of Hawaiian groups. "But it was even
> more uncomfortable to let this matter continue the way
> it had been, knowing that the truth is being handled in a
> cavalier fashion."
>
> There are some figures which are 'aumakua, "which
> would have been sacred to a particular family."
>
> "But you couldn't say," as the Hawaiian groups have
> claimed, "that they were sacred to all the people," he said.
>
> Kane said he has heard criticism for his position. He said
> the ki'i is clearly carved in a secular, rather than sacred,
> style, and wouldn't qualify even if a Hawaiian religion
> survived today. (Wright A31)

With the help of a $125,000 donation by the Office of Hawaiian
Affairs (OHA), the ki'i has been returned to Hawai'i and is currently
housed at the Bernice Pauahi Bishop Museum. But its return was
not as a religious or sacred object. Such situations have become
more common, and it is more evident that continual use of the claim
of religious or sacred importance will be looked at more carefully.
This "cavalier" usage of alleged sacredness may actually diminish
the mana of the argument, especially if the claims are shown to be
unfounded.

Mana is not a fragile concept. When the late "Papa" Richard
Lyman, then a trustee for the powerful Bishop Estate, asked me what
I thought of the geothermal drilling issue, I simply reminded him of
Pele. If Pele is who she really is, then I would not have any fears that
she could not take care of herself. If the drilling was a good thing then
it would go on, but if it was not good then Pele would resolve it in her
own way. She didn't need protest groups and lawyers to reveal her will.

This legend, or sense, of mana continues to persist, for it was
reported in 2002 in the *Honolulu Advertiser* that the old Kona
Lagoon Hotel on the island of Hawai'i would finally be torn down.
The cause?

Some people think the Kona Lagoon Hotel was cursed from the
start. Surrounded by ancient temples and archaeological sites, it was

built on the dwelling place of supernatural twin sisters, 'aumakua
who took the form of lizards, according to Hawaiian legend.

> Security guards hired to watch the property when the
> 462-room hotel closed in 1988 were frightened at night,
> said Joe Castelli, who lives at the neighboring Keauhou
> Kona Tennis and Racquet Club.

> "They told me that they would see lights up there and
> hear Hawaiians singing and talking . . . but when they
> got there, they didn't find anything. So they said they
> just didn't go anymore," Castelli said. (Hurley A1)

It is not important whether this is true or not, unless you want to
tell spooky ghost stories around a camp fire. What is important about
this report is that the belief in the 'aumākua is given such attention
today. It is telling us that even if the formal temple worship and its
related kapu system have ceased, mana exists and endures because
people continue to recognize and believe in it.

The danger to the integrity of mana comes when traditional
religious beliefs and practices are used for other reasons and
purposes. When this usage is revealed not to be based in the
tradition, it can have the effect of lessening people's belief in their
own culture and also the belief of others in that culture. When this
change is accepted as being traditional, it can dramatically alter the
actual tradition, for good or bad.

The late Lakota theologian Vine Deloria, Jr. witnessed this trend
among Native Americans.

> Sweat lodges conducted for $50, peyote meetings for
> $1,500, medicine drums for $300, weekend workshops
> and vision quests for $500, two do-it-yourself
> practitioners smothered in their own sweat lodge—the
> interest in American Indian spirituality only seems
> to grow and manifests itself in increasingly bizarre
> behavior—by both Indians and non-Indians. Manifestos
> have been issued, lists of people no longer welcome on
> the reservations have been compiled, and biographies of
> proven fraudulent medicine men have been publicized.
> Yet nothing seems to stem the tide of abuse and misuse

of Indian ceremonies. Indeed, some sweat lodges in
the suburbs at times seem like the opening move in a
scenario of seduction of naive but beautiful women who
are encouraged to play the role of "Mother Earth" in
bogus ceremonies. (*The World* xvii)

How do we move from the past tradition to the future? I was
visiting the island of Moloka'i in the 1970s, and I asked a family
friend, Mary Horner, if we could visit the grave of her late father,
the Rev. Mitchell Pau'ole, who had been the unofficial "mayor" of
Moloka'i and a leading kahu 'pastor' of a Hawaiian Congregational
church. While we were at the grave site, it dawned on Mary that
it was almost one year to the day since her father had died and
in passing conversation she said that her father had told her that
we (modern-day Hawaiians) should not be frightened of the past.
After all, we are descendants of those people some called pagan and
heathen. He told her, "We don't do what they did, but we respect
them because they are our ancestors."

So, what does one do when walking upon an ancient trail or
entering a historical or archaeological site? I think most people go
there to learn and understand, and if that is the case, then the key
word is respect. That does not mean one has to believe or one has
to have an offering in hand. We may well be wise to consider the
traditional proverb "to walk gently upon the trail, not picking or
touching, not lingering too long with the intent of destroying or
doing something malicious lest the god becomes angry."

1. Webber drew this full scene at Waimea, Kaua'i in January, 1778, depicting the trading of goods and the replenishing of fresh water from a pond in the dead center of the drawing. This is the earliest view of the Hawaiian islands and people. There also exists another drawing of the same scene without any people in the foreground.

2. In this detail of Webber's village scene, it is interesting to note the child reaching for the woman. The seated male appears to have a series of tattoos on his right shoulder and extending down his arm that look like the tattoos on the male Webber also drew while at Kauaʻi. The group is surrounded by foodstuffs, including a bird to their right and a water gourd, coconuts, and bananas to their left. All the men's malos 'loin cloths' are folded into the groin and do not have an extended front flap. Joppien & Smith (416) have noted the extended long hair of the Hawaiian at the front of the image whose back is facing the viewer, which they identified as a hair-piece or wig, at least one of which was traded for. What they did not comment on is the extended tattoo of chevrons from his waist down to his left foot and down the right side of his back. The color detail of the ʻahuʻula 'cape' is most remarkable, as is the fact that the chief, who is also wearing a mahiʻole 'helmet,' uses his hands to spread it out, probably using inner side loops as seen in some of the existing capes. The crest of the helmet is yellow and the visible side is red. The top of the cape is red followed below by a yellow line, then a field of white feathers with spots of black, and the bottom is red. There is a cord extended to the chief's left side held by his hand. The British fellow has an axe extended in his left hand, and he holds a firearm in his right.

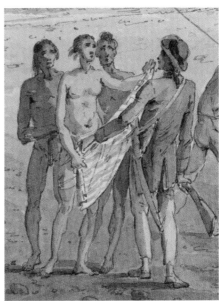

3–4. There exist two slightly different images of the scene on the left, one at the British Library in London and the other, shown here, at the Dixson Library, State Library of New South Wales in Sydney, Australia. In the British Library image, the Hawaiian has long hair, about to the shoulders, while in this image his hair is short. He is holding a bird in his arms, most likely for trade. We can tell that the British fellow is an officer because of the sword he is holding in his left hand. In the detail on the right, a woman is evidently trying to barter a large piece of kapa 'bark cloth' with another officer (identified by the sword and firearm), with two Hawaiian men watching closely behind her.

5. Webber's sketch, preparatory to the composite painting in color plate 1, shows the hale 'house' to the far right with a woman at the gate and two persons at the doorway. The fencing to the far right leading to the gate in front of the house appears to be made from large bunches of sticks connected to form a fence. The house to the left is unusual because it is built upon stilts and not on a stone platform, and because it has no people in the doorway on the elevated porch. This building detail is similar to houses found in Tahiti and suggests that this might be a storage hale.

6. This more detailed drawing of these hale shows many of the elements of the final composite painting. The seated group with woman and child was reproduced faithfully, although a bird at the man's foot and an additional man behind the woman and child were added. The man carrying sugar cane was not retained in the full scene. Instead, there are two men carrying a pig. In this sketch, we see two men conversing at the doorway of the elevated hale.

7–8. According to Cook's journal, they saw several "elevated white objects, like pyramids or rather obe-lisks" (200) while they were at Waimea, and they attempted to go to the one not far from the area depicted in color plate 1. However, the very pond or estuary they were gathering fresh water from prevented them from reaching it. So they walked a bit farther and visited the one pictured in these sketches. These drawings of its interior courtyard and god house have been interpreted as depicting a heiau typical of the island of Kaua'i, in particular, its post and slab 'carved boards' type of ki'i 'images'. Three other details from Cook's journal are of interest. One is the existence of graves in the heiau of both chiefs and sacrificial victims, or "tangata taboo," which Cook describes as occurring in pairs, that is, one sacrifice at the funeral of each chief (203). Another is that the two images in the god house, or "hale mana," were called "Eatooa no Veheina," which Cook translates as goddesses (202). But a more accurate translation is "gods for women," which may not necessarily be female deities. However, the most interesting fact was that Cook described the stone image "near two feet high, covered with pieces of cloth, called bobo [pōpō, to encase with kapa as a bundle], and consecrated to Tongarooa [Kanaloa], who is the God of these people" (201). This is interest-ing because by the 1820s, when missionaries began to describe Hawaiian religion, the worship of Kanaloa was virtually unknown.

9–10. This panoramic view of the north side of Kealakekua Bay by John Webber (with detail of the center right section below) shows the chiefly village of Ka'awaloa. Webber depicts the stone structure towards the point and two village clusters in great detail. But most interesting of all is the very tall hale just right of center that is surrounded by an unusual stone-wall foundation and fence (at the far left in the detail). If we can judge its height by the surrounding coconut trees, then the posts of this wooden fence are extremely high.

11. Moving south around the curve of the bay, this drawing, also by Webber, shows the other village at Kealakekua and is noted for depicting the first image of a man paddling out on a surfboard. To his right is a double-hulled canoe with crab-claw mast and what appears to be seven paddlers and two men seated on a platform. Their cargo is a very long cylindrical object obviously wrapped in layers of white kapa, possibly a stick god similar to that depicted in color plate 18. The stone-walled structure to the extreme right is the heiau called Hikiau.

12. Webber created three images of the formal greeting of Cook by Kalaniʻōpuʻu at Kealakekua that we know of, one study sketch and two, more finished, watercolor paintings. One of these is at the Bishop Museum in Honolulu, and the other, shown here, is from the Dixson Library, State Library of New South Wales in Sydney, Australia and is in excellent condition. A close inspection of the two paintings shows different positions of the men at the prow of the canoe and around the mast. We know that the British expected the paramount chief to board the ships but, strangely, the canoes circled the ships several times before heading back to shore (King, J. 17). Details we can see in the Dixson image include nine mahiʻole 'helmets,' six kāhili 'hand-held feather standards,' and seven ʻahuʻula 'feather capes.' King mistakes the kāhili for spears in his account (King, J. 16). There are fifty-eight passengers on Kalaniʻōpuʻu's canoe and, possibly, nineteen or twenty paddlers. King reports that Kalaniʻōpuʻu's canoe was seventy feet long (King, J. 148).

13. The canoe in the background has nineteen paddlers and contains five pigs as offerings. The canoe in the foreground carries the priest Kao and twenty paddlers. We can see the heads of three large images at the rear. The images are wrapped in many layers of white kapa, similar to the way that the stick gods of Rarotonga in the Cook Islands were prepared. These Hawaiian feathered gods 'akua hulumanu,' as depicted in proportion to the paddlers and the canoe, are bigger than we would expect.

14. I suggest that the chief in the center of the front canoe is Kalaniʻōpuʻu. He holds a kāhili whose top feathers are red and whose body is striped red/white/red and then white. The cape draping his right shoulder is red and yellow and appears to be a full-length cape as it extends down to his knees. If this is so, then it would be the only image of the paramount chief, Kalaniʻōpuʻu. I also suggest that the person to his left, with whom he appears to be in conversation, is probably his aikāne, Palea.

15–16. This large ʻahuʻula is attributed to the paramount chief Kalaniʻōpuʻu, who wears it in the canoe. When Cook came ashore, Kalaniʻōpuʻu took it off to give to him along with his helmet. Both artifacts are now in the Pacific Collection of Te Papa Tongarewa, the National Museum of New Zealand. According to Te Papa, the ʻahuʻula and mahiʻole were part of a private museum in England where a picture of them was painted by Sarah Stone before they were sold at auction in 1806 to a second private museum. That museum was sold at auction in 1819, and both pieces were purchased by Charles Winn whose grandson, Lord St. Oswald, gifted them to the National Museum in 1912.

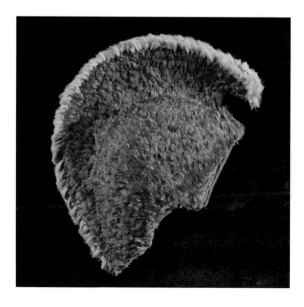

17. This is one of the akua hulumanu 'feathered gods' attributed to Cook's third expedition. It is part of the British Museum's collection in London. It measures 81 centimeters high and 39 centimeters wide.

18. This immense stick god from the Cook Islands was originally part of the collection of the London Missionary Society and is now part of the collection of the British Museum in London. The photograph cannot depict how grand it is, engulfed in layers of bark cloth. The technique is probably similar to that used to wrap the feather god that Webber drew on the canoe shown in color plate 12 .

19. Webber's depiction of these mysterious paddlers masked with gourd helmets has been one of the most influential in shaping people's imagination of Hawaiian culture. There are three passengers: one blowing a conch shell in the rear, one in the middle who seems to be seated on the canoe platform with a pig strapped behind him, and a third seated second from the front in the foreground canoe. Many have suggested that they were of a secret society of priests involved in a religious ceremony. But King's account of their arrival at the ships paints a very different picture. He wrote, "We never saw these masks worn but twice, and both times by a number of people together in a canoe, who came to the side of the ship, laughing and drolling, with an air of masquerading" (King, J. 139).

20. In this detail, the person on the platform is holding a small akua hulumanu 'feathered god,' while the person seated in the canoe cradles another type of feather image that does not have a face. What we can see is a flat surface of red with black specks in rows surrounded by a band of black and sides that also have black specks. The lower part of this object is red. We can presume that the front surface is covered by feathers like the other feathered god images. We can also see, in the colored drawing, the pink and yellow colors of the kapa strips hanging from the bottom rim of the masks. Most contemporary reproductions, probably based on black and white photos, show only white strips.

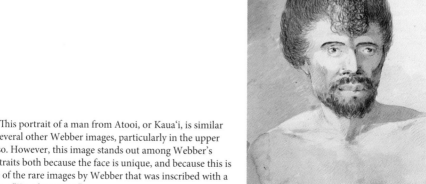

21. This portrait of a man from Atooi, or Kaua'i, is similar to several other Webber images, particularly in the upper torso. However, this image stands out among Webber's portraits both because the face is unique, and because this is one of the rare images by Webber that was inscribed with a name, "Ke-a ka a rona."

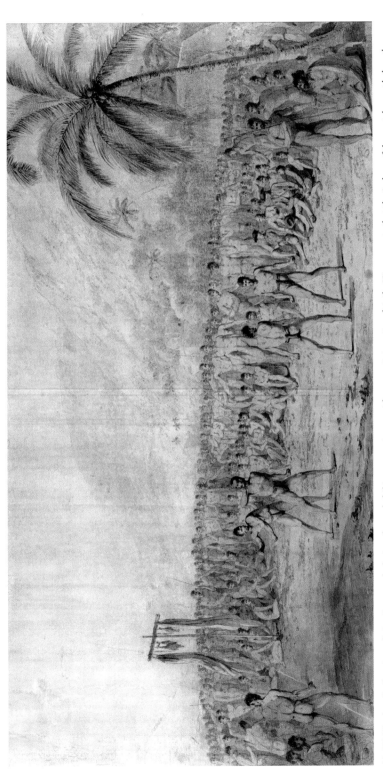

22. Webber's only drawing of a boxing match during the makahiki ceremonies provides some interesting details. King reports that the judges of the matches sat below the banner (King, J. 22–23). There is one British visitor gesturing towards the ground above the pair of boxers on the left, while the other British visitors are seated towards the coconut tree. Again, all the men's malo 'loin cloths' are girded without a frontal flap. Although it appears the audience was primarily men, King gives an account of a wife of one of the chiefs who joined their party, apparently with the aim of "soliciting some trifling presents" (King, J. 165). She was physically abused by her husband, and the British did not know whether or not to intervene on her behalf. They were told not to because of his rank, and the next day they saw the couple behaving as if nothing had occurred (King, J. 165). It was also during one of these boxing events that the British, who by January 28, 1779 were much more familiar with the Hawaiian language, discovered the meaning of the term aikāne (Salmond, *The Trial* 404).

John Webber was in Hawai'i twice as a member of Captain Cook's crew. His first visit was to Kaua'i and Ni'ihau in January of 1778, and his second visit was to Kealakekua Bay in January and February of 1779. Amongst the many sketches and paintings he did during these two visits is this rarely published set of images of birds and fish, which are in the collection of the British Museum. All are signed by Webber, and all but one have the words "Sandwich Isles" written on them. Beyond this, they contain varying degrees of information. Three (numbers 24, 27, and 28) are dated 1779, placing them in West Hawai'i. These same three, as well as one other (number 29), have transcribed names written on them. We see this same variation in the documentation of the fish. All four are labeled "Sandwich Isles," and two are labeled with transcribed names, but none of the four are dated.

23. Unidentified bird by John Webber, undated, possibly an 'ākepa

24. Bird by John Webber, labeled ʻa kie-a-roa [ʻakialoa], dated 1779

25. Unidentified bird by John Webber, undated, possibly an ʻamakihi

26. Unidentified bird by John Webber, undated, possibly a mamo

27. Bird by John Webber, labeled Aka-kan-ne ['apapane], dated 1779

28. Bird by John Webber, labeled He ʻēē vēē [ʻiʻiwi], dated 1779

29. Bird by John Webber, labeled hoo-hoo—the name given by the natives [ʻōʻō], undated

30. Unidentified fish by John Webber, undated, possibly a lae-nihi

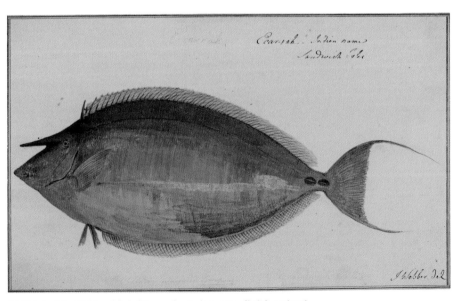

31. Fish by John Webber, labeled Ecar-rah—Indian name [kala], undated

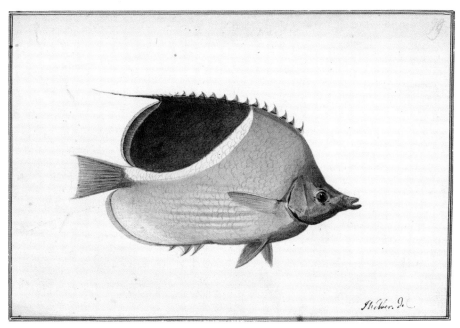

32. Unidentified fish by John Webber, undated, possibly a saddleback butterflyfish

33. Fish by John Webber, labeled Roweeparra or Roupeeparra, undated, possibly a lauwiliwili

34. Louis Choris was a trained artist, and although his contribution is limited as compared to Webber, it is of equal value for its detail, particularly since he arrived in Hawaiʻi in the very last years of Kamehameha's life. This scene of the Russians meeting with Kamehameha has been well studied because Kamehameha, clothed in black kapa, is in it. The late artist-historian Jean Charlot made an exhaustive study of Choris's portraits of Kamehameha. Naturally, the woman next to Kamehameha is his political wife, Kaʻahumanu. I assumed that the young woman next to her would have been Nahiʻenaʻena but have realized that she would still have been a small child at that time.

L. Choris del.

Imp. lith. de Langlumé par. Abel el.

35. Under the banana trees behind the Russians (to the right in the picture) is a young child held in the arms of a woman. This is the second early image of a woman with child (we saw the first in Webber's drawing shown in color plate 1), and in this case it could be a wet nurse or guardian in the court.

36. The structure at the far right is the heiau called Ahuʻena that had been reconstructed by Kamehameha. It was dedicated to the healing gods Kamakanuiahaʻialono and Lonopuha, whose images are visible outside of the structure. The position of Ahuʻena, as well as that of the other structures depicted around what little we can see of the bay, when compared to maps of the area drawn by Henry Kekahuna (Young 13) and Paul Rockwood (Ii 118), gives us a sense of where Kamehameha and the Russians met.

37. Choris painted another house site where he depicted Ka'ahumanu meeting with someone while a group of chiefs and followers waited at the side. It is my contention that this is the back side of the house compound found in color plate 34. We know that the group waiting on the side is definitely of chiefly rank due to the chiefly symbols of kāhili 'feather standard' and feather lei. What is also interesting are the two pigs lying to the far left next to a large pit ringed with stones. We can assume this is an imu 'underground oven' and the pigs are waiting to be cooked.

38. In the text of the chapter on A'o, I point out the probable book or paper that Ka'ahumanu and possibly her Tahitian teacher, Auna, are discussing. He is pointing to it, the very flat object between them.

39. Choris also did a portrait of Ka'ahumanu that shows the fashionable hair styling, first described by Cook's expedition, of using lime on the front band of hair that caused it be bleached white.

40. This is one of the earliest images of urban Honolulu in transition from a village to a major harbor in the Pacific. There are people riding horses and others wearing traditional malo 'loin cloths.' The hale 'houses' are still traditional pili 'grass' houses, but one (the second one from the right) has a canopy over the doorway. The fort protecting the harbor is to the left—there is a sentry standing on the wall between the Western-style buildings. Depicted at the fort is the first rendering of the kingdom's flag, although it appears to have been flying upside down. Contrary to recent folk invention that there was another "secret" flag made, all journals of this time record the flag of the kingdom as composed of the British Union Jack and tri-colored stripes. In the distance, what appear to be another island and clouds are the Wai'anae mountains and the 'Ewa plain.

41. Like the scene of Waimea, Kaua'i by Webber, this drawing by Heddington could also be a composite of village life at Mākaha, Ka'ū, on the island of Hawai'i. To the center right there are two groups of interest. Towards the foreground there are some women gathered and one is looking into a mirror. The group towards the background and left of the person exiting the traditional house doorway is composed of men and women listening, perhaps to someone of authority.

42. John Papa ʻĪʻī (1800–1870) was reared to become the companion and guardian of Hawaiian royalty. ʻĪʻī wrote down the history of events he had personally experienced, especially after reading some of the published articles by Samuel Manaiakalani Kamakau in the Hawaiian language newspapers. He was a member of the kingdom's Privy Council and House of Nobles and, later in his life, served as a member of the Supreme Court.

43. Davida Malo (1795–1853) was trained as a traditional genealogist and educated by American missionaries, attended the Lāhaināluna Seminary in its first class, and was deeply involved in the formation of the Hawaiian government. He wrote the most comprehensive cultural account of traditional Hawaiian society. This particular image is hand-painted and from the collection of the author.

44. Samuel Manaiakalani Kamakau (1815–1876), also a graduate of the Lāhaināluna Seminary, was the youngest of these three native historians and the most prolific writer. Although he was born at the end of the reign of Kamehameha I, he was reared by his grandparents who still lived a traditional life. His grandfather was a priest of the traditional religion, and Kamakau had a vivid recollection of those early days. Kamakau was also one of several Hawaiians who conducted oral history interviews with elderly Hawaiians concerning Hawaiian history and culture. It also appears that he inherited the research of another historian, S. N. Haleʻole.

The following photographs come from the author's collection. These were compiled over the course of a long career as a cultural specialist, researcher, and author and represent modern expressions of many of the values and themes discussed in this book.

45. The author presenting the Hon. David Lange, prime minister of New Zealand, with a model double-hulled canoe at the investiture of Sir Paul Reeves (seated in the middle) as governor-general of New Zealand.

46. Presentation of a Hawaiian flag quilt 'kapa' to Sir Paul Reeves, governor-general of New Zealand, by Hawaiian guests.

47. This is one of three known existing samples of foreign trade cloth from Hawai'i. This sample was collected in 1825 by Andrew Bloxam, a crewmember on the British ship, the *HMS Blonde*. It was this ship, under the command of Captain Lord Byron, that brought the bodies of Kamehameha II and Queen Kalama from England. This sample is a few pieces of cloth, perhaps linen, sewn together to form a bag or pouch using 'olona fiber for thread. It is dyed indigo blue, with a dye that may be either trade dye or native. It was part of Bloxam's collection of kapa samples that did not end up in the British Musuem and is from the author's collection.

48. There are no known images of the despotic chiefs discussed in the chapter on Alaka'i, but there are two very similar petroglyphs of a male figure with a barbed helmet carved into the lava rock, this one at KeahuoLū, and another at Anaeho'omalu. The other known similarity between these two places is that the killing of a high chief took place there. These shared images may be suggestive of such an event.

49–50. Before the historical site of Hikiau heiau at Kealakekua Bay was closed to the general public, the author was able to take these photos of the entrance and of the platform foundation on top of the heiau. This is the location drawn by Webber in his drawing entitled "An offering before Captain Cook in the Sandwich Islands." The heiau wall can be seen to the extreme right in Webber's painting of Kealakekua Bay shown in color plate 11.

51. Hawaiian culture is also finding its way back into schools. These children at Keaukaha Elementary School in Hilo are learning to practice pono both at school and at home. From left to right, Isaiah Paulo, Napahu Lilly, Kainalu Whitney, Maʻalahi Remmers, Kemauka Kahakua show off their "got pono?" t-shirts.

52. Dr. Blaisdell has written about the shift away from the traditional Hawaiian diet to one of Western-style processed foods as one of the major contributors to the significant health problems experienced today by Native Hawaiians.

53. Oratory was an important skill throughout Polynesia, and the kākāʻōlelo was an important position in the chief's council. While we know little of the tradition in Hawaiʻi, the traditional style of oratory is still practiced in many parts of Polynesia. This Samoan talking chief wears a tapa lavalava and bears the symbols of his office, the toʻotoʻo 'staff' and fue 'flywhisk.'

8 Alaka‘i

Traditional Leadership

E ho‘okanaka.
Be someone.
motto of Kamehameha II

✖

E na‘i ‘oukou i ku‘u pono, ‘a‘ole e pau.
Try and undo the good things of mine, it cannot be done.
the attributed last words of Kamehameha

✖

He [a young chief] would have many troubles, live in poverty,
and become a famous ruler.
Kamakau

The word for leadership in the Pukui and Elbert *Hawaiian Dictionary* is alaka‘ina (1986: 472). This word is derived from the root alaka‘i ‘[t]o lead, guide, direct’ (18) and the suffix ‘ana ‘-ing’ (24). Today we see this word used to describe things like student leadership in a hālau ‘school’ or the relationship of a mentor to a student. And it is probably true that this word has always applied to this kind of leadership. I have not seen alaka‘i used to describe an ali‘i.

An ali‘i’s leadership role was unlike that of today’s political leaders who gain power through popular election and lead us in a democratic system of government. In Hawai‘i, traditional governance and the development of leadership were based upon an accident of birth that conveyed rank, status, and a place within the hierarchy. In re-examining traditional sources like the writings of Davida Malo, we rediscover a sense of what traditional leadership was like in Hawai‘i and see that it had many of the qualities of great leadership that are not only timeless but universally held.

One of the biggest clues Malo gives us comes from his chapter concerning the relationship between the ali‘i ‘chiefs’ and the maka‘āinana ‘people.’

> He nui ke ano o na [a]lii, aole like pu, he hao wale kahi alii,
> he uhuki wale kahi alii, he pepehi wale kahi alii, he ohi wale
> kahi alii, he pue wale kahi alii uuku na [a]lii noho pono e
> like me Kamehameha I he alii hoomalu pono ia. (33)

> There were many dispositions of the ali'i. They were not
> alike. An ali'i would be known to only plunder, another
> to up root things, another to kill and another to collect
> or to heap things up. There were a few just ali'i like
> Kamehameha I.; for he was a just and caring ali'i. (177)

There are several things to look at in this statement. The first is how Malo approaches his description. He begins with the negative and ends with the positive. This same approach is used in his other observations, perhaps because it is easier to remember and describe the things that are abnormal or different, and, by a process of elimination, work back to what you really wanted to say.

The ali'i that he refers to—those that plunder, dig up crops, murder, or are greedy—come from a well-remembered tradition that he describes in the following paragraph.

> Due to the misbehavior of some ali'i to the maka'āinana,
> there were often battles fought between the ali'i and the
> maka'āinana. Many ali'i were killed by the maka'āinana
> in battle. The maka'āinana were the opponents of rogue
> ali'i in the old days. (Malo 177)

Malo repeats this statement later in his chapter on politics.

> There were many ali'i who were killed by the
> maka'āinana because they were oppressed.

> These were the ali'i who were killed by the maka'āinana
> because [they oppressed them]. Ko'ihala was killed be-
> cause he overburdened the maka'āinana in [the district
> of] Kā'ū, [on the island of Hawai'i]. Due to this murder
> [the district of] Kā'ū was called mākaha [*fierce*].

> Ko'ihalalani was an ali'i who was killed in Kā'ū. Hala'ea
> was another ali'i killed in Kā'ū. 'Ehunuikaimalino was an
> ali'i who was secretly killed by lawai'a at Keahuolu in the
> Kona [district on the island of Hawai'i]. Kamai'ole was
> another ali'i killed by Kalapana at 'Anaeho'omalu in the
> district of Kona.

> Hakau was the ali'i killed by 'Umi at Waipi'o [Valley]
> in the Hāmākua [district] on the island of Hawai'i.

Lonoikamakahiki was presumed to be expelled in Kona and 'Umiokalani was another ali'i who was expelled in Kona.

Therefore, several of the traditional or old ali'i feared the maka'āinana, but the maka'āinana faced death when the ali'i was pono [*moral, proper or fair*]. (266)

The Despotic Chiefs

The importance of these traditions of the despotic chiefs in the memory of the ali'i is given by the native historian John Papa 'Ī'ī in this account of how Kamehameha passed on these traditions to his son and heir, Liholiho, at the temple of Ahu'ena in Kailua on the island of Hawai'i.

> Whenever there was a meeting in the Ahuena house in the evening, the king [Kamehameha] instructed the heir [Liholiho] carefully as to how to do things, describing the lives of former rulers such as Keakealaniwahine, Kalaniopuu, Koihala, Kamalalawalu, Kauhiakama, and Hakau. Thus Liholiho learned the results of abuse and disregard of the welfare of chiefs and commoners and about farming and fishing and things of like nature. In the discussions with the king the heir derived understanding which has passed down to his heirs of today. (129)

What is in these traditions that is so important to shaping the thinking and behavior of the future ali'i? It should be obvious from 'Ī'ī's statement that Kamehameha hoped his son would figure out which actions and decisions of those chiefs were good or bad and how others reacted to them. 'Ī'ī mentioned the tradition of Ko'ihala, and that is a good place to start because it is lesser known than that of the half-brothers Hākau and 'Umi. Editor Martha Beckwith notes the similarity of plots between this account of Ko'ihala and the story in which "the disaffected old followers of Liloa destroyed Hākau and obtained the chieftainship of Hawaii for Umi" (Green 89).

> An irresolute chief was Ko-i-ha-la. When the chief was visiting in Ko-na, he despatched a messenger to Ka-u with the order for food to be prepared and taken to Wai-ahu-kini, there to meet him. When all was in readiness,

the servants bore it to Wai-ahu-kini. As they sat awaiting his appearance, they saw the chief's canoe heading for Kai-li-kii, so they took up the food again and went on to the place where they expected him to land. Not so! when they got to Kai-li-kii he was heading for Ka-pu-a.

Again the men shouldered the food and followed toward the mountain, but as they reached Ka-pu-a they perceived the chief heading for Ka-alu-alu and they immediately proceeded thither.

By this time they were hungry and tired and they therefore agreed to watch and, if the chief did not arrive shortly, to eat the food themselves. The chief delayed landing, simply sitting idly in the canoe and gazing at the men. So the servants ate the food that had been prepared and then they filled with stones the *ti*-leaf packets in which the fish had been wrapped and the empty calabashes of vegetable food. The chief, seeing these things [Ike ke alii i ka ano e o kanaka — The chief saw the strange behavior of the servants], paddled furiously until he reached Ka-alu-alu. Hence has arisen the proverb, "*Kau ino auwaa o Kaalualu*," that is, "The canoes arrive hurriedly at Ka-alu-alu." Hastening up the beach to the spot where the men sat he cried, "Say! let us eat! let the chief eat!"—"Yes, indeed!" answered the servants. "Here is vegetable food and fish!" Whereupon they stoned the despotic chief to death. (Green 89)

The term used in the Hawaiian text to describe the chief Koʻihala is "hoʻoluhi iʻo," that is, to make truly tired or to overburden. To understand the importance of the servants' actions, we must remember that chiefs were like gods upon the earth. They had rank and status, and if we carefully examine what happened, we can see that Koʻihala's servants loyally continued to follow their chief wherever he went. Things changed when the chief remained in his canoe off shore and just looked at his servants and the food. That is the moment when the relationship broke down because of the chief's insolence and irresponsibility toward the efforts of his people.

As Beckwith has noted, a similar ruse was used to kill the physically and mentally abusive Hākau, the older brother of ʻUmi. It is told in detail in the Fornander account: 'Umi's followers gathered stones, and they "were bundled up into ti-leaf [wrappers], and made to resemble bundles of potatoes" (VI: 200). With the help of some elders who eased Hākau's suspicions, 'Umi, his friends, and followers surprised Hākau and stoned and entombed him with the bundles they had brought with them (Fornander IV: 200–204).

Green's collection also gives the traditions of Hala'ea and Kōha'ikalani, both of whom were killed in the Ka'ū district on the island of Hawai'i. Hala'ea was a chief who coveted all the fish caught by his fishermen. The fishermen respected the demands of their chief until they and they families were forced into near starvation. The Hawaiian text says that "Hoakoakoa na poo lawaia [. . .] a kukakuka iho nei lakou [. . .]" (86). The head fishermen gathered and discussed among themselves how they could get rid of their chief. Their strategy was brilliant because they were able to destroy their chief without diminishing the respect to the chief's rank and status. What they did was simple: they kept on filling the chief's canoe with heavy 'ahi fish until the canoe was ready to sink, and then they all paddled quickly away to watch the chief drown with his coveted fish. The word given to describe Hala'ea is anunu or "greedy" (86–89).

Kōha'ikalani is described as "[h]e alii hoounauna ino" (Green 90) or "causing heavy burdens to be laid upon his people whenever opportunity offered" (91). Kōha'ikalani had his people gather stones to build a new temple, but the priests who came to bless the place realized that the quantity of stones meant the temple would be for human sacrifice, and they warned the people, who were the potential offerings. Taking note of the priests' caution, the people were able to convince the chief to help them by pushing the tree from below while they pulled it from above. The "men pulled at the tree until half the distance up the cliff was covered, then they released the rope. The great tree rolled over on top of the chief and death came to the oppressor [alii hooluhi]" (90–91).

The people were warned by the priests, but they did not retaliate directly. Rather, it was the chief's vanity in taking the role of pushing the log rather than pulling it, a role that should have been for his people, that killed him.

Another despotic chief mentioned by Malo is Kamai'ole. Kamai'ole had taken away the chiefdom from another ruling chief Kanipahu, who was exiled to the island of Moloka'i. Kamai'ole was known for taking the wives of other men and refusing to give them back. "Therefore the maka'āinana were very angry at Kamai'ole. They secretly went to ask [the priest-prophet] Pā'ao how Kamai'ole could be killed" (Malo 298).

Word was sent to Kanipahu calling for his return, but he refused and designated one of his children, Kalapana, as heir. When Kamai'ole traveled by canoe, his canoe would wait until all others had gone ahead, and so at 'Anaeho'omalu, the people and Kalapana, now the designated heir of Kanipahu, waited overnight until all the canoes set sail leaving Kamai'ole's behind. Then they went to kill Kamai'ole (Malo 299).

Among Malo's traditions of chiefs who were killed by the maka'āinana is his statement that "'Ehunuikaimalino was an ali'i who was secretly killed by lawai'a at Keahuolu in the Kona [district on the island of Hawai'i]" (266). This brief passage is the only source we have of a deliberate and outright killing of a high chief by commoners done "secretly." 'Ehunuikaimalino was recognized as the builder of many pathways in the Kona district on the island of Hawai'i and the builder of the famous pu'uhonua 'place of refuge' Hōnaunau (Barrère, "A Reconstruction" 117). According to Kamakau, the chief 'Umi-a-Līloa took over as ruler of 'Ehu's kingdom when 'Ehu was in his old age (*Ruling Chiefs* 19). Typically for the tradition of 'Ehunuikaimalino, of which we are missing many pieces, Malo does not tell us why fishermen would kill such an elderly high chief and in such a manner.

In Malo's concluding chapters on the traditions of the ali'i, he seems to emphasize the difference between good and bad chiefs as being instructive points to remember. We can see this in Malo's description of the very early ali'i, Waia.

> In the words of the Hawaiian Island's people of old,
> Waia('s) chiefdom was very hewa (*bad*), because he went
> about [only] seeking after entertainment, sports and
> pleasures. He had abandoned the orders of his parents
> to be religious (haipule) and to properly care for the

chiefdom, and to care for the maka'āinana [*commoners*]
so that his reign would [be] beneficial. (295)

In Waia we have a chief who is not actively oppressive, but who
is still considered a bad chief because he neglects his duty to properly
care (mālama pono) for both chiefs and commoners.

Other Chiefs Kamehameha Wanted his Son to Remember

To learn about the other chiefs that Kamehameha wanted his
son to know (Lonoikamakahiki, Keākealaniwahine, Kalani'opu'u,
Kamalālāwalu, KauhiaKama), we have to look at the history written
by other native Hawaiian historians, Samuel Manaiakalani Kamakau
and John Papa 'Ī'ī.

The traditions of Lonoikamakahiki (Hawai'i), Kamalālāwalu
(Maui) and KauhiaKama (Maui) are contemporary with each
other. Lono and Kama were rival chiefs and Kauhi was the son of
Kama. Kamakau states that Lonoikamakahiki "proved to be a bad-
tempered chief, who was jealous of his wife because of her beauty,
and frequently gave her a beating" (*Ruling Chiefs* 47). According
to Kamakau, Lono killed his wife in a jealous fit and became
temporarily insane. After wandering in the wilderness and suffering
"cold, chill, hunger, poverty, and lack of clothing," he was able to
recover, and "he attended to the affairs of his kingdom. [. . .] He
became a chief who earned the gratitude of his subjects[1]" (*Ruling
Chiefs* 48).

Kamakau describes Kamalālāwalu as someone who "grew weary
of continued peace with the chiefs of Hawaii, and desired to make
war against the chiefs of Kohala, Kona, and Ka-'u" (*Ruling Chiefs*
55). In waging his war, "Kama-lala-walu, the heedless chief, paid
no attention, but followed the advice of two old men of Kawaiahae
who counseled falsely" (*Ruling Chiefs* 58). He died at the battle at
Pu'u'oa'oaka in Waimea on the island of Hawai'i. Kamakau writes
that Kamalālāwalu "was noted for his fearlessness, and he died
bravely before the chiefs and warriors of Hawaii. He showed no fear
or cowardice, but went forward to meet his death. [. . .] [H]is name
became [. . .] attached to his islands as 'Maui, land of Kama.' Ka-uhi-
a-Kama succeeded as ruler of Maui [. . .]" (*Ruling Chiefs* 60–61).

KauhiaKama had been saved during the battle and escaped back to Maui. According to Kamakau, KauhiaKama was saved by Hinau, a "foster son of Lono-i-ka-makahiki." And strangely, Kamakau adds, "Ka-uhi-a-Kama made Hinau's name a famous one. It was said that Ka-uhi-a-Kama was annoyed with Hinau because he was a favorite of Lono-i-ka-makahiki, and sought means of destroying him. It was said that his [Hinau's] eyes were scooped out" (*Ruling Chiefs* 60).

Later KauhiaKama was captured and taken prisoner to O'ahu where his captors "roasted him in an oven, and [. . .] used his skull as a filth pot" (Kamakau, *Ruling Chiefs* 232). His death and desecration were avenged by Kahekili who "punished the chiefs of Oahu for the evil done by their ancestors and avenged the blood these had shed upon the heads of their children" (*Ruling Chiefs* 233).

Now Keākealaniwahine was a descendant of Lonoikamakahiki. She was the daughter of a woman whose parents were of the highest "marriage" of chiefs, that of a brother and sister. It was said of her mother, Keakamahana, that the chiefs of Kona "recognized one as head over all and they all called her their lord. They left the government to her and exalted her" (Kamakau, *Ruling Chiefs* 61). And her grandmother, Kaikilani, the wife of Lonoikamakahiki, was the first female chief to be given the right and responsibility to rule.

Keakamahana, Kamakau tells us, "despised" her mother-in-law and the oldest daughter of her husband. "She had his mother and daughter killed and their bones mistreated. When Iwi-kau-i-ka-ua discovered that his mother and daughter had been secretly murdered, his mind became possessed with a desire to desert his wife and betray her government to the chiefs of Hilo." He left Keakamahana and lived on the island of O'ahu and married there having a son. This son, upon maturity, went back to the island of Hawai'i and married his half-sister, Keākealani (Kamakau, *Ruling Chiefs* 62).

When Keākealani ruled over Kona, there was a war with the chiefs of Hilo, and the Kona forces lost (Kamakau, *Ruling Chiefs* 62–63). "Kona's chiefs fled to their fortresses, and Keakea-lani and others were taken captive when the Hilo chiefs won. Keakea-lani and her company were sent as prisoners to Maui and to Molokai. Keakea-lani was restored to Kohala where she ruled, in name only, over the districts of Kohala, Kona, and Ka-'u" (Kamakau, *Ruling Chiefs* 63).

Kalaniʻōpuʻu, the paramount chief over the island of Hawaiʻi, was succeeded by Alapaʻi, whose grandfather had been the kuhina kaua nui 'executive officer of war' for Keākealani (Kamakau, *Ruling Chiefs* 76). So the chiefs that Kamehameha was using to instruct his son were not only of recent memory, but they were also closely related and contemporaries of each other.

Kalaniʻōpuʻu was the paramount chief whom Kamehameha served under as a young warrior. Kamakau describes Kalaniʻōpuʻu as "[a] clever chief [. . .] and an able one, famous as an athlete in all games of strength [. . .]. But he had one great fault; he loved war and display and had no regard for another's right over land [. . .]" (*Ruling Chiefs* 79).

In storytelling there are two sides to the telling of the story: that of the story teller and that of the audience. What was Kamehameha trying to teach, to transmit to his son Liholiho, the heir apparent? And what did Liholiho hear? There are many examples that can be drawn out of the lives and experiences of the aliʻi Kamehameha used. We should instantly notice the following traits and behaviors: bad-tempered, jealous, physically and mentally abusive, heedless of good advice, and vengeful.

Hewa and Pono

That kind of behavior is what Malo described as "hewa"—bad and inappropriate, and they are part of the copious list that Malo gives. In fact, Malo devotes a whole chapter in his writings to what we today would call morals or ethical behavior, and in doing so he may have been the only native writer to give us such a detailed account. We might assume, by the sheer number of examples of hewa within these traditions we are told Kamehameha chose for his son to learn from, that the nature of hewa in relationship to the ruling chief was what Kamehameha was trying to emphasize to his son. If hewa is not the appropriate behavior of "a true chief," then what is?

We have already seen the answer to this question in some of the traditions previously mentioned. Malo speaks of a "just and caring" chief (177) "alii hoomalu pono" (33), "to be religious (haipule) and to properly care" (295) "malama pono" (122) for the chiefdom and the commoners. We can start to understand the qualities that make a good chief in this account of Kamehameha's response to his son's behavior.

> While the young chief [Liholiho] and a group of chiefs
> were in their presence, Kalanimoku asked, "What do
> you think? Shall we wrest the kingdom from your father
> [Kamehameha], make you king, and put him to death?"
>
> Liholiho bowed his head in meditation before he looked
> at the gathering, and answered, "I do not want my father
> to die." This reply brought forth the admiration of all of
> the chiefs.
>
> Kinopu, Kamehameha's messenger, returned before the
> company reached Honolulu and told Kamehameha all
> he had seen and heard, including the reply the young
> chief had made. When the king heard what the young
> chief had said he was touched and stated, "He is indeed
> a chief. He did not side with his guardian although he
> knew everything that had gone on. He chose patience
> rather than the kingdom. That is the nature of a true
> chief." (Ii 51)

Malo wrote that "[i]f all the people knew that he was an ali'i haipule [*religious* ali'i], who properly took care of the god (ke akua), then all the people desired that ali'i [to be theirs]. The ali'i haipule(s) were greatly desired persons from the old days. The ali'i haipule(s) were honored persons" (261).

This sentiment was stated to Kahahana, the ruling chief of O'ahu by his prophet, Ka'opulupulu when Kahahana indicated that he wanted to complete a tour of the island restoring "the houses dedicated to the gods" (Kamakau, *Ruling Chiefs* 133).

> 'It is a good wish, O chief! for the gods are the pillars of
> the dominion [. . .]. The gods give such life to a religious
> person, and none shall rebel against his rule. If the land
> becomes poor or suffers from famine or is scorched by
> the sun or lacks fish or servitors, the gods can be found
> in Kahikimelemele. There are two roads for the chief
> to take about the island, one which will support the
> dominion and make it fast so that it shall remain fixed

and immovable, a second which will give the dominion
to others.' (Kamakau, *Ruling Chiefs* 133–134)

    ⮚ So, religious is one word we can use to describe a good leader.

Kamakau tells of how two of the aliʻi, Lonoikamakahiki and
Kamalālāwalu, were able to overcome their hewa through living in
adversity or demonstrating courage and bravery, and then they were
well-remembered aliʻi.

In fact, we find in the traditions of an earlier aliʻi, KihaaPiʻilani, a
similar story of adversity in his youth.

> He patiently bore his troubles knowing that he would
> not die, and that the kingdom of Maui would yet be
> his. He would become a famous ruler according to the
> predictions of those who reared him. ʻHe would have
> many troubles, live in poverty, and become a famous
> ruler.' Kiha-a-Piʻi-lani bore his troubles, his poverty, and
> his homeless state patiently. (Kamakau, *Ruling Chiefs* 22)

It appears that such historical experiences were made part of the
formal education of young aliʻi.

> Furthermore, during the youth of the aliʻi ʻaimoku
> [*paramount chief of district or island*], they were sent out
> to live with wise and skilled people, and to listen first to
> the words of experts and to the important things that
> would benefit their rule. They were to first show bravery
> in combat and in wisdom and to do these things without
> any hesitation.
>
> Furthermore, [these young people] would initially live
> with another aliʻi in a state of poverty, starvation and
> famine so they would remember what these conditions
> of life were like. (Malo 173)

    ⮚ So, another word we can use to describe a good leader is
      patience.

In the statement above, Malo also gives us another clue in the
words, "listen first to the words of experts." If we look back at the

tradition of Kamalālāwalu, we noted that he was heedless of good advice. The disregard for good counsel is also to be found in the tradition of Keli'iokaloa, the eldest son of 'UmiaLīloa.

> While he [Keli'iokaloa] reigned, he took good care of his kingdom, his god, the priests and prophets of the god, and the common people. He lived a righteous life and heeded the teachings of the priests and prophets, but did not mind his father's advice to take care of the chiefs, the old men and old women, the orphans and the poor. When he deserted the advice of the wise, he paid attention to that of fools, thus forsaking the teachings of his father and the learned men of his kingdom. He deserted the god and oppressed the people. (Kamakau, *Ruling Chiefs* 34–35)

Malo even gives us a very vivid idea of how the ali'i sought good counsel.

> When the sun set lamps were light [sic] and the ali'i ate [their meal]. Those who came in to eat with him or her [the ali'i] were called lanika'e. Those who came in late at night were called poho kano. They only talked by lamp light (kukui) and did not eat anything. The people who stayed with the ali'i at the dawn's lamp light were called makou because makou was the name of the lamp. (179–180)

> [. .] If they [the kālaimoku(s)] desired to speak with the ali'i nui then they went to his hale manawa, and sent for the ali'i nui('s) lomilomi [*masseur*] to find the ali'i nui. [When he was located], they all (lākou) secretly conversed together. This conversation was called 'aha kūkā malu, and when it was over they all returned to their own hale(s).

> If the ali'i(s) directly below [in rank of the ali'i nui] wanted to converse with the ali'i nui on matters regarding the chiefdom, perhaps on the topic of war, then the ali'i nui secretly sent for the kālaimoku(s) to talk with him. The ali'i nui listened to all their (lākou) advice (pono) and then they left.

> When the aliʻi nui met (ʻaha ʻōlelo) with all the aliʻi
> below him in rank, he listened only to what every aliʻi
> had to say. If the aliʻi nui recognized what one aliʻi of his
> said, for it was similar to his kālaimoku(sʼ) advice that
> had been secretly heard, then the aliʻi nui agreed to this
> aliʻi(ʼs) words. (266–267)

Maloʻs description of the possible processes of counsel also indicates that it is not just listening that is important for the aliʻi, but it is also important to analyze many views and opinions. In such a dilemma, it appears that an aliʻi would defer to the counsel of his kālaimoku or chief counselor.

    ❧ So, listening and heeding good advice must be added to the
       list of the qualities of a good leader.

Kamakau wrote of Keliʻiokaloa that "he took good care of his kingdom, his god, the priests and prophets of the god, and the common people" (*Ruling Chiefs* 35), and Malo calls Kamehameha an "alii hoomalu pono" (33) ʻchief who is just and caring.ʼ

Kamakau also gives examples of two opposing chiefs on the island of Maui during the time of Kahekili and Kamehameha. Kahekili had appointed Kalanikūpule to rule over Maui.

> Ka-lani-ku-pule was a chief praised for his freedom from
> pretentiousness. He loved the common people, would
> fraternize with the humblest, and was not haughty. He
> was spoken of thus:
>
> *Ku moku paupau*
> *Ko Kanekope - pau e -*
> *Pa-u kahu akua o mua - hilu - e*
> *Ko noho ana i ka haumanumanu*
> *Ko - ki – e*
>
> Standing upon the lowland
> Your chiefly grandeur is gone,
> Your divine state is set aside; although dignified
> You live humbly,
> Very humbly.
> (*Ruling Chiefs* 142–143)

The chiefs of Hawai'i occupied the eastern side of Maui in Hāna and Kīpahulu. Among those chiefs was the younger brother of Kamehameha, KalanimālokulokuiKepo'okalani. Kamakau wrote that, "[h]e protected the rights of the common people, and while he lived in Kipahulu and Hana there was no sugar cane broken off, no potatoes dug up, no pigs roasted. The common people loved him and called him 'The good chief' (*Ke-ali'i-maika'i*) in praise of his kind deeds, and that is why his life was spared when he was about to be made prisoner in war" (*Ruling Chiefs* 143).

In particular, the kindness of both chiefs shows in the way they exercised the chiefly prerogative, for "[a]n ali'i would be known to only plunder, another to up root things, another to kill and another to collect or to heap things up" (Malo 177). These "good chiefs" did not do those things, and they commanded their forces not to touch the property of the commoners.

ᴂ So, we can add caring to the list of words used to describe a good leader.

Another example of the "good chief" comes from the tradition of the chief Kalaunui'ōhua. Although it is not as well remembered as Kamehameha's feat in unifying the islands in modern Hawaiian history, this tradition records the last time before Kamehameha's success that an attempt was made to re-unify the islands since it was first accomplished by the chief Kuali'i.

Again from Malo's account, we learn that Kalaunui'ōhua obtained a great power through being possessed 'akua noho.' Malo tells us that in order to have gotten that power Kalaunui'ōhua had to be "patient enough until the day turns to night" (300). Of course, he wasn't. Nonetheless, the god, Kānenuiākea, took possession of his hand, and "Kalaunui'ōhua was very powerful and if his hand pointed to do battle with another district then this district would flee" (301).

Kalaunui'ōhua was able to conquer Maui, Moloka'i and O'ahu. The ruling chiefs were spared and made kia'āina 'governor,' "*Lit.*, prop [of the] land" (Pukui and Elbert 1986: 146) under Kalaunui'ōhua's rule. However, when he engaged the island of Kaua'i in battle, the power of his hand departed, and Kalaunui'ōhua was defeated by the ruling chief, Kūkona. Kalaunui'ōhua, Kamalu'ōhua of Maui, Kahoku'ōhua of Moloka'i, and Huai[ka]pouleilei of O'ahu were taken prisoners, known as hua.

> Kūkona was kind to them and one day he stayed alone with these captured hua. Kūkona seemed to fall asleep (moe uku la), but he was really not asleep. He was pretending (ho'okalakupua) so he could observe them from the inside of his ahu [*blanket*].

> The hua thought that he was fast asleep and they plotted to kill him. The hua of O'ahu, Moloka'i and Hawai'i vowed [in agreement] to kill him.

> Kamalu'ōhua, who was Maui's hua, said, 'We must not harm (hana 'ino) Kūkona, because he has been good to us. We are in his hands. He has not killed us, therefore we should be fair [hana maika'i] to him.'

> Then Kūkona got up. He said to them, 'My rest has been good. You people plotted to kill me and he is the one who saved me.' (Kamalu'ōhua was the one he pointed to.)

> They admitted it and Kūkona said [to them] that because of the fairness of Kamalu'ōhua's thought, 'You shall all receive my pardon (pōmaika'i), because he thought that life is a very important thing as is the protection of living.

> Because of the pono [*just or goodness*] of Kamalu'ōhua, I will send you all back. You will return in victory to your own islands. I have no thought of ruling over you. You and your lands will be the same as before.' (Malo 302)

Now comes Malo's point.

> Because of the life of Kūkona, Kamehameha I remembered it. This is why Kamehameha spared Kaumuali'i at their meeting in Honolulu on the island of O'ahu. (302)

In the Hawaiian text, the now familiar words maika'i and pono are used to describe the actions of both chiefs: Kalaunui'ōhua's treatment of his hua is "hana maika'i," and Kamalu'ōhua's wisdom is "pono." But what is more remarkable is Malo's point that Kamehameha had heard the tradition before, remembered it, and then followed its wisdom when he had the opportunity to do so.

As our examples have changed in their nature from emphasizing hewa to emphasizing pono so must our question: What and who is a good chief? We have learned there are two different words in Hawaiian for *good*—maikaʻi and pono. We have seen how Kamehameha's younger brother was given the name Kealiʻimaikaʻi 'the good chief' because of his good deeds and kindness. We also recall that Malo calls Kamehameha a pono chief 'a just or fair' chief. This title tells us that his goodness is derived not only from his behavior, but from his morals and decision-making as well.

The Pono of Kamehameha

What made Kamehameha pono? Although Malo makes the claim, he doesn't explain in detail why. However, Kamakau does so in a way we call helu, that is, to count or account for his greatness. And yet we must be a bit cautious, for even Kamakau reveals that Kamehameha "did this in order that the people might speak of his kindness and of the pains he took to care for the chiefs and the people; the orators were instructed to speak of his kind acts" (*Ruling Chiefs* 178).

This is the account Kamakau gives of Kamehameha.

- ❧ Kamehameha had a deliberative council consisting of his counselors and chiefs [. . .] and these persons handled the affairs of government in matters of war or of the welfare of the people (*Ruling Chiefs* 175).
- ❧ Kamehameha always listened to the advice of orators, diviners, kahunas, and men of skill (*Ruling Chiefs* 181).
- ❧ He sought out men who had knowledge of old methods of warfare and made them members of his council (*Ruling Chiefs* 175).
- ❧ Kamehameha made laws to protect both chiefs and commoners, prohibiting murder, theft, wanton destruction of property, the taking of property without cause, robbing the weak, praying to death, and laws to observe the tabus of the gods (*Ruling Chiefs* 175–176).

- He also regulated the fishermen (*Ruling Chiefs* 176).
- He used himself to take part in the work, no matter what kind it was (*Ruling Chiefs* 176).
- He placed restrictions on sea fisheries for periods of five months [. . .] (*Ruling Chiefs* 177).
- He also appointed kahunas as craftsmen [. . .].Wai-pa' he appointed at the head of all these crafts (*Ruling Chiefs* 176–177).
- He appointed tax gatherers for large and small properties [. . .], the larger lands paying larger taxes and the smaller lands smaller taxes (*Ruling Chiefs* 177).
- Kamehameha selected men to act as teachers in the arts of wrestling (*ku'ialua*) [and other sports] [. . .], the configurations of the earth (*papa hulihonua*), wound healing (*lonopu'ha'*), and all the arts of the kahuna (*Ruling Chiefs* 178).
- Kamehameha built heiaus for his gods (*Ruling Chiefs* 179).
- Kamehameha established yearly feasts as a time of rest from labor [. . .] (*Ruling Chiefs* 180).
- He was a patient chief and did not instantly avenge an injury (*Ruling Chiefs* 181).
- Kamehameha respected his wives and gave them wealth and honor (*Ruling Chiefs* 183).

Fornander adds to this reputation.

> He 'lii naauao loa o Kamehameha, he 'lii hana pololei, he 'lii oluolu, he 'lii lokomaikai, he 'lii malama kanaka (V: 477).

> Kamehameha was a very wise king, and was honest, kind, charitable and humane (V: 476).

There are a lot of stories about Kamehameha that underscore these points.

The first concerns an old man whom Kamehameha had overheard praying before drinking his 'awa. The old man concluded his prayer asking for the preservation of the life of Kamehameha, "Let Kamehameha, the good king, live to be old [. . .]." Kamehameha appeared and asked for some 'awa to drink but was told by the old man that he had used his last bits and pieces and had no more.

Kamehameha promised the old man that he would share "a little 'awa" with him and then commanded that a huge amount of 'awa, food, and kapa (clothing) be sent to the old man (Kamakau, *Ruling Chiefs* 182).

Kamakau then tells us, "At another time Kamehameha saw an old man with his grandson on his way home" carrying a heavy load of kī roots. Kamehameha wanted to help the old man carry the load, but the old man believed that Kamehameha was a robber, and he invoked the kapu 'law' that Kamehameha had proclaimed prohibiting robbery and the molesting of old people. The old man declared when asked if Kamehameha is a good chief, "Yes, Pai'ea is a good chief. He makes the old man and the old woman to sleep [without fear] by the roadside. He is a good chief; it is his favorites who are bad and rob others" (*Ruling Chiefs* 182–183). When Kamehameha had put down the old man's load, he told the old man not to mention to anyone that this deed had been done. When the old man was overtaken by some of Kamehameha's people, they asked the old man if he had seen Kamehameha pass by, and then the old man realized that it was Kamehameha who had carried his load.

Another short story about Kamehameha was contributed by Mary Kawena Pukui to Laura Green's collection of folklore. It took place after the conquest of O'ahu when a young warrior in Kamehameha's forces claimed to be the "youngest brother" of Kamehameha. His claim was treated as a loud boast, and the young warrior was reported to Kamehameha. The chief sent for the young warrior and in a loud voice said, "Listen! is it true, this thing that I have heard, that you, boaster, have called me, the king, your elder brother?" (Green 31).

The young warrior said that it is true, and Kamehameha was surprised and asked who told him so. The young warrior exclaimed that it was none other than Kamehameha himself when he declared in his rally cry, "'Forward, my brothers, till you drink the bitter waters!' [. . .] When the king heard this just reasoning, he laughed and bade his retainers prepare a feast for his youngest brother" (Green 33).

Although Kamehameha was in his later years when he received the Russian explorer Golovnin, the captain noted the following characteristics of the aged chief and now king.

Tameamea is already very old; he claims to be seventy-
nine years of age. [. . .] he is alert, strong and active,
temperate and sober, never takes strong drink, and eats
very moderately. In him one observes a most amazing
mixture of childish behavior and ripe judgment and
actions that would not disgrace even a European ruler.
His honesty and love of justice are demonstrated by his
behavior. (192)

It should be pretty clear that the idea of pono is much broader in
its meaning than can be described by a single word like *just* or *fair*. In
the closing to *'Ano Lani*, I suggested that pono is at the root of what
Hawaiian leadership is about, "its relationship of rights, privileges
and responsibility to the people" (Ching, Chun, and Pitzer 140).

Malo sums up this broader description of pono in leadership.

If the maka'āinana knew of the mistakes (hewa) of the
ali'i who did wrong, then the maka'āinana also knew of
the righteous ali'i who truly did pono.

The ali'i who slept a lot (hiamoe loa), who indulged in
pleasures and sports (puni le'ale'a), and who was always
arguing, was accused as being cursed, greedy, stingy and
tight.

The ali'i who was moderate, kind, hono mālie [quiet in
manner-Emerson's translation], humble, patient, was
an ali'i greatly desired by the maka'āinana and greatly
beloved.

The ali'i who did wrong while ruling was not a bit beloved
by all the people of his chiefdom. But the ali'i who did
make things better while ruling was continually beloved.

The ali'i who made things better while ruling was liked to
a powerful person, because of his true pono [*goodness*].
The ali'i who spoke badly of another ali'i was hewa [*at
fault*], because of what he said.

If an ali'i 'ai moku spoke badly about another ali'i 'ai
moku, then only the ali'i who spoke badly was at fault to

the aliʻi who had nothing to do with it (noho mālie) [*lit.,
to be still*].

Therefore, the aliʻi who made things better while ruling
was never accused [of anything]. That was how things
were from the old days until now. (269)

Today we face a situation where increasing numbers of divergent
groups claim sovereignty and leadership. Added to this is the outside
pressure by media- and American-influenced politics for a unified
Native Hawaiian response and plan. Today's challenges demand the
kind of traditional leadership formulated by Kamehameha.

But what makes his legacy and style of leadership seem nearly
impossible to duplicate is that it has become legendary.

The night before Kamehameha was born, we are told, a comet
was seen in the Hawaiian sky. Kamakau tells us, "It is said that there
was rain, thunder, and lightning on the night when Kamehameha
was born" (*Ruling Chiefs* 68). He also says "[t]he night was very
rainy. It was hard to find a fit place for the birth, and it was hence on
one of the *lanai* adjoining the guest-house that the mother suffered
the first pains of childbirth" (*Ruling Chiefs* 67).

Then Kamakau adds more drama to this account.

A numerous guard had been set to await the time of birth.
The chiefs kept awake with the guards [for a time], but
due to the rain and the cold, the chiefs fell asleep, and
near daybreak Ke-kuʻi-apo-iwa went into the house and,
turning her face to the side of the house at the gable end,
braced her feet against the wall. A certain stranger was
outside the house listening, and when he heard the sound
of the last bearing-down pain (*kuakoko*), he lifted the
thatch at the side of the house, and made a hole above.
As soon as the child was born, had slipped down upon
the tapa spread out to receive it, and Ke-kuʻi-apo-iwa
had stood up and let the afterbirth (*ewe*) come away, he
covered the child in the tapa and carried it away. When the
chiefs awoke they were puzzled at the disappearance of the
child. Kohala was searched that day and houses burned.
(*Ruling Chiefs* 67)

The heightened drama of this birth and the reason for the disappearance of the new-born baby comes from the words of a rival chief, Keawemauhili.

> Pinch off the tip of the young mulberry [wauke] shoot.
> (Desha 26)

To the modern, and somewhat Hollywood-influenced, mind, this smacks of those heroic, greater-than-life scenes of Moses in the basket among the reeds. Some of the stories of Kamehameha's youth and early adult life—the moving of the Naha stone that fulfilled a prophecy of greatness, or the fending off of the spears of forty warriors—might have come from the feats of Hercules for their sheer strength, daring, and bravery or from the legends of King Arthur.

This engraving shows Kamehameha warding off the spears of many warriors.

The point of these traditions is not whether they are right or wrong. These traditions were told and embellished to give Kamehameha all the qualities of a demi-god embodied in a chief and leader. In many ways, it is a similar approach to that of the writers of the Christian gospels who sought to emphasize the fulfillment of the words of the prophets of the Old Testament in the life of Jesus of Nazareth, or of the scribes who told of the compassionate deeds of Buddha.

I wrote the following ten years ago about the fabled image of Kamehameha.

> By immortalizing Kamehameha to mythical proportions we have also idealized his standards of leadership and conduct, his *pono*, as the measure of leadership in the Native Hawaiian community. [. . .]
>
> Unlike *aliʻi* before him, Kamehameha forged a new way of governance that might meet the challenges enabling his people to survive in a greater world, but one based in continuity with traditions. The success of that formulation has challenged each generation since his time to uphold or surpass it, until there comes another who will remake it in a way never done before. Until that time his *pono* endures.
>
> Perhaps during a night that is very rainy, when there is thunder and lightning, in what the people of old called ʻIkuwā, the season of the roaring surf, thunder and cloudbursts, the din and voices of the gods in the elements, another child will be born to the hushed whispers of, ʻIs this the one? Is this the next Kamehameha?ʼ (Ching, Chun, and Pitzer 143)

This idealization, and now myth, of Kamehameha is still very pervasive and may take on further epic and popular proportions with the promise of two Hollywood-style biographical movies about him.

However, it would be clear to anyone who thought about it that Kamehameha was only human, and it is not hard, if we look a bit closer at the accounts of his life, to discover his frailties and faults. One of the younger wives of Kamehameha informed Hiram Bingham of his abusive nature.

> Kalakua, the late governess of Maui, who gave me much of Kamehameha's domestic history, says of him, ʻ*He kanaka pepehi no ia; aole mea e ana ai kona inaina.*

He was a man of violence,—nothing would pacify his wrath.'

And,

[Kalakua] said she was once beaten by him, with a stone, upon her head, till she bled profusely, when in circumstances demanding his kindest indulgence and care, as a husband. (Bingham 54)

In 1809, the same year her father had died, Ka'ahumanu, it was reported, took a young lover. He was Kanihonui, a nephew of Kamehameha through his half-sister, Kalanikaulihiwakama on their mother's side (Keku'iapoiwa).

Ka-'ahu-manu was under the influence of liquor when she first gave way to her desire and, ignoring Kamehameha's prohibition, slept with Ka-niho-nui; and she continued this practice while Kamehameha was away worshiping in the god house until the guard [. . .] finally informed the chief; and Ka-niho-nui was put to death. [. . .] He was a great favorite with Kamehameha and with all the chiefs as well, for he was unusually good-looking, finely formed from head to foot [. . .]. He was just nineteen [. . .]. It was wrong in Kamehameha to put the boy to death, but he was killed not only for breaking the law for taking the property of another. Kamehameha [. . .] feared lest, if Ka-'ahu-manu had a lover among the chiefs, it would lead to her rebelling against his rule, drawing her relatives away with her, and thus destroying the commoners. There was a rumor that rebellion was brewing, and hence he put his own [foster] son to death in order to put fear into the hearts of the chiefs. (Kamakau, *Ruling Chiefs* 194)

Kamehameha used a similar strategy of imposing fear upon a population during his war campaigns. It was this fear held by the commoners of the raiding parties of Kamehameha that led to his near death in Puna at the hands of the fishermen there. Kamakau gives a short version of the event.

[. . .] Kamehameha and Ka-haku'i paddled to Papa'i
and on to Kea'au in Puna where some men and women
were fishing, and a little child sat on the back of one of
the men. Seeing them about to go away, Kamehameha
leaped from his canoe intending to catch and kill the
men, but they all escaped with the women except two
men who stayed to protect the man with the child.
During the struggle Kamehameha caught his foot in a
crevice of the rock and was stuck fast; and the fishermen
beat him over the head with a paddle. Had it not been
that one of the men was hampered with the child and
their ignorance that this was Kamehameha with whom
they were struggling, Kamehameha would have been
killed that day. This quarrel was named Ka-lele-iki,
and from the striking of Kamehameha's head with a
paddle came the law of Mamala-hoe (Broken paddle) for
Kamehameha.*[2] (*Ruling Chiefs* 125–126)

A slightly different version was re-told nearly a hundred years
later by Desha. In this version, Kamehameha peacefully attempted to
converse with the people of the area.

We entered there because we saw some fisher-folk
mending their nets. However, the remarkable thing was
that when they saw us they ran away. I attempted to call
to them, but they would not listen and only increased
their speed. (214)

This revisionist history should not surprise us, as it is common
with the stories of Kamehameha. Another famous, or infamous,
example is the kapu Kamehameha placed upon the cattle given to
him by Captain Vancouver, which protected them and allowed them
free range. The end result was an environmental disaster, a part of
Kamehameha's legacy that is not often recounted.

The pervasiveness of the myth of Kamehameha as an ideal
leader makes it hard for us to tease out those qualities that defined
traditional leadership, and especially with Kamehameha, to really
see what it was about him that made his contemporaries describe
him as pono. Add to this the fact that the myth is still being created,

and it becomes even harder. In the popular contemporary song *Hawaii 78*, written by Mickey Ioane and recorded by the late Israel Kamakawiwoʻole, we see another layer of the myth being added when the song talks about highways and condominiums, traffic lights and the modern city life and asks "how would he feel if he saw Hawaiʻi now" (Kamakawiwoʻole 8–10). It goes on to imply that he would be devastated by the Hawaiʻi of today, projecting a modern sense of loss onto him as a logical extension of his pono. And yet, when we go back to the writings of Kamakau we find quite a different image.

> How would it be to have a steam engine at Hilo to make salt until the land is full to overflowing? Or if a steam engine could spout clouds of steam, that would descend and irrigate the mountains of Hualalai so that Kailua might become a land of rivers. That would delight Kamehameha as a result of changing old things for new. (*Ruling Chiefs* 409)

In the current political atmosphere of overt morality, could a personage like Kamehameha survive? Would his strong leadership overcome his frailties? Would he be electable?

We know the legacy of the virtues of pono was exemplified by Kamehameha's grandson and heir, Kamehameha IV when he and his wife, Queen Emma, personally solicited funds from the citizens of Honolulu to build a hospital that would serve a greater population than private doctors could. The monarchs would establish the beginnings of royal patronage that would provide for the social, educational, medical, and spiritual care of Native Hawaiians and those less fortunate in the islands. The institutions they started still exist today as the aliʻi trusts of Bernice Pauahi Bishop, King Lunalilo, Queen Emma, and Queen Liliʻuokalani.

If pono really means that much to the culture, then it ought to be taught and held in great esteem. This appears to be happening more today than just a few years ago. But where in the educational system, formal or ʻohana ʻfamilial,' is it being allowed to be practiced and nurtured? You can teach so-called "values," but if there is no daily application or recognition, then why bother? And the situation gets worse when you consider the political realities that face traditional

This portrait of Kamehameha IV and Queen Emma soliciting funds for the building of Queen's Hospital was based upon accounts of their going into the streets of Honolulu

leadership today. Because our government structure today is not culturally based, there is a sharp divide, and an inherent inequality, between popularly elected officials and traditional leaders. Trustees for the Office of Hawaiian Affairs are popularly elected like any other political office-holder, and trustees for the major ali'i trusts are selected through the court system. Because they are incorporated in the state, these, and other, organizations use a system of selecting their leaders that is not culturally based. Traditional leadership can never be practiced and nurtured in such an environment where the venues for it to exist and thrive are so limited and marginalized.
If the idea and ideal of traditional leadership are to have any significant influence upon our lives, then it must be consciously cultivated.

    ~ Traditional leadership needs to be taught and transmitted to future generations as the way to live and govern.

As Kamehameha had learned the traditions of the chiefs, probably when he was young, so he passed them down to his own son and heir, Liholiho. Through ʻĪʻī's recollections we know that Kamehameha realized that Liholiho had come to understand the responsibility of traditional leadership after some sought to have Kamehameha removed for the death of Kaʻahumanu's favorite, Kanihonui. Kamehameha's response to Liholiho's decision was this.

> ʻHe is indeed a chief. He did not side with his guardian although he knew everything that had gone on. He chose patience rather than the kingdom. That is the nature of a true chief.ʼ (Ii 51)

> ๛ An environment where traditional leadership can be nurtured and practiced needs to be established.

Kamakau asked, "But upon emerging from the school and seeking a place in which to show their skill, what do they find? [. . .] All this learning concerning the circuit of the sun, the planets, the comet, and the nature of the atmosphere of the heavens, even delving down the bowels of the earth like a spider—of what good is it? Where is it leading?" (*Ruling Chiefs* 375). In the same way, today we can ask where we will find opportunities for traditional leadership to be practiced. In other Pacific Island societies, there are councils of chiefs and elders where debate and decision-making are practiced and refined. In such environments, observers can see and hear how speech is used and how decisions are reached through counseling together. The practice of hoʻoponopono used the skills of traditional leadership. But who and where are the traditional leaders, or haku, in the ʻohana today?

> ๛ Traditional leadership needs to be held in esteem, and traditional leaders recognized as equal to, or greater than, elected politicians and popular celebrities.

Kamakau tells us that when Kamehameha sent Haʻaloʻu to meet the prophet Kapoukahi, "Haʻaloʻu knew that no man who understands deep things should go unrecompensed [. . .]" (*Ruling Chiefs* 149). But today what is the reward for traditional leadership and wisdom? In the rarest instances it appears to be a piece of paper, called an award, and maybe a large wooden calabash or ornamental digging stick ('ō'ō). Is that enough to sustain and encourage the pursuit of traditional leadership?

The priest-prophet Ka'opulupulu advised his ruling chief Kahahana that,

> 'Elua na'e alanui o ke ali'i e hele ai e ka'apuni i ka 'āina.
> 1. 'O kēia alanui lā, he alanui 'au'a kēia, 'o [ka] mākia huli honua aupuni kēia, pa'a ke aupuni, 'a'ohe e naue. 2. 'O kēia alanui lā, he alanui lā, he alanui hā'awi aupuni kēia i waho. (Kamakau, *Ke Kumu Aupuni* 86)

> There are two roads for the chief to take about the island, one which will support the dominion and make it fast so that it shall remain fixed and immovable, a second which will give the dominion to others. (Kamakau, *Ruling Chiefs* 134)

The same advice should be heeded when asked why traditional leadership is still necessary in these modern times.

Endnotes
[1] *Ke Au 'Oko'a*, Jan. 12, 1871.
[2] *Ka Nupepa Ku'oko'a*, Mar. 9, 1867.

9 Kākāʻōlelo

Traditions of Oratory and Speech Making

The composers of genealogical chants such as koʻihonua,
haʻikupuna, and kamakua, were men learned in the art who
knew the family lines and were skilled in oratory and state-craft.
Kamakau, *Ruling Chiefs of Hawaii*

✂

Those skilled in speaking and
crafts (hana maoli) were called noʻeau and noʻiau.
Malo, *Ka Moʻolelo Hawaiʻi*

✂

ʻO ka poʻe kālaiʻāina a me ka poʻe kākāʻōlelo, ua nalowale
loa lākou, akā, he poʻe akamai kaulana loa lākou
ma ka hoʻoponopono loea ʻana i ke aupuni.
Kamakau, *Ke Kumu Aupuni*

✂

To a Maori there is a feeling of disappointment with Honolulu.
One would like to stand up on a marae and make a speech
but this is the area of the Pakeha. There are plenty of Hawaiians
here as tram conductors, policemen and other positions.
Sir Peter Te Rangi Hiroa Buck to Sir Apirana Ngata,
27 August 1927

The Gospel according to John begins "In the beginning was the Word [. . .]." The missionary translators for this Gospel chose to use the original Greek *logos* instead of a Hawaiian word. Perhaps they thought the closest equivalent, ʻōlelo, did not express the depth of the word, although translators in Tahiti and Aotearoa (New Zealand) chose to use native terms. It could be that the missionaries here did not learn from their Hawaiian assistants of the proverb "I ka ʻōlelo no ke ola, i ka ʻōlelo no ka make" (Pukui, *ʻŌlelo Noʻeau* 129) 'In the word is life and in the word is death' (Author's translation), which emphasizes the care one needs to place upon what one says and how one says it and on the reliance given to the spoken word.

In a society with no written language—with perhaps the exception of petroglyphs, images, and symbols carved onto lava—what one said, what one remembered, and what one passed on were survival itself. It is said that priests had to memorize all prayers and chants and had to recite them without flaw, else the invocation would not be answered.

This might explain why there is a pause during the high ceremonies on the temples when the priest turns to the high chief and asks a very simple question, "How have the prayers been?" And the high chief answers whether everything had been done all right or not.

Speaking, or speech making, is still a very powerful, respected, and vital part of the culture of the Pacific Islands. In the Western Polynesian islands of Sāmoa, Tonga, and Fiji, orators are esteemed as messengers of wisdom, politics, and culture. In Aotearoa they captivate the attention of locals and visitors on the *marae,* or the traditional grounds, of Māori meeting houses.

> In the Cook Islands the orator of the ariki (high chief) was termed the vaʻa-tuatua (speaking mouth). In Tahiti the office was termed orero (speech). [. . .] Specialization reached its highest in Samoa where a class of hereditary talking chiefs termed tulafale developed. (Buck 166)

In Hawaiian traditions, oratory has been nearly forgotten and hardly studied. Although the importance of Hawaiian language is demonstrated by the increasing number of immersion schools in the state, what one says and how one speaks have yet to be rediscovered.

The title kākāʻōlelo is commonly thought of in its biblical usage as a *scribe*, someone who records information. Today *kākāʻōlelo* is more commonly translated as secretary. However, kākāʻōlelo is the traditional title for an orator, and it is derived from the words kākā meaning to "strike, smite, dash, beat, chop [. . .]" and ʻōlelo, "to speak" (Pukui and Elbert 1986: 117, 284). *Kākāʻōlelo* literally means "to fence [with] words" (119), which sounds more like what lawyers do in courtrooms or politicians do during debates, and reveals how we still use oratory or public speaking today to persuade others. Furthermore, Buck adds that in Hawaiʻi "the kaka-olelo seems to have had the additional function of relating historical stories for the entertainment of the chiefs" (166).

In his article on Polynesian oratory, Buck also noted that "[t]he ancient procedure in Hawaii, where matter-of-fact customs of Western civilization have replaced it, offers an interesting line of study for some student" (167). However, since that time, it appears no one has pursued that challenge, perhaps because our primary

Hawaiian resources, like the writings of the nineteenth century scholars Malo, Kamakau, and 'Ī'ī, have little to offer about kākā'ōlelo.

Oratory in Polynesia

The importance of the orator's position and craft in Hawai'i can be detected by looking carefully at other Pacific Island cultures where we may be able to identify elements similar to those seen in our traditional society.

Among the Māori, oratory "has always been a main avenue for the achievement and exercise of power," and "oratory remains a key technique for persuasion and policy-making" (Salmond, "Mana" 45–46). This is emphasized in the criteria Māori use for those who are orators.

> *Whaikoorero* is governed by an elaborate series of regulations, which vary from tribe to tribe and which stress its dignity as a style of speech. Speakers must qualify by age, seniority of birth (i.e., a younger brother or sons of a living father should not speak), and competence in the conventions of *whaikoorero*, before they may venture to stand upon the *marae*. Women are strictly prohibited to speak in most areas, and any infraction of this rule is summarily punished. (Salmond, "Mana" 47)

The function of orators in Sāmoa is similar where they "pride themselves on their cunning and cleverness. If he wishes to accrue fame, power, and goods, an orator must be continually 'on the move,' seeking arenas for political and oratorical encounters" (Shore 244). While oratory shares this sense of status throughout the Pacific, in traditional times orators had both rank and status.

It is hinted that there was a traditional class of orators in Māori society. "The *rangatira* was an executive chief, chosen for his ability in warfare and oratory, and senior descent was not essential for this role" (Salmond, *Hui* 13). Orators (*'orero*) in Tahiti were sometimes chiefs who spoke for themselves, while others had staff orators to present their ceremonial greetings, public announcements, parliamentary exhortations, and so forth, for them (Oliver 1,031).

Oliver gives this example dated 1799.

> This afternoon the natives held a public meeting near the
> British house when the peace between Otoo, Pomerre, &
> this district was again ratified & confirmed. As all public
> business is transacted between persons called Taaoraro
> or orators, the speakers for Otoo & Pomerre were seated
> on the ground, opposite to each other, about 15 yards
> asunder, each having a bunch of green leaves in his
> hand, (perhaps) as tokens of peace; and there harangued
> upon the subject of their meeting. The spectators kept at
> a proper distance. Otoo was present, but did not seem to
> take much notice of what was doing. (1,031)

Oliver gives a description of the Tahitian orator that is consistent
throughout the Pacific Islands as having "[a]n impressive presence, a
sonorous and tireless voice, mental agility, a memory full of striking
imagery, a knowledge of social etiquette and political realities—all
of these were essential to effective oratory in the domain of tribal
affairs" (1,031). However, he adds that it is not "clear just who such
staff orators were" (1,031). He hints that they were probably not from
the lower classes and more likely chiefly relatives. He also adds that
it is not clear "how they were compensated for their labors, if indeed
they were compensated directly in the form of deliberate payment for
services" (1,031).

The role of orators in Sāmoa is much more clearly defined.
In Sāmoa they are "titled," that is, they are of a class or rank of
men among chiefs who hold a certain title or name. Buck visited
American Sāmoa in 1927 and quickly came to understand the
function and relationship of the chiefs and their talking chiefs. He
wrote to Ngata describing his observation.

> If a chief's party went on a trip round the island (a
> malaga it is called), his party had to know the faʻalupega
> of each village. Under such conditions, it can be
> readily understood that the duty of attending to the
> ceremonial speeches, division of food etc, became
> entrusted to particular chiefs. They became the talking
> chiefs or tulafale and in time attended to all the business

and ceremonial aspects of village life. The office also
became hereditary and in time the tulafale added
to the ceremonial and rendered himself absolutely
indispensable to the social organisation. In fact the
high chief became a figure head and the tulafale the
counsellors and real rulers of the tribe. They are the
scholars and keepers of the tribal lore. The tulafale
apportioned the amount of food each family head, matai,
had to contribute to the village feasts etc. He was in
close absolute touch with the community and with the
other tulafale in the village, he ruled the roost. The fines
and penalties for infringement of law and custom were
adjudicated upon by the tulafale. (Sorrenson I: 57)

What Buck observed continues today as another anthropologist,
Bradd Shore, relates this particularly detailed account in which an
orator (*tulāfale*) describes his role.

The *tulāfale* really suffers in his service to the *aliʻi*. The
aliʻi just sits, and the only hardship he suffers is the
giving of money and mats to the orator. But the orator—
if he hears that guests have arrived, he is off in a flash to
greet them. [. . .]

He comes back with the *ālaga* [leg joint of pork reserved
for senior orators]. [. . .] It's the hard work that wins
the handout [*lafoga*]. That thing called an *aliʻi*, we really
have pity for him, for he gets only poverty. The *aliʻi*—he
gives away and gives away, but the orator gets everything
for free. He gets his money, fine mats, tapa cloths. The
aliʻi, he just stays put, sits still, and suffers for giving
everything to the orator. (244)

Given these clearly defined roles, one would think the
relationship between the *aliʻi* and the *tulāfale* would be formal and
clear, but Shore points out it is far from that. "Within village affairs,
the *faleʻupolu* (body of orators) has interests that are remote from
any specific tie with *aliʻi*. The balance between the active, functional
role of the orators and the more passive dignity of the *aliʻi* is often
unstable" (244).

Another of Shore's informants, described as "an elderly *aliʻi* with a particularly acute analytical capacity" (242), gave this description of the differences between *aliʻi* and *tulāfale*.

> The separation between the *tulāfale* and the *aliʻi* happened like this. This is my opinion on the matter. There are two things within each person: the power to command [*faʻatonuga*] and the power to execute those commands [*faʻataunuʻuga*]. *Each person has both of these potential powers.* This is how that class, the *tulāfale*, became important. They were not, in the old days, called *tulāfale*. But that title began with the Tui Manuʻa when he said to those bearers, "I shall call you *tulāfale* and I shall assign to you the job of realizing or executing my dignity [*laʻu afio*]. So that the Tui Manuʻa held on to the *pule* [authority/secular power], but the realization of that *pule* was given to these other men.
>
> [. . .] Today we have this group of people called *tulāfale* who are like slaves, because of what happened in Manuʻa. We have the class of *tulāfale*. These men carried the dignity of the Tui Manuʻa. Things have changed since those days, but that is how we have today people who give the orders, and people who carry them out. (emphasis in original) (242)

It is apparent from Shore's work that Samoan orators wield great power and influence in their society, although he also states that the balance between the orator and the *aliʻi* is occasionally upset. A possible solution to this problem for some villages has been the combination of both titles, a *tulāfale-aliʻi*.

> He [a tulāfale-aliʻi] may speak on his behalf, holding flywhisk and staff as any senior orator would. He also has certain rights associated with aliʻi status, such as a special kava name, a taupou title, the right to sit at the matua tala (front post) of the meeting house or to wear a tuiga (headdress). The tulāfale-aliʻi may give away fine mats and money as an aliʻi, but he may also receive them in his capacity as orator. The dual status enables the chief to keep a tighter control over his political and economic affairs. (Shore 245)

Hawaiian Orators: The Kālaimoku

While a single person may function as both *tulāfale* and *aliʻi* in Sāmoa, he does not function in both roles at the same time. Hawaiian scholar Davida Malo described a similar relationship for the Hawaiian aliʻi and his head counselor, the kālaimoku. In fact, Malo's only reference to the role of an orator is in reference to the kālaimoku, which is surprisingly quite similar to the description of the Māori *rangatira*: "The person skilled in the oratory [kākāʻōlelo] of the chiefdom was the kālaimoku [. . .]," and "Those skilled in speaking [ʻōlelo] and crafts (hana maoli) were called noʻeau and noʻiau" (178).

Malo says that, like the *tulāfale*, the kālaimoku and the kahuna pule kiʻi 'priest in charge of the prayers of the images or gods' "ran the chiefdom. They guided the head [aliʻi nui] of the chiefdom to where they had thought it was best [to go]" (258). Malo says that the kālaimoku was in charge of matters concerning war and the protection of the things of the aliʻi nui(ʻs) chiefdom.

The authority and influence of the kālaimoku appears to be greater than that of other aliʻi, although the kālaimoku did not necessarily have to be an aliʻi. Malo tells us that when the aliʻi nui consulted with his chiefs, he may or may not have taken their advice.

> If the aliʻi nui recognized what one aliʻi of his said, for it was similar to his kālaimoku(sʻ) advice that had been secretly heard, then the aliʻi nui agreed to this aliʻi(ʻs) words. If the aliʻi nui knew that what the aliʻi(s) had to say was not like the advice of the kālaimoku(s), then the aliʻi did not agree with them. That is how the ʻaha ʻōlelo [council of chiefs] of the aliʻi(s) was held. (267)

Kamakau also associates the role of the "orator" with giving advice and counsel. He suggests that the kākāʻōlelo had been schooled not only in the history and deeds of former and present chiefs but also in the words they had used.

> Some time ago your servant (*kauwa*) sent for some of the old people who had lived in the time of Ka-hekili and of Kamehameha I, and we talked about how the government was administered in their day. The old

men said, "In the time of Kamehameha the orators
(*po'e kaka'olelo*) wcre the only ones who spoke before
the ruling chief, those who were learned in the words
spoken by the chiefs who had lived before his day. When
the chief asked, 'What chief has done evil to the land,
and what chief good?' then the orators alone were able to
relate the deeds of the chiefs of old, those who did good
deeds and those who did evil deeds, and the king would
try to act as the chiefs acted who did good deeds in the
past." (*Ruling Chiefs* 399)

The chiefs disputed about the succession while
Kamehameha was living, and Kamehameha asked the
opinion of men skilled in genealogies and of the orators
and those who knew about government in ancient days.
Some of the chiefs and governors thought that the old
standards should not count in the succession. But the
skilled men told Kamehameha that in order to keep
the kingdom united as he left it and prevent its falling
to pieces at his death, he must consolidate it under one
ruler and must leave it to an heir who was in the ruling
line from his ancestors. (*Ruling Chiefs* 429)

The actual functions of the kākā'ōlelo are known in detail,
particularly the actions of Nā'ili and Nāmaka, described in more
detail in the chapter on Ho'oponopono. Nā'ili was an ali'i 'chief'
of Wai'anae, said to be "kekahi kanaka akamai i ke kākā'ōlelo"
(Kamakau, *Ke Kumu Aupuni* 7) 'a person skilled in oratory' who
intervenes in a battle between the chiefs of Maui and Hawai'i against
O'ahu. He was able to disengage the battle, meet with each side to
broker a joint meeting, and then broker peace, not just an end to the
fighting. Nā'ili is able to accomplish this remarkable task because of
his understanding of genealogies and relationships.

Nā'ili was the brother of a woman named Kamaka'imoku, who
was the older relation of the chiefs of Maui and Hawai'i, in particular
Kalani'ōpu'u and Keōua. This is an important piece of information
because those two chiefs were fighting on the side of the invading
chief of Hawai'i named Alapa'i against the O'ahu chief named
Peleiōhōlani. The second piece of information Nā'ili knew is that the

warring chiefs were related, for the name of Keōua had been given by Peleiōhōlani (Kamakau, *Ke Kumu Aupuni* 7, 62). This cessation of conflict also added to the repertoire of orators, Kamakau noted.

I ka pau ʻana o ka hana kuʻikahi e hoʻopau i ke kaua, hoʻi maila ʻo Peleiōhōlani me kāna kākāʻōlelo, ʻo Nāʻili, me kona mau aliʻi a me kona mau koa ma Koʻolau o Molokaʻi. No laila i ʻōlelo kaena iho ai ka poʻe kākāʻōlelo o Hawaiʻi, me ko Maui, " ʻO Peleiōhōlani, ke keiki a Kū, o Hāna." (*Ke Kumu Aupuni* 11)

At the end of the war Kamehameha-nui became ruling chief of Maui. Pele-io-holani retired to Koʻolau on Molokai with his adviser [kākāʻōlelo] Na-ʻili and his chiefs and fighting men. The counselors [kākāʻōlelo] of both Hawaii and Maui boasted, "Pele-io-holani, the son of Ku, belongs to Hana!" (*Ruling Chiefs* 75)

While visiting the islands in 1840, Captain Charles Wilkes was able to obtain a bit of information about a class of genealogist-historians whose counsel would provide sound leadership.

[. . .] the influence of a certain class of men whose business it was to give instruction and rehearse the proverbs handed down from their ancestors. These men often prophesied that judgment would follow if these were neglected; but, notwithstanding, as may readily be supposed, bad rulers contrived to evade the taboos and rules [. . .] (IV: 35–36)

We are able to have a sense of the role of the orator in traditional Hawaiian society from such bits and pieces of information. We have to do the same gathering of information in order to understand what they said; what they meant; and why people, especially the ruling chiefs, listened, or did not listen, to them. It is from the remembered (sometimes brief) speeches and responses that we can detect some of the meaning, the emphasis, the wording, and the arts of traditional oratory. We can discover the structure of oratory by first looking once again to other areas of Polynesia.

The Structure of Oratory in Aotearoa and Sāmoa

There is a structure to Polynesian oratory. Māori oratory has the following generic descriptions, for there are regional variations, of the basic elements found in *whaikōrero*: A speech may begin with a *whakaarara* or *whakatūpato*, a loud warning or shout invoked by the speaker, which is followed by a *tauparapara* or chant that "establish[es] the orator's claim to esoteric knowledge." [. . .] However, "[t]hese *tau* are not always used; on informal occasions they are not really appropriate, and some speakers do not know any" (Salmond, *Hui* 160).

A Māori kaumatua, or elder, speaking in the marae meeting house in Waikato, Aotearoa.

The main body of the *whaikōrero*, as Salmond notes, is "still highly stylised, but unlike the opening chants it is not completely predictable in wording [. . .]. Skilled orators use poetic sayings with an off-hand deftness [. . .]. They coin poetry of their own, or launch into vivid, witty prose, leaving aside the standard structures altogether" (*Hui* 164–165). However, Salmond concludes that "[t]he usual patterns are, all the same, extremely important. They dominate the great majority of speeches and give *whaikōrero* its poetic, structured quality. The use of these phrases, plus a predictable broad sequence of topics, make a general study of *whaikōrero* possible" (*Hui* 165).

By comparison, in Samoan oratory '*lāuga*,' there appear to be distinctions that depend on the place it is delivered, such as at ceremonies or meetings.

> In ceremonial exchanges, the delivery of the lauga is both presented and received with particular attention to all details that enhance the sacred nature of the occasion and make everyone proud of participating in it. In a fono [meeting] however both the speaker and the audience are less concerned with performance per se and some of the canons of verbal art are lifted. . . participants are too worried about what is coming next. The delivery of the lauga in a fono is more like a 'job' that needs to get done than an honor or occasion for the proud display of verbal skills. (Mallon 133)

According to Mallon, who is basing his chapter on the works of two scholars, Tatupu Fa'afetai Mata'afa Tu'i and Alessandro Duranti, there are several parts, or *vāega*, to Samoan oratory. "The structure works as a guide or framework that the orator will work with to suit the requirements of the occasion" (133). The following is compiled from the work of both scholars.

1. Folasaga (also called tuvaoga or paepae-ulufanua) – the introduction or opening address, which includes the fa'alupega, the ceremonial style and the address of an individual, village or district.
2. 'Ava – the kava presentation.
3. Fa'afetai i le alofa o le atua – the references to ancestors and the expressions of gratitude and thanks to God.
4. Taeao – literally, mornings. The recounting of important events in Samoa's history.
5. Pa'ia – greetings of the sacred titles. A reminder of the power of mythical historical figures and their descendants.
6. Faia or mataupu – the agenda.
7. Fa'amatafiga o lagi – literally, the clearing of skies. The wishing of good luck, peace and prosperity to the visitors and then to the orator's own party. (Mallon 133)

There are some common points in these two descriptions of the structure of Polynesian oratory that we may expect to find in Hawaiian literature. We must use some investigative insight and look very carefully for clues, even the most circumstantial, as to where a person was speaking, who they were speaking to or for, and how people reacted to what they heard. We may also ask ourselves such questions as why the speaker chose to say such things and whether he or she could have said otherwise.

Patterns of Speech in Hawai'i

A good example of what we are looking for can be found in the speech given during the council of chiefs at Pohukaina in Honolulu in 1830, where they had gathered to "discuss financial matters" (Kamakau, *Ruling Chiefs* 300), but what they heard were accusations against Liliha, the guardian of the young King Kamehameha III. Kamakau gives a detailed description of that event.

> A few days later a council of chiefs was held at the stone house at Pohukaina where were gathered chiefs, commoners, and foreigners to discuss financial matters. Three chiefesses spoke for the chiefs, Ke-ahi-kuni Ke-kau-'onohi, Ka-ho'ano-ku Kina'u, Kuini Liliha. Ke-kau-'onohi opened with the words which appear so often in newspapers today and which I then heard for the first time—"Hawaii of Keawe, Maui of Kama-lala-walu, Oahu of Kakuhihewa, Kauai of Manokalanipo." [. . .] Kina'u spoke in the same way. Then Liliha spoke to the people: "Chiefs and people of my chief, hear me. The stink of my name and that of my husband Boki has spread from Hawaii to Kauai. It is said that we do evil and that we have led the young king to do evil, and so he has been taken away from me. But we are not guilty; it is the white people and the naval officers who are guilty; it is they who tempted the king, and the blame has been put upon me. But I admit I have done wrong." At these words both native and foreigners shed tears. Then Ka-heihei-malie, who had been sitting on the stairway during the council, rose and spoke about the goodness of God and

urged the people to listen to the words of Ka-'ahu-manu
and Kau-i-ke-aouli and of Nahi-'ena'ena. Then she
added, drawing a figure from the communal method
of fishing for swordfish, "In the time of Kamehameha
the fishermen swam together in a row, and if one got
out of line or lagged behind he was struck by the sharp
nose of the fish. So those who do not follow God's word
and do not obey our king, but fall out of line, they shall
be struck by the sharp sword of the law, so do not lag
behind lest you be hurt." As these words fell upon the
ears of the people, they applied them to Liliha and raised
an uproar and talked of war against Ka-'ahu-manu and
the chiefs. (*Ruling Chiefs* 300–301)

We are told immediately that there was a very diverse audience
gathered, and this was a council of chiefs held at Pohukaina, in some
sort of large building, for some had been "sitting on the stairway
during the council" (*Ruling Chiefs* 300). The area called Pohukaina
is on the "Diamond Head" side of the 'Iolani Palace grounds. There
are three women who speak. They are all chiefs, and each is allowed
to give an address. One of them begins her speech by poetically
referring to all the major islands and their respective historical
ruling chiefs. Kamakau says that this was the first time he had
ever heard that phrasing, but that it had become quite common in
local newspapers. Another form of this address was used again at
Pohukaina a few years later after the death of Ka'ahumanu and was
recorded by 'Ī'ī.

When the king had left on his journey, Kinau gathered
the chiefs, the lesser chiefs, members of the court, and
the people at Pohukaina and began a proclamation to
them, "O you of Hawaii, great island of Keawe; Maui,
island of Kama; Oahu, of Kuihewa; and Kauai, of Mano
. . . Harken to this, you who are from great Hawaii, land
of Keawe, to Kauai, island of Mano. Our royal mother
Kaahumanu is dead [. . .]."

When Kinau finished speaking, Kekauluohi stood up to
speak. "Here am I, of Hawaii a Keawe, of Maui a Kama,
of Oahu a Kuihewa, and of Kauai a Mano. I add my

approval to the words we have just heard. Our *makua*
have gone on their journey, and we have inherited
their duties under the guidance of these children of
Kamehameha. What she has told us is to look after each
other's welfare, and I approve of this."

The multitude expressed their admiration of the two
who spoke, for none had ever heard these words before.
(159)

This clue shows how formal speeches were created with the use
of introductory poetic phrases or proverbs. In this case she uses the
major islands and chiefs to acknowledge all the people of the islands.
Kīna'u's introduction is answered by Kekāulu'ohi, who gives her
support. It is most interesting that 'Ī'ī had noted the admiration of
the audience and that no one "had ever heard these words before"
(159). And so here we have an example of the use of an introductory
phrase or chant to open a speech, as seen in the Māori and Samoan
structure.

Returning to the third speaker in Kamakau's account, we
see that Liliha's speech is so powerful that it makes both natives
and foreigners cry. Why? In her speech she admits and accepts
responsibility for those wrongs. This is what is known as a mihi and
is deserving of the reaction she got; in fact, that response would be
expected in the process of ho'oponopono.

Everything is not over, as we would expect, for suddenly from the
shadows, or rather from the stairway, another chief gets up to speak
and begins her speech referring to the "goodness of God" and to
words attributed to the ruling chiefs and the king himself (Kamakau,
Ruling Chiefs 300). These may have been used either to protect her
position or to give it a sense of legitimacy by using what was said
before to emphasize her point(s). However, she concludes by adding
a traditional proverb about communal fishing. Why does she add this
at the end of her speech?

This proverb appears to sum up the essence of what she was
saying about following the directives of the king and the chiefs. It is
the graphic illustration of her point. We can see, however, that the
audience has a different interpretation in mind once they have heard

the proverb, for they react in outrage with cries, not of emotion, but for warfare and revenge. What happened in a matter of minutes, and why is it that a few words strung together in such a manner can emotionally pull people in radically different ways?

Kaheiheimālie's use of this proverb to underscore the importance of toeing the line enrages those listening to her because it seems to contradict, or put down, Liliha's previous honest and emotional admittance of guilt. It is like a slap in the face, and the result is a cry for war.

While some poetic phrases give an opening, the retention and use of proverbs in speech making is also evidently a most powerful tool or weapon. These proverbs appear to us today as quick phrases of color and illustrative wisdom, but when they were spoken they were part of a speech or conversation. Salmond remarks that "[i]n all speeches, proverbs, historical and mythological allusions decorate the topical structure, and although the audience can broadly predict its content, still the artistry of its expression holds their interest" (*Hui* 171).

Hawaiian Proverbs as Remnants of Speech Making

Parts of many speeches remain with us today in the form of proverbs. The motto used for the state of Hawai'i is an example of this idea of the evolution of such wise sayings. The phrase "Ua mau ke ea o ka 'āina i ka pono," attributed to King Kamehameha III, is well memorized, although perhaps not well translated or understood in its original context. King Kamehameha III is reported to have said this during a speech at Kawaiaha'o Church after the ceremonies held in an open field on the outskirts of Honolulu, a place now known as Thomas Square. The occasion was the restoration of the sovereignty of the kingdom following the illegal seizure and occupation by the British under Captain Lord George Paulet. It is unfortunate that the only records of the king's speech that still exist are in accounts of the events of that day, and this now famous proverb. What most people have not heard is what he said a few months earlier when the seizure and occupation began. His Majesty had issued a proclamation.

> [. . .] chiefs, people, and common[er]s from my ancestor,
> and people from foreign lands? Hear ye, I make known

to you that I am in perplexity by reason of difficulties
into which I have been brought without cause; therefore
I have given away the life of our land, hear ye! But
my rule over you, my people, and your privileges will
continue, for *I have hope that the life of the land will be
restored when my conduct shall be justified.* (italics added
for emphasis) (Kamakau, *Ruling Chiefs* 364)

In this proclamation Kamehameha III uses the term "the life
of the land," the key words of the motto. In the last line of the
proclamation he refers to the restoration of that life, and to the
idea that his decisions and actions will be justified. That word in
Hawaiian is pono. Therefore, the speech he gave a few months
later at Kawaiahaʻo appears to have been a response to his own
proclamation, and the well remembered phrase literally means
that the life of the land, or the sovereignty, (ke ea o ka ʻāina) of the
kingdom would always exist (e mau) when there was justice as he,
himself, had been vindicated (i ka pono).

We still do not know what he actually said beyond this remnant
of his speech. But we do know that it provides a good example of
how many proverbs, including the following, came to be.

- ❧ When Kamehameha heard of this he consulted his counselors
  and those men who understood wise sayings, and they coined
  this phrase, "The fish have entered the net; they are gone into
  the bag." (Kamakau, *Ruling Chiefs* 161)
- ❧ "Open the sluice gate that the fish may enter!" (Kamakau,
  Ruling Chiefs 133). This phrase is attributed to Kaʻopulupulu,
  the high priest and prophet of Kahahana of Oʻahu.
- ❧ They would have been like the words of Mahu-lua to her son,
  Ku-aliʻi, "Take care of the god, and take care of the big man,
  the little man, and the fatherless." (Kamakau, *Ruling Chiefs* 8)
- ❧ When the Kauai chief saw for the first time, by the ovens
  they had left, the size of the camp which Kamehameha had
  occupied he said, "Where a big squid digs itself a hole, there
  crab shells are heaped at the opening." (Kamakau, *Ruling
  Chiefs* 159)

> "Make the chills run up and down, make them teeter like the tail of a plover, make them flutter like the long feathers of the *koaʻe* bird in the wind, sway like the *ʻuwaʻu* bird in the calm, make them scatter and hold their breath!" (Kamakau, *Ruling Chiefs* 153–154). This was the rallying and battle cry of the chief Kaʻiana.

> "Ka-ʻula-hai-malama plays hide and seek; Ke-ku-hau-piʻo (Stands-leaning) is her father; she leans on the canoe side and rests against the back of the canoe (*Peʻekue Ka-ʻula-hai malama, o Ke-ku-hau-piʻo he makua hilinai aʻe i ka palekai, kalale moku aʻe mahope*). This means that she tries to shield the true offender by dodging direct questions" (Kamakau, *Ruling Chiefs* 333).

> "But it was they [the chiefs] who were the wanderers; the people born of the soil remained according to the old saying, 'It is the top stone that rolls down; the stone at the bottom stays where it is' (*O ko luna pohaku no ke kaʻa ilalo, ʻaʻole i hiki i ko lalo pohaku ke kaʻa*)" (Kamakau, *Ruling Chiefs* 376).

> "In the year 1765 a quarrel arose among the descendants of the chief Ke-kau-like Ka-lani-kuʻi-hono-i-ka-moku. [. . .] The quarrel arose through a certain soldier of the guard named Ka-hahana [. . .]. The chiefs distributed fish to the people and left out this man and his wife. [. . .] The Hawaiian text reads, 'I leʻaleʻa ka ʻai ana a na ʻlii i ka ʻai, a me na laulau, me na hoʻolua, a me ka iʻa, ʻono kana ʻai ana me na wahine; i ke ka ʻole ia i ka pohuehue, kaikoʻo ke awa, popoʻi ka nalu, ʻaʻole i ikeia ka poe nana e heʻe ka nalu.' [The chiefs enjoy eating *poi* and *laulau* and meat cooked in ti leaves and fish. Food eaten with the wives is delicious because the *pohuehue* vine had not been smitten to cause rough sea in the harbor where the billows roll so that the riders of the surf could not be seen.] This hidden threat refers to the practice of beating the waves with a length of *pohuehue* (*convolvulus*) vine such as grows by the seashore in order to secure good waves for surfing. [. . .] [That is, anger rises in the heart and he will be avenged.]" (Kamakau, *Ruling Chiefs* 83).

Some of these excerpts were taken from the middle of battle, some from actual meetings of the councils, and others from conversations. They are "poetic" because many times they use objects and actions in nature to describe human behavior. This should not be surprising for a culture that prizes observation as one of its primary learning skills (aʻo) and honors an avoidance of conflict or directness, as found in the process of hoʻoponopono. The use of such sayings targets a limited audience who, by their actions or behavior, should recognize the intended similarities.

Their inventiveness also shows signs of competition and debate, which is evident in the speeches heard at the council of chiefs at Pohukaina. This spirit of competition is seen in *lāuga* and *whaikōrero*, too.

> Oratory can be intensely competitive, and a good or bad performance affects the prestige of not only the orator but also those he represents. Competition is usually strongest for the right to address or speak to an assembly first. The debate over who has this privilege can last a few minutes or more than an hour. [. . .] Engaging in this type of activity is called faʻatau, which literally means 'to provoke contention'. It is in this competitive aspect of oratory that the skills, character and knowledge of an orator first reveal themselves. (Mallon 133–134)

> For most of the time they are listening to one speaker after another through the ritual paces, and they do get bored. The speakers listen to each other in case there is something they can elaborate on later, but the rest of the audience chat, doze, smoke and otherwise divert themselves. [. . .] [T]he occasional brilliant speech stands out all the more; the audience snap out of their passive monitoring of the ritual, and really begin to listen. When a succession of such speakers stands on the *marae*, each one picking up comments, embroidering on them, making jokes or giving vivid accounts of history, taking up errors and subjecting the perpetrator to good natured ridicule, the *marae* comes alive with attention. (Salmond, *Hui* 165)

Riddling Contests as a Form of Speech-making

Such competition of Māori orators was also known in Hawaiian traditions, but as the game of hoʻopaʻapaʻa or "riddling contest." Beckwith gives a vivid description of this art form.

> In such a contest high stakes are set, even to life itself. In more homely usage the art consists in betting on a riddle to be guessed, in a brag upon which the opponent has been induced to put up a bet, or in merely playing with language in a way to entangle the opponent with contradictory and seemingly impossible meanings. Puns were delighted in as a way of matching an opponent or fulfilling a brag. Taunts after the manner of "stringing" a less sophisticated rival must be met with a jibe more bitter. One series of objects of a kind must be matched with another, or a forgotten item, no matter how trivial, added. One object proposed must be met with another analogous in every detail, or its antithesis [. . .] the contestant being careful in every case to follow exactly the words of his opponent, which he must show to apply equally well to the parallel he has chosen. Real knowledge is necessary for such a contest. (*Hawaiian Mythology* 455)

Beckwith uses the actual dialogue between two contestants as a prime example of the form of hoʻopaʻapaʻa, but Kamakau tells of a historical contest between two adults who are both skilled in kākāʻōlelo. Nāmaka was a person well known during the reign of Kalaniʻōpuʻu. He is said to have attached himself to a chief ʻʻimi haku' through the multitude of skills he possessed in the areas of kālaimoku 'administration,' ke kākāʻōlelo 'oratory,' ke kūʻauhau 'genealogies,' ka lonomakaihe 'spear throwing,' ke kuhikuhipuʻuone 'advising the location of sites,' ka lua 'wrestling,' ka lele, 'leaping off cliffs,' and ke kilo 'observing the signs and omens,' all of which he learned on the island of Kauaʻi (Kamakau, *Ruling Chiefs* 111). In this tradition Nāmaka was said to have been challenged by another highly skilled person named Pakuanui of Nuʻuanu on the island of Oʻahu. He was said to have been a skilled person in kākāʻōlelo and lua. Kamakau tells that Pakuanui was "the father of Ka-ʻele-o-waipiʻo, a man of learning of Kamehameha's day who lived at Kailua and composed the dirges to Jesus" (Kamakau, *Ruling Chiefs* 111). They engaged in a series of wrestling moves until finally Pakuanui was able to deftly maneuver Nāmaka over the cliffs of Nuʻuanu, although Nāmaka is said to have been able to use his skills in cliff leaping to land safely below (Kamakau, *Ke Kumu Aupuni* 64).

The other skills he possessed were learned through some formal training, and the implication here is the possibility that hoʻopaʻapaʻa also involved formal training. Beckwith notes that in other Pacific Island cultures skill in the play and use of language was acquired through schools. She writes that "In Tahiti, the study of enigmas and similes, called paraupiri, was a favorite pastime in the schools and women might take part as teachers. Artificial language, proverbs, and plays on words belonged to the aliʻi period of Tahiti [. . .]." In the Marquesas there were "schools of learning [. . .] in which pupils learned the legends, genealogies, and chants. [. . .] Contests of wit were held between the masters of learning [. . .]" (*Hawaiian Mythology* 462).

The example given of "[t]he chiefs enjoy[ing] eating *poi* and *laulau* and meat cooked in ti leaves and fish" is a poetic allegory of "[f]ood eaten with the wives is delicious because the *pohuehue* vine had not been smitten to cause rough sea in the harbor where the billows roll so that the riders of the surf could not be seen" (Kamakau, *Ruling Chiefs* 83) and demonstrates the Hawaiian skills and knowledge needed to create and use such a poetic invention. The opening phrase describes a very happy and delightful occasion, especially with its description of food and pleasure. For men to eat with their wives is considered to be ʻai noa 'free eating,' which is without any restrictions or prohibitions. The speaker then attempts to liken this pleasurable activity to a more dangerous and menacing event when stormy surf hits the harbor causing any brave surfer who dares ride it to be hidden from sight in the swells. Of course, it is thought that the pounding 'kā' of the morning glory vines 'pōhuehue' is the cause for the waves to pound in the first place. What an odd thought for us today—people getting to feast and enjoy themselves because someone has not done a certain ritual to cause violent weather to form. What has that got to do with revenge? Perhaps it could be saying that you are lucky this time to enjoy yourself and get away with it, but when someone does get into the course of action, then look out, because the results will be dangerous, like surfing when one shouldn't. This is cultural guessing until we can understand the context or the circumstances in which this was said. It is an example that demonstrates how important it is to have a working knowledge of Hawaiian language and culture to be able to grasp the depth of meaning of Hawaiian poetry and oratory.

If we investigate a little deeper, we find that, according to Kamakau, there was a quarrel that occurred "through a certain soldier of the guard named Ka-hahana who belonged to Ke'e-au-moku [. . .]. This man went every day to his plantation and when he returned at night his wife cooked the taro tops. The chiefs distributed fish to the people and left out this man and his wife. [. . .] [T]he chiefs were constantly depriving the people of their fishing rights" (*Ruling Chiefs* 83). Kahahana spoke his words about feasting and surfing and outfitted himself in his war gear. He then began to kill others, and this started a battle known as Kalae'ili'ili. Knowing this bit of information, we can see that the feasting chiefs were indeed the real chiefs of Waihe'e who feasted on such foods but did not share them fairly, and Kahahana would be the one to beat the pōhuehue vines. That is, his anger had built up and exploded like the swells rolling into the harbor, the ones the chiefs liked to pass their time surfing.

Kahahana is able to put together the factors that he has seen as the disturbing behavior of the chiefs: their pleasure in surfing and feasting on the many food resources of Waihe'e, while he and his wife are left to only eat the lū'au taken from his own fields. Even though his words describe his inner anger, they still depict the beauty, the creativeness, and the genius of Hawaiian oratory that we find somewhat in chant and song composition today.

Non-verbal Communication

Perhaps equally important in oral traditions, and with oratory, is the use of non-verbal communication tools such as a club or instrument to emphasize speech, the inflection or tone of voice, facial expressions, and other means that make the act of speaking into a performance worthy of being remembered.

Where oratory is active, in Aotearoa or Sāmoa, one can see orators use a club, a cane, or a long pole (*to'oto'o* in Samoan or *tokotoko* in Māori) to extend their words physically in space or to denote their status as an orator. In Māori *whaikōrero,* speeches "are illustrated with a wealth of gesture, tailored to the meaning of the words and graphically underlining them. A man who speaks with his hands in his pockets is scorned; people say that this is a sign he does not speak his mind" (Salmond, *Hui* 172). Such details are rare or lacking in the literature of Hawai'i, but there are some fragments that indicate the possibility, indeed probability, that these communication tools did exist.

For example, Kamakau tells us of a council held on O'ahu for the chief Kahahana to consider the request of the Maui chief Kahekili, his "foster father," to claim the ivory that drifted ashore at Kualoa. The priest-prophet Ka'opulupulu was called for and "the question put, and Ka-hahana told him that he was willing to grant these things to his parent in return for his up-bringing. The kahuna *bowed his head* [...]" (italics added for emphasis) (*Ruling Chiefs* 129).

A similar action was used by Kamehameha to denote shame, regret, and perhaps even disapproval in the following example.

> Kinopu ordered the keepers of the pond to lower fish nets, and the result was a catch so large that a great heap of fish lay spoiling upon the bank of the pond.
>
> The news of the huge catch reached Kamehameha, who was then with Kalanimoku, war leader and officer of the king's guard. *The king said nothing at the time, but sat with bowed head and downcast eyes, apparently disapproving* of such reckless waste. Had they caught enough for a meal, perhaps forty or twenty, nothing would have been said. However, Kalanimoku, apparently knowing why the king kept his head bowed, commanded Kinopu to release most of the fish. Kinopu's act became common knowledge [. . .]. (italics added for emphasis) (Ii 49)

Some speeches, such as the announcement of the transition of governance after the death of Kamehameha, may be remembered because they are part of the pageantry of historical events that enhance the presentation and performance. Kamakau gives this account of the gathering of the council of chiefs at Kamakahonu, or Kailua Bay.

> On the day when the title of Kamehameha II was given
> him there were gathered to the council the chiefs in
> full regalia, the governors all in their feather robes, the
> war leaders, lesser chiefs, and the soldiers under arms.
> Ka-‘ahu-manu was regent and chief counselor, and Ka-
> lani-moku was chief of the war leaders. [. . .] After the
> prayer by the chief kahuna asking blessings upon him,
> Liholiho came out dressed in great splendor wearing
> a suit presented him from England with a red coat
> trimmed with gold lace and a gold order on his breast,
> a feather helmet on his head and a feather cloak worn
> over his shoulders. He was accompanied by two chiefs as
> escort, one on either side, all in so dignified and orderly
> a manner [. . .]. He was there met by Ka-‘ahu-manu, who
> spoke as follows: "O heavenly one! I speak to you the
> commands of your grandfather. Here are the chiefs, here
> are the people of your ancestors; here are your guns;
> here are your lands. But we two shall share the rule over
> the land." (*Ruling Chiefs* 219–220)

Malo gives a slightly different version of this event, to which he said he was an eyewitness. He said that Keōpūolani was the one who announced that the kingdom would be left to Ka‘ahumanu: "Kaahumanu met all the chiefs and people on the sandy beach, part in the water, and delivered orders to all . . . was one of the true native grandeur and majesty . . ." (qtd. in Malo xv). Without the re-enforcement of the pageantry of the chiefs, Ka‘ahumanu's speech could have been heard as just orders. This appears to be the case when she was nearing her own death and her speech was recorded in the first Hawaiian language newspaper *Ka Lama*.

> [E] na ‘lii, e na kanaka, e hoolohe mai, e hooikaika
> oukou a pau i ka pono, e malama i ke kauoha a ko kakou
> Haku a Iesu; a me ka olelo a ko kakou mau hoahanau,
> ma ka pono, oia wale no ka‘u mea i hele mai nei e h[a]
> i aku ia oukou i ke ola, oia ko‘u makemake; e huli kakou

a pau ma ka mea e olaʻi ko kakou mau uhane; aole oia e haalele mai iaʻu. ("No ke kauoha")

Oh chiefs and people, listen [to what I have to say]. All of you must take strength in doing what is right and to follow the commandments of our Lord, Jesus; and the words of our cousins [the missionaries], in doing what is right, that is what I have to say to you all who are living, and that is my wish. We all must turn to the one who gives us salvation to our souls. He has not departed from me. (Author's translation)

This is an important speech, but it is not as well remembered today as the parting words of other dying chiefs such as Līloa, who said to ʻUmi, "live humbly."

Oratory Today

Today Hawaiian oratory is being heard again, although it is restricted to community gatherings and meetings. It is greatly influenced by speakers who have some relationship to the Māori of Aotearoa, those who have either traveled there or have hosted or been in the presence of Māori who have come here. This imitation may not be a bad thing, for at least the Hawaiian speakers follow a Polynesian format, though it is a Māori one. Recently during personal introductions at a retreat for a Hawaiian organization, a woman introduced herself as "My mountain is such-and-such, my land is such-and-such, my river or water is such-and-such, and my sea is such-and-such." That is a form taken straight from the whaikōrero, the oratory of the *marae* (meeting house) of the Māori; however, there is a similarity in Hawaiian oral traditions as found in the birth genealogies. Kamakau says of himself, "The lands of Manuaula in Kamananui is the placenta from the Lihuʻe cliffs of Kukaniloko to Wahiawa at Pooamoho, the land of my ancestors of my father. The placenta and the land of my mother are from Waikele to Kalauao, the Ewa of Laakona" (Chun, *Nā Kukui* 17). There is a genuine relationship to the land, perhaps not expressed in the same poetic usage as with the Māori for mountain, river, and people, "Taranaki te maunga, Taranaki te wai, Taranaki te tangata ʻTaranaki

is the mountain, Taranaki is the river, and Taranaki are the people,'"
but by the traditional practice of burying the parts of the afterbirth
into the land.

Much has been forgotten about this important art form,
particularly in light of the claim to be "from an oral tradition," but
all is not completely lost. If there is a serious desire to resurrect
Hawaiian oratory, it can be done, for the means to its restoration
have been clearly articulated to us, the living descendants of these
kākāʻōlelo.

- ❧ We know that good orators needed to have a working
  knowledge of genealogies, history, and proverbs. These
  skills can be learned, and a vital part of this is to practice
  the traditional learning, especially observation. It is very
  apparent, even from the Māori and Samoan structures of
  oratory, that observation, careful listening, and good analysis
  of insights make a good orator.
- ❧ The skills of the hoʻopaʻapaʻa can be revitalized through
  language schools, instruction, and competition. Hawaiian
  churches and ʻohana 'families' once retained such skills
  through what was known as hoʻomanaʻo or "remembrance"
  of Hawaiian biblical phrases that would be recited from
  memory and even added to by another person as if in
  competition.
- ❧ Equally important is the need to practice oratory in
  appropriate settings. We should know by now how important
  context is to speaking, and opportunities for formal speech in
  different settings are necessary if this art form is to be revived
  at both meetings and ceremonies, formal and informal.

The revival of Hawaiian oratory may further elevate the usage
of Hawaiian language to one of dignity and honor, but it should
also instill the sacredness of the word. It may well be, as Beckwith
describes it, that we will find our "chief artistic expression"
(*Hawaiian Mythology* 463).

10 Hoʻonohonoho

Traditional Ways of Cultural Management

In the time of Kamehameha the fishermen swam together in
a row, and if one got out of line or lagged behind he was struck
by the sharp nose of the fish.
Kaheiheimalie in *Ruling Chiefs of Hawaii*

✄

If a group worked together to compose a chant the leader
would ask each composer to give a line; if there were eighty
composers the chant would contain eighty lines, and these
would be combined into a single composition. Two, three,
or more composers could work on a single chant.
Kamakau, *Ruling Chiefs of Hawaii*

In Hawaiian there are two words that were used to describe what
management is about: hoʻoponopono and hoʻonohonoho. I have
seen both of them used to describe how a chief ruled. Although today
we associate the word hoʻoponopono with a process of reconciliation,
it had a broader meaning before people began to refer to it with that
single intent. If we broaden what we now think of as the process of
hoʻoponopono to apply it to larger groups, we can see that a leader
or a council of leaders may engage in a similar process to make
decisions and carry them out.

Hoʻonohonoho has a similar kind of intent. The act of noho (that
is, to live) combined with the causative *hoʻo-* (to make), as in to make a
living or to provide a living, suggests more of a system of doing things,
what we now think of as management. I have seen this term used more
often to mean governance. But can it also describe a "cultural" kind of
management? Our modern world of money and of the marketplace is
made complex by the need for a high degree of cooperation between
people. In business, greater efficiency saves on costs and increases
profits. We manage money, goods, services, and people, and we even
try to manage time. If there is such a thing as "cultural" management,
and I believe there is, then the way that we choose to manage all these
things should reflect the culture we use to make our decisions. We
should be able to detect traditional ways our ancestors managed their
world and, if we are practicing "cultural" management, to see those
traditions continued in our practices today.

Management is a term we can associate with two groups: the large, corporate organizations, whether private, government, or not-for-profit and the personal, represented by family or community-based groups. In traditional Hawaiian society, the closest thing to the first group was the aliʻi 'chiefs' and their relationship to people 'kānaka.'

Corporate Management: The Aliʻi

The complexity of the aliʻi's style of rule covers several inter-related concepts and values. Its hierarchy, or protocols, and its methods of collection and redistribution of wealth seem to have operated in ways that we see in large corporations and organizations. Davida Malo gives us this description.

> [. . .] the chiefdom was thought to have [only] one body like a human being. [There being] a head, hands, feet and the smaller body parts. There are many parts to this one body and so this was the same with a chiefdom. It had many parts to its body.
>
> The chiefdom's real body was the people, from the makaʻāinana [*commoners*] to the aliʻi(s) [*chiefs*] who were directly below the aliʻi nui [*high chief*]. This was the real body of the chiefdom [. . .]. The aliʻi nui, who was higher in rank, was the real head of the chiefdom. The aliʻi(s) directly below the aliʻi nui were like the shoulders and chest of the chiefdom. The kahuna [*priest*] of the kiʻi(s) [*images*] was the right hand of the chiefdom, the kālaimoku [*chief counsellor*] was the left hand of the chiefdom. That was how the people of old had worked [this system] out.
>
> The koa [*warriors*] were the right foot of the chiefdom. The mahiʻai [*farmers*] and the lawaiʻa [*fishermen*] were the left foot of the chiefdom. These people labored at every task [and they] were the small parts of the body [attached to] the larger parts of the chiefdom. [. . .]
>
> There were two important body parts: that of the kālaimoku and the kahuna pule kiʻi. They ran the chiefdom. They guided the head [aliʻi nui] of the

> chiefdom to where they had thought it was best [to
> go]. They guided the head of the chiefdom there. If the
> head of the chiefdom refused their guidance then the
> chiefdom might be turned over to someone else, because
> of the mistakes of the head, the ali'i nui. (258)

We can see from this vivid description how the roles and relationships of the various offices and positions worked. The inter-relationship hints at the cooperation needed for such a body to function effectively.

The Despotic Ali'i: The Wrong Kind of Leadership

Malo also points out, however, in the last part of the description, what might happen when things don't go right, what might be called, in today's terms, an internal hostile takeover. As we have seen in the chapter on Alaka'i, there are several good examples of this from the traditions of the so-called "despotic" ali'i of the Kona and Ka'ū districts on the island of Hawai'i, and they show us some of the dynamics and limitations of this relationship.

In the tradition concerning the ali'i Kōha'ikalani, told in the chapter on Alaka'i, he had his people gather stones to build a new temple, but the priests who came to bless the place realized, from the quantity of stones, that the temple would be used for human sacrifice, and they warned the people whom they saw as the potential victims.

Apparently an abusive leader could be removed if it was done within the confines of the society and culture. We saw this in the tradition of the ali'i Ko'ihala whose servants remained faithful to him as they moved from place to place, but became disloyal when he behaved with insolence and irresponsibility toward them. I emphasize the cultural aspects of this tradition of Ko'ihala because the patience of the servants follows a cultural response to the ali'i. Historian John Papa 'Ī'ī tells of an event that occurred in his own homeland of Waipi'o on the island of O'ahu that illustrates that kind of cultural response to the ali'i's commands.

> Kaimihau answered, "You cannot do this, for we were
> not told of it by our leaders. If Kalanimoku had made
> this request through our own leaders, we should have

heard of it and therefore done nothing to prevent the removal of the canoe. If you persist in the idea of taking the canoe, day may change to night and night to day without its budging from its resting place. All things left here at Waipio are protected, from the sea to the upland, and we shall not let them go unless we hear from our own leaders." (77)

'Ī'ī also describes an abuse of power that revealed contrary behavior and the waste of resources.

Kinopu ordered the keepers of the pond to lower fish nets, and the result was a catch so large that a great heap of fish lay spoiling upon the bank of the pond.

The news of the huge catch reached Kamehameha, who was then with Kalanimoku, war leader and officer of the king's guard. The king said nothing at the time, but sat with bowed head and downcast eyes, apparently disapproving of such reckless waste. Had they caught enough for a meal, perhaps forty or twenty, nothing would have been said. However, Kalanimoku, apparently knowing why the king kept his head bowed, commanded Kinopu to release most of the fish. Kinopu's act became common knowledge [. . .]. (49)

In this instance we see how a chief, Kalanimoku, could follow through on his ruling chief's sensitivity to the extravagance and abuse of authority and could impose damage control over the situation. Kamehameha's sensitivity shows an appreciation for the management and control of precious resources and is a sign of being a good 'pono' chief.

When we consider the ali'i system of management and whether it might be useful today, we must consider that the roles, and the rank and status that came with them, had a deep relationship to the culture. Being an accidental product of birth, they were more than mere titles, and the system worked because the people were deeply engaged in the world view and way of life that incorporated these traditional roles.

Incredible as it may seem, in the 1970s, there was serious consideration from the president's office at the University of Hawai'i of incorporating traditional Hawaiian family terms for use by the campus leaders. Titles such as Haku (senior family member) would be used in an attempt to "localize" the administration. What was not considered was that those terms have a deep cultural relationship that requires cooperative use with the people that recognize the authority it carries. Wise council from Native Hawaiian faculty ended any consideration of such a plan.

In traditional Hawaiian society, the rank and status conferred by the system upon an individual depended upon who that individual's parents were. This was then directly related to what kapu 'restrictions' were enforced in one's presence. Consider these protocols described by Malo.

> If the ali'i was eating and people were bent down on
> their knees, then whose ever knee came up was killed. If
> a person went with the ali'i on a kia loa [*a long, light and*
> *swift canoe*] canoe, then that person was put to death.
>
> If a person unfastened the ali'i('s) malo, cape or kapa,
> that person was put to death. There were many other
> kapu that people [broke and] were put to death. The ali'i
> had many kapu(s). (176)

It all sounds rather trivial, but some ali'i were so kapu, such as those under the kapu moe, that they avoided going out in the daylight, for their shadows were considered kapu, and the penalty for their shadow falling on a person was death. To say that this made getting an idea to, or communicating with, the ruling chief a problem is an understatement. We know from Malo that there were several stages in an evening when the ruling chief consulted with others.

> When the sun set lamps were light [*sic*] and the ali'i ate
> [their meal]. Those who came in to eat with him or her
> were called lanika'e. Those who came in late at night
> were called poho kano. They only talked by lamp light
> (kukui) and did not eat anything.
>
> The people who stayed with the ali'i at the dawn's lamp
> light were called makou because makou was the name of
> the lamp. (179–180)

We also know from Malo that the ali'i had other means of counsel.

> [...] the ali'i nui secretly sent for the kālaimoku(s) to talk with him. The ali'i nui listened to all their (lākou) advice (pono) and then they left.

> When the ali'i nui met ('aha 'ōlelo) with all the ali'i below him in rank, he listened only to what every ali'i had to say. If the ali'i nui recognized what one ali'i of his said, for it was similar to his kālaimoku(s') advice that had been secretly heard, then the ali'i nui agreed to this ali'i('s) words.

> If the ali'i nui knew that what the ali'i(s) had to say was not like the advice of the kālaimoku(s), then the ali'i did not agree with them. That is how the 'aha 'ōlelo of the ali'i(s) was held. (267)

Malo's description tells us how the ali'i not only managed their time, or how it was managed for them, but also how they managed the advice they were getting from so many different sources. If Native Hawaiian leaders today seek or manage advice in a similar way, then perhaps this is a cultural practice that has been retained.

Management of Natural Resources

Related to the kapu of the ali'i is the kapu system imposed upon resources. We find that certain restrictions 'kapu' were imposed for religious, mythical, or historical reasons on certain plants, animals, and other natural resources. The kapu that prevented men and women from eating together and dictated what women could not eat (pork, bananas, and shark, for example) were based upon the traditional events of the chief Wākea and his wife Papa. A kapu about fish and fishing was also invoked in Hawai'i. Such a kapu was imposed on the 'ōpelu 'mackerel scad or *Decapterus pinnulatus* and *D. maruadsi*' and aku 'bonito, skipjack, or *Katsuwonus pelamis*.' Malo tells us in the traditions about the prophet Pili that when Pili arrived in the islands his canoe was "accompanied by two fish, the 'Ōpelu and the Aku" (144).

When the wind blew on the ocean, the Aku struck the
side of the canoe and the ʻŌpelu rippled the surface of the
ocean until the wind died down and the ocean was calmed.
That is how Pili and the others sailed to and landed in the
Hawaiian Islands. Therefore, prohibitions were made on
the Aku and the ʻŌpelu in the old days. (144)

The memory of this event became part of the religious
ceremonies. Malo tells us that both fish "were always worshipped
every fishing season" (273).

There were other iʻa that were worshipped, but the rituals
were different from those associated with the ʻŌpelu and
Aku. These iʻa were the ones that surfaced (lana) and
there were a lot of them visible during Kau [*Summer*] and
Hoʻoilo [*Winter*]. During Kau the ʻŌpelu was fished for
and during Hoʻoilo the Aku was fished for.

During the month of Hinaiaʻeleʻele, the ʻŌpelu were
snatched and eaten while the Aku was made kapu. Any
one including the aliʻi [*chief*] could not eat the Aku. If
someone had been heard to have eaten the iʻa, then he
or she was killed. ʻŌpelu were eaten during the month of
Kaelo and then the eating [of ʻŌpelu] was over.

During the month of Kaelo, the Aku was taken (unuhi),
and eaten while the ʻŌpelu were made kapu. No one
could eat that iʻa. Anyone heard of having eaten the
ʻŌpelu was killed. (273–274)

Malo gives us a very good description of the rituals involved in
the worship of these two fish.

When the ʻŌpelu was being fished, the poʻe lawaiʻa
[*fishermen*] gathered at the heiau Kūʻula during the
evening with their ʻupena ʻaʻei [*fine fishing nets*]. A Puaʻa
[*Pig*] with Maiʻa [*Banana*], Niu [*Coconut*], food and
kapa to sleep on were brought [along] and there the akua
lawaiʻa [*fishing god*] was worshipped.

During the ceremonies all the people sat in a circle, then
the kahuna came with a container of water. There was

limu [*seaweed*] and 'Ōlena [*Turmeric root*] placed inside of the container. The kahuna began the pule huikala [*ceremonial cleansing prayer*]. [. . .]

Then, all the men slept in the mua [*men's house*] that night. No one could secretly leave to go back to [his] own house to sleep with his wife. Their sleeping in the mua was kapu (*restricted*), from daylight to nighttime.

Then all the wa'a lawai'a [*fishing canoes*] set sail to sea. The Pua'a(s) were baked and when the po'e lawai'a returned [home] with i'a, then the kahuna prayed and placed the Pua'a on the lele [*sacrificial altar*] with Mai'a, Niu, other foods and the kahuna('s) rites of pule [*prayer*] were over.

All the people ate [the food]. When the feasting was over, then the pule was prohibited (pāpā). Worship was over and all was made noa [free from restrictions].

That is how the worship of the po'e lawai'a who casted for Aku and those who used 'upena was done. (274)

Not all the restrictions imposed had the same function or effect. Another well-known restriction was imposed on certain plants associated with the volcano and the volcano goddess Pele. The Rev. William Ellis noted this when he was taken to the volcano on a tour. When we compared the kapu on the two fish to what Ellis described at the volcano, we can see how much of a difference ritual has to do with the word choice of *kapu* or *lāhui*.

He [Makoa, their guide] objected strongly to our going thither, as we should most likely be mischievous, and offend Pele or Nahoaarii, gods of the volcano, by plucking the ohelo, (sacred berries,) digging up the sand, or throwing stones into the crater, [. . .]. (141)

There is an apparent distinction for such a restriction because Ellis tells us that the word used for the restrictions at the volcano is *lāhui* and not *kapu*.

> [the ohelo berries] were rahuiia, (prohibited,) until some
> had been offered to her [Pele], and permission to eat
> them asked. (162)

> It [tabu] is a distinct word from rahui, to prohibit, as
> the ohelo berries at Kirauea were said to be prohibited,
> being tabu na Pele, sacred for Pele, and is opposed to the
> word noa, which means general or common. (278)

Later in his journal Ellis gives us this distinction between lāhui
and what he describes as kapu.

> Although employed for civil as well as sacred purposes,
> the tabu [kapu] was entirely a religious ceremony, and
> could be imposed only by the priests. (279)

The different usage becomes more apparent when Ellis describes
the restricted 'ōhelo plant being offered to Pele, for there are neither
priests nor religious ceremonies involved.

> They did not use much ceremony in their
> acknowledgment; [. . .] they turned their faces towards
> the place whence the greatest quantity of smoke and
> vapour issued, and, breaking the branch they held
> in their hand in two, they threw one part down the
> precipice, saying at the same time, "E Pele, eia ka ohelo
> 'au; e taumaha aku wau ia oe, e ai hoi au tetahi." "Pele,
> here are your ohelos: I offer some to you, some I also
> eat." (163)

I first encountered the word *lāhui* in this usage when I was living
in Aotearoa (New Zealand) in 1984. Someone had drowned offshore
whose body could not be recovered. The local Māori tribe placed
a *rahui* upon the ocean so that no one could go fishing or gather
any shellfish. I asked my host, a Māori bishop, the reason for the
prohibition, and he explained it in two ways. The first was in respect
to the spirit or soul of the deceased, and the second was to let the
ocean "rest," that is to allow the body to decompose or be eaten and,
after a period of time, removed as waste from the fish's and shellfish's
own bodies.

This detailed comparison of the two words is important because it tells us that kapu, which is related to worship, is not the only word for prohibition, and because it dispels the common misperception that somehow kapu are related to environmental issues. The reason I want to stress the religious connection to kapu is that not all kapu had environmental implications and outcomes. In the tradition concerning the high chief 'Umi, we find a kapu imposed even on how a fish is handled after being caught.

> Fish tossed between the legs became defiled and
> were not acceptable as offerings to the god. Such fish
> were despised by the god. Therefore 'Umi traded
> with another person for fish that were handed out
> and not tossed between the legs. (Kamakau, *Ruling Chiefs* 11)

I don't think anyone today would knowingly object to whether a fish was tossed above or between a fisherman's legs. However, there is some interest in re-thinking something like the traditional kapu, especially for those practices that do have a definite environmental impact such as the kapu on 'ōpelu and aku. It stands to reason that a ban on fishing of a single species for an extended period of time will result in either increased or sustained numbers of fish to be fished. Likewise, as there is more fishing being done today with more sophisticated fishing technology, it should be no surprise that the availability of fish has dramatically decreased. Therefore, an interest has developed in considering restrictions on fishing that are reminiscent of traditional kapu.

The creation of a marine preserve at Hanauma Bay, with a dramatic increase in the marine life population, visibly demonstrates what can happen when such restrictions are employed and enforced. More recently, proposals were made by the state government to impose restrictions on fishing around the island of Ni'ihau due to complaints by the island's residents "that fishing boats from other islands were aggressively fishing the Ni'ihau reefs and reducing their ability to maintain a subsistence fishery. The new rules would allow no outside fishing, and no sale or barter of Ni'ihau-caught fish by Ni'ihau residents" ("State proposes restrictions" B2).

Over a hundred people, including the author, showed up over a weekend to kōkua 'help' in digging out nearly a century of accumulated soil and debris from an old ʻauwai 'ditch' system.

It is probably safe to assume that our ancestors noticed the increased numbers of fish after the kapu had been lifted. However, we should realize that they were not engaged in environmental or resource management for economic production. They practiced this form of management because they had a relationship with the fish; in fact, the aku and ʻōpelu were thought to be ʻaumākua, familial gods or guardians, to the descendants of the prophet Pāʻao (Valeri 28).

Another system of the management of natural resources, which some link to the development and wealth of the aliʻi, is the way in which water was developed for different kinds of island agriculture. The linguistic link between the word for water 'wai' and *waiwai* which can mean "valuables," "riches," or "treasure," is an indicator of how precious water is to Native Hawaiians (Handy and Handy 57). True or not, the management of water has been seen by archaeologists as being crucial to the development of the rank and status of the ruling chiefs. (For more information see Spriggs and Chun; Kirch, *Feathered Gods*.) Agricultural sites have revealed several agricultural systems that manage and distribute water through irrigation. The constant flow of fresh water provided the resource to expand cultivation and production of crops, especially kalo 'taro,' and other food and plants used for clothing. These systems were used in areas now considered harsh and dry, areas such as North Kona on the island of Hawai'i.

As the theory goes, the increased production of foods developed into a surplus the ali'i (and the community) used for trade for other goods not found in their area, and like in other civilizations, this led to an increase in fine arts and crafts, or wealth. Greater production might mean more trade, but there are also some side effects like the greater possibility for warfare to defend the increased wealth or for expansion.

We do not practice this type of cultural management of water today, for we do not engage in such intensive agriculture. In a reversal of the traditional management system of water, we now allow excess water from storms to be diverted directly into the ocean instead of allowing the flooding of the plains. This wastes the excess water and pollutes the coastal shores with silt that could enrich working agricultural fields. This has worked until now because instead of engaging in intensive agriculture, we use land for urban development—houses, shopping centers, and businesses, for which water is drilled instead of relying on springs and ever-flowing streams. But with the increased likelihood of droughts and augmented water consumption by a growing population, it will be interesting to see if planners, environmentalists, and politicians take to considering traditional hydrology and adapt it to modern conservation.

Management of Labor

Laulima, literally "many hands," is the Hawaiian word for cooperation. In Hawaiian society, community development meant the communal use of labor in a cooperative effort. Large construction projects—large temples, irrigation canals, and the like—were efforts that required a lot of hands to complete. However, there were differences in the level of cooperation as we have seen in the traditions concerning Ko'ihala and Kohaikalani. Abusive and oppressive demands do not encourage cooperation even if you have the rank and status to demand it. Kamakau gives an example of the opposite, a tradition where a chiefly command was fulfilled beyond even the aliʻi(ʻs) expectations of cooperative labor. The event was the building of the luakini 'temple' on the hill called Puʻukoholā. Kamakau tells us that "Kamehameha abandoned war and adopted the advice of Ka-pou-kahi and his aunt Haʻaloʻu, to build a house for the god [so to defeat his rivals]" (*Ruling Chiefs* 154).

> When it came to the building of Puʻu-koholaʹ no one, not even a tabu chief, was excused from the work of carrying stone. Kamehameha himself labored with the rest. The only exception was the high tabu chief Ke-aliʻi-maikaʻi [Kamehameha's younger brother]. It is said that when this chief saw Kamehameha carrying stone, he too lifted a stone and started to carry it on his back to Puʻu-koholaʹ; but when Kamehameha saw him packing the stone on his back he ran and took it away saying, "You stop that! You must preserve our tabu. I will do the carrying!" Then he ordered Ka-paʻa-lani and some others to take that rock out into mid-ocean so far that land was no longer visible and throw it overboard. (*Ruling Chiefs* 154–155)

Volunteers pass rocks to create a small diversion dam at Hālawa Valley on Molokaʻi to create a water supply to feed into a restored ʻauwai 'ditch' system for loʻi 'kalo fields.'

In *Native Planters in Old Hawaii*, Handy and Handy, with the collaboration of Mary Kawena Pukui, note the difference between "household enterprise" and the capital works of the aliʻi.

Laulima in household enterprise, family feasts and the
like, was spontaneous. But in the building of taro *lo'i* and
irrigation ditches, and of fishponds, it was organized and
supervised by *konohiki* carrying out orders of their *ali'i*. (307)

There are few descriptions of such communal work, possibly
because much of the commentary on agriculture was from the
perspective of the individual farmer. Kamakau readily admits that
large-scale agriculture really lies with the ability of someone of high
rank and status to organize a large labor force.

If the planter were a chief, the work was easy, for he had
from a hundred to a thousand workers to do his work for
him. The chiefs' *lo'i* were therefore large. This was also
true of a prominent person or one with a large family
(*'ohana*) and many kinfolk (*makamaka*); he too had a
large *lo'i*. Those who had no help had a small *lo'i* [. . .].
(*The Works* 33)

Restoration of lo'i 'kalo fields' in lower Hālawa Valley, Moloka'i

We also have the traditions of the menehune, a mythical people
who epitomize cooperation and capital projects. The menehune
model a chiefly labor unit except for one drawback. According to the
traditions, if, for whatever reason, the project they were constructing

was not finished by dawn, it would remain unfinished. In this regard, cooperation and good relationships are imperative for the project to be finished on time, for any disruption would, more than likely, lead to the project being left undone.

> It is said that in constructing a heiau it was the custom for a chief over a large district to line up all the men under him and pass the stones from hand to hand until all was in place, much like [. . .] barn raisings in pioneer life. The time element is important in these Menehune structures, especially as the workers themselves become purely mythical beings and night is the time of their activity. (Beckwith, *Hawaiian Mythology* 333)

These menehune traditions would have been told to inspire increased labor, but in many instances they explain, or are used to explain, some unfinished project or geographical oddity in the landscape. Their exploits were based upon, and modeled, the kind of communal labor we find described for more "human" activity.

> On the day of treading the *lo'i* was filled with water, and the owner of the patch made ready plenty of "food" (poi), pork, and "fish." It was a great day for the men, women, and children, and no chief or chiefess held himself too tabu to tread in the patch. Every man, woman, and child bedecked himself with greenery, and worked with all his might—trampling here and there, stirring the mud with his feet, dancing, rejoicing, shouting, panting, and making sport. (Kamakau, *The Works* 34)

Handy and Handy recount Kamakau's description of such an event.

> Dry taro was [. . .] sometimes planted by a team of men working in unison. Such work was termed *ha'aheo* (aristocratic), probably because such planting was done for an *ali'i*. The field was burned over, then mulched. The bundles of *huli* were prepared. The men went fishing and ate a good meal, while the women prepared pandanus and *'ilima* garlands for the necks and heads

of their men. At the field, each man, garlanded and
carrying his digging stick (ʻoʻo), and his bundle of huli,
took his place [in line]. Then, holding the ʻoʻo in the
right hand and the huli in the left, each man thrust in the
stick slantwise, and into the hole so made, tossed a huli.
"They turned this way and that as they moved backwards
like a school of paiʻea crabs, and a fine sight it was to see
as they swayed hither and thither." (105)

ʻĪʻī also describes what he had seen in the clearing of a field.

The bulrushes were as nothing, for they were cleared
away in a single day. Some men cut the rushes, some
dug them out, some built mounds, and others covered
the mounds with the rushes. Much food was provided
for the noonday meal of the workers, who then resumed
their work until evening. (68)

Fishing, as with farming, appears in the descriptions and
commentaries to be more of an individual activity. But to make larger
catches, both in numbers and size, a communal effort was needed.

Less formal was the community cooperative undertaking
in lagoon fishing called hukilau, when fish were driven
into a sweep net to which were attached at either end
long ropes with dried ti leaves tied along their lengths.
(Handy and Handy 307)

Another traditional means of communal fishing was alluded to
in a speech given during a very emotional meeting of the Council of
Chiefs at Pohukaina in Honolulu in the 1830s. This event, known as
the Pahikaua war, has been described in more detail in the chapters
on Hoʻoponopono and Kākāʻōlelo. Kuini Liliha had been accused of
being a bad influence on the young king, who was in her care. Her
plea brought tears to those gathered, and Kaheiheimālie, another
female chief, responded to those pleas.

Then Ka-heihei-malie, who had been sitting on the
stairway during the council, rose and spoke about the
goodness of God and urged the people to listen to the

words of Ka-'ahu-manu and Kau-i-ke-aouli and of
Nahi-'ena'ena. Then she added, drawing a figure from the
communal method of fishing for swordfish, "In the time
of Kamehameha the fishermen swam together in a row,
and if one got out of line or lagged behind he was struck
by the sharp nose of the fish. So those who do not follow
God's word and do not obey our king, but fall out of line,
they shall be struck by the sharp sword of the law, so do
not lag behind lest you be hurt." (Kamakau, *Ruling Chiefs*
300–301)

Although Kaheiheimālie uses this reference to make a point
about conformity more than cooperation, she tells us of an extremely
interesting form of communal fishing and cooperation. The
swordfish or "a'u" (*Istiophoridae*) is not a small or ordinary fish, and
the method she describes so graphically places people swimming in
the open ocean attempting to "herd" the large fish into being caught.
Cooperation is needed to remain as a group, perhaps to make the line
of swimmers appear as if it were a larger fish or predator, presumably
driving the a'u towards fishermen in canoes.

Feasting: The Management and Sharing of Food

In these descriptions there is a common element that I find
extremely intriguing about traditional communal labor, the sharing
of food by feasting. It is an element that I was reminded of when
reading a story in the morning newspaper about the simple event
of a barge landing at Kalaupapa. One must realize that the barge
landing at the isolated peninsula once referred to as a leper colony is
a once-a-year event to deliver large commodities such as cars, trucks,
appliances, and furniture. It was after the spectacle of the unloading
of and gawking at the goods that

[d]uring a break in the unloading, nearly everybody in town
joins a community lunch on the steps of the store, where the
menu includes chili and rice, Polish sausage, macaroni salad
and chocolate cake. The lunch, a thank-you for workers
unloading the barge, is the only time when so many people
in Kalaupapa get to eat together. (Leidmann A2)

As an act of gratitude, and perhaps of the sharing of one's wealth, we find that community efforts in labor management often result in feasting. Feasting itself is a community event, as described in *Native Planters in Old Hawaii.*

> *Laulima* likewise was in order in the preparation of community feasts, when wood for fuel must be brought in quantity for the ground ovens, and foods were brought in large amounts, including fish, hogs, dogs, chickens, taros, sweet potatoes, yams, bananas, *kukui* nuts, and coconuts.

> In family enterprise such as was involved in erecting a new house, most of the work was done by *'ohana* (kith and kin), but neighbors would lend a hand. So it was also with family feasts (*'aha'aina*). The wealth of a family was that of many competent hands willing to apply themselves to crude and skilled labor, rather than in material possessions, goods which were to be used or given away. (Handy and Handy 307)

Like farming and other activities in traditional Hawaiian society, feasting was conducted by both chiefs and commoners. Kirch points out that "for the *maka'ainana*, [there] were small feasts (usually focused on the sacrifice of a pig) to celebrate the cutting of a new canoe, or the successful harvest of a set of irrigated taro terraces [. . .]. The chiefs, in contrast, could virtually be found feasting every day of their lives" ("Polynesian Feasting" 178). Kirch's article emphasizes the political and religious implications of feasting for the chiefs that became a "daily reminder of the immense gulf of social distinctions that separated *ali'i* from *maka'ainana*" ("Polynesian Feasting" 180). Without that hierarchy today, what is practiced in feasting is the lū'au, and it is typically a family or community event.

Feasting: The Management of Labor

The idea of feasting as a metaphor for cultural management is something that I wouldn't have considered if I had not read about a video turned corporate management workshop tool called *Fish*. The article described a public relations executive who was visiting Pike Place (public farmers') Market in Seattle. He was intrigued by the fishmongers and how they dealt with the customers by making a show out of the orders. He saw that they were having fun while they worked, which made their job enjoyable. He recorded the whole thing and started to spread the word through sales of the video and workshops that work could and should be fun. His observation was that improved working conditions, such as creating a fun environment in which to work, produced better cooperation among the workers.

If I recorded the preparations for a traditional feast that we now call a lūʻau, what would we expect to see?

Our family lūʻau, from a child's point of view, were more like frantic events than what I think of as celebrations. There was the gathering of food, the preparation of the food and the grounds, the decorating, the entertainment, and the clean up. In other words, work. I remember peeking into the kitchen to see all the women working, either chopping or stirring, and then behind the house were all the men tending a huge mound of dirt and burlap bags with vapors of steam rising up from it. They were drinking beer rather than working at that stage.

The initial stage of a lūʻau is the planning: what is the menu, and, therefore, what are the resources we will need? Firewood, stones, burlap bags, banana stumps, and kī leaves are just the basic things required to have an imu or umu 'underground oven.'

Ellis gives this very early description of the construction of an imu.

> The oven was a hole in the earth, three or four feet in diameter, and nearly a foot deep. A number of small stones were spread over the bottom, a few dried leaves laid on them, and the necessary quantity of sticks and firewood piled up, and covered over with small stones. The dry leaves were then kindled, [. . .].

> When the stones were red-hot, they were spread out with a stick, the remaining fire-brands taken away; and when the dust and ashes, on the stones at the bottom, had been brushed off with a green bough, [. . .] hot stones were then placed on these leaves, and a covering six inches thick of leaves and earth spread over the whole. (147)

It must be considered when planning the menu who and how many are to be invited. What specialty or regional items like ʻōpihi, ʻōpae, hīhīwai, wana, and other side dishes need to be ordered, that is, asked for from relatives or friends, or bought?

The "who would do what" was more of a matter of "who had what"—someone who had the stones used for the imu was probably the one to be in charge of the oven. Someone who could get limu 'seaweed' probably would bring it cleaned and ready to be used.

All of this was pre-planned, and of course there would be many more details to be worked out than are necessary to explain here. Approaching the day of the feast, the home where the event was to be hosted became a focal point for drop-offs and a work center. Not only was food being prepared, washed, chopped, mixed, and seasoned, but flower lei and decorations were also being made, sometimes by the same group of people and sometimes not. The imu was dug and the fire lit to heat the stones. The pig was delivered and "dressed," or prepared for cooking.

On the day of the feast, before the guests arrived, the smaller ones, under the supervision of older children or young adults, helped prepare the tables and chairs and set up the decorations. Usually the hosts were the ones in charge of barking out the orders. In our family, I am told that my uncle and aunt's lūʻau were so popular that people stood on the sidewalk in a line that curved around the neighborhood as they waited to be greeted.

This is an early missionary description of such a feast put on by and for the locals.

> [The food] is placed on the ground, before the group
> for whom it is designed, who, lounging on their mats
> in the attitude of the ancient Romans, partake of it with
> one hand, while they recline upon the other. Servants
> separate the meat with their hands, wiping them
> occasionally *in their mouths or on their naked arms or
> legs*; after which, all eat from the same dishes, using their
> fingers in place of forks and spoons. (Stewart 134–135)

Today, the lūʻau is elevated onto a table surrounded by chairs rather than being on the ground. But there is still the monumental

The baked pig and the laulau bundles of kī-leaf wrapped foods are taken out of the underground imu.

task of cleaning up with the goal of getting the household back to its normal living condition as quickly as possible. I don't recall something called a clean-up committee. It was done when most of the guests had left and the entertainment had become more family oriented or had stopped altogether. Everyone except my brother, who was handicapped, spontaneously started to grab things and move them. Rubbish was collected and dumped, chairs folded, table matting crumpled and discarded, and food taken to the kitchen where a massive washing detail was in progress. Soon enough, there was only a tent standing. The lūʻau was a complete success.

What was going on here? What happened to the stereotype of the lazy Native Hawaiian kānaka who could only play their ʻukulele under the shade of a tree instead of doing hard manual labor?

When one starts to analyze this whole process, one can see several managerial practices being utilized effectively. First of all, there is the planning and development of goals and of objectives designed to achieve those goals. There occurs a meeting or conversations to pre-plan, which involves several things: an inventory of human and natural resources needed to accomplish the goal (the planning of the menu), an assessment of facilities (where we are going to have the lūʻau), and a timetable for deadlines, which were mentally recorded.

What follows are networking to obtain goods and services (getting ʻōpihi and other hard-to-find foods and goods), the allocation and designation of resources and assignments (what aunt so-and-so is going to make, and whether uncle is in charge of the imu), and the purchasing of any materials and their storage (paper plates, napkins, etc.). There begins the assignments of tasks (so-and-so is to be in charge of . . .) and allocation of tasks to personnel (who are mostly junior or younger members).

As the event approaches, the coordination of certain tasks is done. For example, foods that can be prepared several days ahead are prepared and frozen. The day before the event, one can see the pace of activities accelerate as members work on pre-assigned tasks, either learning new and simple tasks or heading for tasks they already have skills in. For instance, the preparation of ake, or raw liver, is a delicate task that requires specific skills, and hence, only those with experience are allowed to do it.

Arguments over processes and assignments are usually arbitrated by the host or senior members of the family. In what I can remember of such incidents, experience is usually the guide as to what method or what person is chosen.

With an inherent understanding of the goal, that is, the success of the lūʻau, and a display of hospitality, it is no wonder no clean-up committee is necessary to follow up at the end. I have even seen guests picking up litter and trays as they leave and emptying them in garbage cans on their way out to their cars. It may be that most of the guests are relatives or friends and their instinctive action provides a lead for others to follow. It certainly emphasizes the point that they are not hired help brought in to pick up the dirty dishes.

This entire process of feasting demonstrates an ability at organization and management that is phenomenal and can be found with many other indigenous peoples where feasting plays such an important role. It also shows that fundamental elements emphasized in modern techniques of management are also being practiced in traditional societies, and therefore, are not necessarily strange or foreign to indigenous peoples.

Now let us consider the harder questions. Would it be possible for a corporate type of organization to have done the same thing, that is, to organize and put on such a feast for perhaps hundreds of people, with the same sort of budget and resources? And then, why is it that Native Hawaiians seem to have difficulties, either creating corporations or heading them if we are so successful in an operation like feasting? What makes the lū'au a success?

I believe one answer lies in relationships; the kinship, obligations, respect, and honor, and the need to reciprocate are the motivation that creates the desire for success. This is the cultural element, and I think it is an element that corporate management really strives hard to foster among its mostly non-related employees to achieve success. But it does seem to be elusive in a corporate culture.

I remember my father, who, in his younger days with his friends, loved to build stone walls in a local masonry style. One day his boss at work needed a stone wall built at his house, and my father went there to help him build it. He told me later that after it was all done, his boss wanted to give him a hundred dollars for helping him. My father was surprised and insulted, and although he never said why, I believe it was because he did it out of friendship, out of heeding the request of someone he knew and respected who needed help. The payment, if there was to be one, might have come later when he needed help too, not in the form of immediate cash.

This also reminds me of a story of two famous native carvers from the Canadian Northwest, I believe they were Charles Edenshaw and Mungo Martin, who would give each other gifts of their work. The gift giving escalated as one tried to out-do the other. They soon reached a point where they had to stop, for they had forgotten that the initial reason for the gift giving was to further the bond of friendship, and now the gifts were actually destroying that relationship. In the end, it is the relationship that is important, not the gifts or the act of giving. The item and the action are only means to develop and strengthen the emotional bonds.

Borrowing a phrase I have heard in corporate management meetings and workshops, how can non-related workers "buy in" to such a level of cooperation and relationship? Although kinship is a very influential factor in traditional society, I do not believe it is the only contributing factor for the success of a lū'au or for the traditional examples of communal work we have seen. Relationships, particularly among non-relatives, are built upon not only reciprocity of obligations but, I believe, more importantly, upon respect and trust. How can one create that among non-kin folk?

Culturally based Management: Some Stories

I have worked at several organizations and agencies whose main purpose or mission is to help Native Hawaiians. There has always been a lingering question about whether they are Hawaiian organizations or organizations that just happen to serve Hawaiians? What would it mean to be a Hawaiian organization? Does that mean having more Native Hawaiians as workers at all levels, especially at the top? Does it mean using the Hawaiian language? And perhaps most importantly, does it mean adopting Hawaiian culture as part of how business is done?

At two of those organizations, the top levels were indeed occupied by Native Hawaiians, elected or appointed. At both places at least a token amount of Hawaiian language was used, especially as greetings over the telephone. At both places, to a limited degree, some form of Hawaiian culture was encouraged, usually as a social means of bringing the staff together. Native and non-native staff-members were also encouraged to learn more about Hawaiian culture and society as a means of being better able to understand and communicate with clientele. One of my tasks was to develop materials and workshops to help facilitate that learning and appreciation. When I think back, both at times even used hoʻoponopono as a means to attempt to reconcile personality conflicts and disagreements. In both cases, it worked for about two weeks before things reverted back to business as usual.

The story of the third organization is much longer and more detailed because there had been a serious effort made to change the way services were being provided to people.

In an effort to promote better access, appropriateness, and accessibility of services for Native Hawaiians, we spent hours upon hours talking about the way things were actually being done and about how we could integrate culture into our work. We developed a list of guiding principles to improve such services. Among the ways we thought we could improve accessibility were the following:

      ❧ Staff should be sensitized through appropriate training in the history, culture, values, and needs of the population they intend to reach and serve.

      ❧ Staff should familiarize themselves with and respectfully acknowledge the issues of importance to Native Hawaiians.

      ❧ There should be a mechanism in place to provide ongoing assessment and evaluation of staff sensitivity to client needs.

      ❧ Programs should provide a setting in which sensitivity, supportiveness, and mutual respect can flourish.

      ❧ Programs should promote the appropriate integration of traditional Native Hawaiian [practices] into existing services.

All nicely said and well intended, but nothing was done. There was a lot of resistance. There were a lot of excuses, but I think the most important one, and the least said, was that people didn't know how to do it. We had developed some very good and high-minded principles, and people agreed with them, but we didn't really have a course of action for how to implement them within a bureaucratic system. A majority of the staff knew that they had to do something different, and many of the non-natives and some of the younger native workers realized that this meant they needed to really make an effort in order to understand and learn another culture (Hawaiian). Although as an organization we were still cautious about imposing things on workers, we concluded that it was critical for each staff member to accept and understand their own culture. However, there was still reluctance to impose upon staff, and it was always hoped that change would come from an individual's own motivation and good will.

It was also painfully recognized that many of the families served by the organization did not have a deep cultural base and were struggling to get by in modern Hawaiʻi, too. The organization's leadership recognized this situation as an opportunity to become a cultural bridge for both staff and families so we could be the best helpers in their lives. These were very fine and high-minded principles, which, over time, could easily be forgotten. However, we did a most unusual thing, albeit half-heartedly, in order to prevent that. The staff was given the opportunity to explore and examine its own organizational culture.

A committee was formed to determine the core competencies needed to do our work and to relate those competencies to core values that would guide that work. We framed the core values as taking care of each other; working together and building relationships; striving for pono; sharing compassion; and believing (trusting) in the capacity and capabilities (resiliency) of others and self. This language made it easier to translate and transform them into Hawaiian concepts and terms, and this is what we came up with:

1. Laulima — Cooperation is the key to success
2. Poʻokela — Strive to do your best
3. Kuleana — Consider the feeling of others
4. Aloha — Love one another
5. Kūpono — Trust in each other

Even with this list, a note of explanation had to be attached because some staff had particular and personal interpretations of those Hawaiian terms we wanted to use. We would have had a Tower of Babel unless we could develop a common understanding of that final list of terms.

It had taken seven years for us to come to this point, and there was still some resistance, and some outright rejection, but now among only a small number of workers. Discussion and dialogue, workshops, retreats, and countless administrative meetings slowly furthered this process until the turning point occurred at a gathering for everyone. We listened to an outside consultant, who was a Pacific Islander, tell a story about "two giants" who symbolized the two different approaches being used and advocated to accomplish the organization's goals.

The metaphor of two competing giants, who used the same resources in each trying to out-do the other with neither ever being able to complete the task, was compelling. The story was so memorable that for some time thereafter the staff kept referring to the "two giants."

Something clicked among some very influential workers, for they met that evening, and when everyone gathered again the next day, this group presented a response by telling a story they had created.

Their story was a like a dream and a nightmare and, in hindsight, it spoke about their own understanding of what they had heard the morning before. They were now retelling it in their own way.

They believed they were on an island where they had found a baby that had drifted there and needed help, and they were able to help. This was satisfying and gratifying to them. As time passed they helped more and more babies who drifted ashore until one day they realized that they were surrounded by too many infants. They had neither the will nor the resources to help them all anymore. They realized that so much effort had been placed upon helping individuals that they did not realize that something greater was happening elsewhere which was the source of the problem of drifting babies, and that unless they knew, understood, and could do something about it they would keep doing what they had always been doing, only benefiting a few.

Finally all the documents, guiding principles, and statements made sense to them. Culture as the way their clients were living and responding or not responding to the world is the source, the cultural base, to which they truly needed to guide their clients to be able to make the most appropriate responses and help.

This new enthusiasm turned into a set of organizational documents that, in turn, needed to be translated into something that could be easily conceptualized. Here we turned to a graphical illustration of what this culturally based management might look like. We chose a linear or horizontal direction to emphasize that cultural practices remain constant as the primary basis for the decision-making, planning, and actions that ultimately result in the outcomes.

On the left, a circle of images represented the various aspects of Hawaiian culture—language, performing and visual arts, elders, and family—that were important for the organization. To the right of this, five framed images represented visualizations of the five values chosen to guide our work (aloha, laulima, kūpono, kuleana, and poʻokela). And to the right of these, a table surrounded by chairs represented the importance of discussion and dialogue. A row of chevrons in the background indicated the directional flow of the implementation of these ideas by everyone in the organization, whether the chief executive officer, office staff, or groundskeepers.

And looming above all the stages was a Hawaiian proverb from Pukui: "Hili hewa ka manaʻo ke ʻole ke kūkākūkā ʻDiscussion brings ideas together in a plan'" (ʻŌlelo Noʻeau 106–107).

This proverb was central to the experience we had had up to that point. What had seemed to be endless meetings underscored how important discussion and dialogue were for those people who would be affected by any decision. We realized that if people could be involved from a very early stage, could be heard and valued, and then be a part of the decision making process, they would, more than likely, buy in to the change. The process, as it emerged, used elements and skills taken from hoʻoponopono to help facilitate focused discussion. It also provided opportunities for those gathered to value, recognize, and affirm diverse opinions and to work for an agreement by all.

The final step, illustrated on the extreme right of the graphic to represent the end point of the process, was the involvement of our clients. As the users of our programs and services, they needed to have a voice in the process that would create those programs and services and in the partnership through which they would be delivered. As an organization, we would no longer be working for our clients, but working with them.

The graphical representation had been the culmination of a process that brought all the shareholders together to create a model that we thought gave us a chance to improve how we accomplished our work. However, this model was never implemented. By the time we had been able to put it all together from concepts down to graphic art, the leadership had changed, and they were no longer interested in culture as the basis for the management. This was a major disappointment for many, including me, who had put so much effort and trust into this process. But in hindsight, it was a valuable exercise that would be a great resource for others the next time around.

Hana Hou, Another Attempt

Several years later, a step in that direction was taken at a workshop attended by Native American, Hawaiian, and Canadian elders and youths. As their facilitator, I knew this was a diverse group with some participants attending for the first time, and it was important for them to discover some common understanding and bond. I used a simplified model of the process described above to elicit from each participant what he or she believed were important virtues and values of their native culture. Many of the participants told stories or gave examples from their personal experience to describe what they meant, and through this discussion we were able to develop a list.

When our list was getting long and people were becoming exhausted, we moved to the next task. This was to describe how they practiced those listed virtues and values among their families, communities, and people. Again, many stories were told, and a long list was developed.

These two lists identified their shared cultural base, which led to the next question: What virtues and values did they carry over into their organization, in this case a church? This time, they listed and described aspects of their native ministry and discovered that many of these also applied to cultural activities and practices done outside of the church organization.

But, they also spoke of a frustration for the limitations cultural practices had in a non-native organization and of their desire to be an indigenous church. This led to asking them what more they would need to do to have a church that they felt was home. Once again, they were able to provide several ideas and descriptive stories of their experiences in what they termed a "journey."

In reviewing all the lists and ideas, we sat back in awe at how much effort had been put in, and people began to see things in a new way.

> ∾ We all realized how important it was to discover a common cultural base of virtues and values from which we could share our own experiences and stories. In doing so, we also became more familiar with each other, going beyond introductions to a deeper understanding of each other.
> ∾ We realized how important the sharing of stories and personal experiences were for teaching and transmitting cultural wisdom that cannot be defined in single words or short phrases. We really appreciated the stories as a means of indigenous communication that should not be dismissed or demeaned.

- ❧ We acknowledged that all this took time. Time was needed to tell all the stories, and time was needed to listen, to comprehend, and to reflect.
- ❧ We discovered that when cultural virtues and values are practiced in an organization as they are in families and communities and among the people where they originated, there is less tension and anxiety, especially among indigenous peoples, stemming from not understanding what is expected of them.
- ❧ We realized that an organization that wants to be indigenous needs to be clearly committed to being supportive and encouraging. We know from experience that limited, or qualified, commitment leads to tokenism and failure.
- ❧ We believed that from this process a truly indigenous organization can be developed, its operations and administration defined and described by the cultural experiences and stories we have in us and by the ways they appear in practice in our daily lives. In this regard, we must create a multitude of opportunities for those, both native and non-native, who do not share our common cultural base to do the things that will reinforce our stories and allow them to actively participate and to be able to tell their own stories.

Culture and Business

There is another side of our traditions that few people appreciate, most likely because many of us have not taken the time and effort to read accounts of the very earliest encounters between Native Hawaiians and the Euro-American explorers, adventurers who basically stumbled upon these islands. From the arrival of Cook in 1778 until nearly sixty years later, the journals and diaries of captains and crew are full of interesting first-hand observations, including many on the subject of trade.

When we relive these events through their eyes and words, we must remember that the Europeans, and later the Americans, did not know that these encounters represented the end of a nearly five-hundred-year period of isolation. From these accounts we can learn what, if anything, Native Hawaiians understood about business.

Trading as the First Encounter: This Little Piggy Went to Market

The first encounter of the Hawaiians with the ships led by Captain James Cook upon their unanticipated arrival at Niʻihau and Kauaʻi took place in January of 1778. It was far from the romantic image of friendly hordes of natives in canoes, and there is no evidence that the Hawaiians thought these Western explorers could be gods. The encounter appears to have been prompted by curiosity and suspicion and to have ended with trading.

The English saw the canoes approaching, and when they got close, they were greeted in a language so similar to the Tahitian the English had learned while in Tahiti that the two groups were able to communicate. Cook noted that the canoes had piles of stones in them that he thought the natives had brought along to defend themselves, but having no need of them, they dumped them into the ocean. The natives in the canoes could not be convinced to board the ships, so Cook lowered some brass medals tied to a line, and the natives returned the line with ʻākule ʻmackerel' tied to it. This was done again and some small nails were given, which Cook noted the natives valued "more than any other article" (192). Cook wrote

> For these they exchanged more fish, and a sweet potatoe;
> a sure sign that they had some notion of bartering; or,
> at least, of returning one present for another. They had
> nothing else in their canoes, except some large gourd
> shells, and a kind of fishing-net; but one of them offered
> for sale the piece of stuff that he wore round his waist,
> after the manner of the other islands. (192)

And then,

> As soon as we made sail, the canoes left us; but others
> came off, as we proceeded along the coast, bringing with
> them roasting-pigs, and some very fine potatoes, which
> they exchanged, as the others had done, for whatever
> was offered to them. Several small pigs were purchased
> for a sixpenny nail; so that we again found ourselves in a
> land of plenty [. . .]. (193)

However, when the English changed their trade items, they learned how practical the natives were.

> When we shewed them some beads, they asked first, "What they were; and then, whether they should eat them." But on their being told, that they were to be hung in their ears, they returned them as useless. They were equally indifferent as to a looking-glass, which was offered them, and returned it, for the same reason; but sufficiently expressed their desire for *hamaite* and *toe* [names for iron and the face of an adze], which they wished might be very large. (Cook 194–195)

Cook's detailed observation of the Hawaiian reaction to the infamous trade bead reveals that Hawaiians recognized value in certain items and that value was based upon desirability for use, not for beauty or adornment. Hence, trade beads were "useless," but iron was desired because it could be made into rare and valuable tools.

Without the presence of any chiefs, the Hawaiians of these very first encounters showed a remarkable understanding of how to interact with such total strangers. The English were, at first, taken aback when the Hawaiians came on board the ships and, awed by what they saw, attempted to take all sorts of objects. In order to stop such behavior, Cook had to establish the idea of trading, rather than taking, or in his words, stealing (195), as the means to acquire goods they desired. The Hawaiians got the message and complied so well that Cook made the following observation.

> These people merited our best commendations, in this commerical intercourse, never once attempting to cheat us, either ashore, or along-side the ships. Some of them, indeed, as already mentioned, at first betrayed a thievish disposition; or rather, they thought, that they had a right to every thing they could lay their hands upon; but they soon laid aside a conduct, which, we convinced them, they could not persevere in with impunity. (205)

When the next foreign explorer, La Pérouse, captain of a French scientific expedition, arrived at the islands of Hawai'i and Maui, he would notice that trading with the natives was not as easy. He noted in May of 1786 that the Hawaiians were now well aware of the value of the items they had to trade and of what they wanted in return.

> Our pieces of old iron hoop strongly excited their
> desires, and they showed no want of address in making
> a good bargain to procure them. They steadily refused
> to sell any quantity of cloth or number of hogs in the
> wholesale way, aware that they might derive more profit
> by the separate sale of each individual article. (41)

After the turn of the century, Russian explorers would comment on how much more accommodating and sophisticated native traders had become in dealing with foreigners through learning of foreign language(s) and customs. Captain Lisianskii's account from 1804 illustrates this change.

> Coming up onto the deck, the first islander grasped
> the hand of everyone he met with the words "How
> do you do?" He had picked the phrase up from some
> Englishman or other living on the island, of course. [. . .]
> The first had brought out a hog weighing some two and
> a half *pood*. Broadcloth was requested in exchange for it.
> There being none aboard, the natives carried it back to
> the shore. (Barratt 29)

He also noted how their needs and wants had changed in the eighteen years since La Pérouse's visit, iron hoops no longer being the prized commodity they had been.

> Though the islanders were exchanging their goods for
> knives or small mirrors readily enough, it was our printed
> cloth and striped ticking that they really prized. [. . .] And
> they put a high value even on plain canvas. On the other
> hand, they would hardly deign to look at the iron hoops
> with which we were, it seemed, too abundantly supplied.
> (Barratt 31)

Lisianskii is describing a classic case of the concept of supply and demand. Iron had become commonplace, and the new desired commodity was woven cloth. If they couldn't get that, then the Hawaiians didn't want to trade at all. He even noted that in just a month's time the price of things had increased: On 15 June, trade continued as before, only evertything [sic] except birds became more expensive. (Barratt 35)

When Lisianskii returned ten years later, in 1814, he complained about the disadvantage foreign ships were at when it came to trade, even going so far as to blame other foreigners, in particular naive American whalers, for spoiling the system by, apparently, being too generous in their dealings.

> [. . .] the natives were the worst of profiteers. By general agreement, they would firmly maintain the price of any ware that one of them had sold us. And should one man happen to make a good sale, it was known in all the craft around. At once, all demanded the same price for a similar article. Iron, which was once held in great esteem here, is now worth almost nothing, though the islanders will still take it quite willingly in the form of bars. During our own stay, the most wanted goods were simple canvas, printed cloth, scissors, little knives with pretty handles, and mirrors. For the pieces of iron hoop that secured us six or ten coconuts or two bunches of bananas on the island of Nuku Giva [Nuku Hiva], we could get only the most insignificant objects at Karekekua [Kealakekua]. Ovigi [Hawai'i] has indeed changed greatly over the past ten years, everything now being far more expensive than earlier, as the appended price list shows. The prevalence of these high prices must certainly be attributed to the United States vessels, as many as eighteen of which sometimes call in a single summer to take on all the provisions needed for the remainder of their voyages. (Barratt 46)

His fellow Russian explorer, Golovnin, arrived in the islands in 1818 and also commented on the high prices for commodities and the increased skill of the chiefs in manipulating the market. He noted their sophistication in collecting information about the arriving foreign ships, their crews, and their cargo to use as an advantage in trading.

[. . .] the inhabitants brought quantities of vegetables,
fruit, and chickens for sale, but no hogs. However, the
prices were so high that it did not pay to buy anything;
for instance, in exchange for two watermelons they
wanted a jackknife or a tableknife or a pair of scissors;
the same was asked for a melon. Iron they valued at next
to nothing, and offered mere trifles in exchange for sheet
copper. (177)

The Sandwich Islanders have become very expert and
prudent in their trade, especially their ruler, Tameamea.
The proof of this is the fact that he employs several men
from among the chiefs of lower rank who speak some
English, whose duties consist of visiting foreign ships
and finding out from the sailors the type and amount
of cargo and the number of people aboard, so that
Tameamea may set his price for goods and provisions
accordingly. (203)

When the first American scientific expedition arrived in the
islands in 1840 under the command of Captain Charles Wilkes,
trading in Honolulu, at least, had evolved to become a very real
market economy. Pickering wrote that Honolulu "is a new and
flourishing commercial town," adding that "[i]t was a novelty in
Polynesia to see persons along the roads, bringing wood, charcoal,
and provisions of various kinds, to supply a market" (88). But in
the countryside coins were not yet in use. Pickering described
arriving "at the coast about twenty miles from Hilo [. . .] and we
even experienced difficulty in purchasing provisions, as coin was not
valued" (95).

In a span of about sixty years, Native Hawaiians had developed
a very keen sense of trading, commodities, and dealing with
foreigners on their own terms. Through the observations recorded
in ships' journals and other firsthand documentation, we can see the
development of keen and crucial skills by both chiefs and commoners
in order to become serious traders in a market economy. They had
learned these skills so well that ships' captains would be prompted
to write their complaints, even as early as 1786, of the profiteering
nature of their native counterparts.

The Brave New World

In the 1980s, a lot of attention was given to the fact that few Native Hawaiians were involved in the business world. One reporter wrote,

> [p]erhaps the biggest reason Hawaiians aren't in business is the recurring belief by Hawaiians themselves that their culture and business don't mix. [. . .] If the number of Hawaiians who feel they can combine culture with business increases, the chances are greater that a Hawaiian business community will emerge. (Kephart 20, 22)

From the early explorers' descriptions of trade and of the skill the Hawaiians acquired in a span of just a few years, it would seem that a vigorous business community might have evolved among Native Hawaiians. But the case study of management in a Hawaiian organization made it clear that this is not the case. The change seems to have come in the shift from trade, in the sense of bartering, to a market economy that used money. An editorial in *The Polynesian* from 1848 sheds some light on the much more difficult time Native Hawaiians had in making the transition to the abstract concepts of time and money.

> Much has been said against Hawaiians on the score of their business transactions—want of punctuality in engagements; a disposition to overreach—deception and dishonesty. Hawaiians have had no time-pieces in ages past; they have been accustomed to make no account of time—they waste days and weeks without once dreaming that they have lost any thing. [. . .] The deep poverty of this people leads them to wish all they can get for the trifles they may have to dispose of to foreign visitors. They have seldom the means of estimating the actual worth of what they carry to market; but their own wants and destitution they do know; and these are often the exact measures of their demands. ("Piety or No Piety" 33)

Because I have condensed the story of how we developed a working model for cultural management, I have failed to really express how long it took to develop and the extent of the emotional struggle for all those involved. The integration of traditional culture and corporate culture is not an easy task. The dominance of Western culture with its emphasis on non-relational hierarchy and a style of corporate structure that doesn't easily integrate cultural ways makes it even more difficult. It is easier to slip into token measures such as using Hawaiian terms for non-cultural policies and standards than it is to truly integrate the two.

The choice of culturally based management is a deliberate one, and its integrity is based upon keeping it as the standard. But what can an organization expect to gain from making that choice? As we have seen from the examples of the familial (feasting) and the organizational (corporate) models, the key elements are relationships and trust. In terms of management, those two elements can translate into long-term loyalty, increased efficiency and production, better personnel interaction and cooperation, staff "buy-in," easier transitions to change, and, possibly, more Native Hawaiians involved in business. It might also answer the bedeviling question of whether an organization is a Hawaiian organization or an organization that serves Hawaiians.

Traditional Hawaiian society, from the examples we have seen, utilized methods of management that no longer function today. However, when we look at how early Hawaiian society functioned, we are amazed at the results of these practices in comparison to some of the styles and systems of management used today. This has prompted serious interest in adapting some traditional ways in modern life for the regulation of such things as fishing and water usage.

Today much of management is focused upon outcomes like profit margins, efficiency, and compliance to regulations and laws. Accomplishing those kinds of outcomes often comes at a human cost of interpersonal relationships and community, and for Native Hawaiians those kinds of situations can be a source of conflict that needs to be reconciled through the integration of cultural practices into corporate life. And the extension of culturally based concepts into corporate culture might work if there were an organization bold and brave enough to take a risk in moving the theory and model into reality.

11 Kapu

Gender Roles in Traditional Society

He hana nui loa ka ai kapu ma Hawaii nei, he hana kue loa, he hana kaumaha he hana pono ole loa, iwaena o ke kane a me kana wahine iho [. . .]
Malo, *Ka Moʻolelo Hawaiʻi*

O na kane no hoi kekahi poe loea ma ke ano hana malo a me ka pau wahine. He poe hapa no nae ka poe i ao ia ma ia aoao; ua kapa ia lakou o ka poe hooluu a kapalapala a Ehu.
Kamakau, *The Works of the People of Old*

Not long ago the word *kapu* posted on a tree or fence meant "keep out" and, being in Hawaiian, it seemed a polite way to phrase a warning. To many visitors, not knowing Hawaiian, it didn't mean anything, or as some local comedians suggested, it may have been someone's name. The "keep out" warning actually comes from a tradition of kapu as restricted or prohibited, and in that sense it is usually associated with traditional Hawaiian religion. However, keeping people away from a sacred site is only part of the meaning of kapu. Its origins and its traditional usage have more to do with the separation of gender roles than with traditional religion. For this reason, I have chosen the word *kapu* to be the title of this discussion of gender roles. We do not have a word for gender roles in Hawaiian. The kapu, which created many of the roles for men and women in traditional Hawaiian life, comes closest to describing this idea.

A discussion about the roles of men and women is also bound to touch upon sex and sexuality. Most of the traditions, oral or printed, were far more open about sex and sexuality than we are in today's culture. This discussion can help reveal how our own thinking, prejudices, and world view influence the way we look at traditions concerning gender roles and sexuality.

The Traditions of Wākea and Papa

The separation of roles and tasks—and even of the act of eating together—by the kapu was due to an incident caused by sexual desire in the marriage of the chiefs Wākea and Papa. It is hard to imagine how such an event resulted in dictating what men and women do every day of their lives. But this event was powerful enough to define religion and politics for traditional Hawaiian society.

It began with the chief Wākea's desire to secretly sleep 'moe malu' with his daughter Ho'ohōkūkalani without having her mother, his wife, Papa, know. A bargain was struck between Wākea and his priest, Komo'awa, as a way to seclude Papa away for four nights. In return for her separation from Wākea it was declared that certain foods would be kapu or restricted for women to eat, and that women would not eat with men in the mua or men's house. Papa agreed to these orders.

After Wākea and Ho'ohōkūkalani had slept together, Komo'awa tried to wake Wākea from his sleep so the chief could sneak back to the men's house, but even with the reciting of a prayer chant, saying it louder and louder, Komo'awa could not wake Wākea.

> When the daylight came, Wākea finally got up and covered (pūlo'u) [his head] with a kapa [*bark cloth*]. He returned to the mua thinking that Papa had not seen him. But Papa had seen Wākea and she quickly ran and entered into the mua and quarreled with him. Wākea tried to appease (hoihoi) Papa by saying "sweet" things (me ka ho'ole'ale'a). Papa was appeased and they were separated. (Malo 294)

Malo tells us the foods prohibited for women to eat in an act called 'ai kapu 'restricted foods or eating' were pigs, coconuts, bananas, red colored fish such as kūmū 'goatfish,' and other types of fish such as ulua 'jackfish,' shark 'manō niuhi,' turtle 'honu and 'ea,' pahu 'trunkfish,' porpoise 'na'ia and nu'ao,' whale 'koholā,' manta and sting ray 'hīhīlua, hailepo, and hīhīmanu.' However, he adds, "[t]his list is incomplete of these things that could cause a woman to be put to death for eating these things while she was carefully watched" (158–159).

Another result of this incident was the banning of women from entering into the mua, or men's house, where the men worshiped and ate, and the banning of men from entering the hale pe'a, or house for menstruation. The penalty for anyone breaking the ban was death. "The husband could go in only into the wife's hale 'aina [eating house], but the wife could not enter into the husband's mua [because it was considered kapu]" (Malo 159). The men's eating house, or mua, served also as their place of worship and for the initiation of young boys to adulthood, and this could be a major reason why women were not allowed there. In fact, Kamakau states that it was the "ceremonial offering of ʻawa" that made the mua restricted, hence, men and women were kept to separate houses (*The Works* 132).

This event was important enough to be recalled and woven into in the creation chant Kumulipo, although in a different form than the account described by Malo.

We learn from lines 1800 and 1801 of the chant that two of the sacred or restricted ʻkapu' nights were called Kāne and Hilo (Beckwith, *The Kumulipo* 124), but the restricted plants and foods are very different from those described by Malo. They are called "ʻai lani makua," ʻparental heavenly' or ʻchiefly' foods, and included the "ʻape" which is itchy, "ʻakia" which is bitter, "ʻauhuhu" which is insipid, "ʻuhaloa" which is medicinal and the "laʻalo," a type of kalo which is "manewanewa," a term used to describe rites to counteract a family curse of sickness (Beckwith, *The Kumulipo* 233). It may be that these plants, called ʻai lani or "heavenly food," had a sacred connotation and as such, were another category of things made kapu, or prohibited, for women.

Wākea's secret desire turned into something greater than he might have bargained for, and it would have developed like a bad cover-up to a major crime unless it was used to explain the differing roles of men and women. It established what is known as the kapu system which divided roles and labor between genders; set restrictions on whom one could eat with and what one could eat; evolved into a system of rank and status, and the protection of both, for the aliʻi or ruling chiefs; set up the priesthood as the intermediaries for the aliʻi and created a government that incorporated religion into its ruling system. The kapu system defined how people lived until it ended in 1819.

This very restricted and divisive system of governance and living has been portrayed in many accounts of Hawaiʻi and has often led to the questioning of traditional ways. But it is clear that this questioning is greatly influenced by modern perceptions of the roles of women and men. For example, it was once questioned in cultural quarrels as to whether it was "culturally correct" for women to paddle canoes, especially when the time came to consider if women could compete in the canoe competition from the island of Moloka'i to Honolulu. This bias, according to Linnekin, can also be found in the way Hawaiian society has been interpreted and analyzed. She quotes a recent study by Valerio Valeri to demonstrate this point.

> Women are excluded from the production and cooking
> of these [important] foods. . . . At most, they are given
> the task of appropriating some secondary foods—which
> in a way are "residual," like the women themselves:
> shellfish, mollusks, seaweed, small crustaceans, and so
> on. Sometimes they are able to grow sweet potatoes
> ('uala), a little-prized tuber reserved for marginal land,
> which has the dubious honor of being associated with
> the excrement of the pig Kamapua'a. (Linnekin vii)

Linnekin takes Valeri to task writing, "Valeri's characterization of Hawaiian women as 'marginal' and 'passive' in the context of the sacrificial religion strikes me as a characteristically Western male view of women and moreover, if I may be forgiven for indulging in a stereotype myself, a very Mediterranean male attitude" (viii).

Gender Roles in Pre-contact and Post-contact Hawai'i

The traditions are pretty clear that the separation caused by the 'ai kapu was a fundamental part of Hawaiian life. Accounts of the segregation of women from much of the religious and political life of temple worship are generally true. Women were not allowed into the temple grounds. Instead they had to worship at a smaller site located outside. As Malo states, "the husband did all the key outdoor tasks and his wife did the indoor tasks [. . .]" (159).

It is easy to imagine the separation of tasks based upon gender where men do all the hard labor such as farming and fishing and women do tasks associated with, or located near, the home such as making kapa or bark clothing, and gathering shellfish and seaweeds along the shore. This is a simple picture and follows a pattern of society that has been taught for a very long time. However, because

This detail of the household of Kālaimoku (Kalanimoku) from
"Îles Sandwich: Maisons de Kraimokou, 1819" by J. Alphonse
Pellion shows a woman beating kapa and a man holding the tools
of battle.

of the ʻai kapu, men were also responsible for the cooking and
preparation of food. This is probably due to the prohibition banning
women from touching and eating the various foodstuffs. Kamakau
agrees with Malo, but he adds something more.

> All the work outside the house was performed by the
> men, such as tilling the ground, fishing, cooking in the
> *imu*, and furnishing whatever the women needed in the
> house. This was the common rule on Kauai, Oahu, and
> Molokai, but on Maui and Hawaii the women worked
> outside as hard as the men, often cooking, tilling the
> ground, and performing the duties in the house as well.
> At the time when Kamehameha took over the rule from
> Hawaii to Oahu it was not uncommon to see the women
> of Hawaii packing food on their backs, cooking it in the

> *imu*, and cultivating the land or even going fishing with
> the men. On Maui the men showed their wives where
> their patches were and while they went to do other work
> the women brought the food and firewood from the
> uplands and cared for the *imu*. (*Ruling Chiefs* 238–239)

We cannot be sure of the period of time Kamakau is referring to, whether he is talking about pre- or post-contact island life, but his reference to the time after Kamehameha established rule over all the islands (1810) may indicate the loss of numbers in the male population due to warfare and or foreign diseases. Conflicts throughout history repeatedly show how warfare reduced the number of males in a society and affected the jobs that had been traditionally dominated by men.

Many of the traditions show pre-contact society to be more complex and flexible. We know that men were the priests and that religion was male dominated. Even the "major" gods of the temples were male gods. Major roles in traditional society were male dominated, such that "[t]he composers of genealogical chants such as the *koʻihonua*, *haʻikupuna*, and *kamakua*, were men learned in the art who knew the family lines and were skilled in oratory and state-craft" (Kamakau, *Ruling Chiefs* 241). Yet, there is an obscure reference made on the last day before the ships of Cook's expedition left after he was killed, about the role of women as possible priests on the island of Niʻihau. It is from the journal of James Burney who was on the H.M.S. *Discovery* and reports

> There are at Neehou many priests and, what we have not
> seen at any other of these Islands, priestesses, who all
> act as if they were inspired by some supernatural power,
> performing numberless mad and strange pranks. (11)

David Samwell, one of the surgeons, identified the old woman who encountered Captain Cook when the British went ashore on the island of Niʻihau as Waratoi or Walakoʻi. He made this entry in his journal for January 31.

> [. . .] she performed daily some religious Ceremonies
> as we supposed them to be, & offered Up some small

pigs as Sacrifices for some purpose, and used many
Extravagant Gestures like the Thracian Priestesses of old
as if possessed with some fury [. . .] (Beaglehole 1,085)

When the British returned to the leeward islands of Kaua'i and
Ni'ihau, the old woman, Walako'i, came specifically to see them.
Samwell recorded the event in his journal on Saturday, March 6,
1779.

This morning an elderly woman called Waratoi who had
made herself remarkable at Neehaw by her extravagant
behaviour when we were there last year, & was generally
known by the Name of the Mad Woman, arrived here
from that Island & came on board the Discovery; when
she came along side she made a Speech & on coming
upon deck shed Tears & seemed much affected at seeing
some of her old Acquaintance again, she was dressed
in the stile of a bedlamite with red & yellow rags flying
about her, however she had sense enough to cast them
off on having a better dress presented to her. (Beaglehole
1,226–1,227)

Later on Tuesday, March 9, 1779 her husband came to the
ships and Samwell describes him as being "mad as well as his Wife"
(Beaglehole 1,229). The next day, Wednesday, March 10, Samwell
would come to a conclusion about this order of priests.

[. . .] the Priests every day bring a small pig or two &
sacrifice them at the feet of some of the Gentlemen
ashore, at the same time making Speeches & using many
extravagant Gestures as if they were mad or inspired,
which make us doubt whether Waratoi & her Husband
be frantic or no as they both belong to the Priesthood [. . .]
(Beaglehole 1,229)

On Sunday, March 14, Walako'i came back to the ships and
Samwell noticed that she was scarified from "her neck & shoulders
marked with blisters raised by the Caustic Juice of some Vegetable
which she had put on herself on receiving the News of the Death
of a great Chief at Atowai, whose name was Tairemai [Ka'ilima'i]."

Samwell thought that she used the juice of the mokihana bush to cause the welting (Beaglehole 1,230). And the next day as the British set sail to find the furthest leeward they were told existed, Moku papapa, Walakoʻi and her husband got into a canoe with a gift of a very large iron dagger and departed back home.

How did the British determine these people on Niʻihau to be priests and priestesses? We do not know. However, the citation is of great interest because Burney noted the role these women have is different from what they have seen on the other islands.

It is also apparent from mythical traditions that women, particularly those of rank and status, were involved in another, typically male, role—warfare. In the traditions of ʻAukelenuiaikū, the high chief, a woman named NāmakaoKahaʻi appears with a feather garment made for warfare ka paʻu ai kaua (Fornander IV: 53). And in historical traditions, Kamakau writes that on January 1783 at a battle in Honolulu between the chiefs Kahekili of Maui and Kahahana of Oʻahu, "Ka-hekili's wife Kau-wahine was also a noted fighter" (*Ruling Chiefs* 136). In fact, according to Malo, the lives of women chiefs and those of rank and status (wāhine koikoi) were quite different from that of their counterparts in farming and fishing communities.

> As for the lives of women at the aliʻi(ʻs) residence, they did not beat kapa nor stamp designs on to the pāʻū(s) and malo(s). [. . .] Composing mele [*chants or songs*] in the name of the aliʻi(s) was a principle (sic) activity of the women associated with the aliʻi. (183)

Women in the farming and fishing communities not only beat and stamped designs on to bark clothing 'kapa,' they had to prepare the inner bark of the wauke 'paper mulberry,' and to soften and bleach it. They did the labor-intensive work of pounding the strips of inner bark to produce a felt-like material suitable for clothing.

> Women of the kuaʻāina worked with their husbands. They climbed [down] to the sea to bind in circular bundles (he piʻi nō i kai i pōʻaʻaha) Māmaki (uhai Māmaki), Maʻaloa, pōuluulu [*Breadfruit shoots*], and palaholo. After gathering these materials (uhai) [they are soaked in salt water to be soften (sic)], they are made into

kapa [*bark cloth*]. The women would beat these materials
into kapa, then designs were stamped on to the pāʻū(s)
and malo(s). She supplied her husband, children, the
haku ʻāina(s) and friends, and even had some to trade for
what they lacked (kō lāua hemahema). (Malo 183)

As Linnekin suggests, this activity may have been a source of
power for women because the production of kapa was essential for
daily clothing, religious usage, and tribute gifts for the chiefs. Kapa
was in great demand, and these women were the main suppliers.

These [mats and kapa] are important tasks for women
which are very beneficial. Women's work is known as
kūʻonoʻono [*wealth*] and loea [*skill*] [. . .]. They were
considered to be a source of waiwai [*wealth*]. (Malo 171)

However, Kamakau reports that women did not make all the
kapa.

The furnishings for the inside of the house were made
by the women. [. . .] The women also made the tapa
coverings for the sleepers [. . .]. They made tapa also for
the clothing of men [. . .]. Men who were disinclined
to follow manly pursuits were taught to be experts in
making loincloths and women's skirts and were called
"dyers and printers of Ehu." (*Ruling Chiefs* 238)

Kamakau tells us men were the only ones who made a certain
type of kapa called hamoʻula or kuaʻula.

The work of making *hamoʻula*, or ribbed tapa [another
name for *kuaʻula*], was the work of men, not of women.
(*The Works* 112)

It was specially made in a site that covered two acres or more,
and it "was enclosed with a flimsy fence of palings two or three *anana*
in height. The palings were bound tightly, and dried banana leaves
were laid against the outside. This was the fence for the painting
and dyeing yard. All the supplies of the people inside were kapu"
(Kamakau, *The Works* 112).

An elderly Samoan male beating tapa 'kapa' in Savai'i, Sāmoa

Why was this particular type of kapa made by men and only by men? Why the secrecy, for the finished product only supplied more clothing for men and women?

Perhaps part of the answer comes from the fact that the protectors of those who made and printed kapa were two sisters, La'ahana and Lauhuki, but 'Ehu, the "originator of ribbed tapa, *kua'ula*, became the male *'aumakua* for those who colored *kua'ula*, *hamo'ula*, *waili'ili'i*, *u'au'a*, and such tapas" (Kamakau, *The Works* 116). Did the dyers and makers of ribbed kapa need to have been male, too? Or was there something particular about the tasks of dyeing and making the ribbed grooves on the kapa that required only men to be involved?

Knowing its cultural use or its importance might help to determine why men were the only ones to make this particular kapa. However, we are aware of only one culturally related example of the use of ribbed kapa. A piece of ribbed kapa was found in one of only two known examples of a unique sennit corded casket or kā'ai. This find may not represent its only cultural use, but at this point it is the only example we have (Rose 37).

It is also important to re-examine what Kamakau had said concerning this reversal of roles, and I have italicized the words for emphasis: "Men who were *disinclined to follow manly pursuits* were taught to be experts in making loincloths and women's skirts and were called 'dyers and printers of Ehu'" (*Ruling Chiefs* 238). In the original Hawaiian text it reads, "'O nā kāne nō ho'i kekahi po'e loea ma ke 'ano hana malo a me ka pā'ū wahine. He po'e hapa nō na'e ka po'e i a'o 'ia ma ia 'ao'ao; ua kapa 'ia lākou 'o ka po'e ho'olu'u a kāpalapala a 'Ehu" (Kamakau, *Ke Kumu Aupuni* 233). We learn from this that the men who were taught this art were called the dyers and printers of designs of 'Ehu, so this may indicate that at least that portion of the work, with particular colors and designs, was a male role. The part about "manly pursuits" is more ambiguous. The word Kamakau uses is *po'e hapa* which usually translates to "half," but in this case may mean of "limited" skills, or perhaps with some disability. How the word "hapa" can be related to gender is a very good question.

Aikāne: Just a Friend or a Whole Lot More?

The common problem of mistranslation, and subsequent misunderstanding, of Hawaiian terms for gender roles is also found in the word and role of the aikāne. Its current use as a term for men to call a friend, or buddy, is interesting since its literal translation has more of a sexual connotation.

A re-translation of aikāne as something more than a friend has to take into consideration our modern attitudes and perceptions about male gender roles and relations between men. For instance, it is a stereotype today to make a judgment about the sexuality of men who display female mannerisms. Yet in *Nānā I Ke Kumu* it was noted that "[f]eminine appearance or a soft voice was not considered evidence of homosexuality" (Pukui, Haertig, and Lee II: 110).

Captain King, one of the officers who accompanied Captain Cook in 1778–79, wrote in his journal of the young chief Palea, who is the declared aikāne of the ruling chief of Hawai'i, Kalani'ōpu'u.

This account can open our eyes and minds to a very different attitude concerning male sexuality and its possible role in traditional society. We must remember that the accounts written by the crew of Captain Cook's ships are the earliest written eyewitness accounts we have of traditional Hawaiian society, and as such, contain details of the actions seen as well as cultural attitudes of both native and foreigner.

> Among the chiefs that came on board the *Resolution* was a young man called Pareea, whom we soon perceived to be a person of great authority. On presenting himself to Captain Cook, he told him that he was *jakanee* to the king of the island, who was at that time engaged on a military expedition at Mowee, [. . .] it was observed that the *Discovery* had such a number of people hanging on one side, as occasioned her to heel considerably; [. . .] Captain Cook being apprehensive that she might suffer some injury, pointed out the danger to Pareea, who immediately went to their assistance, cleared the ship of its encumbrances, and drove away the canoes that surrounded her. (Barrow 385)

The young man's authority was corroborated in the journal of Mr. Burney.

> Parreear was always zealous in advising & assisting to punish offenders & several instances happened of his beating them when we excused & let them go, and taking their canoes from them. Indeed on all occasions Parreear was proud of displaying his authority & frequently without much feeling for his countrymen. (Sahlins, *Historical Metaphors*, 43)

A modern analysis of this event is given by Anne Salmond in one of the most recent re-interpretations of the events of Captain Cook's journey.

> Palea, a handsome young man who soon confided that he was Kalani'opu'u's *'aikane* [male lover], seemed to exercise considerable authority. After restoring order on the decks of the ships, he escorted a small, emaciated man named Koa'a on board [. . .]. Koa'a, a priest and

a distinguished warrior, approached Captain Cook
reverently, presenting him with a length of red bark-
cloth which he wrapped around his shoulders [. . .]
before giving him a large pig and quantities of fruit and
root vegetables. After dinner in the Great Cabin, Koa'a
and Palea conducted Cook, Lieutenant King and an
unarmed party ashore [. . .]. (*The Trial* 395)

Kamakau also identifies Palea's relationship with Kalani'ōpu'u
as being aikāne (*Ke Kumu Aupuni* 54). The relationship of aikāne is
described by Davida Malo in his descriptions of the reign of several
ancient ruling chiefs. He says that during the reign of Līloa it was said
that the chief

[. . .] had hana ma'i [*masturbation*] with a sleeping
companion. [. . .] in secrecy without letting anyone else
know [that he did so].

This is what was remembered during the time Līloa
reigned. Līloa had made a certain person his favorite
(punahele). [. . .]

Upon Līloa('s) death, people asked this punahele, "What
did you know [that got you] your punahele status from
Līloa?" This person said, "He performed hana ma'i on
me on [between?] my thighs."

The friends of theirs listened, and hence, moe 'aikāne
[*sleeping with companions*] was well established (pa'a loa)
from that time on until the time of Kamehameha I. (304)

Malo's tradition of Līloa is looked upon as the earliest example
of the aikāne relationship, but Malo, in an earlier chapter, also tells
us that Wākea had an aikāne. This revelation was brought to light
after examining Malo's original handwritten manuscript in a chapter
on the kauwā, or slaves, which had been revised so that portions
referring to aikāne were deleted. The following is the translation of
the unedited text, with the deleted text in brackets.

During the time of Wākea, he had an 'aikāne (*male
companion*). [Ha'akauilanani was his name.] It was not

> heard of as to how he had become an 'aikāne of Wākea
> [perhaps it was done in trade], who knows? When Papa
> left Wākea, Papa went to sleep with his 'aikāne. They had
> a child named Kekeu. [. . .] [they have become] ancestors
> of those true 'aikāne in the Hawaiian Islands. [. . .] If a
> "free" person (someone without any restrictions) slept
> with, perhaps an ali'i and children were born, then they
> were considered true 'aikāne. (Malo 184)

What does Malo mean by a "true" aikāne? Is it, as suggested, a person (male or female) whose status was noa, or free, and not just someone involved in a male homosexual relationship? Or did the concept of aikāne change under the reign of Līloa to be only that of a male companion? British accounts cannot completely clarify this for us, because the British did not understand what the relationship of aikāne was. They did learn its meaning later as they remained on the island of Hawai'i. David Samwell made this entry to his journal on January 29, 1779 during the Makahiki festival.

> Another Sett of Servants of whom he has a great many
> are called Ikany [. . .] and their business is to commit
> the Sin of Onan upon the old King. This, however
> strange it may appear, is fact, as we learnt from frequent
> Enquiries about this curious Custom, and it is an
> office that is esteemed honourable among them & they
> have frequently asked us on seeing a handsome young
> fellow if he was not an Ikany to some of us. (Beaglehole
> 1,171–1,172)

Samwell's commentary is the earliest foreign confirmation that the term aikāne is in reference to a sexual relationship rather than one of being a "close friend or companion." He seems bothered by it, as evidenced by this second bit of commentary in his journal.

> [. . . they] have as many Concubines and Wives as they
> please, and a number of young fellows under the Title of
> Ikany whose office has been before explained, & we have
> great reason to think that that Unnatural Crime which
> ought never to be mentioned is not unknown amongst
> them. (Beaglehole 1,184)

He also alleges that Kamehameha also engaged in an aikāne relationship, writing in his journal on February 10, 1779.

> Kameha-meha got nine [daggers] of them for his Cloak.
> He with many of his attendants took up his quarters on
> board the ship for the Night: among them is a Young
> Man of whom he seems very fond, which does not
> in the least surprize us as we have had opportunities
> before of being acquainted with a detestable part of his
> Character which he is not in the least anxious to conceal.
> (Beaglehole 1,190)

But that was not the last of his observations and comments about the aikāne, for as the British were finally departing the islands and they were off the island of Kaua'i, Samwell witnessed this incident when the attention was directed to one of the British crew members.

> Karan-koa [Kalanikoa; he was the son of Kiha and
> Ka'apuwai (ftn. 3)], brother to Teeave by the father's
> side, being on board the Resolution to day and seeing
> a handsome young fellow whose appearance he liked
> much, offered six large Hogs to the Captain if he would
> let him stand his Ikany for a little while, such is the
> strange depravity of these Indians. (Beaglehole 1,226)

Although Linnekin, in her study of gender and rank says it "may have been a homosexual relationship [. . .] in any case intimate association with a chief, whether homosexual or heterosexual, was a recognized route to higher status" (100). Malo, however, is quite clear about the sexual role of aikāne and their close relationship to the chief(s).

> Those who slept with women were rare to find in the ali'i('s)
> residence. Most slept without the company of women. Many
> slept with 'aikāne [*male companions*]. The sleeping of males
> together was widespread at the ali'i('s) residence. (181)

But was the status of aikāne synonymous with the authority displayed by Palea, or was it closer to that of a punahele (favorite)?

Kamakau refers to Palea as Kalaniʻōpuʻu's punahele. This was also the status of Līloa's aikāne. It well may have been a combination of the relationship, which gains access to the high chief, and the status as a punahele, that granted a person like Palea authority in the name of the high chief.

The Observations of Gender Roles After Cook

Kamakau tells us that women played a great role in society, but it is difficult to know whether or not he is referring to pre- or post-contact society.

> The men stood along the width of the field [to plant
> sweet potato] with their backs to it and began digging.
> [. . .] Women followed with the slips, dropping two into
> each planting hole and other women placed them side by
> side [. . .] (*The Works* 24)

> In the morning there would be octopus spearing, it was
> announced to the men and women. There would be many,
> many of them, some on canoes and some afoot carrying
> spears [. . .] (*The Works* 70)

> [. . .] a kahuna went to the mountains to hew down a
> tree for the canoe [. . .] men and women went up to
> the mountains to drag it down, and many pigs were
> provided for them. The dragging of a canoe (*kauo waʻa*)
> was a great occasion. (*The Works* 119)

Later, early missionaries, too, noted the various roles of women.

> The old men were most of them dressed in a kihei, as
> were also some of the women, but many of the latter
> wore only a pau of native cloth wound round their loins
> [while farming at Papapohaku]. Their black hair was
> in several instances turned up, and painted white all
> around the forehead, with a kind of chalk or clay [. . .]
> (Ellis 132)

Among the chiefs, women were seen to be involved in the making of chiefly ornaments. This may have been a pre-contact activity and carried on after contact, for Malo comments, "It was a lot of labor for the female aliʻi to make lei huli kua" (189).

> [. . .] the females, especially those attached to the
> households of the chiefs, spend much time in making
> articles of ornament; in the braiding of human hair
> for necklaces; trimming and arranging feathers for
> wreaths and kahiles; polishing tortoise shell and the
> ivory of whale's teeth, for finger rings, and the handles of
> feathered staffs, &c. (Stewart 150)

During the post contact period John Papa ʻĪʻī saw that women in the chief's court, no matter their rank or status, were not exempt from hard labor.

> [. . .] a proclamation was sent to the women of the
> court to fetch and spread grass on the field early in the
> morning. This proclamation required all the women
> who served in the court, chiefesses of lesser rank and
> notables, to fetch grass from Kawaiahao. (54)

One of the most interesting of these observations was reported by John Whitman, who was in the islands from 1813 to 1815.

> The women also have their boxing matches and under
> similar regulations. They however do not box under
> the same Etour moco moco [*Akua mokomoko* 'fighting
> God'] as the men, it being necessary that theirs should be
> made especially for females, the mens being tarboo and
> the womens nore [*noa*]. (Linnekin 30–31)

It is also probable that the status of women had begun to change after the arrival of Captain Cook and his expedition since women played a unique role in the trade for foreign goods. Women provided sexual favors for the British crew with or without the consent of men for an increased accessibility to trade goods, especially iron (Linnekin 56–58, Sahlins, *Historical Metaphors* 41).

Women of high rank played an increasing role in the governance of the kingdom from the ending of the kapu system in 1819, especially since the two heirs and sons of Kamehameha were too young to govern after his death. In fact the role of the kuhina nui or premier became a position filled only by women.

The role of a woman warrior also continued into post-contact times. Kamakau recorded that it was a "koa wahine" (woman warrior) who sounded the initial alarm that the Kaua'i rebels were attacking the loyalist fort at the battle of 'Aipua'a on July 24, 1823 on the island of Kaua'i. "Kahala-i'a and his men were awakened by the ringing of the bell and the shouts of a woman warrior who cried, 'Here come the Kauai warriors after the arms! here [sic] come the rebels! the [sic] men of Hawaii still hold the fort! it [sic] is not taken for Kauai!' " (*Ruling Chiefs* 267).

A Girl Named Keākealani

The increasing status of women that occurred after the arrival of Captain Cook was was not unprecedented. Years before— several generations before the time of Kamehameha—a greater cultural shift to the kapu system had happened on the island of Hawai'i as a result of the birth of a baby girl.

Upon the death of the ruling chief, Lonoikamakahiki (the same chief who introduced the Makahiki, an annual tribute of rites and games, a sort of Hawaiian Olympics), his children did not become rulers. Instead authority went to "[t]he children of Kanaloa-kua'ana [. . .] and their descendants became rulers" (Kamakau, *Ruling Chiefs* 61). Rule passed to the offspring of Keli'iokalani and Keākealanikāne. They had a daughter named Keakamahana.

> Ke-aka-mahana was made ruler of Hawaii, but not the whole of it for there were other chiefs over Hilo and Hamakua. [. . .] Chiefs of Kona recognized one as head over all and they all called her their lord. They left the government to her and exalted her. Their ruler was Ke-aka-mahana, a woman. This sacred woman, Ke-aka-mahana, was married to Iwi-kau-i-ka-ua, a chief of Hawaii. Their rank was not equal as his was lower than hers for hers was of *pi'o* rank, and her family included the tabu chiefs of Kauai. [. . .] She was one of the *pi'o* rank because her parents were brother and sister, Ke-li'i -o-ka-lani and Keakea-lani-kane. When Ke-aka-mahana was born she was

taken to Kauai to be reared, and when the chiefs of Hawaii desired a sacred ruler over their government they went to Kauai to bring her back. (Kamakau, *Ruling Chiefs* 61–62)

Keakamahana did not like the mother and older daughter of her husband, Iwikauikaua, and she had the two women killed. When this happenened her husband left her to live on Oʻahu and had a son there named Kāneikauaiwilani, in whom he nurtured the chance for revenge. Like a bad made-for-television movie, Kāneikauaiwilani, when he grew up, went back to Hawaiʻi to marry his half sister, Keākealani, the daughter of Keakamahana and Iwikauikaua. The chiefs of Kona continually fought with the chiefs of Hilo over the many resources that were under Hilo's control. In time, things got worse for the chiefs of Kona, and when they were finally defeated, Keākealani and her people were captured and sent as prisoners to Maui and Molokaʻi. When she was finally released she ruled over the districts of Kohala, Kona and Kaʻū, but "in name only" (Kamakau, *Ruling Chiefs* 63).

John Papa ʻĪʻī emphasized that Keākealaniwahine [the term *wahine*, or "female," is added to distinguish her name from the other Keākealani who was male and had the term kāne added to his name] was the paramount chief of the entire island, and as such, had more status and privileges than would normally be associated with a woman.

> Keakealaniwahine was once the ruler of all Hawaii, and was succeeded by her son Keawe i Kekahialiiokamoku. Keakealaniwahine was brought up with the *kapu moe*. As there was no other chiefess her equal, she was kept apart, with the chiefs who had the right to the prostrating kapu, and away from places where people were numerous. Her houses, surrounded by a stone wall, stood on an elevation above Keolonahihi in Holualoa, North Kona. She was thought to be a chiefess who would care for the welfare of the people and for the kingdom, and would understand how to benefit it and bring it prosperity.
>
> Later, when she became the ruler, she was in charge of all the heiaus on Hawaii. She offered human sacrifices in the

six *luakini* heiaus of the six districts of Hawaii [. . .]. It was
said that whenever a ceremony was performed at these
heiaus she wore a skirt of *ninikea*, a soft white tapa made
by women who were skilled in the art.

Though a woman, Keakealaniwahine was permitted
to enter the heiaus to give her offerings and sacrifices.
However, she was not allowed to eat any of the offerings
and gifts with the priests and the men, who ate by
themselves. She participated only in the ceremonies,
for men and women continued to eat apart from the
time of Wakea, because of Hoohokukalani. [. . .] Thus
Keakealaniwahine ate in her own house of the food
permitted to women. The only men who ate with the
women were those who prepared the food of the chiefess
and who had the privilege of serving it to her. (Ii 159–160)

The ruling male chiefs and priests dramatically changed their
world through this radical but practical shift to accommodate a
woman, who had been born of greater rank and status than any of
them. The next shift to the kapu system would have to wait several
generations until the time of Keōpūolani and Kaʻahumanu, direct
descendants of Keākealaniwahine. They were the two women
deliberately sought by Kamehameha to be his wives in his quest to
conquer and unify the islands, and who would initiate the eating
freely with men and the eating of unrestricted foods upon his death.

Keōpūolani was a "niece" of Kamehameha—her grandfather,
Keōua Kupuapāikalani, was Kamehameha's father. Her high rank
and status, based upon the model of the union of Wākea and
Hoʻohōkūkalani, came from her parents who were half-brother and
sister, and her paternal and maternal grandfathers, Kalaniʻōpuʻu and
Keōua Kupuapāikalani, who were half-brothers and who also shared
the same wife, Kalola PupukaoHonokawailani.

According to Kamakau, Keōpūolani was

[. . .] for whom these tabus were made and who had
benefit of them. [. . .] even Kamehameha had been
obliged to uncover and remove his loin cloth in her
presence; (*Ruling Chiefs* 224)

She became his wife only through his conquest after defeating the chiefs of Maui. "It has been said that because Kamehameha I did not obtain his high chiefess [Keōpūlani] through appeal to Kahekili and others, this was the reason for the great inheritance war between Kamehameha I and Kalanikupule at Wailuku, Maui [. . .] As a result of this victory of Kamehameha, he obtained this very high sacred chiefess" (McKinzie 28). The term *inheritance war* mostly refers to Kamehameha's desire to have his children inherit the highest possible rank through Keōpūolani. We see this practice again with another notable wife of Kamehameha's, the younger sister of Kaʻahumanu, Kaheiheimālie Kīnaʻu. She had two daughters, Kamamalū and Kīnaʻuwahine, and Kamehameha wished them to become the wives of his "grandsons" [a term he used for his own sons] by Keōpūolani. By these unions of sisters and brothers, they would achieve an even higher rank and status within his immediate family.

While Keōpūolani could be considered Kamehameha's sacred wife, Kaʻahumanu could be considered his political wife for she brought him the natural resources of eastern Maui needed for his war campaigns as well as the great armies of her father, Keʻeaumoku Papaiahiahi, who was descended from Keākealaniwahine. Kamakau called this marriage an "alliance [. . .] Kamehameha's long control of the government was due to this wife alone; through her all the chiefs became reconciled to Kamehameha [. . .]" (*Ruling Chiefs* 311).

Long after their marriage, after Kamehameha had gained control of the islands, we see evidence of how great Kaʻahumanu's strategic importance had been to Kamehameha when her father, Keʻeaumoku on his death bed, warned Kamehameha that "None of the chiefs is strong enough to conspire against you. There is indeed one who might succeed in such a rebellion, your wife [Ka-ʻahu-manu]; but if you are careful rebellion may be avoided." Upon this advice, Kamehameha fearing for the stability of his government, [. . .] made Kaʻahumanu the pillar and cornerstone for the state by making her body kapu (forbidden) so that if any high chef slept with [her], he was considered a rebel, and he was put to death and his land confiscated (Kamakau, *Ruling Chiefs* 189).

Keōpūlani and Kaʻahumanu, together, were instrumental in ending the restrictions imposed upon men and women by the kapu from the time of Wākea, Papa, and Hoʻohōkūkalani. The conditions for their actions had been in place for a long time, perhaps waiting for the precise moment when they could be acted upon. Malo reminds us of some of the pre-contact traditions.

> Furthermore, several people were given the task as unprohibited eaters for chiefly women and for women of rank (wahine koikoi). These people ate with these women as they had prepared the women's food. They were called several names such as ʻai noa and ʻai pūhiʻu. (159)

This sanctioned free eating was allowed only after the death of the ruling chief, and only the men who had prepared the food could eat with high-ranking women. However, when the new paramount chief had been installed and the kapu reinstated, then this free eating ended.

A range of speculation has developed as to the motivation for the ending of the kapu: from the redistribution and denial of land holdings by the chiefs, to the increase of power and ambition on the part of high-ranking female chiefs after centuries of male domination, to political control by the new ruling family of the Kamehamehas. The arrival of Captain Cook created further challenges for the religious-political system of the Hawaiians' world view, as well as for their ideas of the way things should be (Linnekin, Sahlins).

Whatever the motivation, the death of Kamehameha in 1819 created the opportunity for dramatic action during the traditional mourning rites, including the eating together of men and women. The decision to make this mourning practice permanent was made by the very young heir Liholiho (Kamehameha II), and the result was the ending of all the rituals and preferences given to the chiefs. This decision was backed by the remaining high chiefs of his father's old court, his mothers Keʻōpūolani and Kaʻahumanu, and his uncle Kalanimoku. Kamakau thought it was strange for a "tabu chiefess [. . .] one for whom these tabus were made and who had benefit of them," to have agreed to such a decision and to cooperate in its enforcement. However, he stated it correctly that when "Ke-opu-o-lani, the only remaining high tabu chiefess, gave up the tabu with the consent of all the chiefs, the tabu system fell" (*Ruling Chiefs* 224).

It was during this important point in the transition from chiefs
to king, from an isolated society to one open to the world, that
with some irony, women with greater rank and status than the men
around them influenced the end of the kapu begun so long ago by
Wākea and Komoʻawa.

Linnekin's reading of the historical tradition leads us to believe
that "women become more important than ever as points of access
to power and as politically powerful figures in their own right. By all
accounts, as premier (*kuhina nui*) and regent Kaʻahumanu was the de
facto ruler of the Hawaiian Kingdom until she died in 1832" (72).

She adds that "with the demise of the sacrificial cult that legitimated
conquest, male Hawaiian *aliʻi* seem to have lost some of their *mana*,
their efficacy and directedness. [. . .] The fall of the indigenous religion is
only one of many factors in the demoralization of male chiefs. But if
[. . .] the tabus were a way in which men exerted some control over
women, then *aliʻi* men may well have suffered differentially from the
loss of that ritual system" (73). This makes sense when one considers
how male-dominated the kapu system had been for the chiefs and
others of rank and status. The union of political power and religious
authority imposed through Komoʻawa with Wākea increased the
power of male priests and chiefs over the limitations imposed upon
high-ranking women (Papa). The eventual overthrow of the kapu
system cancelled that power and authority and resulted in limitations
on the roles of the male chief in the new society.

Linnekin concludes her study by suggesting that

> the segregation of men and women under the *kapu*
> system gave women a degree of autonomy, even a
> certain ritual leverage over men. The social standing of
> Hawaiian men *and* women has been radically abridged
> since 1778. A society with far different notions of
> women's proper place became dominant in the islands.
> [. . .] Whether Hawaiians have internalized the Western
> model of male-and-female is quite another question, and
> one that has yet to be answered. (239)

Defining a proper role for Native Hawaiian men today is
one of the challenges being actively explored in Native Hawaiian

communities. Many Hawaiian males, who seem to identify only with men of rank and status, such as aliʻi and warriors, seek to revive some sort of traditional role for men through lua 'traditional wrestling or martial arts,' protocol, and leadership. Men have dominated the leadership roles of Christianity, but their influence is lessened when the major Christian denominations, locally and nationally, keep native clergy and laity in subservient organization roles. A solution may be found in some sort of culturally recognized roles for men as those found in Aotearoa 'New Zealand,' where oratory is reserved for men, and women have other defined roles in these rituals of protocol and encounter. I once asked an elder Māori woman at a marae gathering what she thought about the separation of roles, and whether she felt women should be allowed to speak on the marae 'sacred courtyard area for rituals of encounter.' Her answer, in light of the above discussion, still echoes with wisdom and reality, "We [Māori women] don't mind all the wind that is spoken because we know when and where and who make the decisions anyway. So let the men have their moment in the sun. It's only talk."

A difficulty Linnekin alludes to is determining how much modern American culture has influenced, and continues to influence, the Native Hawaiian discussion of gender roles and sexuality. While I was working at the Queen Liliʻuokalani Children's Center, a fellow worker brought in a project involving Hawaiian male teenagers on the island of Kauaʻi. Reviewing his proposed project so that it might be culturally appropriate, I returned it with one major concern. The group was to print t-shirts with a design of an over muscled male posing in a manner of a body builder or weight lifter. My objection was that the image was a modern image from contemporary American culture. I told him that traditional culture would want to lead youth to become responsible, nurturing, and caring adults who can benefit their extended family, or ʻohana. The motto of Kamehameha II was hoʻokanaka, to be someone. Today, it could also be hoʻomakua, to be adult or an elder, that is to have respect because people know who you are and what you must and can do.

The re-definition of gender roles in contemporary Hawaiian life must, I believe, be culturally based in order to take hold in a community of responsible and contributing members. If they are not, the re-invented roles will serve only for celebrations and holidays. This culturally based approach can be achieved if we develop these roles as proposed by Martin Brokenleg in his work on youth at risk, encompassing roles for both men and women that emphasize these four guiding principles: a sense of belonging, mastery, independence, and generosity (Brendtro et al. 45). Otherwise the roles of men and women will allow them only to play at culture rather than to live it.

12 Hewa
The Wrong Way of Living

The king was the one who did wrong, but fault was put
on an innocent person. Perhaps the king's conscience
within him knew that what he had done was wrong and that
he should repent, thus shortening the matter and letting it end.
'Ī'ī, *Fragments of Hawaiian History*

✖

Though he alone was thought to have committed
the misdeed, the whole family was held guilty.
'Ī'ī, *Fragments of Hawaiian History*

In 1985 I had the opportunity to travel with the late Moses
Keale, Sr., chairman of the Office of Hawaiian Affairs (OHA), to
visit the northern Pueblo (Tewa) peoples. New federal funds were
being released for a Native Hawaiian arts and crafts program, and we
went to New Mexico to visit their similarly funded program in Santa
Fe. After lunch with representatives of the Eight Northern Indian
Pueblos, they informed us that there was a celebration beyond the
mesas, in the mountains at Taos. They said there was a traditional
Native Hawaiian dance group being honored there. Before we left,
one of them told us, half jesting and half warning, to beware of the
clowns, the *koshare*, during the celebrations as they tended to pick on
the obvious tourists.

We got to Taos Pueblo and saw the crowd gathered in a very
large semicircle at the main plaza. I spotted the Hawaiians sitting
down on the dirt on the other side of the circle. We heard loud
laughter and shouting, and a cry of anguish. The clowns had entered
the crowd, and one had put a large watermelon up the shirt of an
unsuspecting tourist to make him look pregnant. The clowns were
painted in black and white stripes, and some had two long pointed
tips on their heads. As they came along the semicircle, that's when
Moses indicated it was time to go. He had his beautiful, white,
Tahitian baby palm hat on, and it was not going to a clown.

The tradition of clowns and clowning around is found in many
Native American cultures. Some traditions speak of this group as
formerly being a very powerful priesthood that did something wrong

The author and Moses Keale, Sr. (in his Tahitian baby palm hat) with Dr. Susan Guyette and Walter Dasheno of the Eight Northern Indian Pueblos Council in San Juan Pueblo, New Mexico

and, thereafter, had to lead a life of misbehavior or doing things backwards. At these feast days, their task of comedy, sometimes becoming very pointed abuse, is to point out, by providing a mirror image of the world, how things really should be done. If their victims know the difference between good and bad behavior, then their shame is revealed through embarrassment, and the public display might be all that is needed to have misbehavior corrected. In Hawai'i, we don't have the role of clowns in our traditions, but we do have some characters who acted like clowns or tricksters.

We find tricksters, such as the coyote or rabbit in the southwest United States, in indigenous cultures throughout the world. Tricksters are a little bit different than clowns. Their bad behavior is more likely to be intentional. They not only use trickery to get what they want; they lie, cheat, deceive, and even seem to do magical feats.

The stories in Hawai'i most closely belonging to this form are the traditions Beckwith called "kupua stories." She wrote that they had "a regular pattern" (*Hawaiian Mythology* 404).

> The kupua is born in some nonhuman form, but
> detected and saved by his grandparents, generally on
> the mother's side, who discern his divine nature. He is
> precocious, becomes speedily a great eater, predatory
> and mischievous. (*Hawaiian Mythology* 404)

Even though she states that "[k]upua stories are admittedly
fiction, although often credited as fact" (*Hawaiian Mythology* 404),
we recognize that causes for the child's bad behavior range from
rejection at birth to identification with a missing parent, in these
cases the father. What is thought of as rascal or mischievous behavior
inherent to the child, what some today would call "acting up," is
evidently based upon the child's early experiences trying to establish
some sense of belonging and relationship to others.

The tradition of 'Ōpelemoemoe and his son, Kalelealuaka, is one
of these kupua stories. The son's bad behavior and tricks are a sign of
his vying for attention that underscores his deep desire to know who
his father is and, therefore, who he is himself.

> Hele aku la keia [Opelemoemoe] a hiki i ka wahine,
> noho iho la laua, a hala he mau anahulu, hapai ka
> wahine i ke keiki.
>
> I loko o keia wa, olelo aku o Opelemooemoe: "E, ke hoi nei au
> i Oahu; eia ka'u kauoha ia oe, i hanau ae he keiki kane, kapa
> oe i kona inoa, o Kalelealuaka, a i manao e imi ae ia'u, eia ka
> maka la, he ihe." Noho aku la ka wahine o Kalilikookalauae,
> a hanau he keiki kane, kapa iho la i ka inoa o Kalelealuaka,
> hanai iho la a nui. He keu ke kolohe a me ka eu; mimi iho
> la kela i ka umeke a me ka ipukai, pela ka hana mau ana.
> Nolaila, lele aku ka makuakane kolea papai ia Kalelealuaka,
> uwe kela a olelo aku ia Kalikookalauae ka makuahine: "Ea! E
> kuu makuahine, e hai mai oe i ko'u makuakane;" hoole aku
> ka makuahine, aole ou makuakane e ae, o kou makuakane iho
> la no ia. No ke koi pinepine o Kalelealuaka i ka makuahine,
> e hai mai i kona makuakane. Hai aku o Kalikookalauae ia
> Kalelealuaka: "Ae, he makuakane kou, o Opelemoemoe ka
> inoa. (Fornander V: 171)
>
> 'Ōpelemoemoe went to the woman and they lived
> together. After several weeks (anahulu) had passed she
> was pregnant with child.
>
> During that time 'Ōpelemoemoe said, "Oh, I have to go
> back to O'ahu. I have to tell you this, if a boy is born give
> him the name of Kalelealuaka, and when he wants to

find me this is the sign of my love for him, a spear." This woman, Kaliliko'okalaua'e remained there, and she gave birth to a son and called him Kalelealuaka and raised him up until he was mature. But he was a rascal full of energy. He even urinated in the food bowls and did all sorts of things like that. Therefore his stepfather (makuakāne kōlea) beat Kalelealuaka, and he cried and spoke to his mother, Kaliliko'okalaua'e. "Mom! Tell me who my real father is." His mother refused to and told him he had no other father but his stepfather. Kalelealuaka didn't give up and kept asking his mother until she finally told him who his real father was. Kaliliko'okalaua'e told Kalelealuaka, "Yes, you have a real father whose name is 'Ōpelemoemoe. (Author's translation)

The most renowned kupua in Hawaiian traditions is Māui [Maui], whom Martha Warren Beckwith, the first anthropologist-folklorist in the islands to study and translate traditional Hawaiian stories, named as our master trickster. Later, in 1955, her successor in the field, Katherine Luomala, renamed Māui as a "South Sea Superman." She gave this description of this pan-Polynesian kupua or demi-god.

When the world was still new, Maui turned the already hide-bound social order topsyturvy, and according to the insulted gods, he tried to dissolve the entire physical and social universe into its original chaos. His exasperated parents, who thought him a bad boy, called him with obvious restraint "that nasty joker" and "that revolting child." His lawlessness made him so unpopular in his village that he finally had to move to the underworld until gossip and anger died away. The gods, who had long since abandoned him, were as anxious as the villagers about what to expect next from this semidivine juvenile delinquent who tried to usurp their power and privileges and whose misbehavior was on a cosmic scale. The gods were disturbed because Maui had learned magic from them after they had rescued him, an ugly misbirth cast away by his mother with a prayer, and had tenderly reared him until he decided to return to the earth to seek his mother and other

> relatives. Maui spent his brief but eventful life in trying to
> prove to the gods that he knew more magic than they did
> and in trying to impress the homefolks by his adventures.
> Instead, he angered and alarmed everyone, until at last only
> a flock of silly, chattering little birds would have anything
> to do with him. (85)

We are all too familiar with the acts of Māui: snaring the sun to slow down the day, fishing up the islands, or obtaining fire because all of these helped our ancestors' miserable plight. Those stories have been told and retold, especially in children's books. They play to our desire to see the lowly triumphing over the mighty and powerful. However, Māui's epic tradition involved other feats as well. He also separated the sky and earth. He rescued his mother from an eel and his wife from an eight-eyed bat. He had to be rescued from being sacrificed by his mother and younger sibling. These stories, and there are many variants of them, make Māui seem like the Superman we are more familiar with who is there to look after and protect the weak and lowly. But Māui is no Clark Kent, and the story of his death, which comes because he had made himself "unpopular with his tricks" (Beckwith, *Hawaiian Mythology* 233), underscores his motivation for all these feats—his need to receive attention and a sense of belonging, perhaps even love, that he misses from his relatives.

> Maui goes to live in Hilo on Hawaii and makes himself
> unpopular with his tricks. He one day visits the home of
> Kane and Kanaloa and their party at Alakahi in Waipio
> valley and attempts to spear with a sharp stick the bananas
> they are roasting by the fire. He is detected and his brains
> dashed out. They color the side of Alakahi peak and tinge
> red the shrimps in the stream. A rainbow is formed of his
> blood. (Beckwith, *Hawaiian Mythology* 233–234)

Examining what happens in the stories of Māui's feats sheds a little more light on why Luomala uses the term juvenile delinquency to describe Māui's use of his super powers.

Obtaining fire from the mud hens is his first feat. He first had to catch one of them, and then to threaten the little bird to convince it to reveal the secret. He then "rubs a red streak on the mud hen's

Some of Māui's feats are well known, while others are less well known. This print by Dietrich Varez shows Māui lassoing the sun in order to show it down.

head out of revenge for her trickery before letting the bird escape" (Beckwith, *Hawaiian Mythology* 230).

His second feat is to slow down the sun by lassoing the sun's rays until eventually the sun has to plead for its life. In one version of the story, after accomplishing his task Māui "then turns to punish Moemoe, who has derided his effort. Moemoe flees until overtaken north of Lahaina, where he is transformed into the long rock beside the road today" (Beckwith, *Hawaiian Mythology* 231).

When Māui goes fishing with his brothers they hook a giant fish in order to make the islands one. In some versions a canoe bailer found floating on the water is involved, which turns into a beautiful woman. In one version, Māui's mother had warned about this bailer; however, he picks it up anyway, causing his brothers to turn and look, and resulting in the fish getting away and islands not being united (Beckwith, *Hawaiian Mythology* 232).

In the West Maui versions, Māui's mother and her young child, who is an owl, come to rescue Māui from being offered as a sacrifice. His half-brother, the owl, gets Māui and sets him free so that Māui's mother "sits down, covers him with her clothing and pretends to pick fleas. Thus he is saved" (Beckwith, *Hawaiian Mythology* 231). In the O'ahu versions, it is Māui who saves his wife from the eight-eyed bat, Pe'ape'amakawalu. Māui "cuts off the chief's head and flies away with his wife to Oahu, where he drains all eight of the bat's eyes in a cup of awa" (Beckwith, *Hawaiian Mythology* 233).

In the traditions, Māui may punish the mud hens for deceiving him by rubbing the bird's forehead so hard it turns red, but in the following stories of the chiefs the violence has deadly results, and they are playing for keeps. We see in these traditions how the concept of hewa intensifies from mischief and misbehavior of a child to deceit and plotting, jealousy, and physical violence of adults.

Several generations before the 1779 arrival of Captain James Cook on the island of Hawai'i, these mythical traditions of kūpua, younger and older brothers, and tricksters entered historical reality when the paramount chief Līloa had another son, whom he named 'Umi.

'Umi had been conceived through an affair with a woman named 'ĀkahiaKuleana. As if patterned after the 'Ōpelemoemoe story, Līloa had left her with child and with personal items to symbolize his paternity: his own clothes, whale's tooth pendant, and war club.

Kamakau tells us that Malo recorded an early written account of 'Umi while they were members of the first Hawaiian Historical Society in Lāhaināluna (Malo vi, ftn.). This is Malo's account.

> While he [Līloa] was staying there, he went to bathe in the stream of Kahoea, This area is close to Kealakaha. He found 'Akahi[a]Kuleana there. She was coming back from bathing to purify herself as she was over her period. (Later she was to join her husband, that was the way women of that time did things) and her female kauwā stayed at the embankment of the water to bring her pā'ū [*clothing*].

> Līloa saw a beautiful woman and Līloa desired this woman. He seized her and said, "We must sleep together." The woman saw Līloa and consented.

The two [of] them slept together and when they were finished sleeping, Līloa saw that she had been menstruating (pohā). Līloa asked this woman, "Say, are you not menstruating?" She said, "Yes, I am. I have been for a while" ('o ko'u mau ana mai la nō ia.)

Līloa said to her, "You are probably pregnant." She thought so, too. Then Līloa asked her, "Who are you? What is your name?" She told him, "I am 'Akahi[a]Kuleana. My parent is Kuleanakapiko." Līloa said, "Then you may be a 'sister' of mine." And she said, "That may be so."

Then Līloa instructed her about the child, "If the child born is ours, if it is a girl, well, you will name her after your side, but if it is a boy, then you will call him 'Umi."

'AkahiaKuleana said, "What will be their [the boy or girl's] sign that will readily indicate that they are your children as an ali'i?"

Līloa gave [her] his malo [*loin cloth*], his niho palaoa [*Whale's tooth pendant*] and his club, saying, "These are the sign of our child and when he or she grows up, you will give these things to him or her." Then, 'AkahiaKuleana agreed to Līloa('s) instruction and 'AkahiaKuleana gave [the objects] to her kauwā to take care of the symbols of Līloa to be given to the child.

When this conversation was over, Līloa went and made a Kī leaf malo for himself and he put it on.

When he returned to his hale, his people saw that he was wearing a Kī leaf malo and not his own malo. They said, "Līloa has gone mad. He does not have his own malo on. He is wearing a Kī leaf malo."

Līloa stayed there until the relaxing of the kapu of the heiau [Maninini] was complete. Then he returned to Waipi'o to his permanent residence.

After these days, 'AkahiaKuleana was indeed pregnant with 'Umi. Her real husband thought that it was his child and he did not know that the child was Līloa('s).

When the child was born, the mother named him, 'Umi, because that is what Līloa wanted the child to be called after he had conceived (wai kō ai) the child [with 'AkahiaKuleana].

This child, 'Umi was raised up until he was mature. It was said when 'Umi('s) [step] father [the husband of 'AkahiaKuleana] went to farm and came back that he found 'Umi had eaten up all the food, so he beat 'Umi up.

'Umi was beaten by his step-father (ka makua kōlea ona) as 'Umi had eaten up all the food, i'a [*fish*] and everything else. The step-father abused him (hana 'ino), because he thought that he was the real father of the boy. 'Umi was very depressed as was 'AkahiaKuleana at 'Umi('s) beatings.

Therefore, 'Umi secretly asked 'AkahiaKuleana, "Do I have another father? Is this my only father?"

'AkahiaKuleana told him, "Your father is in Waipi'o. His name is Līloa." 'Umi said, "I must go to my [real] father." His mother said, "Yes, you should go."

When 'Umi had eaten all the food, the step-father again beat him up. Then 'AkahiaKuleana said, "My husband, this is not your son you are beating."

Her husband was angry and sarcastically said, "Who is the father of your son, is it Līloa?" 'AkahiaKuleana said, "Yes, Līloa is [the father] of my son."

The husband said, "Where are the signs that this child is Līloa('s)? This is my son, because you are my wife."

'AkahiaKuleana called her kauwā, "Bring [me] the objects of Līloa('s) that were left for 'Umi."

'AkahiaKuleana said to her husband, "Now you know who is the father of the child." And he saw [the objects and realized] that he was not the father of the child.

After this conversation, 'AkahiaKuleana carefully advised 'Umi about his journey to Waipi'o to [see] Līloa.

'AkahiaKuleana put Līloa('s) malo on 'Umi. She placed the palaoa on 'Umi and [gave him] the club. (305–307)

Like 'Ōpelemoemoe, 'Umi is mistreated and abused by his stepfather. He asks his mother if he has another father, and even after he is claimed by Līloa, 'Umi still has to endure the abuse of his older half-brother, Hākau. Malo does not give us a lot of detail about the relationship between the two brothers, but he does say "His [Hākau's] naʻau [*Lit., intestines, but fig., heart*] was angry at 'Umi. Hākau spoke rudely to 'Umi while Līloa was still alive. Līloa was sadden[ed] for 'Umi because of Hākau('s) anger" (308). Malo also tells us that "Hākau mistreated 'Umi so that he could drive 'Umi away" (309). A good portion of the tradition now is devoted to how 'Umi is able to emerge from obscurity to claim the chiefdom and triumph over Hākau, and it is this part of 'Umi's story that is mostly remembered today. Beckwith placed him among the "usurping chiefs" (*Hawaiian Mythology* 389). Anthropologist Valerio Valeri recognizes that 'Umi's life starts off as "an impure but extraordinary birth. His powers are manifested at first in the form of disordered, 'mischievous' behavior" (278). Valeri also describes 'Umi as "the usurper and conqueror par excellence" (211). 'Umi's story is of "the conquering enemy" transformed into a "'legitimate' king" (279).

This interpretation of a political struggle is important, too, but I do not believe it is the most compelling reason to tell this story, unless you happen to be the younger relative of a weak ruler. 'Umi's story is important because it is about relationships: his relationship with his mother and stepfather, establishing a relationship with his biological father, with his half-brother, with his friends and allies, and more importantly, with himself by discovering his own identity.

This type of tradition is not new. It is the same story that has enraptured adults and young adults alike in Tolkien's Lord of the Rings trilogy and that thrills young readers in Rowling's Harry Potter series. Like them, 'Umi's story is also about doing the right thing. I don't believe 'Umi set out to overturn the prevailing order of things as Māui did. 'Umi was not out to destroy his older bother. In Kamakau's version of the story, Hākau actually started his reign well-intentioned and "lived a just life." But then he changed.

> After Liloa's death, Hakau took over the government,
> and the chief ['Umi] lived under him. In the first years
> of his reign Hakau observed the teachings of his father,
> the kahunas, and counselors, and lived a just life. [. . .]
> But in the later years of his rule he was lost in pleasure,
> mistreated the chiefs, beat those who were not guilty of
> any wrongdoing, and abused the priests of the heiaus of
> his god and the chiefs of his own government. 'Umi was
> also abused by Hakau and was called the child of a low-
> born slave. [. . .] Hakau was jealous because 'Umi-a-Liloa
> was handsome and good. (*Ruling Chiefs* 9–10)

Eventually, he developed into an abusive leader to his loyal followers, as demonstrated by the following event that caused two of his own priests to turn against him.

> At one time the old men, Nunu and Ka-kohe, were
> indisposed through taking a purge. They sent a man to ask
> Hakau to send them food, fish, and 'awa. Hakau answered
> with insulting words, reviling them in such a way as to
> humiliate them. The old men began to plot to give the
> kingdom to someone else. (Kamakau, *Ruling Chiefs* 12)

> After remaining there a few days the old men went home
> pretending friendship for their lord and nursing hatred
> and grudge in their hearts. Nunu and Ka-kohe were high
> priests of the priestly class of Lono. (Kamakau, *Ruling
> Chiefs* 14)

Abuse, mistreatment, unnecessary beatings, and jealousy are the causes that legitimized 'Umi's violent overthrow of his older brother and later invoked fear in high chiefs about the potential danger of younger relatives.

Some of the causes of 'Umi's difficult relationship with his older brother are to be found in this excerpt from the paragraphs Malo uses to describe the term hewa in his chapter concerning what was hewa and pono.

> If the eyes of a person sees something to covet, but the
> heart does not desire it, then the hewa will not remain

(pili). But when the eyes see something and the heart desires it, then the thought will increase there [in the heart]. The source of this is kuko [*desire*], li'a [*a strong desire*], ulukū [*nervousness*], ho'okaha [*to extort*], ho'omakauli'i [*avarice*], 'i'ini [*craving*], and halaiwi [*to look at longingly*] with the idea to secretly take and acquire the object. These hewa were called 'aihue [*theft, to steal*].

Furthermore, there were many reasons for desiring another person's wealth. There was ho'ohalu [*to stare wide eyed*], maka'ala [*watchful*], kia'i [*to look at*], ho'okalakupua [*elusive*], ho'oeleiki (*to bear a grudge*), ho'opa'ewa [*to cause wrong*], and ho'opā'ē'ē [*to cause one to go astray*]. And with these ideas one could kill someone at some lonely spot to get that person's wealth. These hewa were called pōwā [*robbery*] and murder was the means to do so.

Furthermore, if a person decided to increase his or her possessions by taking someone else's, who had much more, then the first thought was to pākaha [*to cheat*], lawe [*to take*], kipa [*entice*], hao [*plunder*], uhuki [*to pull up or uproot*], kā'ili [*snatch*] and 'ālunu [*greed*]. There were many other types of hewa.

Furthermore, if a person let another know what was going on or the truth of the matter, and it turned out not to be so after they were through talking to each other, then there were many reasons for this to have occurred [in the heart]: ho'opunipuni [*lying*], wahahe'e [*deceit*], 'alapahi [*falsehood*], pālau [*to tell tall tales*], kūkahekahe [*jest*], palolo [*gossip*], kokahe ["*the lie unclothed*," Emerson's translation], pahilau [*to tell lies*], and other such numerous thoughts.

Furthermore, if a person decided to do hewa to another, then there were many thoughts there [in the heart]. The first was 'aki [*malign*], 'aki'aki [*slander*], ni'ani'a [*false accusations*], holoholo'ōlelo [*gossip*], makauli'i [*covet*], ka'ameha'i [*elusive*], kuene ["*belittling*,"

Emerson's translation], poupou noho nio [*pretense to knowledge or skill*], ho'owalewale [*tempting*], luahcle [*seduce*], kumakaia [*to betray*], ho'olawehala 'ōpū 'ino'ino [*malicious accusation*], lawe 'ōlelo [*tattle*], and pūonioni [*contentious*] and there were other similar and numerous thoughts.

If a person thought badly of another, then there were many thoughts there [in the heart]. The first is huhū [*anger*], inaina [*temper*], 'a'aka [*bad temper*], kē'ē [*shrieking angrily*], nanā [*quarrelsome*], kūkona [*being crossed*], nāhoa [*defiant*], mākona [*nasty*], kala'ea [*rude*], ho'olili [*provoking jealousy*], ho'omāku'e [*to scowl*], ho'oko'iko'i [*to treat harshly*], ho'oweliweli [*to threaten*], and other similar thoughts which were so numerous.

Furthermore, if a person decided to kill someone due to a fault [hala], then there were many thoughts there [in the heart]. The first was pepehi [*murder*], hailuku [*stoning*], hahau [*beating*], kula'i [*pushing over*], 'umi [*strangulation*], ku'iku'i [*fighting*], papa'i [*hitting*], hāko'oko'o [*leaning on*], ho'okonokono [*to entice*], and other similar thoughts which were so numerous.

This was a person of hewa. (186–187)

This is an amazingly descriptive and long list of what was observed and recognized as bad behavior. Hewa is manifested as jealousy, anger, and mistrust; as a cycle of escalating violence between perpetrators and victims that results in abuse both physical and emotional, shame, humiliation, and revenge. We can see all of these played out in the traditions of chiefs.

Acts of Hewa in the Traditions of the Chiefs

From the time of 'Umi until the unification of the islands under Kamehameha, there were localized and inter-island conflicts between chiefs caused by usurping of power and status, the control of resources, the pressures of increasing populations, and natural disasters such as famines. In the story of KihaaPi'ilani, whose sister was 'Umi's wife, Kiha, through his wife, asks her father for some farmlands in the district of Hāna. When he asks what lands Kiha wants, she says, "The lands my husband told me to ask for are Honomaʻele, Kaʻeleku, Kawaipapa, the two Wananalua and Koali." Interestingly enough, he "bowed his head in silence" in response (Kamakau, *Ruling Chiefs* 27).

> Then raising it, he said, "Your husband is no commoner. He is a chief, Kiha-a-Piʻi-lani. [. . .] I shall remain loyal to his older brother [. . .]. Your husband does not want farm lands for the two of you, but is seeking means to rebel against the kingdom. The lands of Honomaʻele and Kaʻeleku supply the ʻohiʻa wood and ʻieʻie vines of Kealakona to build ladders to the fortress. Kawaipapa supplies the stones of Kanawao that are used in battle [. . .]. (Kamakau, *Ruling Chiefs* 27)

What was the problem between the two brothers, Lono and Kiha, sons of Piʻilani, the late paramount chief of Maui?

> It was said that there were two heirs to the kingdom, Lono-a-Piʻi-lani and Kiha-a-Piʻi-lani [both nephews of ʻUmi] [. . .] the government went to Lono-a-Piʻi-lani. [. . .] In the first years of Lono-a-Piʻi-lani's reign all was well, and the people were content.
>
> Lono-a-Piʻi-lani took care of Kiha-a-Piʻi-lani, and the latter cared for the people by giving them food. Lono-a-Piʻi-lani became angry, for he felt Kiha-a-Piʻi-lani was doing it to seize the kingdom for himself. [. . .] The ruling chief's taro patch was smaller, for the latter [Kiha-a-Piʻi-lani] saw to it that his patch exceeded in size. Therefore Lono-a-Piʻi-lani grew very angry with him and abused him. He humiliated him over food and fish, and so they fought. The briny water which held *ohua* fish [and squid] was thrown into Kiha-a-Piʻi-lani's face; the tips of the squid's tentacle clung to his eyes.
>
> Lono-a-Piʻi-lani sought to kill Kiha, so he [Kiha] fled in secret to Molokai. [. . .] He patiently bore his troubles knowing that he would not die, and that the kingdom of Maui would yet be his. (Kamakau, *Ruling Chiefs* 22)

This reminds us of a famous Cantonese proverb, "yan mu sam doi fu [. . .], no family holds its wealth for over three generations" (Chen n. pag.) that warns that wealth and power accumulated by the first generation will later be squandered by the third. It appears that 'Umi's descendants also seem to follow a pattern of at first upholding what is pono only to disregard it later.

> Ke-li'i-o-kaloa was 'Umi-a-Liloa's eldest son [. . .]
> While he reigned, he took good care of his kingdom,
> his god, the priests and prophets of the god, and the
> common people. He lived a righteous life and heeded the
> teachings of the priests and prophets, but did not mind
> his father's advice to take care of the chiefs, the old men
> and old women, the orphans and the poor. When he
> deserted the advice of the wise, he paid attention to that
> of fools, thus forsaking the teachings of his father and
> the learned men of his kingdom. He deserted the god
> and oppressed the people.
>
> These were his oppressive deeds: He seized the property
> of the chiefs and that of the konohiki of the chiefs, the
> food of the commoners, their pigs, dogs, chickens, and
> other property. The coconut trees that were planted were
> hewn down, so were the people's kou trees. Their canoes
> and fish were seized; and people were compelled to do
> burdensome tasks such as diving for 'ina sea urchins,
> wana sea urchins, and sea weeds at night. Many were the
> oppressive deeds committed by this chief Ke-li'i-o-kaloa.
> (Kamakau, Ruling Chiefs 34–35)

When 'Umi's other son, Keawenuia'Umi had "learned of the unjust rule of Ke-li'i-o-kaloa and the burdening of the common people, he was filled with compassion for the chiefs and commoners of Kona" (Kamakau, Ruling Chiefs 35). Kamakau also tells us that after this defeat Keli'iokaloa's children "did not inherit the land" for it was taken over by their uncle. Keawenuia'Umi became the paramount chief of the entire island, and his rule was passed on to his descendants (Ruling Chiefs 36). When he died the island was divided up between his sons, one of whom was Lonoikamakahiki.

Lono-i-ka-makahiki was a son of Keawe-nui-a-'Umi, and
was chief of Ka-'u and Puna. He was sole ruler over those
two districts on Hawaii. He was married to a chiefess,
named Ka-iki-lani-kohe-pani'o [. . .]. Lono was a chief who
did not heed the advice of his priests and counselors, and
so his wisest counselors deserted him and sought a better
lord. Thus did Lanahu-'imi-haku and others leave him to
seek a lord who listened and heeded advice [. . .] with the
hope that he was a righteous chief who listened to all that
the priests and counselors taught him.

While Lono lived with his wife, Ka-iki-lani, he proved
to be a bad-tempered chief, who was jealous of his
wife because of her beauty, and frequently gave her a
beating. [. . .] There were some people there who wished
to tease because they disliked the chiefess and were
jealous of the beauty of her face and form. They thought
of finding a cause for her to be killed by being beaten.
[. . . They] called out, "O chiefess Ka-iki-lani of Puna,
the youth of the dark cliff of Hea sends you his regards."
[She disregarded them.] [. . .] But the mischief-makers
still called loudly, making mention of her lover, in this
manner, "O Ka-iki-lani, beautiful chiefess of Puna, your
lowly lover Hea-a-ke-koa sends his regards." Lono and
the chiefs heard, and so did all the people who were
gathered there [. . .]. Lono grasped a block of wood and
cruelly beat his wife, unmercifully smiting her to death.
(Kamakau, *Ruling Chiefs* 47–48)

Lonoikamakahiki became temporarily insane and, in great
remorse, he abandoned everything and went wandering from island
to island. On the island of Kaua'i he was deserted by all his followers
except for one man named Kapa'ihiahilina [. . . and] "they wandered
in the wilderness in poverty and hunger for many months. Lono was
crazed with grief for his wife. Kapa-'ihi-a-hilina took good care of him
as though he were a personal attendant" (Kamakau, *Ruling Chiefs* 48).

But there was still hewa to be found. Kamakau says that after
Lonoikamakahiki regained himself and returned to Hawai'i to rule,
he made Kapa'ihiahilina "a person of importance before the chiefs

and other members of the court. [. . .] but tattlers who were jealous of his being a favorite went to the chief to find fault" (*Ruling Chiefs* 48). Kapaʻihiahilina composed this chant to remind Lonoikamakahiki of what had happened before when they were friends, and it is one of the few places where we see the word hewa invoked.

> *O Lono-i-ka-makahiki ka pua o Kalani,*
> Lono-i-ka-makahiki, offspring of a chief,
> *O Kalani kapu a Keawe i hanau.*
> A tapu heavenly one born to Keawe.
> *Hanau Kalani keʻlii ku halau,*
> The heavenly one was born a chief with great power,
> *He halau nehe Lono mai Kapaʻahu,*
> With the tapu of silence from Kapaʻahu,
> *Ka ʻahuʻula kapu o Ku-malana-hewa,*
> The tapu feather cape of Ku-malana-hewa.
> *Ua hewa, ua hewa e—*
> A fault has been committed—
> *Ua hewa ia na la he hoʻomauhala,*
> The fault is the bearing of a grudge.
> *ʻAʻole ʻano hala i hoʻomau ai e Kalani,*
> It is not a fault to be cherished, O heavenly one!

After recalling the hardship and suffering that they shared wandering together, Kapaʻihiahilina ended this chant of loyalty and friendship for Lonoikamakahiki with these words:

> *Aloha wale ana ka wau ia ʻoe iloko o ka uahoa.*
> I bid farewell to you, who remain in anger.
> (Kamakau, *Ruling Chiefs* 49–52, translated by Pukui)

Lonoikamakahiki's story echoes another one, found on the island of Oʻahu, that of KahalaoPuna. She, like Kaikilani, was said to be young and beautiful. She was supposed to marry Kauhi, a man of importance and responsibility to the paramount chief of Oʻahu, Kākuhihewa; however,

> [s]ome people who were desirous [imihala] of seeing Kahalaopuna put to death [. . .] upon meeting Kauhi made up a slanderous story [olelo epa] against her [. . .]: "How strange indeed was the behavior of your intended

wife, Kahalaopuna! She went dancing two nights now, and on each night had a separate lover." When Kauhi heard this from these men [kela mau kanaka], he said to himself: "I shall indeed kill her for she has taken all the good things from my lord which I gave her. She has now gone and defiled herself." (Fornander V: 188)

In this version Kauhi broke off a branch from an ʻōhiʻa lehua tree and struck her "two and three times" (Fornander V: 190) even as she chanted of her love for Kauhi in which she states, "Like unto a shark is your jealousy of me (Me he mano la no ka lili iaʻu)" (Fornander V: 190–191). And again "Kauhi beat her until she was almost dead" (Fornander V: 190) while Kahalaopuna pleads again.

At this Kauhi again prepared to strike her with the stick to kill her. In her last faint cry she said: "My love to you. Let me kiss you, my husband, ere I depart from this life. Tell our parents of my love for them." Kauhi then said: "Why do you give your orders when you are thus about to die? I shall kill you." With that he struck her with the stick and killed her. Kauhi then dragged the dead body and laid it under the lehua tree, covered it over with leaves and ferns, fixed it so that it could not be seen and returned to his home. (Fornander V: 190)

A further example of hewa that arises from desire is the story of Kamanawa, a high chief and remarkable warrior for Kamehameha. Most people today know Kamanawa from his image, along with his twin brother, Kameʻeiamoku, on the royal coat of arms.

This sound proved to be the wailing over Kamakinki [sic], the wife of a chief of high rank. Strong suspicions being entertained of her having been poisoned by drinking ava, which her husband, Kamanawa, had prepared for her, he was apprehended, together with an accomplice, whose name was Sono. Three days after their arrest, they were put under trial before Kekuanaoa, the governor, as presiding judge, and a jury of twelve Hawaiians. [. . .] They were found guilty by the jury, and Sono confessed on the trial that he had committed one other murder.

The facts in relation to the murder of the chief's wife
were as follows.

The husband and wife had been for some time separated,
because the chief wished to marry another woman,
for whom he had formed a strong attachment. Having
already one wife, this was forbidden by the law, and he
in consequence determined to rid himself of her.
[. . .] Accordingly, a seeming reconciliation was brought
about, and they met at the house of a son-in-law of
Kamakinki to celebrate it by drinking ava. Two bowls
of the liquor were prepared, the one unadulterated,
the other mixed with poison composed of Tephrosia
piscatoria, Daphne indica, and the leaves of a common
gourd (Lagenaria). From the first of these the company
drank, but when Kamakinki called for her share, which
was handed to her by Kamanawa her husband, she, after
taking a few mouthfuls, complained of its bitterness.
On asking if the other cups had tasted so, and being
answered in the negative, she at once accused her
husband of having poisoned her.

[. . .] When Kamanawa drugged the ava, he had doubts
whether it would prove effective, but was glad to find it
so. [. . .] But there was no pardon; and the criminals were
hung on the 20th of October, on the walls of the fort,
the king having gone some days previously to Lahaina.
(Wilkes IV: 30–31)

The Chiefs of the Kingdom—Signs of Remorse and Shame

Along with observations of hewa, the vast traditions also record
the reactions of individuals, mostly chiefs, of remorse and shame.
Previously, in the account of KihaaPi'ilani, his father-in-law, when
asked by Kiha's wife for certain lands that Kiha wanted in the Hāna
district, reacted by bowing his head in silence. What did that mean?
It is the same reaction we saw when 'Ī'ī tells of Kamehameha's
reaction to the waste of fish caught.

The king [Kamehameha] said nothing at the time, but
sat with bowed head and downcast eyes, apparently

The warrior chiefs Kamanawa and his twin brother, Kameʻeiamoku, are depicted on the coat of arms of the Hawaiian Kingdom, as seen on the gates of ʻIolani Palace.

> disapproving of such reckless waste. [. . .] However, Kalanimoku, apparently knowing why the king kept his head bowed, commanded Kinopu to release most of the fish. (49)

A very powerful example of an individual's reaction of shame is seen in an encounter between Queen Kaʻahumanu and her brother Kalanimoku over the apparently wrongful imprisonment of his friend Ka-nuha "who was to be banished to Kahoolawe for using government money belonging to Hawaii" (Kamakau, *Ruling Chiefs* 308). Kalanimoku said, "'I shall use the money of Hawaii as long as I live; after my death it can be used for the government. I am the one to be banished and not my friend Ka-nuha.' At these words Kaʻahu-manu burst out weeping and covered her head in her blankets" (Kamakau, *Ruling Chiefs* 308). Kamakau also writes that

> [. . .] it is well known among the chiefs that Ka-ʻahu-manu snubbed Ku-wahine for winding Ke-ka-ulu-ohi's skirt about herself, and Ku-wahine wailed aloud with shame.
>
> [. . .] Ka-iki-o-ʻewa was Ku-wahine's father, and he was hurt by Ka-ʻahu-manu's snub [. . .]. (*Ruling Chiefs* 393)

The missionary C. S. Stewart witnessed another, similar episode of strong emotions being publicly displayed.

> As we approached, her [Kekauʻōnohi] eyes filled
> with tears, and, with a voice almost inarticulate from
> emotions ready to overpower her, she lifted her
> hand, and, pointing to the scene of intemperance and
> debauchery, exclaimed, "*Pupuka! pupuka!*" "Shameful!
> oh shameful!" and throwing herself backward with a
> convulsive sob, hid her face and her tears in a roll of
> tapa, against which she was reclining. (195)

The reactions of Kaʻahumanu and Kekauʻōnohi remind me of what I have read in Brad Shore's description of one of the pivotal actions of the Samoan equivalent to hoʻoponopono, called *ifoga*, when the head chief or the head of the family publicly revokes shame by covering himself or his head with a mat.

> [. . .] there are traditional judicial processes that operate
> within and between extended families—such as the *ifoga*
> (humbling) that the senior chief of family must undergo
> toward the chief of another group against which an
> offense has been committed. This humiliation involves,
> for the chief, publicly kneeling or sitting before the house
> of the offended group with a mat placed over his head.
> (111)

An extreme response to individual shame is suicide. ʻĪʻī writes of the tragic "suicide because of shame" (99) in the life of the chief Kalaniakua. She was also known as Kalani Kauiōkikilo and was the younger sister of Kekuʻiapoiwa. They were the members of the defeated chiefs of Maui and Oʻahu and became consorts to Kamehameha.

> She [Kalaniakua] died by suicide because of shame at the
> frequent jibes from Liliha about "homeless chiefs, who
> dwell under my protection and that of my *kaikunane*,
> Kamehameha, whose kingdom this is. They destroyed
> our child, these captives whom we brought here from
> Iao." Liliha spoke thus, perhaps, because Kalaniakua

was pregnant by Kamehameha and the child died in her womb.

One day Liliha secretly sent her grandson, Liholiho, to go and cling to Kalaniakua's back while she sat in the open talking with a company of women. While they were absorbed in conversation, the young chief clung to Kalaniakua's back until she reached around for him and placed him on her lap. When Kalaniakua repeated this, Liliha, who was watching was filled with wrath. [Being of highest kapu, Liholiho had the right to climb upon Kalaniakua's back]. (Ii 99)

'Ī'ī writes that Kalaniakua was "despised" (99) and "unhappy" (100), that "[w]e know that grief weighed heavily upon Kalaniakua for the things Liliha had done" (100), and that her actions were "wrong" (100). He says, "They were wrong because of, first, her great regard for her own rank; second, her lack of respect for the kapu of Liholiho; and, third, her destruction of the unborn child [. . .]" (100). This would be a most strange dilemma to reconcile whose actions are the hewa, Liliha's or Kalaniakua's, had not 'Ī'ī concluded with "[a]pplicable here is Solomon's saying, 'The wicked is driven away in his wickedness: but the righteous hath hope in his death. (Ho'okuke'ia ka mea hewa iloko o kona hewa; Lana ho'i ka mana'o o ka mea pono i kona make ana.)' – Proverbs 14:32" (100). His injunction of a Biblical quote referring to hewa leads me to wonder if traditionally hewa really can be equated with wickedness and sin?

Hewa and Hala

When we look at the traditions for instances of hewa we encounter another term, hala. From their descriptions in the Pukui and Elbert *Hawaiian Dictionary*, you might think that hewa and hala were the same thing. There is little difference between the two definitions, and both are heavily overlaid with Christian concepts of sin and guilt. But reading Malo we can conclude that they are not the same thing. Malo uses hewa to contrast to pono in his chapter heading, and then he goes into great detail to tell us that what is not pono is hewa. Hence, if pono is the right way of living, then hewa is its antithesis, its opposite. It is the wrong way of living, not wickedness or sin.

But when we look further, the dictionary does give us clues to help us understand both the similarities and the differences between these words. When we consider the reduplication of *hala* we can guess that *halahala*, or its causative *hoʻohalahala*, will probably mean something like doing or finding more fault. Pukui and Elbert confirm this with their definition of "[t]o criticize" (1986: 51). But the reduplication of *hewa*, *hewahewa*, is not something worse than bad. In this form, it means a "great many, very, vast" (1986: 67), relating to the fourth meaning of *hewa*, but also takes on a second meaning— "[c]razy, demented, wild, aimless" (1986: 67).

When we use the causative form *hoʻohewahewa* it becomes "[t]o fail to recognize" (1986: 67). I think this is key to understanding the difference as well as the similarity in these words.

We see that *hewa* cannot be reduplicated but *hala* can. *Hewa* can only stand alone and does not work in a way in which you can add the prefix hoʻo- to it. The authors of *Nānā I Ke Kumu* gave some clarity to this puzzle when they wrote, "In the traditional understanding of *hala* as a transgression or offense, is a subtle but significant axiom of human relationships: that the wrong-doer and the wronged are linked together by the very existence of the transgression and its chain of after-effects" (Pukui, Haertig, and Lee I :71).

Further clarity between the two words is evident when the matter reaches a point of forgiveness or reconciliation. The word for that is kala. Pukui and Elbert give us a sense of what forgiveness is about when they describe *kala* as "[t]o loosen, untie, free, release, remove, unburden, absolve, let go, acquit, take off, undo [. . .]" (1986:120). There is a compound word *kalahala* which is defined as "[a]tonement, remission of sins; to pardon, absolve from sin [. . .] (1986: 120). The compound *kala hewahewa* means "[t]o give away in an insane manner, as would a crazy person" (1986: 120) based upon the second meaning of *hewahewa*.

I think the tradition of Lonoikamakahiki, mentioned before, is a good example to demonstrate this linguistic anthropology. Lono is a chief with a violent temper whose wife is remarkably beautiful and faithful to him. But she has many detractors who are jealous of her, and they conspired to cause both Lono and his wife harm. We should recall Kamakau's telling of this story.

> While Lono lived with his wife, Ka-iki-lani, he proved to be a bad-tempered chief, who was jealous of his wife because of her beauty, and frequently gave her a beating. [. . .] There were some people there who wished to tease because they disliked the chiefess and were jealous of the beauty of her face and form. They thought of finding a cause for her to be killed by being beaten. [. .] Lono and the chiefs heard, and so did all the people who were gathered there, inside and outside of the shed. Lono grasped a block of wood and cruelly beat his wife, unmercifully smiting her to death. When he saw that she was dead, an unhappy feeling possessed him, and he became crazy with the grief for his wife. (*Ruling Chiefs* 47–48)

Compressed into this story are the elements of jealousy, anger and rage, guilt and shame, extreme grief that develops into madness, and eventual remorse. From this we can see how hewa, this moral quality of misjudgment, can develop reduplicated into hewahewa or madness.

Captain King observed what appears to have been a similar fit of jealous rage between a couple during the makahiki celebration and games.

> At one of the entertainments of boxing, Omeah was observed to rise from his place two or three times, and to go up to his wife with strong marks of displeasure, ordering her, as it appeared to us from his manner, to withdraw. [. . .] However, she kept her place; and when the entertainment was over, joined our party, and soliciting some trifling presents. [. . .] She was accordingly walking along with us; which Omeah observing, followed in a violent rage, and seizing her by the hair, began to inflict, with his fists, a severe corporal punishment. This fight, especially as we had innocently been the cause of it, gave us much concern; and yet we were told, that it would be highly improper to interfere between man and wife of such high rank. We were,

> however, not left without the consolation of seeing the
> natives at last interpose; and had the farther satisfaction
> of meeting them together the next day, in perfect good-
> humour with each other; and what is still more singular,
> the lady would not suffer us to remonstrate with her
> husband on his treatment of her, which we were much
> inclined to do, and plainly told us, that he had done no
> more than he ought. (King, J. 165–166)

It is possible that the presence of the Englishmen produced a non-fatal outcome, even though they did not physically intervene.

What does this all say about the quality of hewa? I think it is very suggestive that hewa is a state of being, reflective of one's mental or moral condition, a state of mind implied in Malo's description of choosing between pono and hewa. Hala is the act of doing something wrong. Archbishop Desmond Tutu describes this ability inherent in being able to choose.

> [T]o do evil is part and parcel of our ability to do good.
> One is meaningless without the other. Empathy and
> compassion have no meaning unless they occur in a
> situation where one could be callous and indifferent
> to the suffering of others. To have any possibility of
> moral growth there has to be the possibility of becoming
> immoral. (13)

Hence, hewa is not a concept for which there can be forgiveness (kala or kalahala). Rather, it is hala that can be forgiven.

Kalahala

We find the concept of kala+hala to be part of the vocabulary of the kahuna ʻanāʻanā kuni, a class of priest not usually thought of today as being associated with healing and whose title has often been translated as *sorcerer*. These kāhuna were responsible for forgiving (kalahala) the trespasses of other persons. As we saw in the discussion of hoʻoponopono, kalahala was one of their duties.

> One of his duties as a *kahuna ʻanaʻana* in his practice
> of *kuni* (*iloko o kana ʻoihana kuni*) was to *kalahala*—

remove the grounds for offense within the victim, and
so remove (*wehe*) the affliction (*make*) sent by another.
(Kamakau, *Ka Po'e Kahiko* 122)

This lesser known aspect of traditional healing practice is
corroborated by Kamakau's contemporary Zephyrin Kahōāli'i
Kepelino in a brief article entitled "Te Tala," reproduced and
translated in Kirtley and Mo'okini (59). Although the translators
rendered it as "counter-sorcery," te tala literally means "to forgive,"
and inserting this definition into the translation gives support to
Kamakau's statement.

> He mea te Tala i pili i na tahuna anaana a pau, O te tahu
> anaana atamai ma te tala ana i ta anaanaia mai e tetahi, oia
> te tahuna oiaio; a o ta mea ite ole ma ia hana, he *holona* ia.

> Elua mea nui iloto o ta anaana, o te *ta*.. mate, o te *tala* ola.
> [. . .] Penei ta hana mua: hootolotolo mua oia ia ia iho, me
> ta imi maopopo i tona lavehala i ta mea i tolohe mai ia ia.
> (Kirtley and Mo'okini 59)

> Forgiveness (te Tala) is something associated with all
> the priests involved with sorcery. The skilled guardian of
> sorcery was able to counter (te tala 'ana) the sorcery of
> another. This was the true priest and one who was not able
> to do so was unskilled (holona).

> There were two important things in sorcery: causing death
> (o te tala mate) and restoring health (o te tala ola). [. . .]
> This is what is first done: he first examines (ho'otolotolo)
> himself, to see what errors and deeds he has done wrong
> against the person who wants to harm him. (Author's
> translation)

These two sources give evidence of the fact that in traditional
society a person could see atonement when faced with the ultimate
punishment of death by sorcery. Kalahala has been perceived by
some as a counter to sorcery more than as healing. But after the
demise of the traditional priesthoods we see in the evolution of
ho'oponopono how important kalahala becomes to the mental and
spiritual healing of Hawaiians.

Guilt and Shame

Ernest Kurtz, in his work with Alcoholics Anonymous, sees a similar relationship between the concepts of guilt and shame. He describes guilt as relating to "an infraction, a breaking of the rules; shame, a literal 'shortcoming,' a lack or defect of being" (4).

> Guilt focuses on the *thing done* and thus reveals itself
> in self-reproaches [. . .] shame attends to *self as do-er*,
> inducing self-reproaches with a very different emphasis
> [. . .]. Too often, therapists settle for the resolution of
> guilt when it is the confrontation with shame that is the
> hurting person's deepest need. (7)

Where have we seen this before? At each implementation of the process of ho'oponopono, whether with couples and families or before large lecture groups, there comes a point where we do not necessarily wish to determine who did what to whom, but what is causing people to inflict so much hurt upon each other. For some victims, that might seem unbearable because of what has been done to them, and that burden becomes even more unbearable when forgiveness is sought from everyone, including the victim. As Kurtz has learned from his experiences with Alcoholics Anonymous, it is confronting the hurt, and not the guilt, that is the deepest need. As he describes the hurt or shame, it

> focuses on the *self*: it is the perception of not just any
> lack or failure, but of the deficiency of the self as self, as
> human being. Shame testifies not to wrong-doing but to
> flawed be-ing. (7)

We should recall what Pukui has said about this stage of ho'oponopono and why it is important for both the perpetrator and the victim to be involved.

> The person against whom the feeling of resentment was
> directed was asked to forgive him, also. If he, in turn,
> bore an ill will and had thought or spoken evil against
> him, he must ask to be pardoned. First the patient
> confessed and was forgiven, then he in turn forgave the

trespasses of the others against him. A mutual feeling of affection and willingness to cooperate had to exist in the family and the household before anything further could be done. (*Ho'oponopono*, audiotape)

This is why I believe Kurtz can write that there is a positive side to the recognition of shame.

> Perhaps surprisingly, despite the depth of self involved in shame's feeling "bad," the sense of shame itself is a good thing—something to be cherished and valued. [. . .] Shame [. . .] despite its negative side that points up failure and falling short, also entails something positive: insight into the reality of the human condition. (7–8)

Kamakau addressed this when he wrote about some of the causes of the depopulation of the islands in pre-contact times. He described the horrible actions committed by certain chiefs out of vengeance that led to a destructive circle of violence.

> Revenge was another great cause of strife in old days; a feud was carried on by the descendants of those involved even up to the time of the coming of the missionaries. Pele-io-holani cherished a feeling of enmity against the chiefs of Molokai for the death of his daughter Ke'e-lani-honua-ia-kama, and at the battle of Kapu'unoni he slaughtered the chiefs and roasted them in an oven at Hakawai in Kalua'aha, and he attacked the commoners inhumanly, all for revenge. Ka-hekili sought to avenge upon the chiefs of Oahu their slaying of the chiefs and commoners of Maui. They had taken Ka-uhi-a-Kama prisoner to Oahu and roasted him in an oven, and they had used his skull as a filth pot. Such acts of vengeance added to the distresses of the people. The chiefs of Hawaii and Molokai retaliated upon Pele-io-holani, as at the oven of Kuna at Waikiki and that of the chiefs at Hekili above Kanela'au in Honolulu [. . .] It is even said that Ka-lani-moku left the body of Ke-kua-o-ka-lani on the lava rocks after the battle of Kuamo'o instead of having it buried according to his rank as chief, [and that

he did this] as an act of vengeance because Ke-kua-o-ka-lani's ancestor, Alapaʻi-nui-a-Ka-uaua, had drowned Ka-lani-moku's ancestor, Ka-uhi-ʻaimoku-a-Kama, at Nuʻu in Kaupo. He was tied and thrown into the sea at Puhele and left to the mercy of the sharks. This left bad blood in the family which broke out at the death of Ke-kua-o-ka-lani. (*Ruling Chiefs* 232–233)

But like Kurtz, Kamakau realized that to end the circle of violence something positive must occur and he suggests,

If the sins committed by the ancestors are thus cherished, they become like a smoldering flame which will burst forth upon the descendants, causing the destruction of chiefs and people. Any feeling of revenge in the hearts of our people should be rooted out [. . .]." (*Ruling Chiefs* 233)

Where Do We Go From Here?

This book began with *Pono* and now ends with *Hewa*. That was a very conscious and intentional decision. It is not hard to recognize that the complexity of modern society, compounded by modern technology, has caused peoples across the world to struggle with choices regarding how to live. Popular culture is full of modern-day myths about good and evil, and we see their confrontation played out in every aspect of modern life, from small-scale and local issues to the way religious ideas of morality influence global politics. The acknowledgment of global environmental problems adds another layer of tension to the total picture.

For indigenous peoples, the Peoples of the land and seas, this situation is even more urgent. We are still faced with issues of identity and culture caused by colonialism, compounded by the continual loss of wise elders and good leadership, and by a population of young people for whom traditional culture and language seem increasingly foreign in their own homes. In a matter of years some indigenous peoples will have lost their home lands, whether because of a rising ocean or whether they are displaced as the melting of the ice pack leads to the extinction of the animals they depend on for food. Ironically it is the issue of global warming that has finally given creditability to the voice and concerns of indigenous peoples. The wisdom and experience of the indigenous peoples of Andaman and Nicobar Islands on December 31, 2004 that allowed them to flee before the arrival of the tsunami caught the attention of scientists and world media (Misra). Environmental activist Sheila Watt-Cloutier's monitoring of the climate changes in the Arctic region and warning of its devastating effect on Inuit life were recognized by the United Nations in 2007 with the awarding of the Mahbub ul Haq Award for Outstanding Contributions to Human Development.

As the world begins to rediscover indigenous knowledge as relevant and increasingly essential to human survival, more challenges for the People arise from the sharing of resources (human and natural) in a market economy, cultural survival in a political landscape of simple majorities, and asserting a role of moral leadership.

As an active participant and observer for the past twenty-five years in various government and private organizations dealing with indigenous issues, I have seen some remarkable achievements and some monumental mistakes. Both results were the consequence of whether or not decisions were made from a cultural perspective and of the depth of understanding the decision-makers had of their own culture. Let me give a "graphic illustration," as the late master slack-key musician Gabby Pahinui used to urge me to do when talking story with him. When the Office of Hawaiian Affairs was located right below the offices of the trustees of the Bishop Estate/Kamehameha Schools, their chairman, Richard "Papa" Lyman, would send for me every once in a while to talk story. Papa Lyman loved to speculate about the multiple and hidden meaning of Hawaiian words, something that drove his fellow trustees nuts. One day our administrator, T. C. Yim, told me he had a call from Papa Lyman and, "you better go up now." This time he wanted to talk about an area in east Honolulu that the estate owned and could possibly develop into a master planned resort-community of hotel-resort, condominiums, and shopping center. It was the last undeveloped area on that side of the island and a place I knew well for spearing uhu 'parrot fish' to bring to a Chinese restaurant to be cooked sweet-sour style. There were burial dunes in the sandy beach area and a fisherman's shelter cave across the main road that had been revealed by a brush fire.

I told Papa that if our ancestors did not have a village there, wouldn't that suggest that they did not believe it was inhabitable. Where was the source of ever-flowing water? If we develop it now, everything would have to be imported to sustain life there. The next day I got a call from one of the estate's land officers who asked if I had been talking recently to Papa Lyman because the project had been shelved.

In the ensuing years we have witnessed heavy downpours and flooding in this area. The entire island has sustainability problems for garbage control, water supply, and other problems that come with urban development. Much of the area has finally been purchased by the government for natural preservation. I would hope that from the clues of the past we would have learned that some places do not need to be "developed," for they already have been developed to their fullest potential.

When asked why he was so knowledgeable, Kamehameha II responded, "Na wai hoʻi ka ʻole o ke akamai, he alanui i maʻa i ka hele ʻia e oʻu mau mākua? *Why shouldn't I know, when it is a road often traveled by my parents?*" (Pukui, ʻŌlelo Noʻeau 251). The problem, as I have tried to point out in this book, is not only knowing what wisdom is, but also knowing how to use it, and that brings us back to choices, and to the cultural basis of pono and hewa. When we look back at Malo's chapter on this subject, we see that he rightfully identifies the source of it all to be "ka manao no o ka naau mai" (42), the thought from the gut or the heart of a person. I believe Malo is talking not about a mere whim or fancy of a person's desire, but the very core and essence of that person's being—when they are so comfortable with making a decision because it is second nature to them. The battle between good and evil, or the choice between them, is not about one over the other; it is about how a person wants to live. When someone realizes this, then decisions and choices become part of the cultural identity through which life is experienced and expressed. It is no wonder that the major religions of the world include in their beliefs such prescriptions as how to eat, dress, and behave. Those morals do not guarantee salvation by themselves, but they certainly give an identity and an anchor to hold on to in a complex world of uncertainty.

A way of living for indigenous peoples is more than behavioral controls. It is more than a tradition or the way that it has always been done. It is about the way we see and relate to the world around us now. The genius of our peoples is in keeping those traditions for future generations to know, but in also reinventing and recreating them for today. That synthesis is the way in which we see and relate to the world around us now. If we cannot live as such then we do not exist as a People, and we are just like everyone else.

13 Afterword

[I]ndigenous forms of governance will never become a reality
if they are not guided by traditional indigenous values.
Dale Turner commenting on the work of Taiaiake Alfred, director
of the School of Indigenous Governance at the University of Victoria, B.C.

There are more virtues, values, and other interesting subjects to
be looked into than what I have covered in this book. I have tried
to present a view of the way we live, think, and behave through the
stories and examples of our ancestors and the people they welcomed
to these islands. In doing this, everyone involved in this project has
discovered things that we did not know about when we started—
information that has challenged the way things had been taught to us
and the way we had believed they were. A colleague told me after a
lunch gathering that, upon hearing about our project, he was pleased
that the Department of Education was involved with a "Hawaiian"
project. He had let the idea go at that, until he began to read the
material and realized how little he knew about us. He said that we
were making a remarkable contribution. Coming to the end of this
book, I hope that we have lived up to his assessment.

In presenting our culture from the oldest sources—both primary
sources of our own people as well as the earliest outside views—I
intended to demonstrate that we have a common and shared culture
and set of values throughout these islands. There certainly was
regional diversity, and remnants still exist today, but the people could
and did communicate with one another and interact together. This
was certainly made clear to the British explorers under the command
of Captain James Cook when, upon arriving at Eastern Maui and
Hawai'i late in 1778, they learned that news of their first landfall at
Ni'ihau and Kaua'i in the spring of that year was common knowledge
throughout the island chain. The British would also discover how fast
venereal disease, and perhaps other infectious diseases (Stannard 74),
had also spread across the islands.

We also discovered from this approach how our cultural
practices and values have changed from that common base,

sometimes slightly and at other times immensely. It has not been my intention to disparage the actions of groups or individuals in how they have interpreted cultural practices and concepts, but to demonstrate by comparison the cultural change, again for good or bad.

Each generation has a responsibility 'kuleana' to ensure that it hands down cultural traditions as it has learned them. This action provides a continuity and link to the source. But each generation also has the right 'kuleana' to interpret those traditions as they relate to their own situation and to add their experience and rendering to the tradition.

There are two examples that come to mind that illustrate this point. The first involves the method of teaching being implemented by a hālau hula 'hula school' where many of the students did not know the language and culture and some were not Hawaiian. I wrote about how this came about when I was asked to put together the biography of kumu hula 'hula instructor or master' Maiki Aiu Lake for the Oxford University Press.

> Her students would learn Hawaiian genealogies, culture, mannerism, legends, poetry and the "beauties of our own Hawaii" (Ariyoshi, 1998, 73). She instituted written instructions because she had been advised by Hawaiian cultural authority and mentor Mary Kawena Pukui that since the Hawaiian language was no longer being spoken it would be better to have things written down. She put up a blackboard in the Studio, which was unheard of, and required her students to conduct individual research and be tested once a month. If they failed they were to leave the training. (Chun, "Maiki Aiu Lake" 2)

The second example involves a dilemma I and my co-workers at the Queen Liliʻuokalani Children's Center faced when we were teaching our staff, professional social workers and others, to offer hoʻoponopono to the families who came to the center for help. We wanted to be true to what Mary Kawena Pukui had desired when she introduced the center to the use of hoʻoponopono: that the families should be engaged in this cultural practice and not be dependent upon professionals to provide them with it.

But, we also had to train staff, both Hawaiian and non-Hawaiian, to take the lead roles those family leaders should have been taking. After deliberating on those factors we developed a program whereby staff would train and work with a mentor, someone experienced in ho'oponopono, and they would also, through experience and teaching, guide the family to learn how to practice ho'oponopono without us.

In both examples I believe the innovation, which was to accommodate the reality of the times, works because the goals were not to deliberately change the tradition but to help in the transferring of cultural knowledge. Today we have several kumu hula with their hālau who are graduates of that experience as well as many cultural practitioners of ho'oponopono who I hope are empowering the families they work with to learn and practice it among themselves.

I also believe we have raised a lot more questions than we have answered, and I can see many new avenues of research coming out of this work. In general, continued analysis of how we are doing things now and in what direction we are headed, particularly with regards to the touchy subjects of sovereignty and politics, would be tantalizing and would help guide us in this journey of self-determination.

There is a lot of work to be done on the territorial period, especially the period right after annexation. This has been the dream of one of my American Studies mentors, Paul Hooper, who knows how little work has been done in this area. Consider these factors: the early territorial legislature was dominated by the Home Rule Party led by Native Hawaiian Robert Wilcox. Wilcox became Hawai'i's first congressional representative, and when he was defeated the second congressional representative was Jonah Kūhiō Kalaniana'ole. Why? Because Native Hawaiians were still the majority of voters. They had been excluded in the Republic of Hawaii by voting rules that would inspire the exclusion of Black (African-American) voters in the "Jim Crow" South of the United States decades later.

Just a few years later, the 1920s saw the enactment of the Hawaiian Homes Act, and hand-in-hand with this, the founding of the Hawaiian civic clubs. A thorough understanding of this time could only benefit us now, as the federal establishment of the "blood quota" codified in that law still dominates Hawaiian politics.

I have yet to see a biography and analysis of the life and contributions of Abigail Kamokila Campbell. I remember her from when I was a little boy wandering around Lanikūhonua and then walking right up to this very tall and imposing Hawaiian woman. An analysis of her role in island politics would be enlightening.

We have seen in this book how traditions and values can be transformed, and the territorial period was one of tremendous impact upon Hawaiians. It was during this time that Te Rangi Hiroa (Sir Peter Buck) wrote in a letter to his pal Sir Apirana Ngata,

> The Hawaiians have turned to American politics in which party influences most of the Government jobs including the appointment of policemen. All the same they are nice lovable people but lack organisation and high incentive. (Sorrenson II: 202)

> The Hawaiians have no leaders, such as you and I would recognise. Any such leader would have taken to the platform or the press and disassociated the Hawaiian people from the Massie case. The abhorrence of the Hawaiian people to acts of violence against women should have been vehemently stressed, and the two accused youths with Hawaiian blood treated as individuals who had departed from Hawaiian ideals through improper assimilation of western culture. (Sorrenson II: 280)

I also regret that the chapter on "Aloha" did not lead up to the present day so we could all understand how such a cultural value has become an economic powerhouse in these islands and how that power affects the very culture and people from whence it came, again, in ways both good and bad. I am afraid that just that subject alone would make a book by itself. Recently there have been several books on the subject of "aloha" related to tourism and economics, some analytical and others bordering on self-help and how-to books. It would be important to discover how all of that compares to the Hawaiian traditions about aloha and hospitality.

What we did find in common throughout all the chapters of this book is the concept of pono. Because of my work translating Davida

Malo's manuscript *Ka Moolelo Hawaii*, I began this project with a
notion that such a concept would run deep through the culture. But
the tremendous number of stories that dealt with some form of pono
has been astounding.

Its importance today is reaffirmed in schools like Keaukaha
Elementary on the island of Hawai'i, whose principal Lehua Veincent
and his faculty and staff have made pono the standard of behavior for
their students and school community. A picture of the students from
the school wearing their "Got Pono?" t-shirts is included in the color
section of this book because they are nā mamo, the generation of the
future.

It is also reaffirmed by Linda Oba, a recently retired teacher
at Olomana School, who introduced the chapter on pono to her
class of incarcerated girls who, at first, just seemed bored. But when
challenged to express what they had read about pono they took
cameras out of the classroom to discover what they could find that
was pono in their midst. As we have discovered in these chapters it
is easier to describe the negative than the positive, and her students
took pictures of the barbed wire fence. They said they could find
something that was pono: a coconut tree beyond the barbed wire that
they could capture if you took the photo at a very tight angle from
the ground and the flowers of tiny weeds growing through the cracks
of the concrete pavement in the courtyard.

One of the students did manage to express herself, and quite
eloquently, in an essay about her thoughts on pono.

> Through the struggle to preserve our culture many
> feel that this generation is careless about the Hawaiian
> traditions. But this is very untrue. We as teens see
> the world in our own ways, and we know that our
> traditions are beginning to die. As much as we want to
> do something about this, we are clueless about what to
> do. What are we suppose to do anyway? We watch our
> elders and we do what we see, we learn what they teach,
> and we perpetuate. If we aren't taught the things that
> the Hawaiian society wants us to learn then what are
> we suppose to teach others and how are we to carry on
> tradition.

I suppose we could answer her with the lists of programs, classes, workshops, books, DVDs, and other materials or with strong words about preserving the culture. This book is another example of the effort being made to inform and maintain our culture and our way of seeing and thinking about the world. There is a lot going on concerning cultural preservation and maintenance, and a lot of funds being allocated to pay for it all. There have been some significant inroads made in a short time, and the present generation and, no doubt, future generations, may take those victories for granted: language recovery, performing arts, hula, and competitive sports, particularly outrigger canoeing. Hawaiian language pre-schools and immersion programs as well as advanced college degree programs in Hawaiian Studies and language enroll students of all ages and of varied cultural and racial backgrounds.

But I believe we must go beyond these efforts if we are, to paraphrase what Martin Brokenleg once preached to a group of us, to do more than the same things we have always done, which get the same results. Linda Oba's student is asking us not only to transmit the cultural practices to her generation but to also empower them with the tools to make those practices a part of their lives. We can tell them the stories, the traditions, but does that make them a storyteller? Linguist Joshua Fishman puts it even more succinctly when he says, "my wife engages in laptop publishing [. . .] for our grandchildren. But let me tell you, the true lap top here is my lap and her lap and the laps of the children's mother and father. That is a bond with the language that will stay with them after we are long gone" (80).

The manner of this book has been to present the intellectual and cultural traditions embodied in the different way we see the world so students like Oba's can make decisions about how and why the traditional stories have meaning to them and create new experiences for their audience, the next generation. What I hope has occurred in reading and reflecting about this book is seeing and knowing, which are the same word in Hawaiian, ʻike. They, too, are cultural practices that manifest our virtues and values. They are equal to, and sometimes more important than, being on a stage or in a sports competition. If you put them into action they can win you the prize. With them you have a presence and the confidence of authority, and you embody what you are doing because it is you. It is your soul and spirit, not acting or replicating.

Two well-known quilters, the late Bessie Like and the late Meali'i Kalama, told me how much emotion was physically transferred into their quilts with every stitch. If they were having a good day Auntie Bessie would complete a whole hoop in one evening, but on another day she might have to remove all the stitches she made because it looked bad. Therefore, Meali'i would say, her quilts were full of herself and her love. They have a certain quality to them, a certain life, and we can see that when we look at them. But in recent years quilters have looked to perfection of stitches and design and their quilts, and these quilts, at least to me, look stiff and lifeless.

One answer to the challenge of cultural maintenance and creativity for this generation and those yet to come is a new strategy that brings together, with equal emphasis, an "indigenous philosophy" and the instant gratification that is so important to the young.

I found this strategy, and the term *indigenous philosophy*, in the recent writings of Dale Turner who advocates for the need for indigenous peoples to have "indigenous thinking and world views" that enable them to engage with Western (dominant society) legal, political, and cultural practices as indigenous intellectuals who can interpret, translate, and engage indigenous philosophy (9).

Turner makes a case for being able to articulate from within an indigenous philosophy that generates "explanations of the world expressed in indigenous normative languages." However, a problem arises when "legal and political discourses of the state do not use indigenous philosophies to justify their legitimacy. The asymmetry arises because indigenous peoples must use the normative language of the dominant culture to ultimately defend world views that are embedded in completely different normative frameworks" (Turner 81). Hence, he is advocating that those indigenous peoples trained in the Western education system need to collaborate more with traditional cultural practitioners as never done before to develop counter strategies in developing the ways, whether they be laws, codes, or programs, for cultural maintenance to truly work for the people and not for the dominant culture. He describes this new strategy in these terms.

> If we take seriously the idea that protecting indigenous
> nationhood is a priority for an indigenous intellectual
> culture, we need to be able to speak and write
> convincingly in indigenous terms *and* be able to change
> how these arguments are used in the institutions
> of the state. Indigenous intellectuals must be both
> philosophical *and* political. But how is this possible? I
> believe part of the answer lies in how well indigenous
> peoples can reconcile an indigenous academic
> culture with the existing forms of leadership found
> in indigenous nations. Thinking about indigenous
> problems, engaging other people's ideas, publishing
> one's thoughts, and holding dialogues with those who
> disagree with us means little if these ideas do not lead to
> transformations in indigenous nations. Those nations
> require intellectual leaders and political leaders to work
> together. (emphasis in original) (Turner 106)

What is this intellectual culture or philosophy? His quotation of Osage English professor Robert Allen Warrior illustrates this point well.

> If our struggle is anything, it is a way of life. That way
> of life is not a matter of defining a political ideology
> or having a detached discussion about the unifying
> structures and essences of American Indian traditions. It
> is a decision—a decision we make in our minds, in our
> hearts, and in our bodies—to be sovereign and to find
> out what that means in the process. (Turner 89)

This is, in essence, what I struggled to say in the first chapter on Pono and why I deliberately choose that term to attempt to label what has to happen "in our minds, in our hearts and in our bodies" to go beyond mere words and lofty ideals. Like many Hawaiian words, *pono* has become so fashionable it is bantered about in a growing number of settings. One of these was an invitation-only event sponsored by the Maui Native Hawaiian Chamber of Commerce where the leading Democratic candidates in the 2010 Hawai'i gubernatorial race, both non-Hawaiians, faced off. As Maui

News writer Chris Hamilton describes the event, "each presented strategies to bring long-sought assistance to the host culture." He added that "Hannemann and Abercrombie often used the word 'pono,' or doing what's right, to explain how they will assist the Native Hawaiian people." Did either candidate know what they really meant when they used *pono*? Do they know what it means to Hawaiians? Or is the word *pono* becoming so over-used that it is losing its original meaning and becoming a trendy catch-all, like *aloha* or *'ohana*, in what, Turner reminds us, is the normative language of the dominant culture.

Although Turner advocates a blend of academic and indigenous cultures, we don't all need to either belong to an elite intellectual class or become politicians in order to know and live our culture. What we do need is to become better decision-makers, recognizing the commonality we share—that elusive ideal of lōkahi or "unity"— and grounding our lives upon the virtues and values that maintain our relationships with each other. We must strive to no longer be practitioners of culture, but to live it daily in our lives as a people from all economic, educational, and social levels. That is what is needed for generations to come—no nā mamo.

Appendix

Hearing for a Deeper Understanding
of Indigenous Knowledge:
Things We Learned from Publishing Indigenous Material
By Malcolm Nāea Chun & Lori Ward

Collaboration, Style and Form

We began our collaboration on a federal Native Hawaiian Education grant-funded project to develop and publish a series of books to help students, parents, and school administrators understand and appreciate traditional indigenous virtues and values. Malcolm came to the project from the Hawaiʻi State Department of Education, and Lori was the editor for the Curriculum Research & Development Group (CRDG) at the University of Hawaiʻi, College of Education. It was a partnership of necessity at first—as part of a grant-funded project, neither had the opportunity to opt out of the project or to choose someone else with whom to collaborate.

We faced several interesting challenges, beginning with the facts that Lori had not worked with indigenous (Native Hawaiian) materials, and American English is Malcolm's second and learned language. Others included the wide range of audiences to address, the use of an indigenous language and sources, and ourselves—in particular, the lack of any relationship upon which we could build. In hindsight, if we were to attempt to do this project over again, it would have been better to have established familiarity and background first. We should have had a party and gotten to know each other better. Collegial politeness and too much cultural sensitivity can blur what should be the obvious presumptions of style and composition. We did not realize how much our own cultural and academic backgrounds would get in the way until we plunged into writing and editing. Eventual we would discover that they did work together, sort of.

Malcolm had completed manuscripts for three of the books while working for the Department of Education, and when Lori began her editing of them she had a multitude of questions. This began our learning curve. Beyond the fine points of editing style, she discovered that at times Malcolm's style of composition left her wondering what she had just read. She also had the issue of having to get up to speed on a large body of research materials that she knew almost nothing about.

What Lori would discover about Malcolm is that beyond being an educator who has taught courses on Hawaiian mythology, literature, and religion, he has translated and published over a dozen primary source books on Native Hawaiian culture. He was raised by his elders in his own language and culture but was educated in a highly formal Western system. Given the modern, and Western, sensibilities of his education, we might expect that he would communicate like the rest of us, and he does not, so we discovered. His writing and thinking reflect his first language, which is indigenous, and at times defies Western readership and editing. Lori, for her part, came to the project with a grounding in the very specific and conservative conventions of academic publishing, a system that comes directly out of Western culture, and that is not, despite the way it may be presented, neutral in its approach to telling a story.

The chapters in this book are peppered throughout with a form of traditional story telling that, as a form of teaching and communication of imagery, is both entertaining and insightful, but, as we found, gets lost in the cultural translation. An example is this discussion of the Hawaiian word *mahalo*, used today to mean *thank you*. British comedienne Tracy Ullman once joked on her television program that when she came to the islands she thought the word *mahalo* meant garbage because it was on all the street trash bins. In traditional literature *mahalo* is used to mean admire, but there was no traditional virtue, and hence, no word for *thank you*. This ends up as a nice story, but one for which Lori would demand a paragraph of explanation, a demand that might or might not be complied with.

This is just one example of the many times when our two approaches clashed. There were many discussions where one of us had to explain the importance of what we were doing to the other. It was interesting to watch the evolution of the process as each came to know the other better and to understand why the work was put together the way it was. We eventually came to a point were we could predict some of the issues and understand each other's point of view, and where each of us could trust that when the other dug in his or her heels on a point, that it was important and should be left as is. But right to the end of this collaboration, there were instances of the culture clash that we had to work to understand and overcome. In other words, and this is not surprising when stated explicitly, both of us remained grounded in our own cultural background and world view and had to constantly keep in mind that ours was but one way of looking at the world or of telling a story, and that not only were there other views, but that these were just as legitimate as our own, and often more appropriate. An interesting lesson that we learned is that these differences were not always hurdles to be overcome. They often came up in areas of process, where we each had to learn to give a little, but they also came up in how we approached content, and in these cases the combination of two approaches sometimes meant that we uncovered new information.

Process-driven conflicts had been there from the beginning, and some had taken more discussion to resolve than others. But the issue came to a head when Malcolm finished his book on what he called cultural management, that is, how Native Hawaiians planned and worked with their resources and labor to complete tasks. In essence, he saw it very differently from modern Western models that are still being used for and by Native Hawaiians and, basically, failing. Besides her unhappiness with the phrase "cultural management" because it seemed to mean something different to her than what Malcolm meant when he used it, Lori could not, as an editor, accept that Malcolm had not cited some of the documents he used to demonstrate the management incompetence in a large Native Hawaiian organization. Things came to an impasse when Malcolm absolutely refused to back down on the issue of citing the documents he wanted to quote. He believed that, not only would citing those sources be embarrassing to those who had been involved, the point being made was a cultural, not an academic, one. As someone who had been there, and was therefore telling the story from first-hand recollection, he believed not only that the sources did not need to be named, but that doing so would be counter-productive to the points being made. Lori delayed working on this book for more than a year, still trying to figure out how to fix this dilemma so it would be publishable. The "ah-ha" moment came for Lori at an advisory council meeting attended by many Native Hawaiians from various educational agencies and institutions. Several of them candidly remarked that if young Native Hawaiians are not able to know and to tell their own story in the current educational systems, then those young people are being denied their history, culture, and identity. She came away from that meeting understanding that if the story could not be told by the storyteller in his context and style, then no one would ever hear it or read it because of the external demands that were stifling it. Cherokee storyteller and writer Thomas King reminds us that in the end what exists today is all that we have got and all that remains to let us know who we are.

> The truth about stories is that that's all we are. "I will
> tell you something about stories," the Laguna storyteller
> Leslie Silko reminds us, "They aren't just entertainment/
> Don't be fooled/ They are all we have, you see/All we
> fight off/Illness and death. You don't have anything/If
> you don't have the stories." (King, T. 92)

First Nation Canadian writer Dale Turner articulates this concept as well, commenting that "[i]ndigenous peoples have their own philosophies, which they apply when articulating their understandings of the world. Indigenous philosophies are rooted in oral traditions, which generate explanations of the world expressed in indigenous normative languages" (81–82). However, re-creating and telling our story may be difficult when a non-indigenous audience, who happens to serve in the role of gatekeeper to the publishing process, does not comprehend the style of storytelling that consists of indigenous philosophies embedded with cultural detail. Little translation or explanation is given because, for an indigenous audience, it is not needed. The problem arises when an indigenous author finds that he must conform to a Western style of expression by reshaping his work to meet all the conventions of Western academic publishing in order to get his work out to a broader audience. Turner found that out, noting that when indigenous peoples use their own traditions in dialogue with the dominant culture of Canada, they discovered only conflict and frustration. In his conclusion on this dilemma he states, "I believe that Aboriginal peoples must think more seriously about the constraints that are unilaterally imposed on the language we must use [. . .]. The fact that our ways of understanding the world are not worthy of equal participation in a dialogue over the meaning and content of our rights is itself a form of inequality" (Turner 26). By providing translation and explanations he finds that indigenous peoples "must use the normative language of the dominant culture to ultimately defend world views that are embedded in a completely differently normative framework." The "dominant culture does not face this hurdle. [. . .] Part of listening to Aboriginal peoples, and thereby facilitating greater Aboriginal participation, must involve overcoming this asymmetry." (Turner 81–82)

A common result for those who work in a cross-cultural collaboration, and who try to address the asymmetry Turner describes, can be mutual frustration and misunderstanding. If all voices are to be valued and heard, then we have to realize there are some irreconcilable differences in style. If we ignore those differences and demand compromise from native writers, we will lose those voices. Everyone should be able to tell their story as they want to tell it.

Cooking 101: The Cook Books

Part of Malcolm's style of storytelling has been to use an innovative method of weaving together the academic disciplines of history, anthropology, and indigenous studies. His innovation is being able to incorporate historical accounts and academic analysis with cultural experience and world-view. Traditional storytelling can be inventive more than revisionist, so he uses primary indigenous sources in the original language as well as Western eyewitness accounts from the journals of explorers and adventurers to confirm patterns of culture or to contradict them. With the digitization of sources that were once rare and isolated, researchers now have great access to very early primary materials that were once the domain of the lucky few, and Malcolm has been able to utilize them in his storytelling so that the reader can understand that he is only the storyteller and not the story inventor. In following this methodology we are able to pattern ourselves in the tradition of academia by providing citations and references that can be cross-checked and referenced while still telling the story in a way that speaks to an indigenous audience.

Of course, the earliest published eyewitness account of Native Hawaiian culture comes from the journal of Captain James Cook, an account that was cut short when he was killed after his great welcome at Kealakekua Bay on the island of Hawai'i. What few realize is that this was not his initial welcome to the islands. His first encounter, less well-known, was with a group of fishermen off the islands of Ni'ihau and Kaua'i. Malcolm had been reading a version of the journal posted on a University of Wisconsin web site but found that only one of the two chapters that dealt with this first visit to Hawai'i was posted. He found another website, this time from a Canadian national archives site, that did include a description of the first encounter, a scene he wanted to describe because it illustrated that the natives were more interested in trading with the foreigners than in fighting and that they did not view them as gods. At this point, he had material from Cook's journal posted at two different web sites, one (the second one he had tried) that included the full journal, and one that included only excerpts. Great, except when Lori began to double-check the references she found that the quotations from the two sites often were not the same. Consider this account of Cook's first encounter with Native Hawaiians from what turned out to be two different printings of "Cook's journal."

> At this time, we were in some doubt whether or no the land before us was inhabited; but this doubt was soon cleared up, by seeing some canoes coming off from the shore, toward the ship. I immediately brought to, to give them time to join us. They had from three to six men each; and, on their approach, we were agreeably surprised to find, that they spoke the language of Otaheite, and of the other islands we had lately visited. It required very little address, to get them to come along-side; but no intreaties could prevail upon any of them to

come on board. I tied some brass medals to a rope, and
gave them to those in one of the canoes, who, in return,
tied some small mackerel to the rope, as an equivalent.
This was repeated; and some small nails, or bits of iron,
which they valued more than any other article, were
given them. For these they exchanged more fish, and
a sweet potatoe; a sure sign that they had some notion
of bartering; or, at least, of returning one present for
another. They had nothing else in their canoes, except
some large gourd shells, and a kind of fishing-net; but
one of them offered for sale the piece of stuff that he
wore round his waist, after the manner of the other
islands. (Cook 191–192)

As we made a nearer approach, many of the inhabitants
put off from the shore in their canoes. We were agreeably
surprised to find, that they spoke a dialect of the
Otaheitean language. They could not be prevailed upon
by any entreaties to come on board. Captain Cook tied
some brass medals to a rope, which he gave to those who
were in one of the canoes; and they, in return, fastened
some mackarel to the rope, by way of equivalent. This
was repeated; and some small nails, or pieces of iron,
were given them; for which they gave in exchange some
more fish, and a sweet potatoe; a sure indication of their
having some notion of bartering, or, at least, of returning
one present for another. One of them even offered for
sale the piece of stuff which he wore about his waist.
(Cook and King 129–130)

Both are nominally Cook's journal, but one was written in the
first person by Cook and the other in the first person seemingly by
someone else, since Captain Cook is referred to in the third person.
Closer inspection found that there were other differences as well.
After doing some research of her own Lori discovered that there
are various versions of "Cook's journal." Some were authorized by
the British Admiralty, while others appear to be done by renegade
printers cashing in on the market demand. We also found that
the first edition of the "official version" has a fairly egregious

typographical error in the very short section that covers Cook's first visit to Hawai'i, a situation that caused a great deal of confusion for us, and that appears to be responsible for the second edition being done by a different printer. Since these are rare books, authorized or not, researchers in their own home town libraries may have historically had access to only one version, which, without the wider access created by the Internet, each considered to be a copy of the single source. What we found, through following Malcolm's research method combined with Lori's editorial process, is that there are stories out there about the sources in this field yet to be discovered—another project for another paper. In the end we compared the texts and decided to use a version found on the web site of the Royal Library in Copenhagen. We chose this version because it was published "by order of the admiralty," it contained both of the chapters that discussed Cook's initial stop in Hawai'i, and the typographical error found in the first edition was corrected.

We were both fascinated with this discovery, and spent quite a bit of time off on this tangent before we felt like we had a clear enough picture of what we were dealing with that we could make a decision about how to move forward. But, having finally made this decision, Malcolm was able to use the authorized journal of Captain Cook to tell stories that, even after two hundred years of scholarly examination, still offer insights into Native Hawaiian culture that can be found nowhere else. Malcolm has noted that when Cook did a walkabout on the island of Ni'ihau, he commented, "The ground, through which I passed, was in a state of nature, very stony, and the soil seemed poor. It was, however, covered with shrubs and plants, some of which perfumed the air, with a more delicious fragrancy than I had met with at any other of the islands visited by us in this ocean" (Cook 218). We have yet to find a botanical identification to that plant. And during that same walkabout Cook encountered a woman who performed a ritual about him that scholars have noted but have not given any analysis or commentary of.

> While the people were engaged in filling four water casks, from a small stream occasioned by the late rain, I walked a little way up the country, attended by the man above-mentioned, and followed by two others carrying

the two pigs. As soon as we got upon a rising ground, I
stopped to look round me; and observed a woman, on the
opposite side of the valley where I landed, calling to her
countrymen who attended me. Upon this, the Chief began
to mutter something which I supposed was a prayer; and
the two men, who carried the pigs, continued to walk
round me all the time, making, at least, a dozen circuits
before the other had finished his oraison. This ceremony
being performed, we proceeded; [. . .] (Cook 217)

Why did she walk around Cook twelve or more times? There
is nothing in later Native Hawaiian sources that would describe or
explain what this ritual was, and scholars have remained silent on the
subject.

After Cook's arrival at Kealakekua Bay in 1779 his journal ends,
and we have to rely on the accounts of his crew, and in particular that
of his successor, Captain James King. His writing is just as insightful as
his predecessor, and in two very minute passages he describes native
ornaments, examples of most of which can be found in collections of
Hawaiian artifacts. However, there is one description that doesn't seem
to match anything we've seen in existing collections.

Instead of this ornament, some of them wear, on their
breast, a small human figure, made of bone, suspended in
the same manner. (King, J. 135)

And sometimes, a small human image of bone, about
three inches long, neatly polished, is hung round the neck.
(Cook 232)

There exist two small pendants, one at the Peabody Essex
Museum in Salem, Massachusetts and the other at the Metropolitan
Museum of Art in New York City, with similar form, although not
made of the same material. Malcolm wrote more about these items in
his doctoral thesis and noted that neither of these institutions has, to
this day, recognized their similarity to King's descriptions.

The voyage also preserved, although in limited numbers, other
rare descriptions of the islands, people, and culture through the
artistry of John Webber.

I Know It When I See It

Storytelling can give vivid descriptions to the human imagination but a picture, as the old Chinese proverb goes, is worth a thousand words, and the vivid images rendered by Webber are the first visual record of the islands and the people who lived there. Most of what we have seen published, going back to the original publication of the account of the journey in the eighteenth century, have been engravings etched onto plates and sometimes colorized by hand. In research terms, that is secondary information because the engravings have been, perhaps as carefully as possible, rendered from the original hand-drawn and painted works by someone who hadn't been there on site to see the images first hand. Malcolm made trips to the repositories that have the original Webber drawings and, with the exception of the Bishop Museum where he was only allowed to see photocopies of what they had, was able to see the original drawings and paintings in person. He went to London to the British Library and the British Museum Archives and then to Sydney to the State Library of New South Wales's Dixson Library. There he was able to see what Webber had actually drawn and painted. He could see details that engravers either could not replicate, excluded, or invented, and he could see the colors that Webber used, which could not be duplicated in black and white engravings.

Webber's drawing of the reception that Cook received when the ships returned from the northwest of America (Alaska and Canada) is one of his most famous images. There seemed to be two originals of this painting, one in the Bishop Museum that is tinted a yellow-orange hue due to an overcoat of varnish, and another in vivid and clear color at the Dixson Library. Why would Webber do two originals of the same scene? Careful examination revealed that he didn't. He made two paintings of the same event but at different moments. A comparison of the two shows that several people in the main canoe have shifted positions. And we believe that we can now identify the facial features of the paramount chief of the island, Kalaniʻōpuʻu. If this is true, this would be the only contemporary image that exists of him.

Another famous drawing of Webber's is the early scene of the British gathering with Hawaiians in 1778 at Waimea Bay on the island of Kaua'i. It may actually be a composite of several pencil drawings that Webber had done to illustrate their encounter while the British explored the area. In the original, with computer enhancement of digitized photos, we can see details like the colors of a chief's feather cloak and helmet or a native holding on to his duck or chicken he may have been trading with one of the crew. We can even see the pond or inlet where the British went to collect fresh water in the central background because it is a light bluish tint in the original.

The most revealing of the drawings for contemporary Native Hawaiians will be the discovery found in the drawing of the now iconic gourd mask. There are no explanations of who the people were or what they were doing when Webber depicted them in a canoe wearing these helmets or mask. None of the masks were collected and none survive in any collection today. Contemporary Native Hawaiians have replicated them to wear at cultural and political events as a symbol of indigenous identity and often include the bark cloth strips hanging from the bottom of the helmet/masks, but they kept them white like the black and white engravings depict them. However, in Webber's original drawing at the British Library Malcolm saw the strips in alternating light colors of faded red or pink and yellow that an engraver could not replicate.

What Did We Learn?

We still agree to disagree and find points that may require clarification; that is nature of collaboration. We both realize that our continual efforts to come to a resolution have been beneficial to readers, judging from their reviews and comments. We recognize how important the material is to the indigenous population today, especially because it provides access through the citations to rare and out of print materials that most readers would not discover on their own. But, in particular, we appreciate how important it is to have made an indigenous, culturally based perspective on Hawaiian virtues and values available. We know the results can be transformative.

As the cultural specialist for this project, working with Lori has made Malcolm very aware of who the target audience can be and of how to tell a story to a wider audience. From Lori's perspective as the editor working with an indigenous writer, the process has made her aware that her training in Western conventions of publishing, presented implicitly as "the" way things are done, is really merely one way things can be done, albeit a very entrenched and dominant way. As the managing editor responsible for maintaining quality control, which, in this case, meant producing a product that met all the conventions typically associated with academic publishing, one of the biggest and most profound lessons she learned is that allowing the work to follow a different framework didn't necessarily mean throwing out all the rules, and it didn't mean producing a product that was not worthy of the standards established by the University of Hawai'i. She finally, after years working on this project, came to understand the asymmetry Turner described, whereby an indigenous writer has to contort his story to fit into the constraints laid down by the dominant culture, and to understand that all it took to change that was one person agreeing to do things differently.

Our disagreements and misunderstandings have also brought better research, clarity of thinking, and explanation of many aspects of Native Hawaiian culture that were either taken for granted or not even considered before. And, most important to Malcolm has been the articulation of knowing, and being able to spell out in words, our manner of communicating, teaching, and thinking through storytelling. It is the validation of our oral traditions in the mass media and means it is possible that we can continue to tell our stories in the manner we are accustomed to in a medium that was so forbidding and foreign. Having said that, there are still moments when he retorts, "Oh, do what you want!" so we can get the material published.

Bibliography

"Affecting Scene." *Religious Intelligencer* [New Haven, CT] 31 Dec. 1825: 488.

"Agency to Reassess Rules on Shark Fishing." *Honolulu Star-Bulletin* 19 June 1999: A3.

Akaka, Abraham K. *Aloha ke Akua.* Honolulu: University of Hawaii Press, 1959.

Allen, Helena G. *The Betrayal of Liliuokalani, Last Queen of Hawaii 1838–1917.* Honolulu: Mutual Publishing, 1982.

"Aloha." *Merriam-Webster's Collegiate Dictionary.* rev. and enl. ed. 1986.

"Aloha." *Shorter Oxford English Dictionary.* 5th ed. 2003.

Andrews, Lorrin. "Aloha." *A Dictionary of the Hawaiian Language.* Honolulu: Island Heritage Publishing, 2003 (originally published in 1865).

Ariyoshi, Rita. *Hula is Life: The Story of Hālau Hula o Maiki.* Honolulu: Maiki Aiu Building Corporation, 1998.

Ashizawa, Becky. "Shark's Guardian Role Valued by Hawaiians." *Honolulu Star-Bulletin* 30 Nov. 1991: A4.

Barratt, Glynn. *The Russian Discovery of Hawai'i: The Journals of Eight Russian Explorers.* Honolulu: Editions Limited, 1987.

Barrère, Dorothy B. *Kamehameha in Kona: Two Documentary Studies.* Pacific Anthropological Records No. 23. Honlulu: Bernice Pauahi Bishop Museum.

——. "A Reconstruction of the History and Function of the *Pu'uhonua* and the Hale o Keawe at Hōnauanu." *The Natural and Cultural History of Hōnaunau, Kona, Hawai'i.* Departmental Report Series 86-2. Honolulu: Bernice Pauahi Bishop Museum, Department of Anthropology, 1986: 117–136.

Barrow, John, ed. *The Voyages of Captain Cook.* Hertfordshire, UK: Wordsworth Editions Ltd., 1999.

Beaglehole, J. C., ed. *The Journals of Captain James Cook on his Voyages of Discovery.* 4 vols. and a portfolio. Vol. 3: *The Voyages of the* Resolution *and* Discovery *1776–1780*, part 2. Originally published by the Hakluyt Society, reprinted by The Boydell Press, 1999.

Beckwith, Martha. *Hawaiian Mythology.* Honolulu: University of Hawaii Press, 1970.

——, ed. and trans. *The Kumulipo.* Honolulu: University of Hawaii Press, 1972. (Facsim. reproduction of the 1st ed. published in 1951 by the University of Chicago Press).

——. "The Romance of Laieikawai." *The Thirty-Third Annual Report of the Bureau of American Ethnology, 1911–1912.* Washington: GPO, 1919.

Bingham, Hiram. *A Residence of Twenty-One Years in the Sandwich Islands, or the Civil, Religious, and Political History of Those Islands.* Hartford, CT: Hezekiah Huntington; New York: Sherman Converse, 1848.

Blasidell, Richard Kekuni. "He Mau Ninau Ola." *Ka Wai Ola o OHA* Fall 1983: 15.

——. *History of Medicine in Hawai'i.* Honolulu: University of Hawai'i Department of Medicine, July 1, 1982.

——. "Ho'okē 'Ai: the Moloka'i Diet." *Ka Wai Ola o OHA* April 1988: 23.

Boggs, Stephen T., and Malcolm Nāea Chun. "Ho'oponopono: A Hawaiian Method of Solving Interpersonal Problems." *Disentangling, Conflict Discourse in Pacific Societies.* Eds. K. A. Watson-Gegeo and Geoffery M. White. Stanford, CA: Stanford University Press, 1990.

The Book of Common Prayer and Administration of the Sacraments and Other Rites and Ceremonies of the Church According to the Use of The Episcopal Church. New York: The Church Hymnal Corporation; Seabury Press, 1977.

Bott, Elizabeth with the assistance of Tavi. *Tongan Society at the Time of Captain Cook's Visits: Discussion with Her Majesty Queen Sālote Tupou.* Wellington, NZ: The Polynesian Society (Incorporated), 1982.

Brendtro, Larry, Martin Brokenleg, and Steven Van Bockern. *Reclaiming Youth at Risk: Our Hope for the Future.* Rev. ed. Bloomington, IN: National Educational Service, 1990.

Brigham, William Tufts. *Ka Hana Kapa, The Making of Bark-cloth in Hawaii.* Memoirs of the Bernice Pauahi Bishop Museum of Polynesian Ethnology and Natural History; v. 3. Honolulu: Bishop Museum Press, 1911.

Buck, Peter H. "Polynesian Oratory." *Ancient Hawaiian Civilization.* Eds. E. S. Craighill Handy, et al. Rev. ed. Honolulu: The Kamehameha Schools Press, 1965: 161–168.

Burney, James. *Journal of James Burney's Log of H.M.S. Discovery, 15 Feb. 1779 24 Aug. 1779.* Sydney, AU: manuscript in Mitchell Library, 1779.

Campbell, Archibald. *A Voyage Round the World from 1806 to 1812.* Honolulu: University of Hawaii Press for Friends of the Library of Hawaii, 1967.

Chen, Kuo Hung. *We Call Our Treasure Tan Heung Shan.* Honolulu: Bank of Hawaii, 1989.

Ching, Linda, Malcolm Nāea Chun, and Pat Pitzer. *'Ano Lani.* Honolulu: Hawaiian Goddess Publishing Company, 1993.

Chun, Malcolm Nāea. "Creation and Re-creation: The First Hawaiian Christian Prayer." *First Peoples Theology Journal* (2001): 115–117.

——, trans. *Hawaiian Medicine Book, He Buke Laau Lapaau.* Honolulu: Bess Press, 1986.

——. *Ka Mo'olelo Laikini La'au Lapa'au, The History of Licensing Traditional Native Practitioners.* Honolulu: Health Promotion and Education Branch; Hawai'i State Department of Health, 1989.

——. "Maiki Aiu Lake" in *American National Biography* On-line Publication, Oxford University Press, New York, 2002

——, ed. and trans. *Must We Wait in Despair, The 1867 Report of the 'Ahahui Lā'au Lapa'au of Wailuku, Maui on Native Hawaiian Health.* Honolulu: First People's Productions, 1994.

——. *Nā Kukui Pio 'Ole, The Inextinguishable Torches: The Biographies of Three Early Native Hawaiian Scholars: Davida Malo, S. N. Hale'ole and S. M. Kamakau.* Honolulu: First People's Productions, 1993.

——, ed. and trans. *Native Hawaiian Medicines.* Honolulu: First People's Productions, 1994.

——. *OLA: Cultural Perspectives of Hawaiian Health Care.* Honolulu: Health Promotion and Education Branch, Hawai'i State Department of Health, 1992.

——. "Understanding Laʻau Lapaʻau." *Perspectives on Health Care and Healing on Kauai: 200 Years of Change* 26 Oct 1988.

Consedine, J. *Restorative Justice, Healing the Effects of Crime.* Lyttelton, NZ: Ploughshares Publications, 1995.

Cook, James. *A Voyage to the Pacific Ocean.* 2nd ed. Vol. 2. London: Printed by H. Hughes for G. Nicol, Bookseller to his Majesty, and T. Cadell, 1785. Online facsim. ed. at <http://www2.kb.dk/elib/bhs/cook/>.

Cook, James and James King. *A Voyage to the Pacific Ocean* [volume II]. Undertaken, by Command of His Majesty, for Making Discoveries in the Northern Hemisphere. Performed under the Direction of Captains Cook, Clerke, and Gore, in the Years 1776, 1777, 1778, 1779, and 1780. Being a copious, comprehensive, and satisfactory Abridgement of the Voyage written by Captain James Cook, F.R.S. and Captain James King, LL.D. and F.R.S., In Four Volumes. London: Printed for John Stockdale, Scatcherd and Whitaker, John Fielding, and John Hardy. 1784. Online facsim. ed. at < http://www.canadiana.org/view/17640/0005 >.

Damon, Ethel M. *The Stone Church at Kawaiahao, 1820–1944.* Honolulu: Trustees of Kawaiahao Church, Star-Bulletin Press, 1945.

Daranciang, Nelson. "Warning piles more bad news on kava." *Honolulu Star-Bulletin* 26 Mar. 2002: A1, A10.

Deloria Jr., Vine. *God is Red.* New York: Dell Publishing Co., 1973.

——. *The World We Used to Live In, Remembering the Powers of the Medicine Men.* Golden, CO: Fulcrum Publishing, 2006.

Desha, Stephen L. *Kamehameha and his warrior Kekūhaupiʻo.* Trans. Frances N. Frazier. Honolulu: Kamehameha Schools Press, 2000.

Dibble, Sheldon. *History of the Sandwich Islands,* Honolulu: Thrum Publishing, 1909.

"Eia Mai Kekahi Mau Laau Kupele A Na Kupuna." *Ka Nupepa Kuokoa* [Honolulu] 16 Nov. 1922: 2.

Elbert, Samuel H. "The Chief in Hawaiian Mythology." *Journal of American Folklore* 69 (1956): 99–113, 341–355; 70 (1957): 264–276, 306–322.

Elbert, Samuel H. and Noelani Mahoe. *Nā Mele o Hawaii Nei.* Honolulu: University of Hawaii Press, 1970.

Ellis, William. *Journal of William Ellis.* Honolulu: The Honolulu Advertiser, 1963.

Emerson, Nathaniel B. *Unwritten Literature of Hawaii: the Sacred Songs of the Hula.* Washington DC: Smithsonian Institution, Bureau of American Ethnology (Bulletin 38), 1909.

"Extracts from the Journal of Mr. Bingham while at Atooi." *Religious Intelligencer* [New Haven, CT] 10 Aug. 1822: 161–164.

"Extracts from the Journal of Mr. Bingham while at Atooi." *Religious Intelligencer* [New Haven, CT] 17 Aug. 1822: 177–180.

"Extracts from the Journal of the Missionaries." *Religious Intelligencer* [New Haven, CT] 13 July 1822: 97–99.

"Extracts from the Journal of the Missionaries." *Religious Intelligencer* [New Haven, CT] 20 July 1822: 116–120.

Finnegan, Ruth and Margaret Orbell, eds. *South Pacific Oral Traditions.* Bloomington, IN: Indiana University Press, 1995.

Firth, Raymond. "Speech-Making and Authority in Tikopia." *Political Language and Oratory in Traditional Society*. Ed. Maurice Bloch. London: Academic Press, 1975.

"'Fish!' the movie." *Honolulu Advertiser* 27 Mar. 2000: B6+.

Fishman, Joshua A. "What Do You Lose When You Lose Your Language?" in Cantoni, Gina, ed. Stabilizing Indigenous Languages. Flagstaff, AZ: Northern Arizona University Press, 1996: 186–196.

Fornander, Abraham. *Fornander Collection of Hawaiian Antiquities and Folk-lore*. 3 vols. Trans. Thomas G. Thrum. Memoirs of Bernice Pauahi Bishop Museum, vols. IV–VI. Honolulu: Bernice Pauahi Bishop Museum, 1916–1919. ('Ai Pohaku Press, Honolulu, facsim. ed., 1999).

Golovnin, V. M. *Around the World on the* Kamchatka, *1817-1819*. Trans. with intro. Ella Lury Wiswell. Honolulu: Hawaiian Historical Society; University Press of Hawaii, 1979.

Green, Laura Spring. *Folk-Tales from Hawaii*. Ed. Martha Warren Beckwith. Honolulu: Hawaiian Board Book Rooms, 1928.

Grossman, Lev. "The Curious Case of Kava." *Time* 8 Apr. 2002: 58.

Haleʻole, S. N. *Ka Moolelo o Lāʻieikawai, The Hawaiian Romance of Lāʻieikawai*, Trans. by Martha Warren Beckwith. Honolulu: First People's Productions, 1997.

Hamilton, Chris. "Candidates for Governor Share Cultural Ideas." *The Maui News* 11 Sept. 2010. http://www.mauinews.com/page/content.detail/id/540295.html

Handy, E. S. Craighill and Elizabeth Green Handy with Mary Kawena Pukui. *Native Planters in Old Hawaii: Their Life, Lore, and Environment*. Bernice P. Bishop Museum Bulletin 233. Honolulu: Bishop Museum Press, 1972.

Handy, E. S. Craighill and Mary Kawena Pukui. *The Polynesian Family System in Ka-ʻu, Hawaiʻi*. Rutland, VT: Charles E. Tuttle Company, 1972.

Hartwell, Jay. "Legal, Religious and Cultural Practices Continue Pele Reign." *Honolulu Advertiser* 25 Apr. 1987: A8.

Hiroa, Te Rangi (Peter H. Buck). *Arts and Crafts of Hawaii, Vol. V, Clothing*. Bernice P. Bishop Museum Special Publication 45. Honolulu: Bishop Museum Press, 1964.

Holy Bible, New International Reader's Version. Grand Rapids, MI: Zondervan Publishing House, 1995.

"Homily." Mercy Center, San Francisco, May 1, 1986.

Hoʻoponopono: Keeping Alive the Gift. Videocassette. The Queen Liliʻuokalani Children's Center, Honolulu, 1999.

Hopkins, Alberta Pua. "Aʻo aku, Aʻo mai, A process of teaching and learning from each other," CC-Md, Episcopal Church, n.d.

———. "Child's Culture vs. School Culture," in *Risky Business: Working with Hawaii's Children*, ESC Hawaii, 1992.

Hurley, Tim. "Kona Lagoon Hotel May be Torn Down." *Honolulu Advertiser* 14 Oct. 2002: A1, A4.

Ii, John Papa. *Fragments of Hawaiian History*. Trans. Mary Kawena Pukui. Ed. Dorothy B. Barrère. Bernice P. Bishop Museum Special Publication 70. Honolulu: Bishop Museum Press, 1959.

Johnson, Rubellite Kawena. "Search for Traditional Values." Paper presented to the Humanities Conference, Honolulu, 1979.

Johnson, Rubellite Kawena and John Kapio Mahelona. *Na Inoa Hoku, A Catalogue of Hawaiian and Pacific Star Names*. Honolulu: Topgallant Publishing Company, 1975.

Joppien, Rüdiger and Bernard Smith. *The Art of Captain Cook's Voyages, Volume 3, The Voyage of the Resolution and Discovery 1776-1780*. Melbourne: Oxford University Press, 1987.

"Journal of Messrs. Richards and Stewart at Lahinah." *Religious Intelligencer* [New Haven, CT] 19 March 1825: 657–659.

"Journal of Messrs. Richards and Stewart at Lahinah." *Religious Intelligencer* [New Haven, CT] 24 Sept. 1825: 258–260.

"Journal of the Mission." *Religious Intelligencer* [New Haven, CT] 14 Aug. 1824: 166–168.

Judd, Laura Fish. *Honolulu, Sketches of Life in the Hawaiian Islands*. Honolulu: Honolulu Star Bulletin, 1928. Rpt. ed., private publishers, Members of the Judd Family, Honolulu 2003.

Kahāʻulelio, Daniel. *Ka ʻOihana Lawaia (Hawaiian Fishing Traditions)*. Ed. M. Puakea Nogelmeier. Trans. Mary Kawena Pukui. Honolulu: Bishop Museum Press, 2006.

Kamakau, Samuel Manaiakalani. *I ka Wa o Kamehameha, In the Time of Kamehameha, Selected Essays by Samuel M. Kamakau*. Trans. Malcolm Nāea Chun. Honolulu: The Folk Press, 1988.

——. "Ka Moolelo Hawaii." *Ke Au Okoa* [Honolulu] 15 Sept. 1870: 1.

——. "Ka Moolelo Hawaii." *Ke Au Okoa* [Honolulu] 17 Nov. 1870: 1.

——. "Ka Moolelo Hawaii." *Ke Au Okoa* [Honolulu] 24 Nov. 1870: 1.

——. "Ka Moolelo Hawaii." *Ke Au Okoa* [Honolulu] 8 Dec. 1870: 1.

——. "Ka Moolelo Hawaii." *Ke Au Okoa* [Honolulu] 15 Dec. 1870: 1.

——. "Ka Moolelo Hawaii." *Ke Au Okoa* [Honolulu] 29 Dec. 1870: 1.

——. "Ka Moolelo Hawaii." *Ke Au Okoa* [Honolulu] 19 Jan. 1871: 1.

——. "Ka Moolelo O Kamehameha I." *Ka Nupepa Kuokoa* [Honolulu] 24 Aug. 1867:1.

——. *Ka Poʻe Kahiko, The People of Old*. Trans. Mary Kawena Pukui. Ed. Dorothy Barrère. Bernice P. Bishop Museum Special Publication 51. Honolulu: Bishop Museum Press, 1964.

——. *Ke Aupuni Mōʻī*. Honolulu: Kamehameha Schools Press, 2001.

——. *Ke Kumu Aupuni*. Honolulu: Ke Kumu Lama, 1996.

——. *Ruling Chiefs of Hawaii, Rev. ed.* Honolulu: The Kamehameha Schools Press, 1992.

——. *The Works of the People of Old, Na Hana a ka Poʻe Kahiko*. Trans. Mary Kawena Pukui. Ed. Dorothy Barrère. Bernice P. Bishop Museum Special Publication 61. Honolulu: Bishop Museum Press, 1976.

Kamakawiwoole, Israel. *IZ, The Songbook Collection*. Warner Bros. Publication, 2004.

Kanahele, Clinton. *Interview with Luka Kinolau*. The Clinton Kanahele Collection, Joseph Smith Library, BYU Hawaii, Laie, HI. http://library.byuh.edu/library/archives/kanahele

Kanahele, George Huʻeu Sanford, ed. *Hawaiian Values*. Honolulu: WAIAHA, 1982.

——. *Kū Kanaka, Stand Tall, A Search for Hawaiian Values*. Honolulu: University of Hawaii Press; WAIAHA Foundation, 1986.

Kepelino. *Kepelino's Traditions of Hawaii*. Ed. Martha Warren Beckwith. Bernice P. Bishop Museum Bulletin 95. Honolulu: Bishop Museum Press, 1932; Millwood, NY: Kraus Reprint, 1978.

Kephart, Linda. "Why aren't Hawaiians in business?" *Hawaii Business* Apr. 1985: 17–22.

King, James. *A Voyage to the Pacific Ocean*. 2nd ed. Vol. 3. London: Printed by H. Hughes for G. Nicol, Bookseller to his Majesty, and T. Cadell, 1785. 14 Apr. 2009 Online facsim. ed. at <http://www2.kb.dk/elib/bhs/cook/>.

King, Thomas. *The Truth About Stories, A Native Narrative*. Minneapolis, MN: University of Minnesota Press, 2003.

Kirch, Patrick. *Feathered Gods and Fishhooks*. Honolulu: University of Hawaii Press, 1985.

——. "Polynesian Feasting in Ethnohistoric, and Archaeological Contexts: A Comparison of Three Societies." *Feasts, Archaeological and Ethnographic Perspectives on Food, Politics, and Power*. Ed. Michael Dietler and Brian Hayden. Washington, DC: Smithsonian Institution Press, 2001.

Kirch, Patrick V. and Marshall Sahlins. *Anahulu, The Anthropology of History in the Kingdom of Hawaii*. 2 vols. Chicago: University of Chicago Press, 1992.

Kirtley, Bacil F. and Esther T. Mookini, trans. and anno. "Kepelino's "Hawaiian Collection": His "Hooiliili Havaii," Pepa I, 1858," *The Hawaiian Journal of History*. Vol. 11. Honolulu: Hawaiian Historical Society, 1977: 39–68.

Kubota, Gary T. "Officials Let Dead Whale Sink." *Honolulu Star-Bulletin* 1 May 2001: A6.

——. "Wasteful Practices of Gill-netters Denounced by Maui Residents." *Honolulu Star-Bulletin* 8 May 2002: A6.

——. "Whale Sanctuary Plans Draw Criticism Over Care." *Honolulu Star-Bulletin* 2 May 2002: A7.

Kurtz, Ernest. *Shame and Guilt*. 2nd ed. New York: Universe, Inc., 2007.

Kuykendall, Ralph S. *The Hawaiian Kingdom, Volume I, 1778-1854 Foundation and Transformation*. Honolulu: University of Hawaii Press, 1968.

La Pérouse, Jean-François de Galaup. *A Voyage Round the World*. Translated from the French, 3rd ed. Vol. 2. London: printed for Lackington, Allen, and Co., 1807: (28-224). 14 Apr. 2009 Online facsim. ed. at <www.americanjourneys. org/aj-131>.

Leidmann, Mike. "Christmas comes to Kalaupapa in summer." *Honolulu Advertiser* 7 Aug. 2003, morning final ed.: A1+.

"Letter from Bartimeus Lalana." *Religious Intelligencer* [New Haven, CT] 1 Apr. 1826: 689–690.

"Letter from the Mission to the Corresponding Secretary." *Religious Intelligencer* [New Haven, CT] 16 Aug. 1823: 164–165

"Letter of the Reinforcement." *Religious Intelligencer* [New Haven, CT] 12 June 1824: 19–21

Liliuokalani. *Hawaii's Story by Hawaii's Queen*. Rutland, VT: C. E. Tuttle, Co., 1964.

——. *The Queen's Songbook*. Text and music not. Dorothy Kahananui Gillett. Ed. Barbara Barnard Smith. Honolulu: Hui Hānai, 1999.

Linnekin, Jocelyn. *Sacred Queens and Women of Consequence: Rank, Gender, and Colonialism in the Hawaiian Islands*. Ann Arbor: The University of Michigan Press, 1990.

Luomala, Katherine. *Voices on the Wind, Polynesian Myths and Chants*. Honolulu: Bishop Museum Press, 1955.

Mallon, Sean. *Samoan Art & Artists, O Measina a Samoa*. Honolulu: University of Hawai'i Press, 2002.

Malo, Davida. *Ka Mo'olelo Hawai'i, Hawaiian Traditions*. Trans. Malcolm Nāea Chun. Honolulu: First People's Productions, 1996.

Manu, Moses. *He Moolelo Kaao no Keaomelemele (The Legend of Keaomelemele)*. Ed. Puakea Negelmeier. Trans. Mary Kawena Pukui. Honolulu: Bishop Museum Press, 2002.

Maunapau, Thomas K. *Huakai Makaikai a Kaupo, Maui (A Visit to Kaupō, Maui)*. Ed. Naomi Noelanioko'olau Clarke Losch. Trans. Mary Kawena Pukui and Malcolm Nāea Chun. Honolulu: Bishop Museum Press, 1998.

Maurer, Oscar E. *Three Early Christian Leaders of Hawaii*. Honolulu, TH: The Board of the Hawaiian Evangelical Association, 1945.

McKinzie, Edith Kawelohea. *Hawaiian Genealogies*. Vol. 1. Ed. Ishmael W. Stagner, II. La'ie, HI: The Institute for Polynesian Studies, 1983.

Mead, Hirini Moko. *Magnificent Te Maori, Te Maori Whakahirahira*. Auckland, NZ: Heinemann Publishers, 1986.

Misra, Neelesh. "Stone Age cultures survive tsunami waves." Associated Press. 4 Jan. 2005 http://www.msnbc.msn.com/id/6786476/

"Mission to the Sandwich Islands." *Religious Intelligencer* [New Haven, CT] 7 Apr. 1821: 721–726.

"Mission to the Sandwich Islands." *Religious Intelligencer* [New Haven, CT] 14 Apr. 1821: 737–741.

"Mission to the Sandwich Islands." *Religious Intelligencer* [New Haven, CT] 5 May, 1821: 785–787.

Nāmakaokeahi, Benjamin K. *The History of Kanalu*. Trans. and ed. Malcolm Nāea Chun. Honolulu: First People's Productions, 2004.

Neil, Christopher. "Hawaiian Rite Planned to Help Ease Rift on Shark Hunt." *Honolulu Star-Bulletin* 1 Dec. 1991: A3.

"No ke kauoha a Kaahumana ma kona make ana." *Ka Lama Hawaii* [Lahainaluna] 28 March 1834:4.

Office of Hawaiian Affairs. *Ho'okipa, Hawaiian Hospitality*. Honolulu: Office of Hawaiian Affairs, 1988.

Oliver, Douglas L. *Ancient Tahitian Society, Volume 2, Social Relations*. Honolulu: University Press of Hawaii, 1974.

Pickering, Charles. *United States Exploring Expedition, The Races of Man: and Their Geographical Distribution*. Vol. IX. Philadelphia: C. Sherman, 1848. Online facsim. ed. at <http://www.sil.si.edu/digitalcollections/usexex/navigation/ScientificText/usexex19_13select.cfm>.

"Piety or no piety at the Sandwich Islands." Editorial. *The Polynesian* [Honolulu] 15 July 1848: 33.

Portlock, Nathaniel. *Voyage Round the World; But More Particularly to the Northwest Coast of America: Performed in 1785, 1786, 1787, and 1788, in the King George and Queen Charlotte, Captains Portlock and Dixon*. London: John Stockdale and George Goulding, 1789. 16 Oct. 2006 Online facsim. ed. at <www.americanjourneys.org/aj-089/>.

Pukui, Mary Kawena. *Ho'oponopono or Setting to Rights*. Rec. 10 July 1958. Audiotape. The Bernice Pauahi Bishop Museum, Honolulu. H-41 G.

——. *'Ōlelo No'eau, Hawaiian Proverbs & Poetical Sayings*. Bernice P. Bishop Museum Special Publication, No. 71. Honolulu: Bishop Museum Press, 1983.

Pukui, Mary Kawena, E. W. Haertig, and Catherine A. Lee. *Nānā I Ke Kumu (Look to The Source)*. 2 vols. Honolulu: Hui Hānai, 1972.

Pukui, Mary Kawena and Samuel H. Elbert. *Hawaiian Dictionary*. Honolulu: University of Hawaii Press, 1957.

——. *Hawaiian Dictionary*. Rev. and enl. ed. Honolulu: University of Hawaii Press, 1986.

The Queen Lili'uokalani Children's Center, Program Division. *Cultural Plan II*. Honolulu: The Queen Lili'uokalani Children's Center, 1999.

——. *He Buke Mele Kamali'i no ka Mō'īwahine 'o Lili'uokalani, A Children's Songbook in Honor of Queen Lili'uokalani*. Honolulu: Queen Lili'uokalani Children's Center, 1999.

"Return of Prince George to Atooi." *Religious Intelligencer* [New Haven, CT] 28 Apr. 1821: 770–773.

Rose, Roger G. *Reconciling the Past, Two Basketry Kā'ai and the Legendary Līloa and Lonoikamakahiki*. Bishop Museum Bulletin in Anthropology 5. Honolulu: Bishop Museum Press, 1992.

Sahlins, Marshall. *Historical Metaphors and Mythical Realities, Structure in the Early History of the Sandwich Islands Kingdom*. ASAO Special Publications No. 1. Ann Arbor: The University of Michigan Press, 1981.

——. *How "Natives" Think: About Captain Cook, for Example*. Chicago: University of Chicago Press, 1995.

Salmond Anne. *Hui: A study of Maori Ceremonial Gatherings*. Wellington, NZ: Reed, 1975a.

——. "Mana Makes the Man: A Look at Maori Oratory and Politics." *Political Language and Oratory in Traditional Society*. Ed. Maurice Bloch. London: Academic Press, 1975b.

——. *The Trial of the Cannibal Dog, Captain Cook in the South Seas*. London: Allen Lane, an imprint of Penguin Press, 2003.

"Sandwich Islands." *Religious Intelligencer* [New Haven, CT] 19 Apr. 1823: 737–741.

Schreiter, Robert J. *Constructing Local Theologies*. Maryknoll, NY: Orbis Books, 1986.

Schütz, Albert J. *Voices of Eden: A History of Hawaiian Language Studies*. Honolulu: University of Hawai'i Press, 1994.

Shook, E. V. *Ho'oponopono, Contemporary Uses of a Hawaiian Problem-Solving Process*. Honolulu: University of Hawaii Press, 1985.

Shore, Bradd. *Sala'ilua, A Samoan Mystery*. New York: Columbia University Press, 1982.

Sorrenson, M. P. K., ed. *Na To Hoa Aroha, From Your Dear Friend: The correspondence between Sir Apirana Ngata and Sir Peter Buck*, 1925–50, 3 vols. Auckland: Auckland University Press, 1986–1988.

Spriggs, Matthew and Malcolm Nāea Chun. "Renaming the Hawaiian Cultural Sequence: Some Suggestions." A Paper for Kenneth Emory's 90th Birthday *Festschrift*. n.p., 1987.

Stannard, David E. *Before the Horror: The Population of Hawaii on the Eve of Western Contact*. Honolulu: University of Hawaii Social Science Research Institute, 1989.

State Department of Health. *Ka Papahana o ka 'Oihana Ola Hawai'i: The Office of Hawaiian Health Status Report*. Honolulu: The State Department of Health, 1991.

"State proposes restrictions on fishing around Ni'ihau." *Honolulu Advertiser* 7 Aug. 2003: B2.

Sterling, Elspeth and Catherine C. Summers. *Sites of Oahu*. Honolulu: Bernice P. Bishop Museum, 1978.

Stewart, C. S. *Journal of a Residence in the Sandwich Islands During the Years 1823, 1824, and 1825*. Facsim. ed. Honolulu: University of Hawaii Press, [1970] 1830.

TenBruggencate, Jan. "The Early Hawaiians Allowed Retribution for Attacks by Sharks." *Honolulu Advertiser* 9 Dec. 1991. A1, A4.

Turner, Dale. *This is Not a Peace Pipe: Towards a Critical Indigenous Philosophy*, Toronto: University of Toronto Press, 2006.

Tutu, Desmond with Douglas Abrams. *God has a Dream, A Vision of Hope for Our Time*. New York: Doubleday, 2004.

Valeri, Valerio. *Kingship and Sacrifice*. Trans. Paul Wissing. Chicago: The University of Chicago Press, 1985.

Wallace, William Kauaiwiulaokalani III. *The Church of Jesus Christ of Latter-day Saints In the Hawaiian Islands from 1850–1900; An Abridgement*. Lā'ie, HI: La'ie Community Association, 2000. http://www.laiecommunityassociation.org/history.html

Wilkes, Charles. *Narrative of the United States Exploring Expedition During the Years 1838, 1839, 1840, 1841, 1842*. 5 vols. Philadelphia: C. Sherman, 1844. 14 Apr. 2009 Online facsim. ed. at <http://www.sil.si.edu/digitalcollections/usexex/follow-01.htm>.

Wright, Walter. "Statue Not Sacred, 2 Experts Contend." *Honolulu Advertiser* 1 June 1997. A27, A31.

Young, David. *Na Mea Makamae: Hawaiian Treasures*. Kailua-Kona, HI: Palapala Press, 1999.

Index

Production Notes for Chun | No Nā Mamo

Cover design by Robin M. Clark and Wayne M. Shishido

Text design and composition by Wayne M. Shishido
with text and display type in Minion Pro

Printing and binding by Sheridan Books, Inc.

Printed on 50 lb. Glatfelter Natural B18 Text, 500 ppi